# VOLUME 1: THE DELIRIUM OF HOPE

IMAGE COMICS, INC

Robert Kirkman - Chief Operating Officer
Erik Larsen - Chief Financial Officer
Todd McFarlane - President
Marc Silvestri - Chief Executive Officer
Jim Valentino - Vice-President
Eric Stephenson - Publisher
Ron Richards - Director of Business Development
Jennifer de Guzman - Director of Trade Book Sales
Kat Salazar - Director of PR & Marketing
Corey Murphy - Director of Retail Sales
Jeremy Sullivan - Director of Digital Sales
Emilio Bautista - Sales Assistant

Branwyn Bigglestone - Senior Accounts Manager
Emily Miller - Accounts Manager
Jessica Ambriz - Administrative Assistant
Tyler Shainline - Events Coordinator
David Brothers - Content Manager
Jonathan Chan - Production Manager
Drew Gill - Art Director
Meredith Wallace - Print Manager
Addison Duke - Production Artist
Vincent Kukua - Production Artist
Tricia Ramos - Production Assistant

IMAGECOMICS.COM

JEFF POWELL
Book Design

ISBN 978-1-63215-194-0

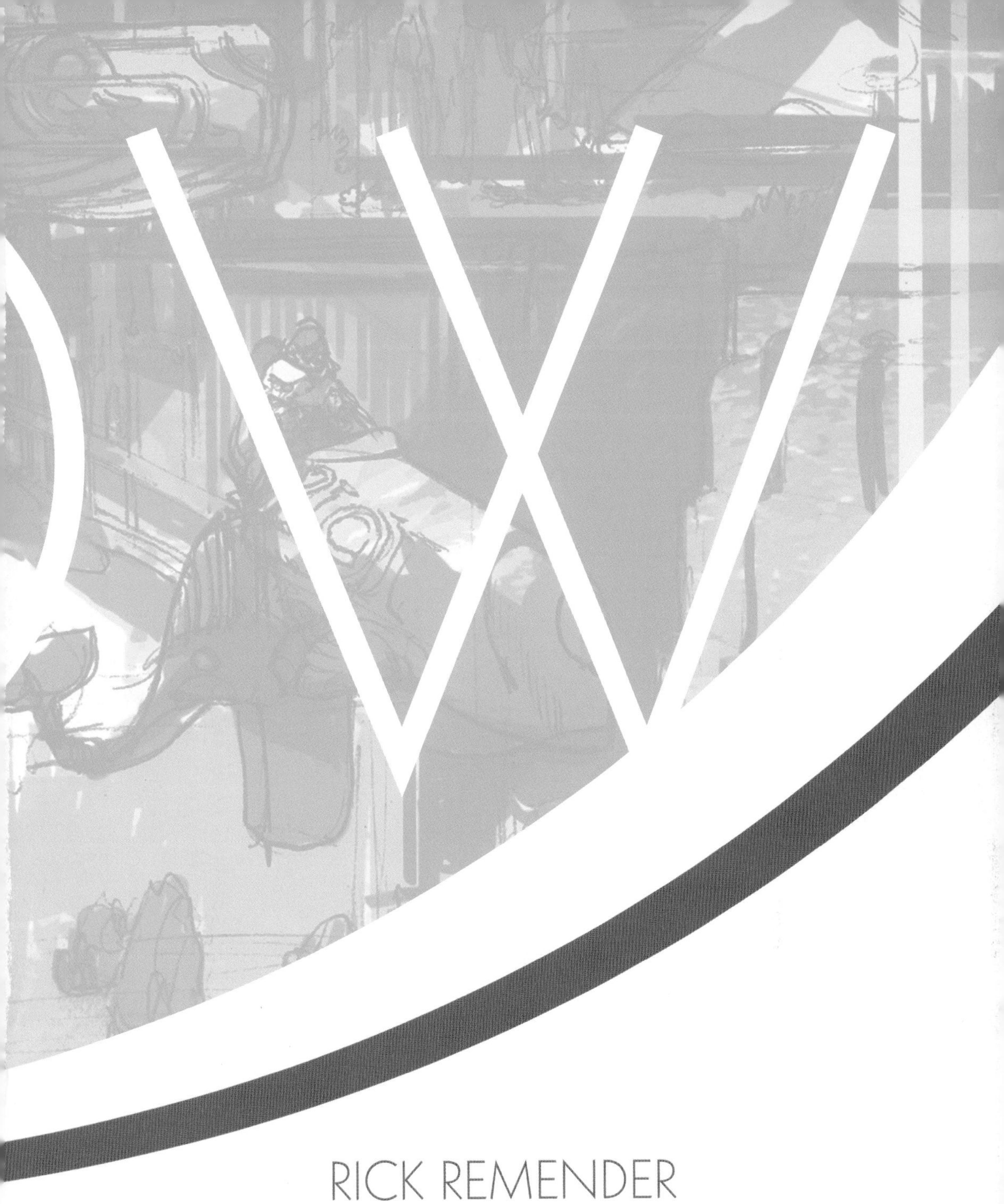

RICK REMENDER

writer

GREG TOCCHINI

artist

MARIANE GUSMÃO

color assistant

RUS WOOTON

letterer

SEBASTIAN GIRNER

editor

Created by Rick Remender & Greg Tocchini

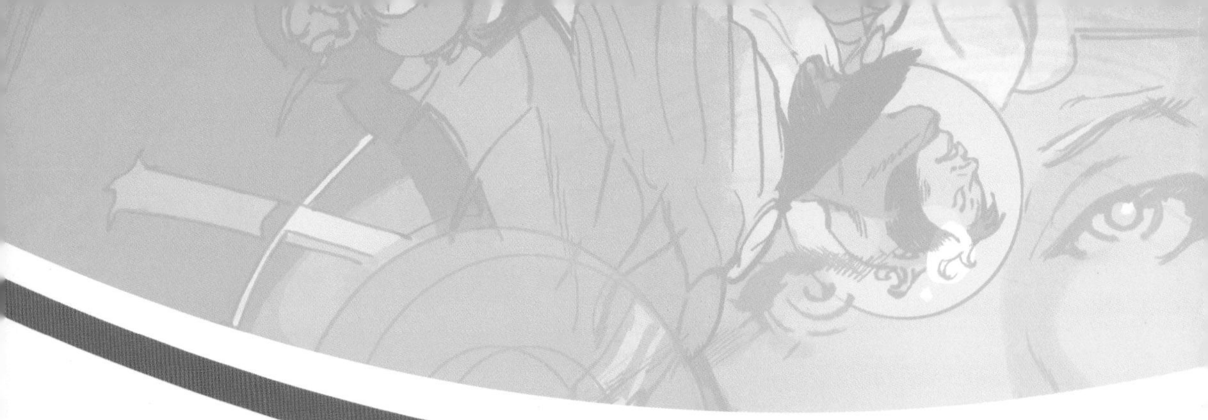

ONE DAY THE SUN WILL EXPAND on its way to going supernova and engulf the entire world. If you're anything like me, then the first time you learned this it sat with you for a bit. No matter how far off into the future it is, its finality is heavy duty.

It's true. I was 7 or 8 years old when I got my first true taste of nihilism.

I remember thinking, "Jesus, what a ...waste of time this all is then. It's all so futile. No matter what we build, no matter what we create, no matter what we accomplish, the sun's going to eat it all up."

I had just, sort of, processed the concept of dying not too many years before, but this was too much. It was hard enough to get my head around my own mortality, but the whole planet? Fuck.

Fast-forward to 2010, when Greg Tocchini and I had just finished *Last Days of American Crime*, and we started looking for our next project together. We both wanted to do something Sci-Fi, but it had to be unique. Had to be different than anything either of us had ever done or ever seen. I spent months writing ideas, but nothing really excited me. I was already doing science fiction in *Fear Agent* and hadn't found that big hook. Something that was different enough to be worthy of Greg's superpower and jive-ass skills.

Then, one fateful afternoon, while reading *National Geographic*, I hit on an article about the timeline of when the sun is actually expected to expand and consume our solar system. It reminded me of my youthful fascination with the concept and got me thinking: that's a great ticking time bomb. That's THE ticking time bomb. It was interesting on a universal level, this affected everyone, all of us, which is usually the first ingredient of "home run material upon which to build a story."

I filled a notebook with ideas: how would mankind survive? What would we do? I guess we could move to the bottom of the ocean to escape radiation while looking for a new planet. But what if we were down there for too long? What

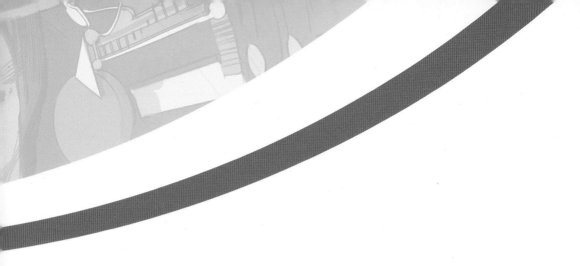

if no probe ever found an inhabitable world? Tens of thousands of years pass and now there's just these few cities left. My world-building brain kicked into gear and we began creating the setting for *Low*.

During the developing years of this book, I began therapy, and the biggest hurdle for me to overcome was learning to develop positive thinking habits. Being pessimistic by nature, this was a challenge. The workbook my therapist had me doing was all about optimism and reminded me of a book an old friend gave me: *Illusions* by Richard Bach. When I was about 25 years old, and thinking of leaving my job at 20th Century Fox Animation to go do comics, this book's ideas about how optimism and conscious thought can shape reality compelled me to just quit my job and give it a try.

Now I realize that in fifteen years I've never once written an optimistic character.

This led me to develop Stel Caine, the eternal optimist who holds out hope against all odds. A perfect fit for this far-future tale of humanity at its lowest point. A perfect character to examine the notion that it's not what happens in life that defines us, but how we choose to deal with it.

And it was perfect timing as during the production of *Low* I began to find my way to a more optimistic state of mind, which has made my life better in almost every regard. I've been more productive, found time to exercise, more time for my family, and increased my workload considerably. Writing Stel's adventures and what she endures, how she endures it, became incredibly cathartic.

*Low* is a story of one woman's eternal optimism, to burden the sorrows and the crushing weight of a world without hope.

It's a story I finally feel ready to tell.

Rick Remender

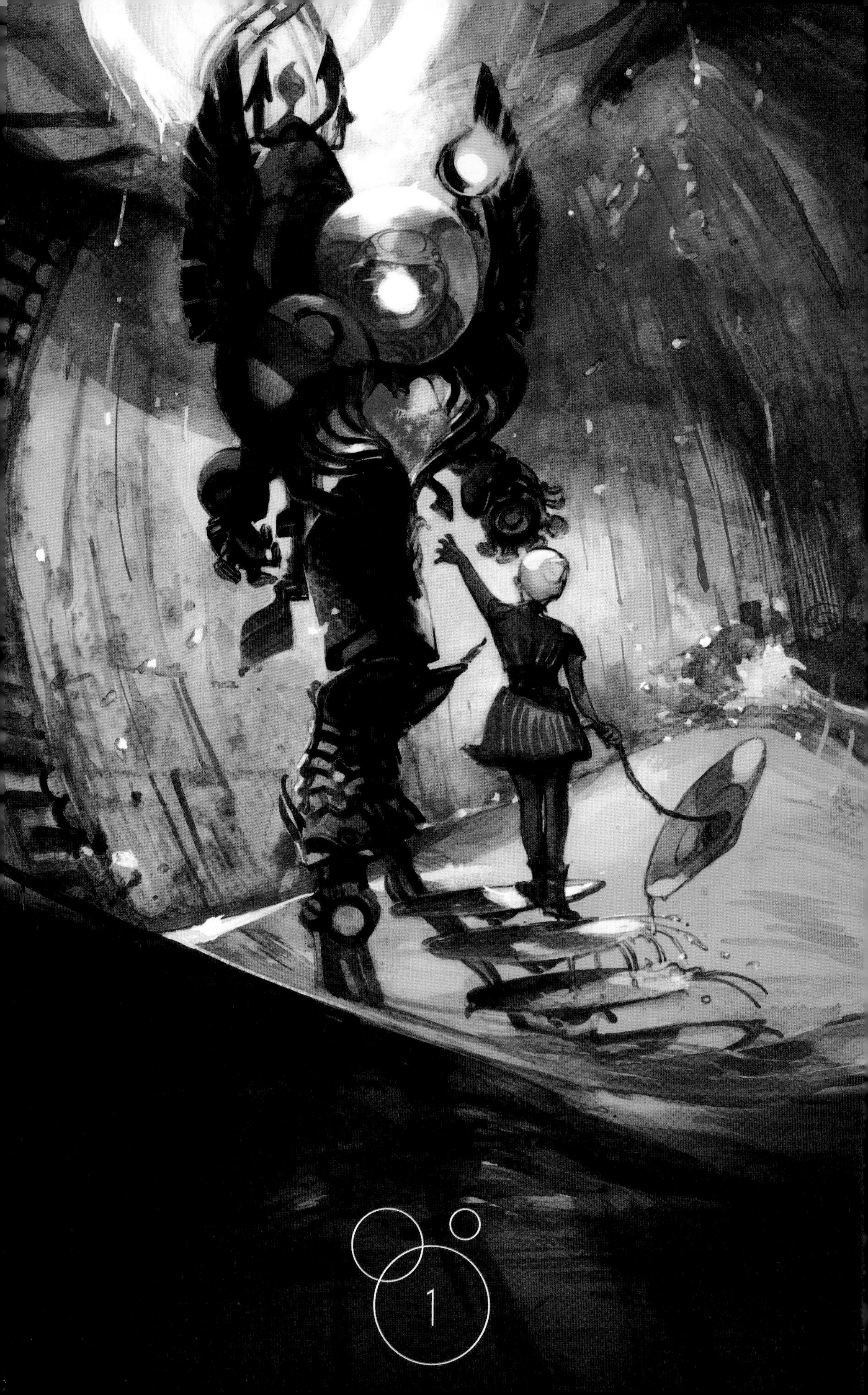

1

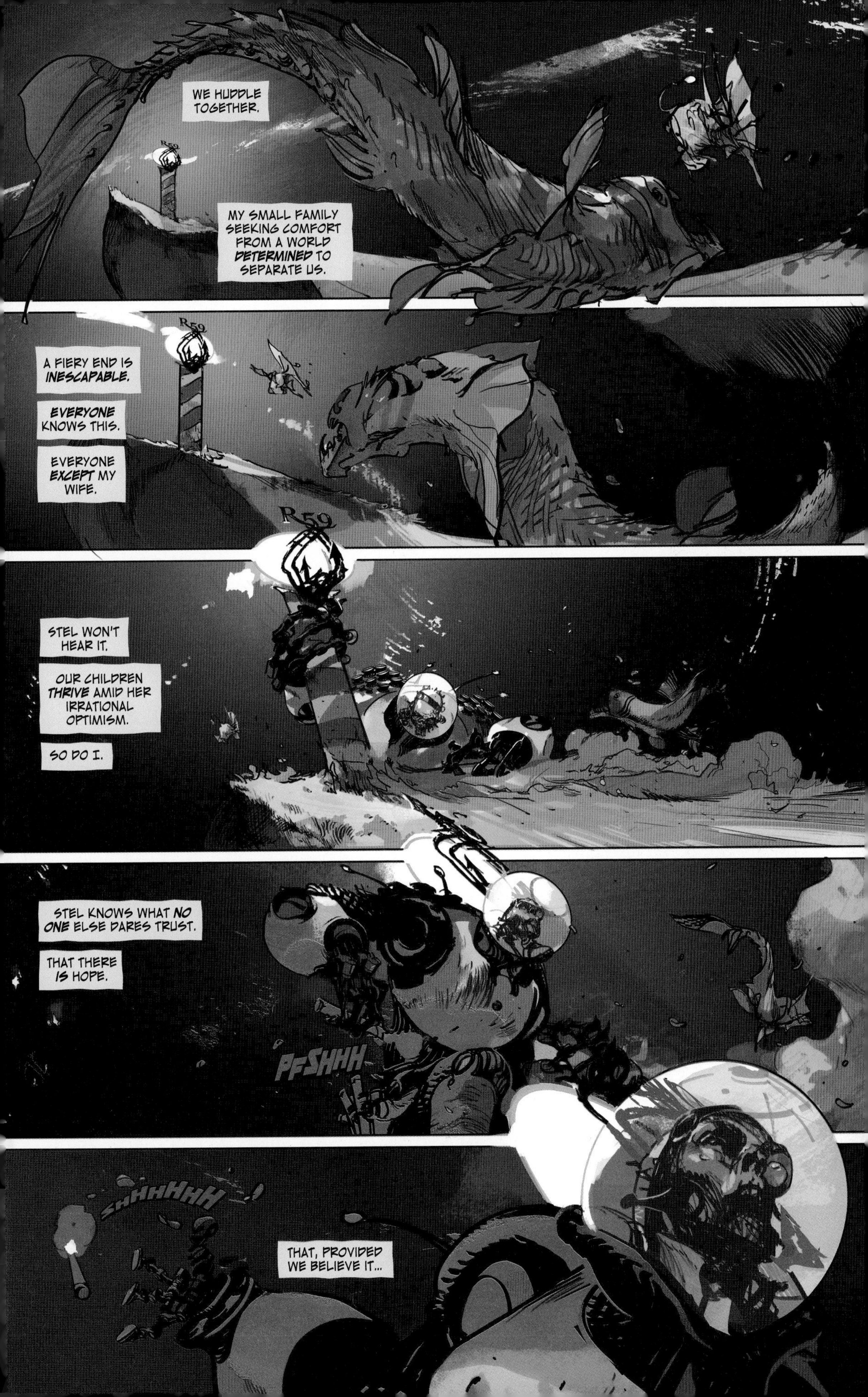
WE HUDDLE TOGETHER.
MY SMALL FAMILY SEEKING COMFORT FROM A WORLD **DETERMINED** TO SEPARATE US.
R59
A FIERY END IS **INESCAPABLE.**
**EVERYONE** KNOWS THIS.
EVERYONE **EXCEPT** MY WIFE.
R59
STEL WON'T HEAR IT.
OUR CHILDREN **THRIVE** AMID HER IRRATIONAL OPTIMISM.
SO DO I.
STEL KNOWS WHAT **NO ONE** ELSE DARES TRUST.
THAT THERE **IS** HOPE.
PFSHHH
SHHHHHHH
THAT, PROVIDED WE BELIEVE IT...

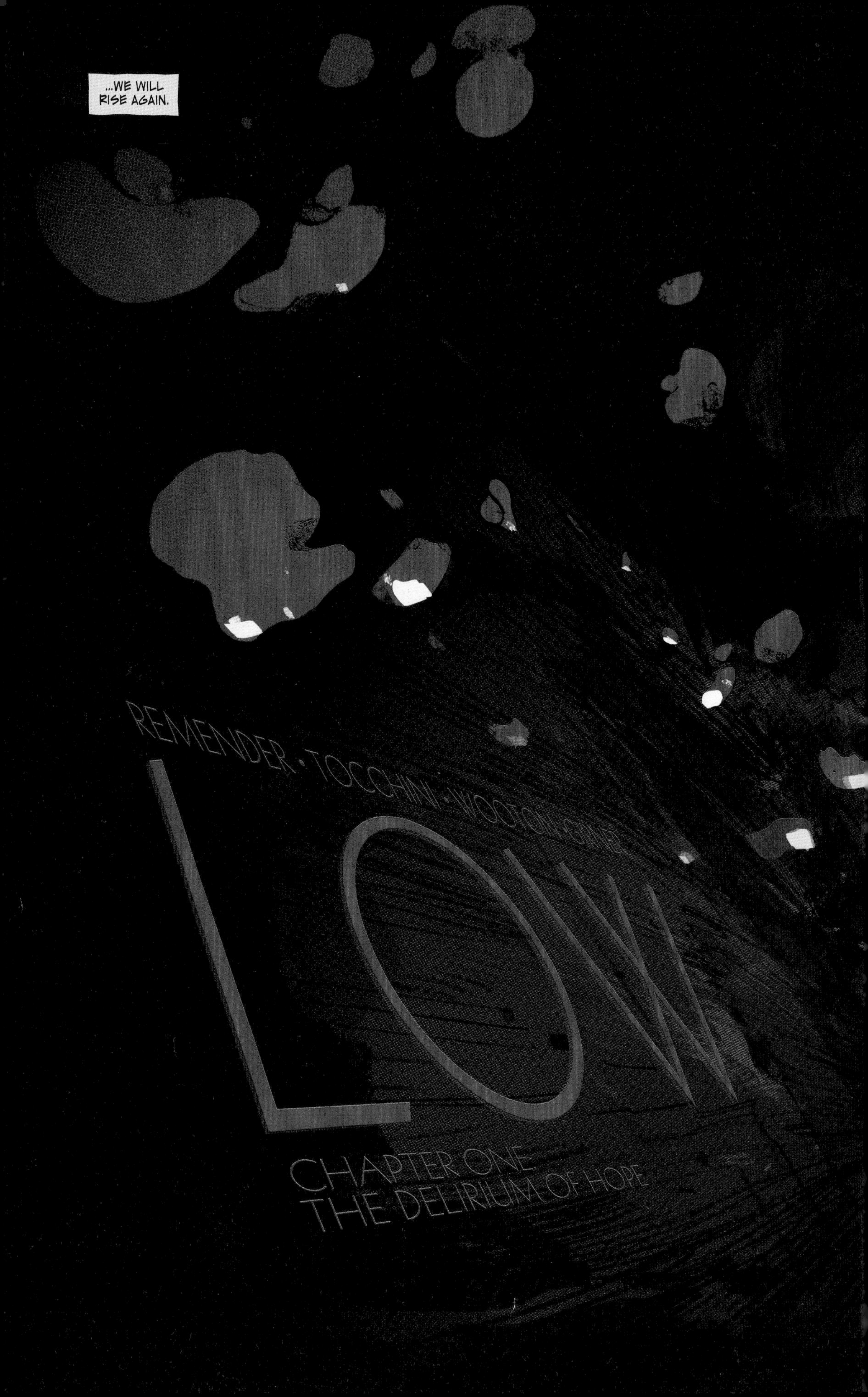
...WE WILL RISE AGAIN.
REMENDER • TOCCHINI • WOOTON • GARNER
LOW
CHAPTER ONE
THE DELIRIUM OF HOPE

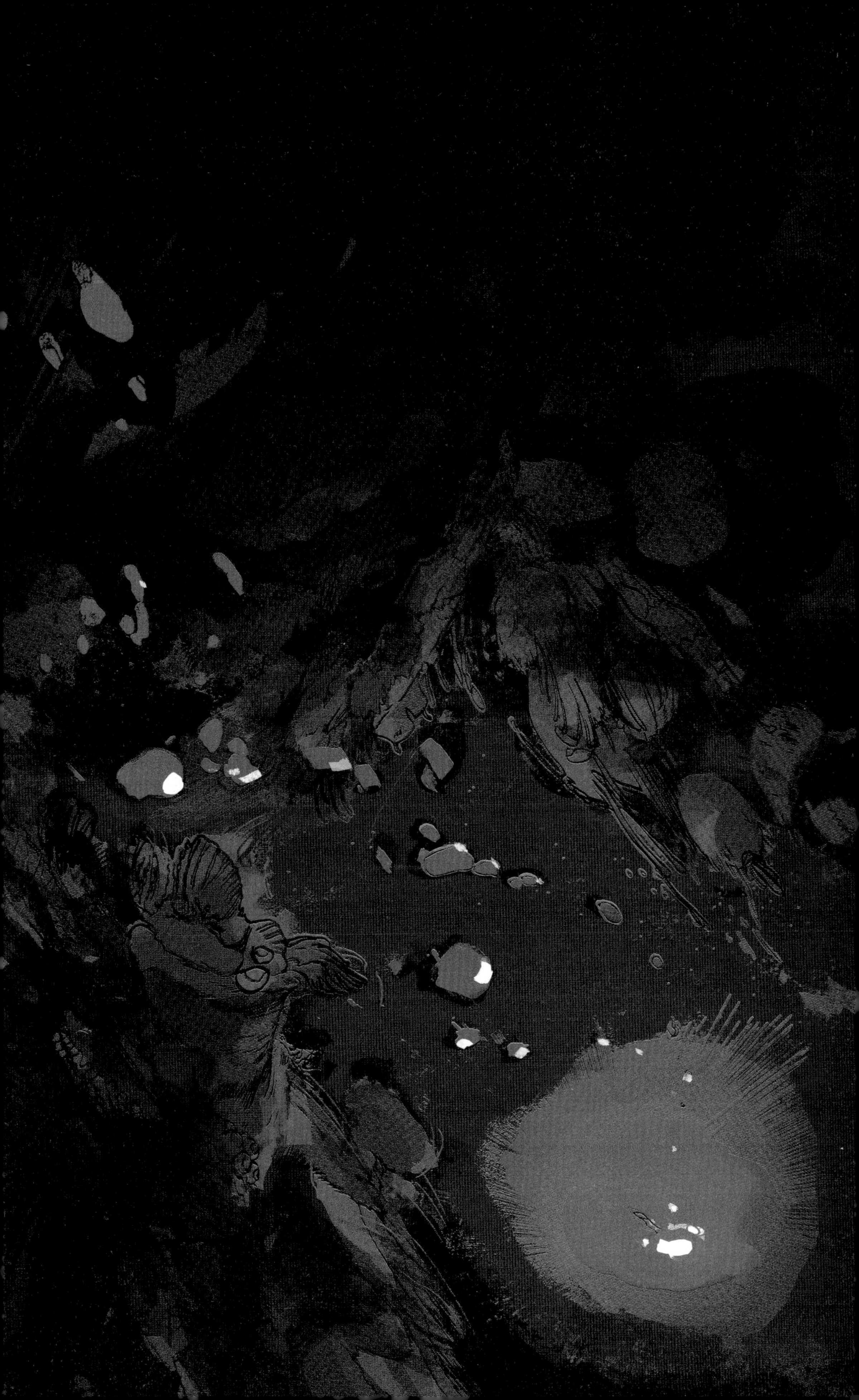

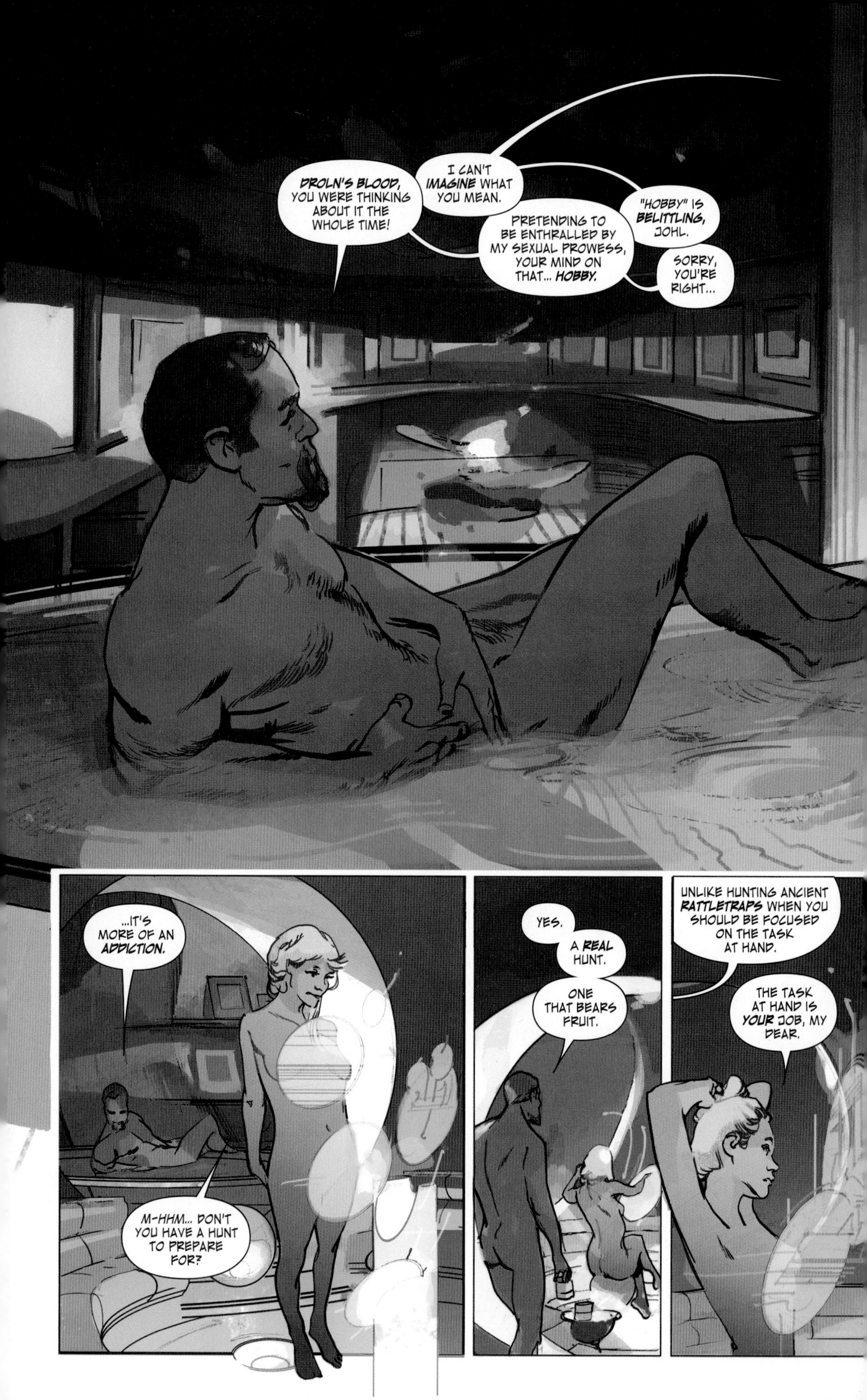
DROLN'S BLOOD, YOU WERE THINKING ABOUT IT THE WHOLE TIME!
I CAN'T IMAGINE WHAT YOU MEAN.
PRETENDING TO BE ENTHRALLED BY MY SEXUAL PROWESS, YOUR MIND ON THAT... HOBBY.
"HOBBY" IS BELITTLING, JOHL.
SORRY, YOU'RE RIGHT...
...IT'S MORE OF AN ADDICTION.
M-HHM... DON'T YOU HAVE A HUNT TO PREPARE FOR?
YES.
A REAL HUNT.
ONE THAT BEARS FRUIT.
UNLIKE HUNTING ANCIENT RATTLETRAPS WHEN YOU SHOULD BE FOCUSED ON THE TASK AT HAND.
THE TASK AT HAND IS YOUR JOB, MY DEAR.

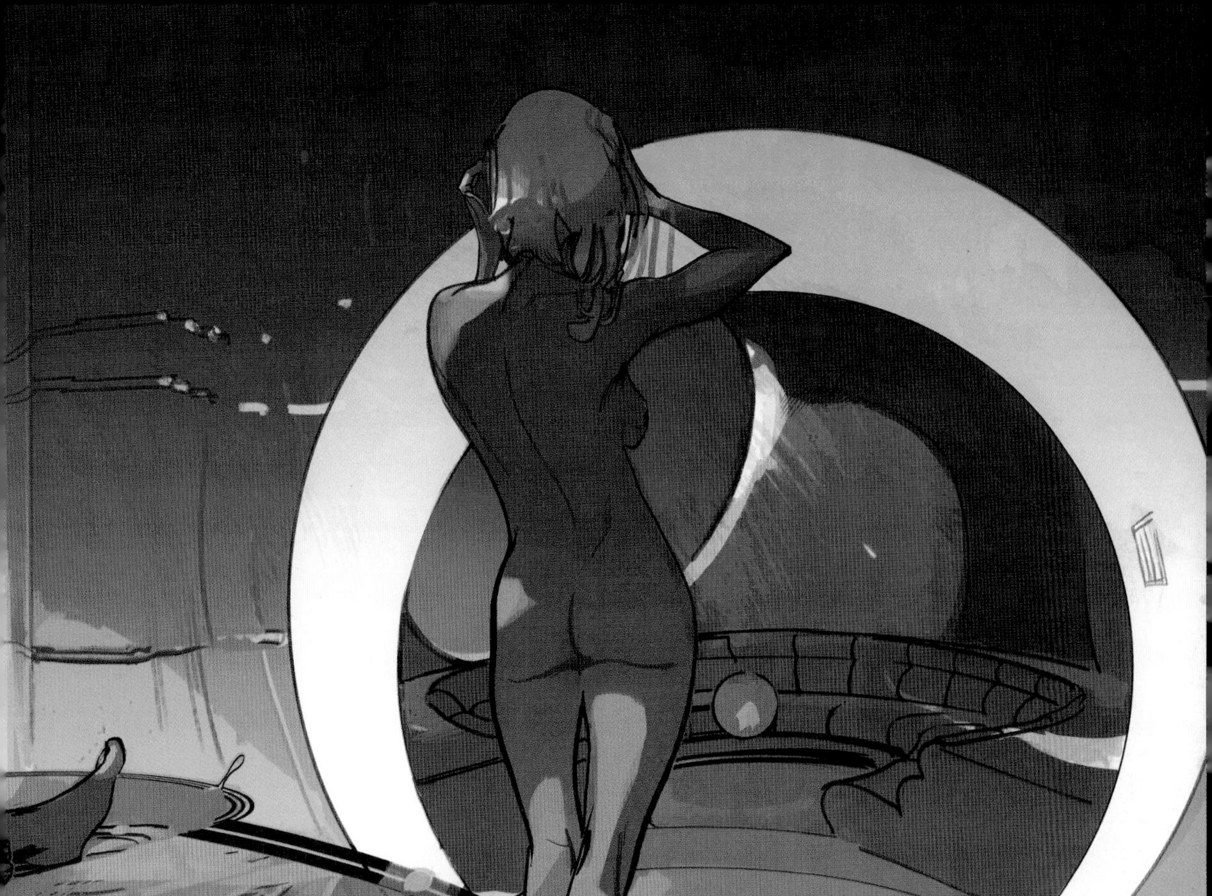

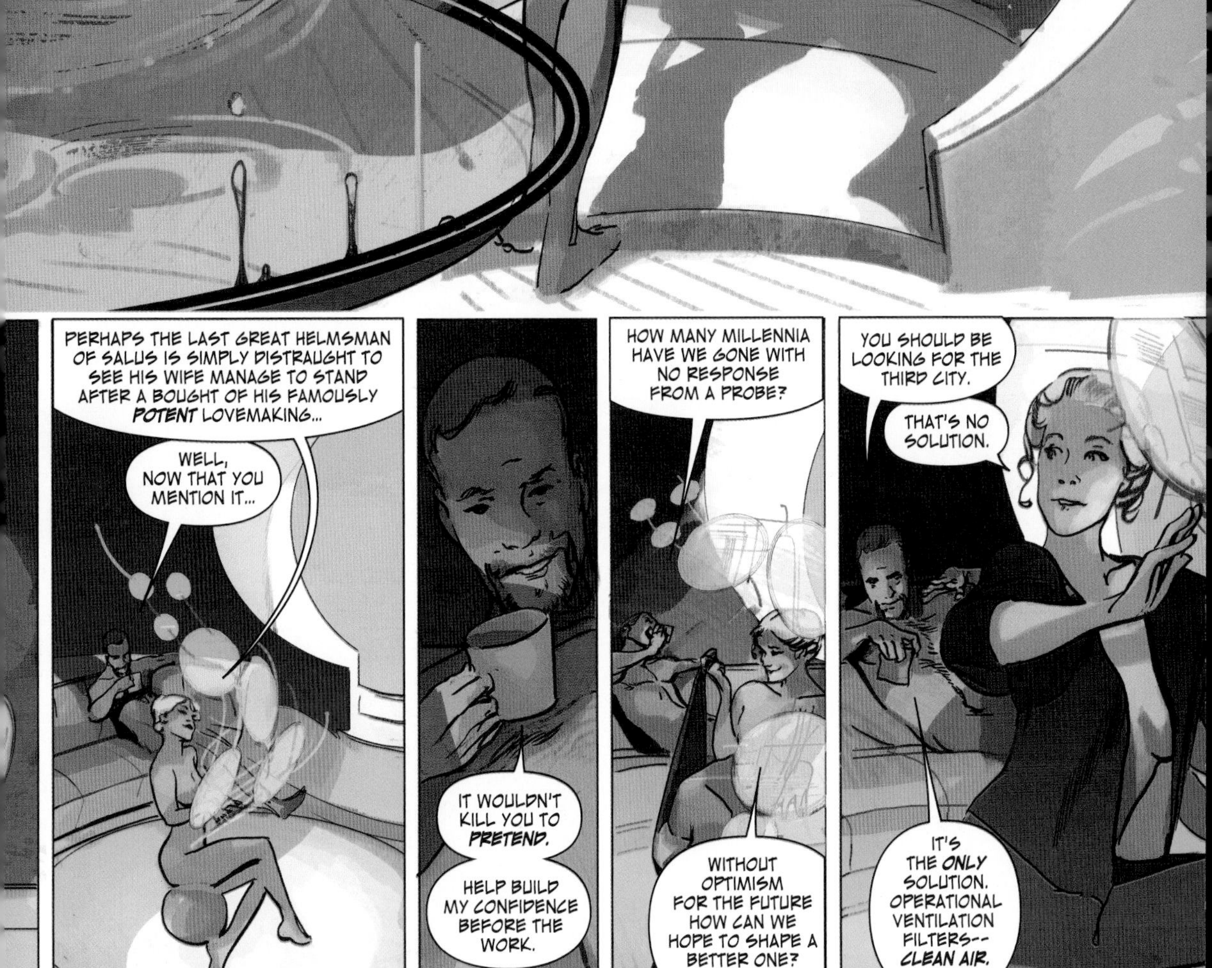
PERHAPS THE LAST GREAT HELMSMAN OF SALUS IS SIMPLY DISTRAUGHT TO SEE HIS WIFE MANAGE TO STAND AFTER A BOUGHT OF HIS FAMOUSLY POTENT LOVEMAKING...
WELL, NOW THAT YOU MENTION IT...
IT WOULDN'T KILL YOU TO PRETEND.
HELP BUILD MY CONFIDENCE BEFORE THE WORK.
HOW MANY MILLENNIA HAVE WE GONE WITH NO RESPONSE FROM A PROBE?
WITHOUT OPTIMISM FOR THE FUTURE HOW CAN WE HOPE TO SHAPE A BETTER ONE?
YOU SHOULD BE LOOKING FOR THE THIRD CITY.
THAT'S NO SOLUTION.
IT'S THE ONLY SOLUTION. OPERATIONAL VENTILATION FILTERS-- CLEAN AIR.

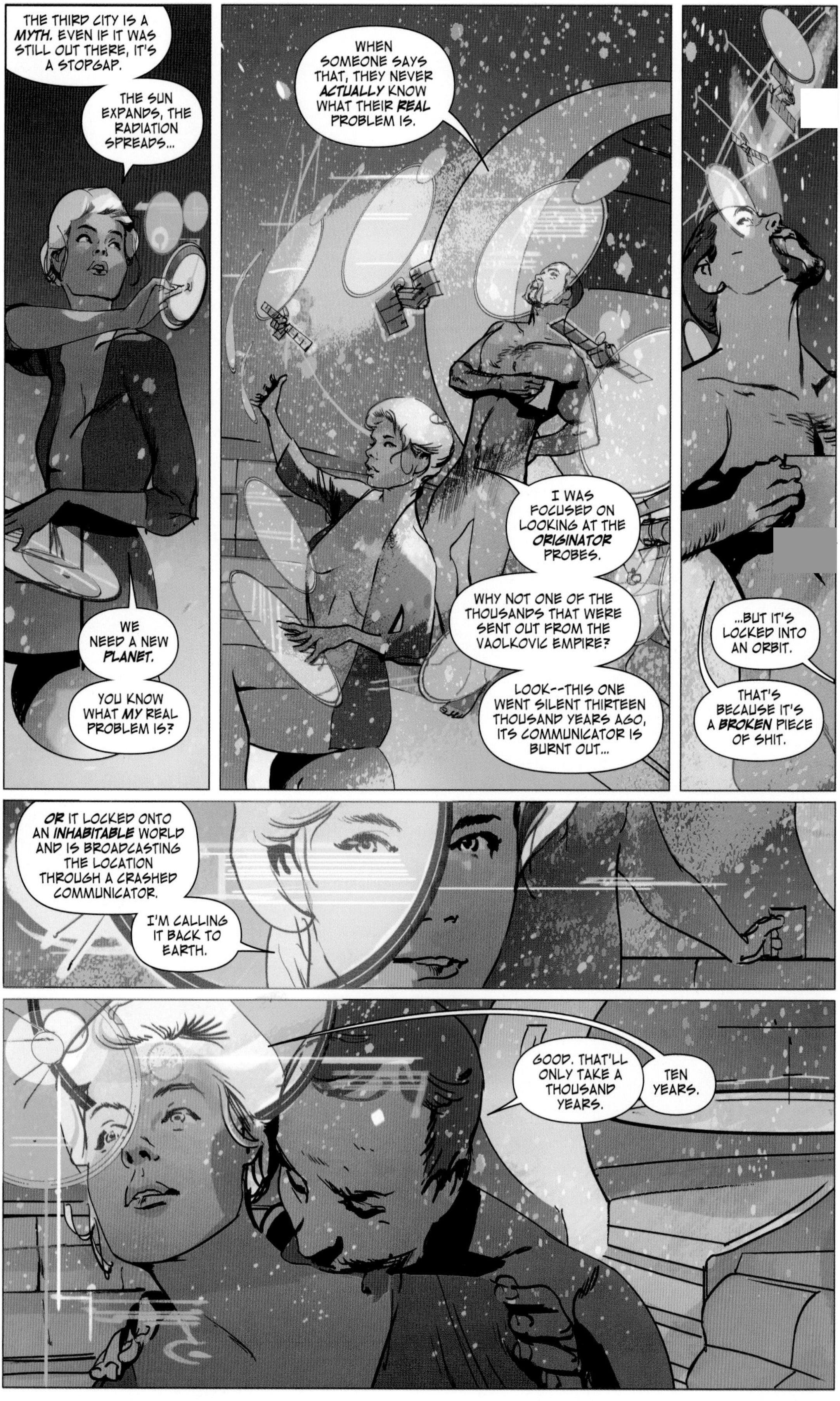
THE THIRD CITY IS A MYTH. EVEN IF IT WAS STILL OUT THERE, IT'S A STOPGAP.
THE SUN EXPANDS, THE RADIATION SPREADS...
WE NEED A NEW PLANET.
YOU KNOW WHAT MY REAL PROBLEM IS?
WHEN SOMEONE SAYS THAT, THEY NEVER ACTUALLY KNOW WHAT THEIR REAL PROBLEM IS.
I WAS FOCUSED ON LOOKING AT THE ORIGINATOR PROBES.
WHY NOT ONE OF THE THOUSANDS THAT WERE SENT OUT FROM THE VAOLKOVIC EMPIRE?
LOOK--THIS ONE WENT SILENT THIRTEEN THOUSAND YEARS AGO, ITS COMMUNICATOR IS BURNT OUT...
...BUT IT'S LOCKED INTO AN ORBIT.
THAT'S BECAUSE IT'S A BROKEN PIECE OF SHIT.
OR IT LOCKED ONTO AN INHABITABLE WORLD AND IS BROADCASTING THE LOCATION THROUGH A CRASHED COMMUNICATOR.
I'M CALLING IT BACK TO EARTH.
GOOD. THAT'LL ONLY TAKE A THOUSAND YEARS.
TEN YEARS.

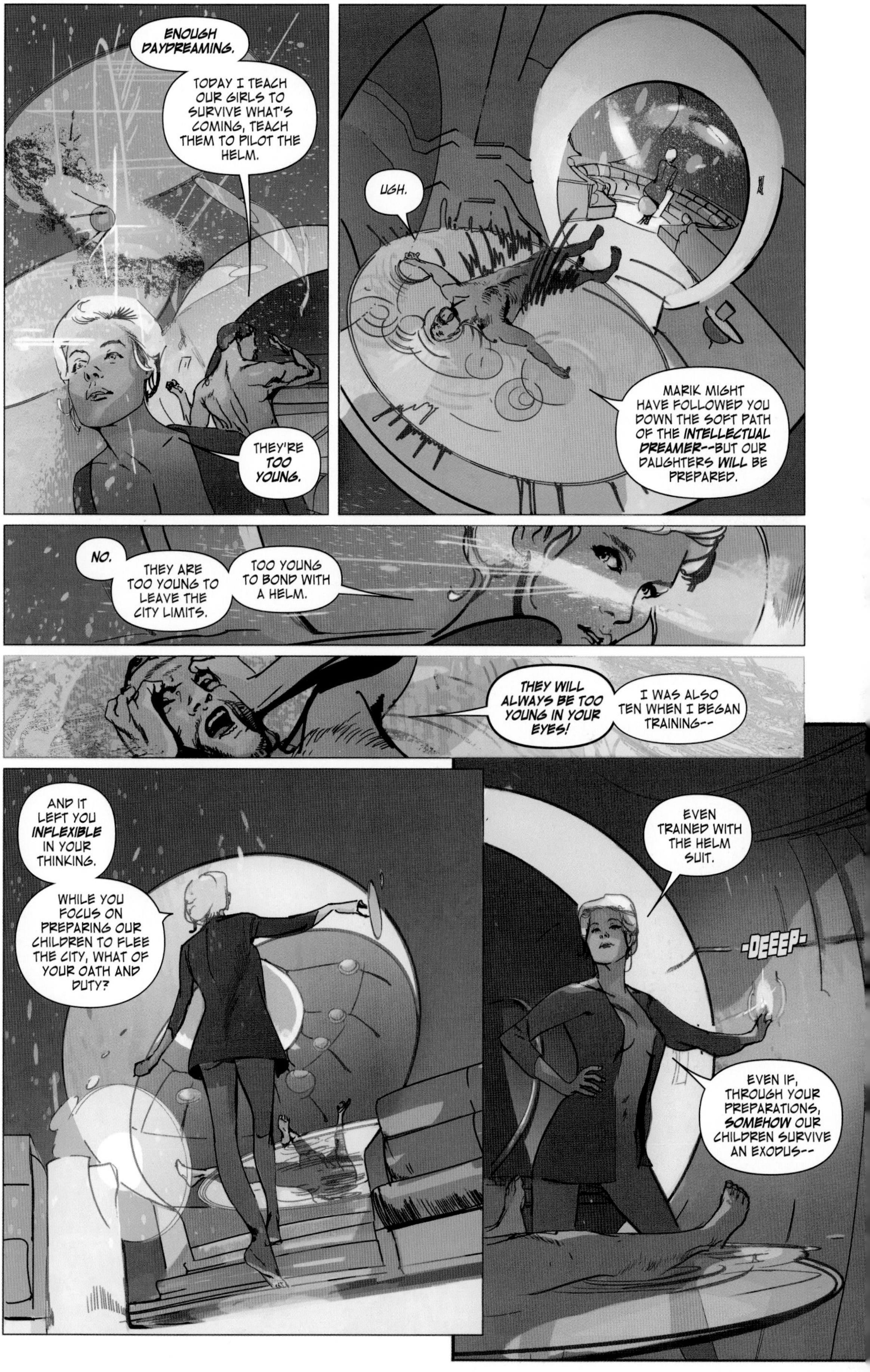
ENOUGH DAYDREAMING.
TODAY I TEACH OUR GIRLS TO SURVIVE WHAT'S COMING, TEACH THEM TO PILOT THE HELM.
THEY'RE TOO YOUNG.
UGH.
MARIK MIGHT HAVE FOLLOWED YOU DOWN THE SOFT PATH OF THE INTELLECTUAL DREAMER--BUT OUR DAUGHTERS WILL BE PREPARED.
NO.
THEY ARE TOO YOUNG TO LEAVE THE CITY LIMITS.
TOO YOUNG TO BOND WITH A HELM.
THEY WILL ALWAYS BE TOO YOUNG IN YOUR EYES!
I WAS ALSO TEN WHEN I BEGAN TRAINING--
AND IT LEFT YOU INFLEXIBLE IN YOUR THINKING.
WHILE YOU FOCUS ON PREPARING OUR CHILDREN TO FLEE THE CITY, WHAT OF YOUR OATH AND DUTY?
EVEN TRAINED WITH THE HELM SUIT.
-DEEEP-
EVEN IF, THROUGH YOUR PREPARATIONS, SOMEHOW OUR CHILDREN SURVIVE AN EXODUS--

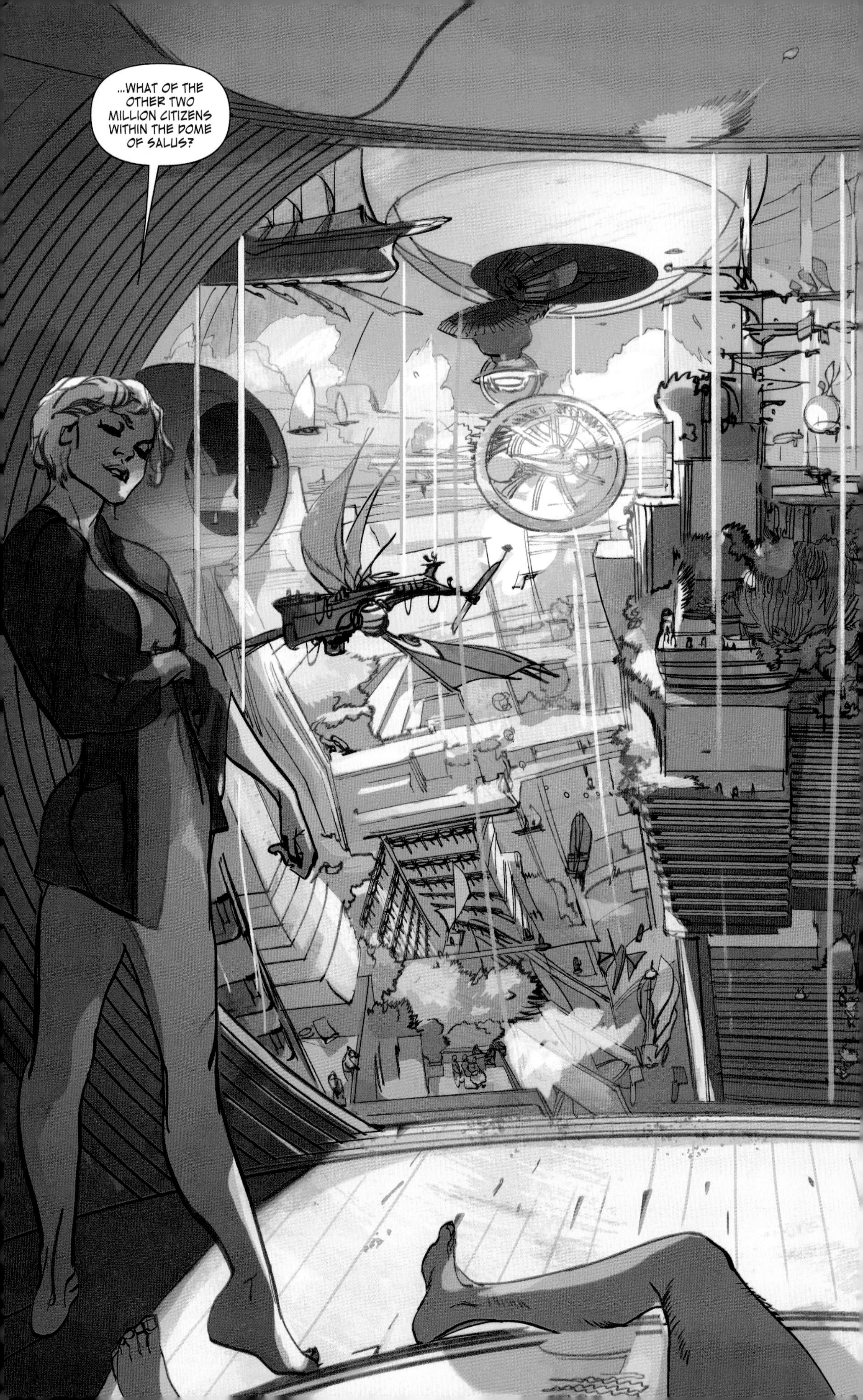
...WHAT OF THE OTHER TWO MILLION CITIZENS WITHIN THE DOME OF SALUS?

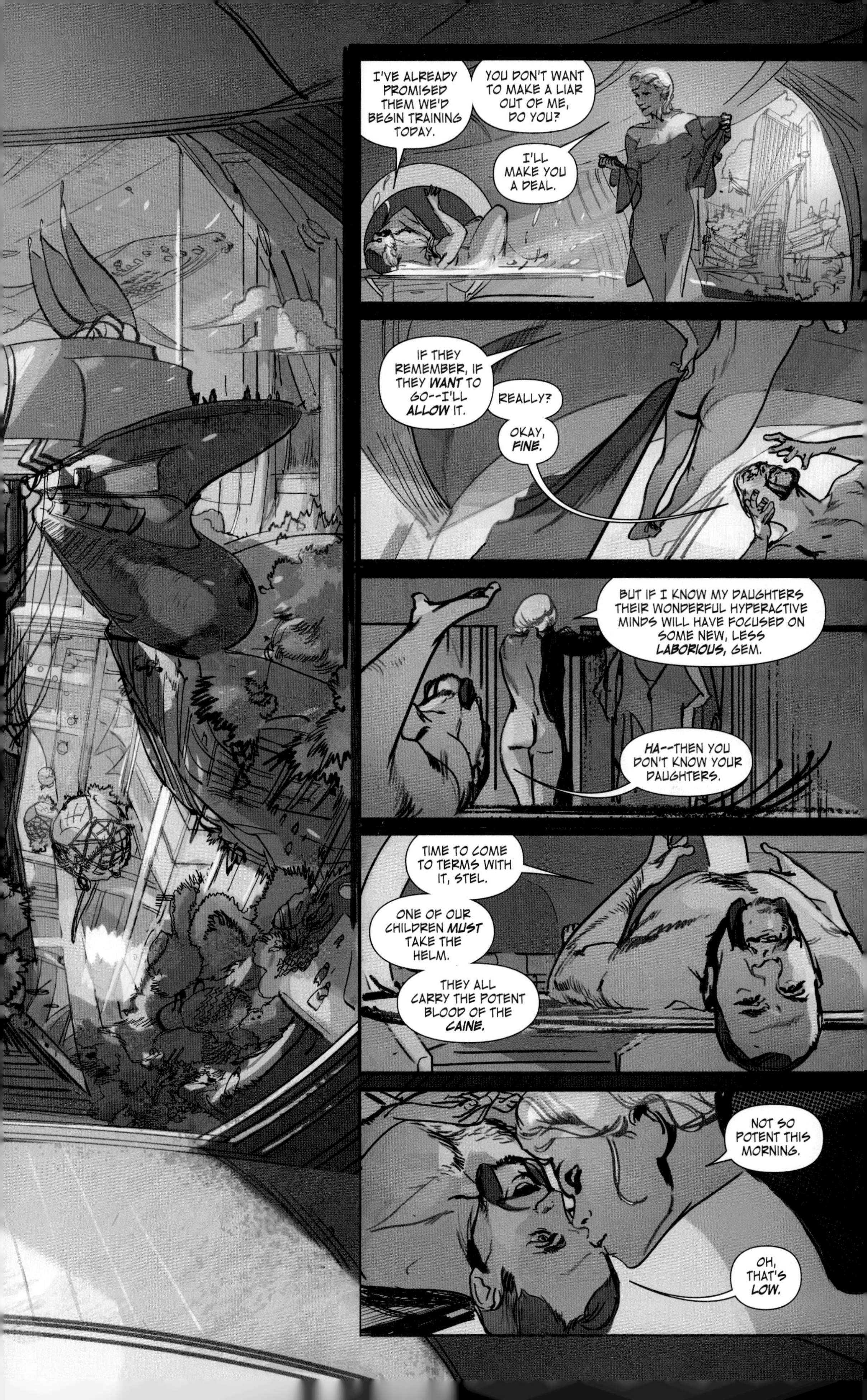
I'VE ALREADY PROMISED THEM WE'D BEGIN TRAINING TODAY.
YOU DON'T WANT TO MAKE A LIAR OUT OF ME, DO YOU?
I'LL MAKE YOU A DEAL.
IF THEY REMEMBER, IF THEY WANT TO GO--I'LL ALLOW IT.
REALLY?
OKAY, FINE.
BUT IF I KNOW MY DAUGHTERS THEIR WONDERFUL HYPERACTIVE MINDS WILL HAVE FOCUSED ON SOME NEW, LESS LABORIOUS, GEM.
HA--THEN YOU DON'T KNOW YOUR DAUGHTERS.
TIME TO COME TO TERMS WITH IT, STEL.
ONE OF OUR CHILDREN MUST TAKE THE HELM.
THEY ALL CARRY THE POTENT BLOOD OF THE CAINE.
NOT SO POTENT THIS MORNING.
OH, THAT'S LOW.

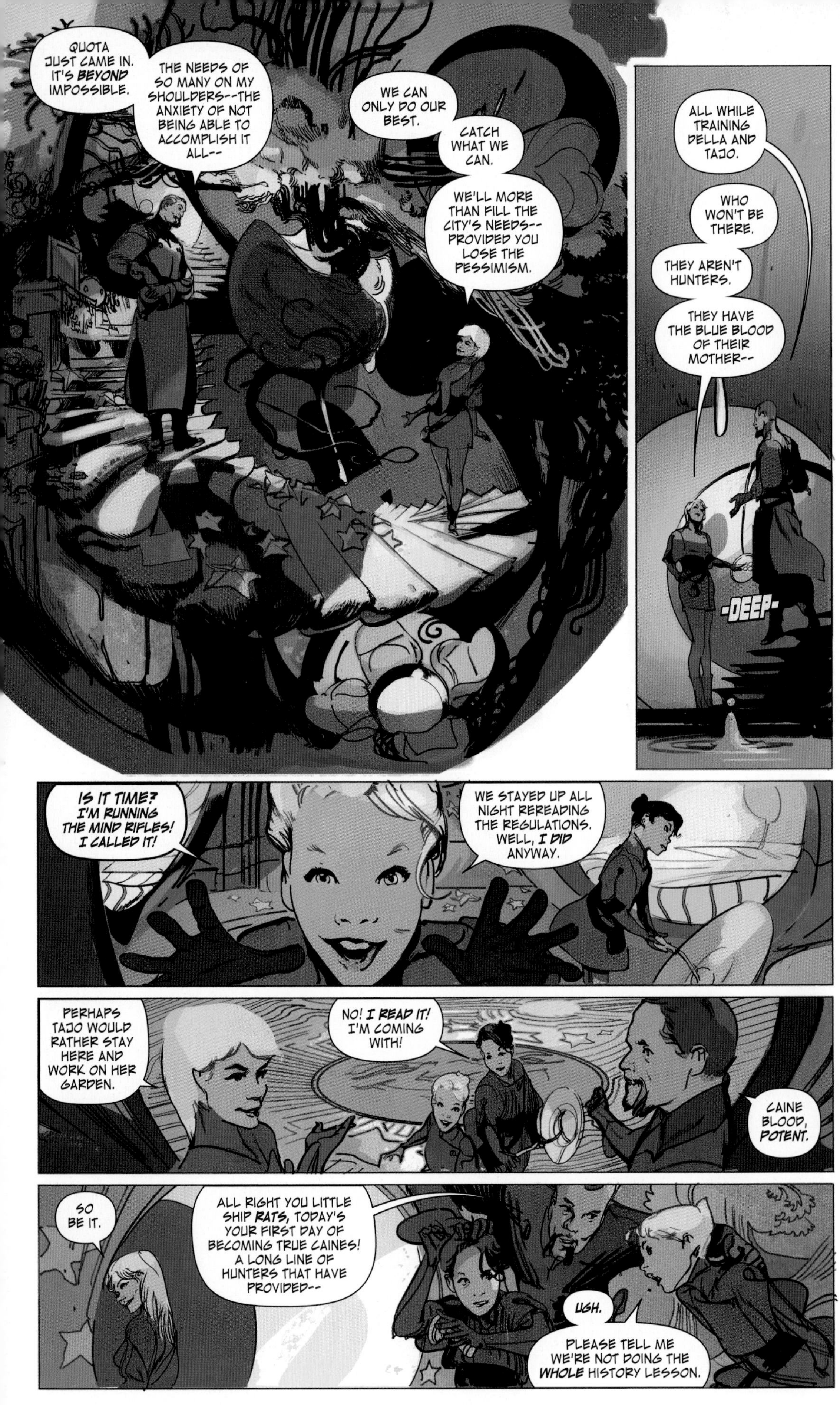
QUOTA JUST CAME IN. IT'S **BEYOND** IMPOSSIBLE.
THE NEEDS OF SO MANY ON MY SHOULDERS--THE ANXIETY OF NOT BEING ABLE TO ACCOMPLISH IT ALL--
WE CAN ONLY DO OUR BEST.
CATCH WHAT WE CAN.
WE'LL MORE THAN FILL THE CITY'S NEEDS--PROVIDED YOU LOSE THE PESSIMISM.
ALL WHILE TRAINING DELLA AND TAJO.
WHO WON'T BE THERE.
THEY AREN'T HUNTERS.
THEY HAVE THE BLUE BLOOD OF THEIR MOTHER--
-DEEP-
***IS IT TIME? I'M RUNNING THE MIND RIFLES! I CALLED IT!***
WE STAYED UP ALL NIGHT REREADING THE REGULATIONS. WELL, ***I DID*** ANYWAY.
PERHAPS TAJO WOULD RATHER STAY HERE AND WORK ON HER GARDEN.
NO! ***I READ IT!*** I'M COMING WITH!
CAINE BLOOD, **POTENT.**
SO BE IT.
ALL RIGHT YOU LITTLE SHIP **RATS,** TODAY'S YOUR FIRST DAY OF BECOMING TRUE CAINES! A LONG LINE OF HUNTERS THAT HAVE PROVIDED--
***UGH.***
PLEASE TELL ME WE'RE NOT DOING THE ***WHOLE*** HISTORY LESSON.

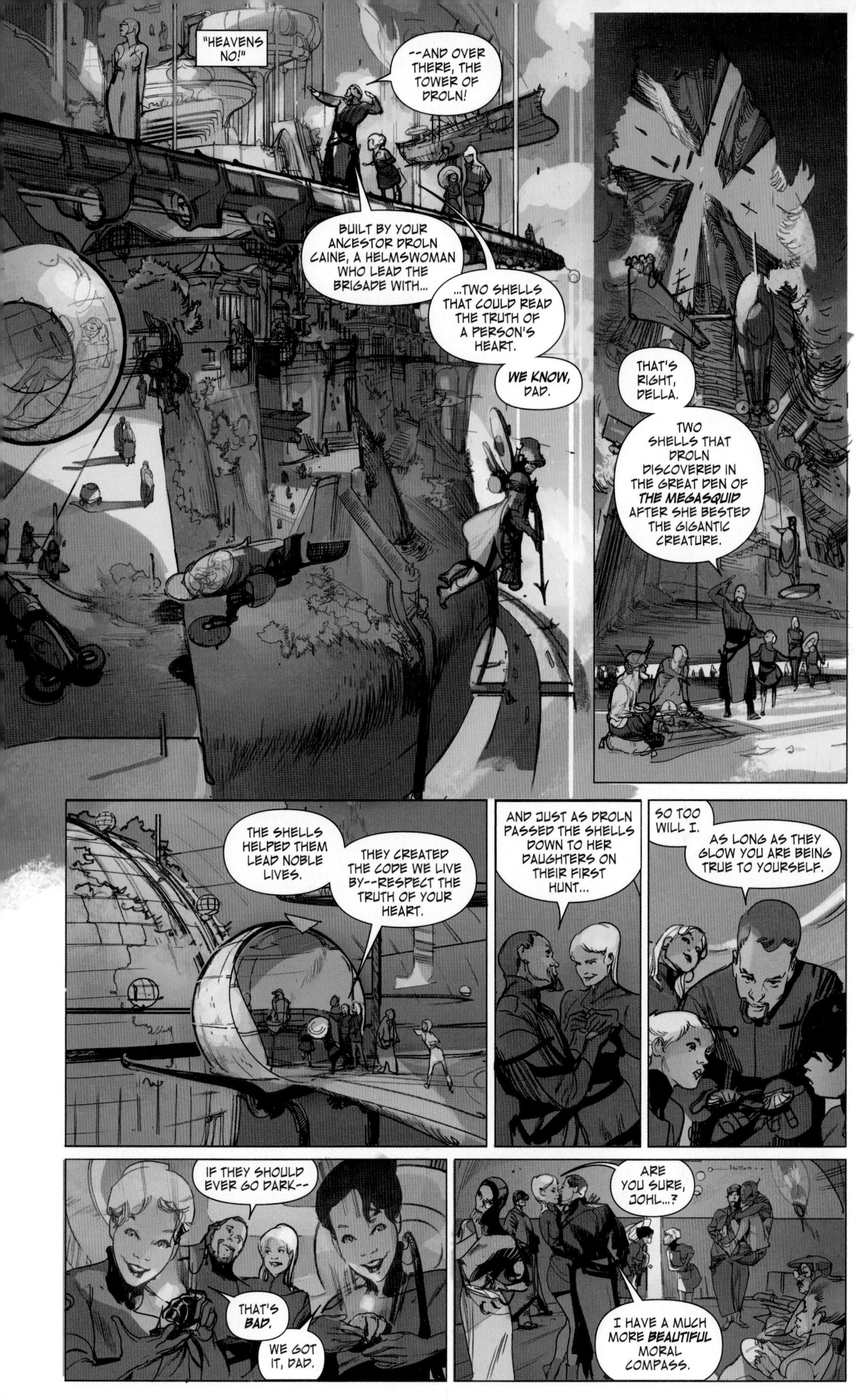
"HEAVENS NO!"
--AND OVER THERE, THE TOWER OF DROLN!
BUILT BY YOUR ANCESTOR DROLN CAINE, A HELMSWOMAN WHO LEAD THE BRIGADE WITH...
...TWO SHELLS THAT COULD READ THE TRUTH OF A PERSON'S HEART.
WE KNOW, DAD.
THAT'S RIGHT, DELLA.
TWO SHELLS THAT DROLN DISCOVERED IN THE GREAT DEN OF THE MEGASQUID AFTER SHE BESTED THE GIGANTIC CREATURE.
THE SHELLS HELPED THEM LEAD NOBLE LIVES.
THEY CREATED THE CODE WE LIVE BY--RESPECT THE TRUTH OF YOUR HEART.
AND JUST AS DROLN PASSED THE SHELLS DOWN TO HER DAUGHTERS ON THEIR FIRST HUNT...
SO TOO WILL I.
AS LONG AS THEY GLOW YOU ARE BEING TRUE TO YOURSELF.
IF THEY SHOULD EVER GO DARK--
THAT'S BAD.
WE GOT IT, DAD.
ARE YOU SURE, JOHL...?
I HAVE A MUCH MORE BEAUTIFUL MORAL COMPASS.

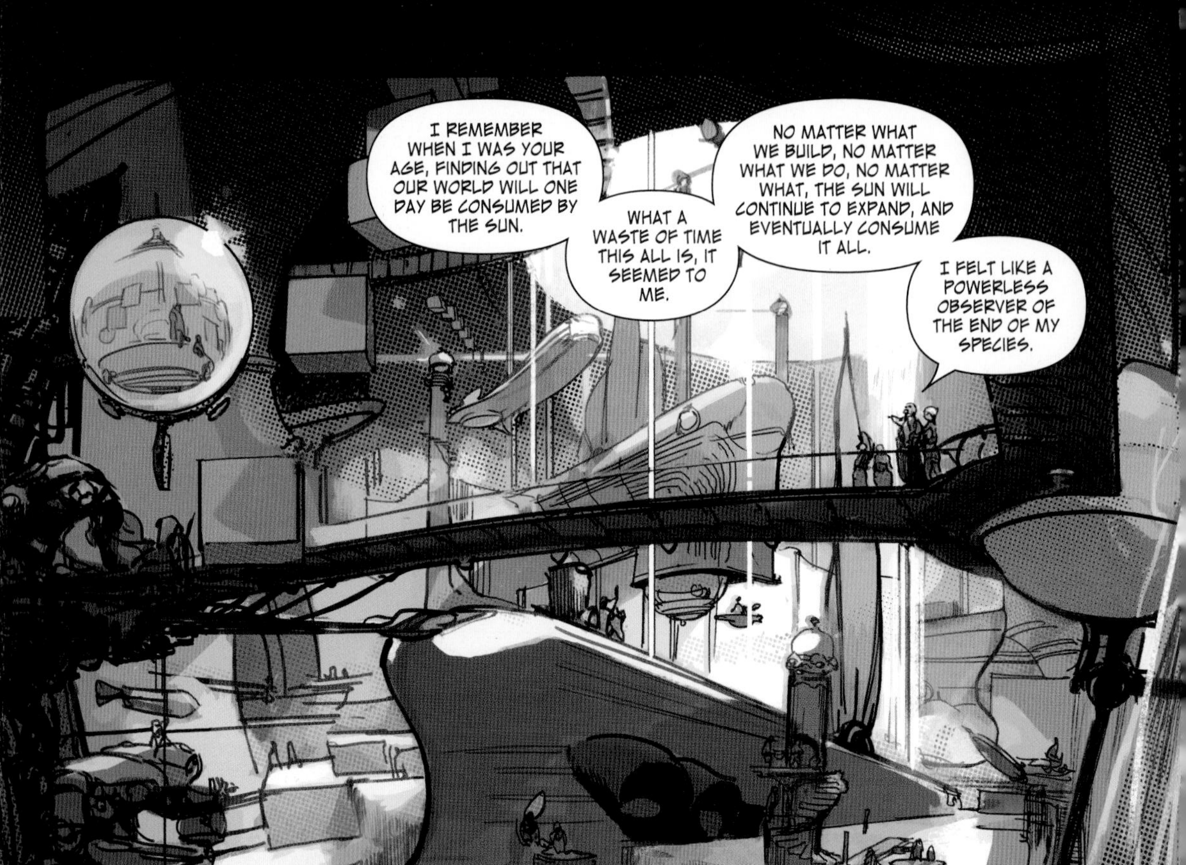
I REMEMBER WHEN I WAS YOUR AGE, FINDING OUT THAT OUR WORLD WILL ONE DAY BE CONSUMED BY THE SUN.
WHAT A WASTE OF TIME THIS ALL IS, IT SEEMED TO ME.
NO MATTER WHAT WE BUILD, NO MATTER WHAT WE DO, NO MATTER WHAT, THE SUN WILL CONTINUE TO EXPAND, AND EVENTUALLY CONSUME IT ALL.
I FELT LIKE A POWERLESS OBSERVER OF THE END OF MY SPECIES.

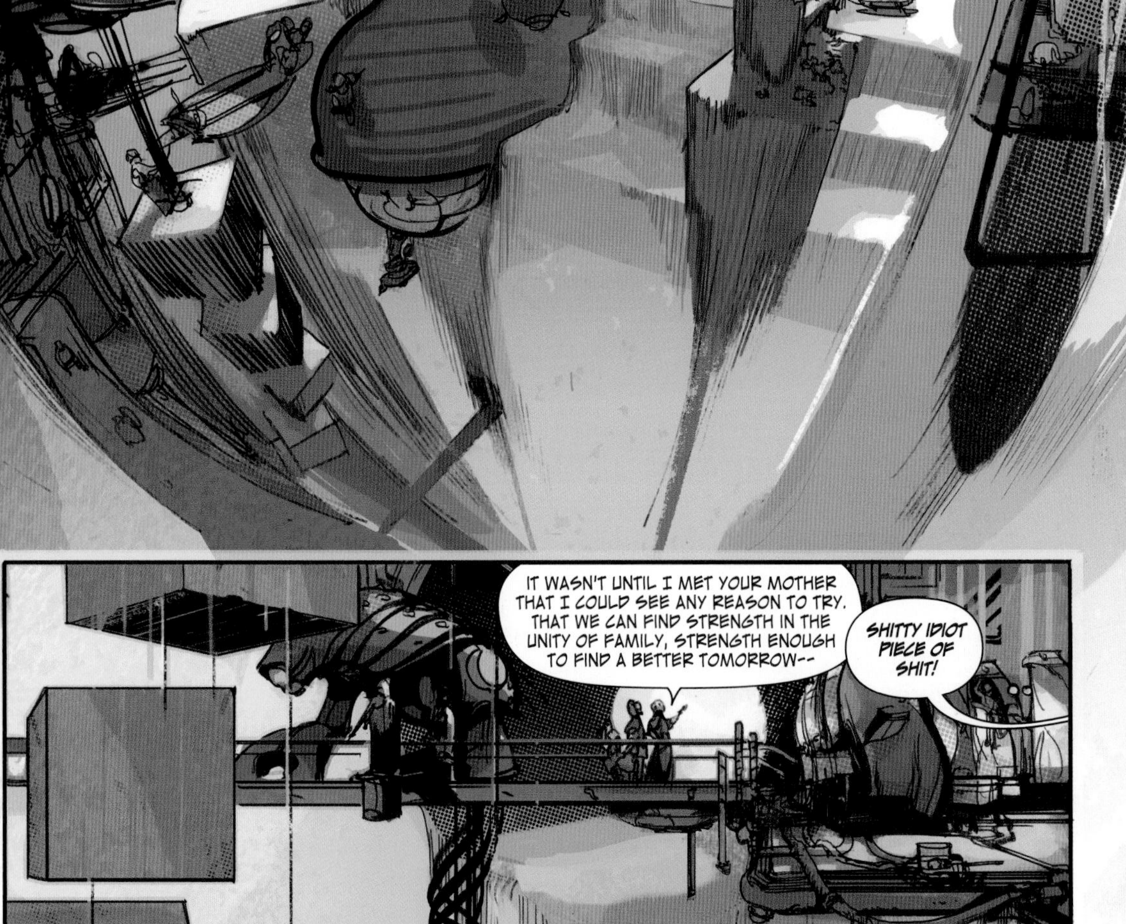
IT WASN'T UNTIL I MET YOUR MOTHER THAT I COULD SEE ANY REASON TO TRY. THAT WE CAN FIND STRENGTH IN THE UNITY OF FAMILY, STRENGTH ENOUGH TO FIND A BETTER TOMORROW--
SHITTY IDIOT PIECE OF SHIT!

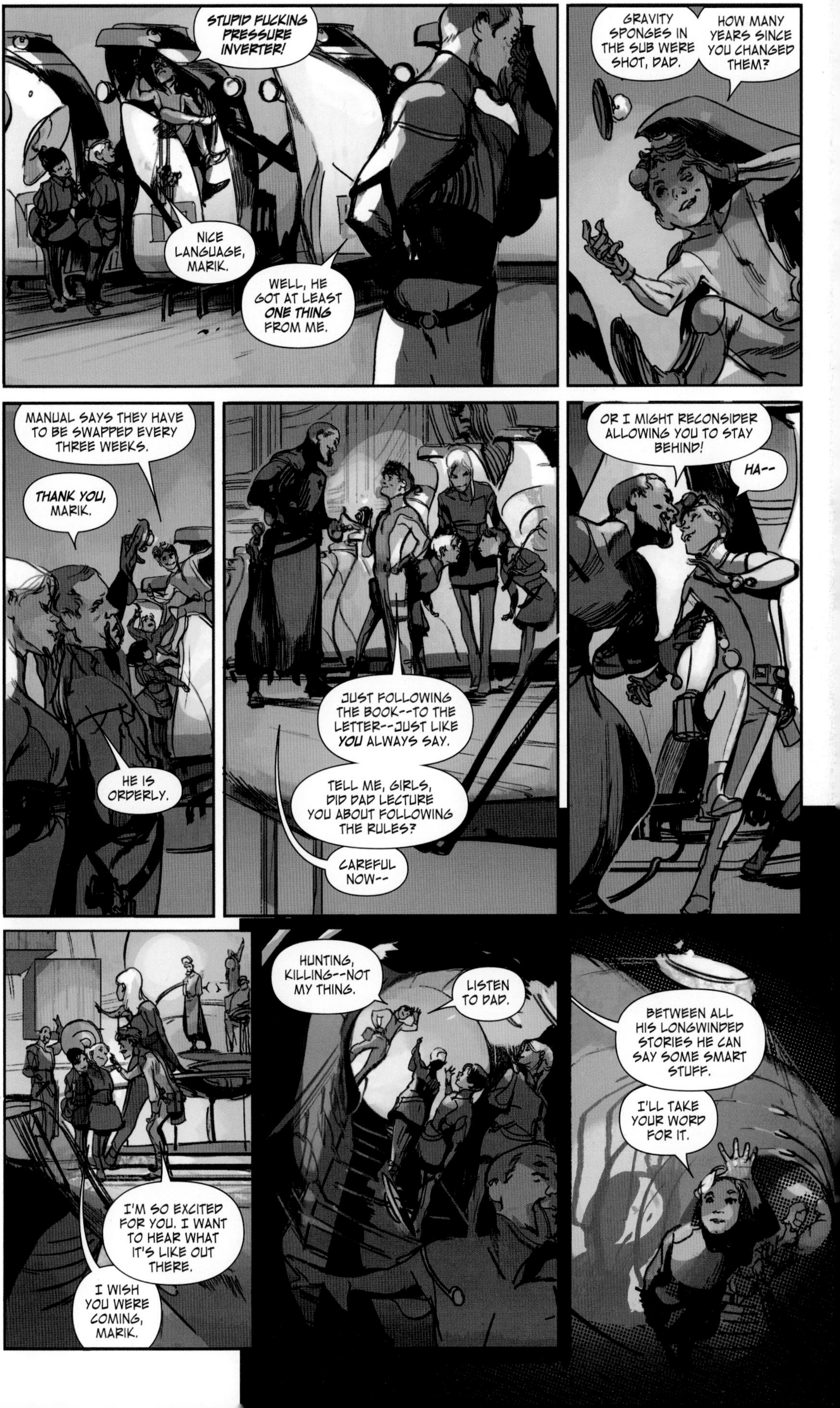
STUPID FUCKING PRESSURE INVERTER!
NICE LANGUAGE, MARIK.
WELL, HE GOT AT LEAST ONE THING FROM ME.
GRAVITY SPONGES IN THE SUB WERE SHOT, DAD.
HOW MANY YEARS SINCE YOU CHANGED THEM?
MANUAL SAYS THEY HAVE TO BE SWAPPED EVERY THREE WEEKS.
THANK YOU, MARIK.
HE IS ORDERLY.
JUST FOLLOWING THE BOOK--TO THE LETTER--JUST LIKE YOU ALWAYS SAY.
TELL ME, GIRLS, DID DAD LECTURE YOU ABOUT FOLLOWING THE RULES?
CAREFUL NOW--
OR I MIGHT RECONSIDER ALLOWING YOU TO STAY BEHIND!
HA--
I'M SO EXCITED FOR YOU. I WANT TO HEAR WHAT IT'S LIKE OUT THERE.
I WISH YOU WERE COMING, MARIK.
HUNTING, KILLING--NOT MY THING.
LISTEN TO DAD.
BETWEEN ALL HIS LONGWINDED STORIES HE CAN SAY SOME SMART STUFF.
I'LL TAKE YOUR WORD FOR IT.

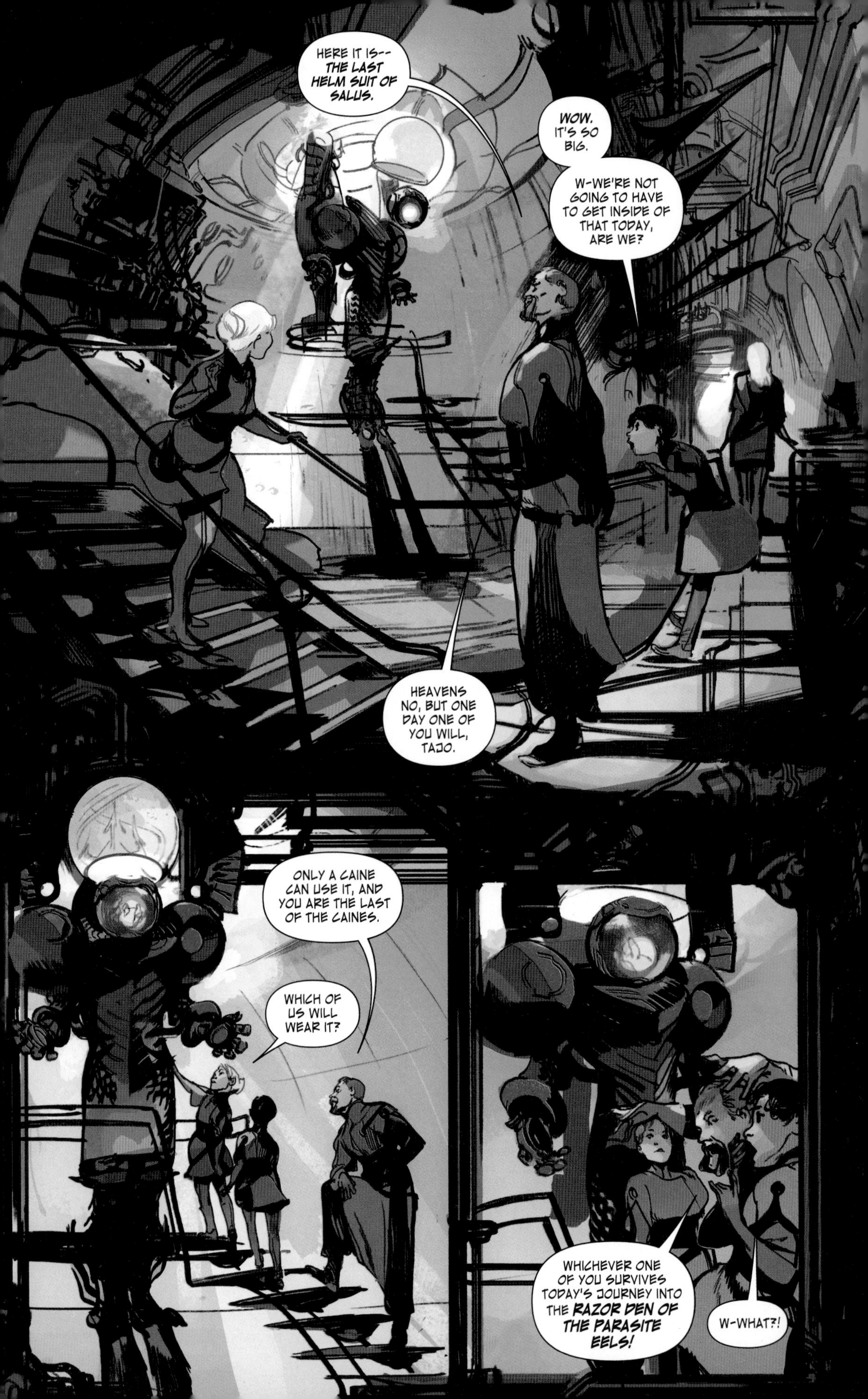
HERE IT IS-- THE LAST HELM SUIT OF SALUS.
WOW. IT'S SO BIG.
W-WE'RE NOT GOING TO HAVE TO GET INSIDE OF THAT TODAY, ARE WE?
HEAVENS NO, BUT ONE DAY ONE OF YOU WILL, TAJO.
ONLY A CAINE CAN USE IT, AND YOU ARE THE LAST OF THE CAINES.
WHICH OF US WILL WEAR IT?
WHICHEVER ONE OF YOU SURVIVES TODAY'S JOURNEY INTO THE RAZOR DEN OF THE PARASITE EELS!
W-WHAT?!

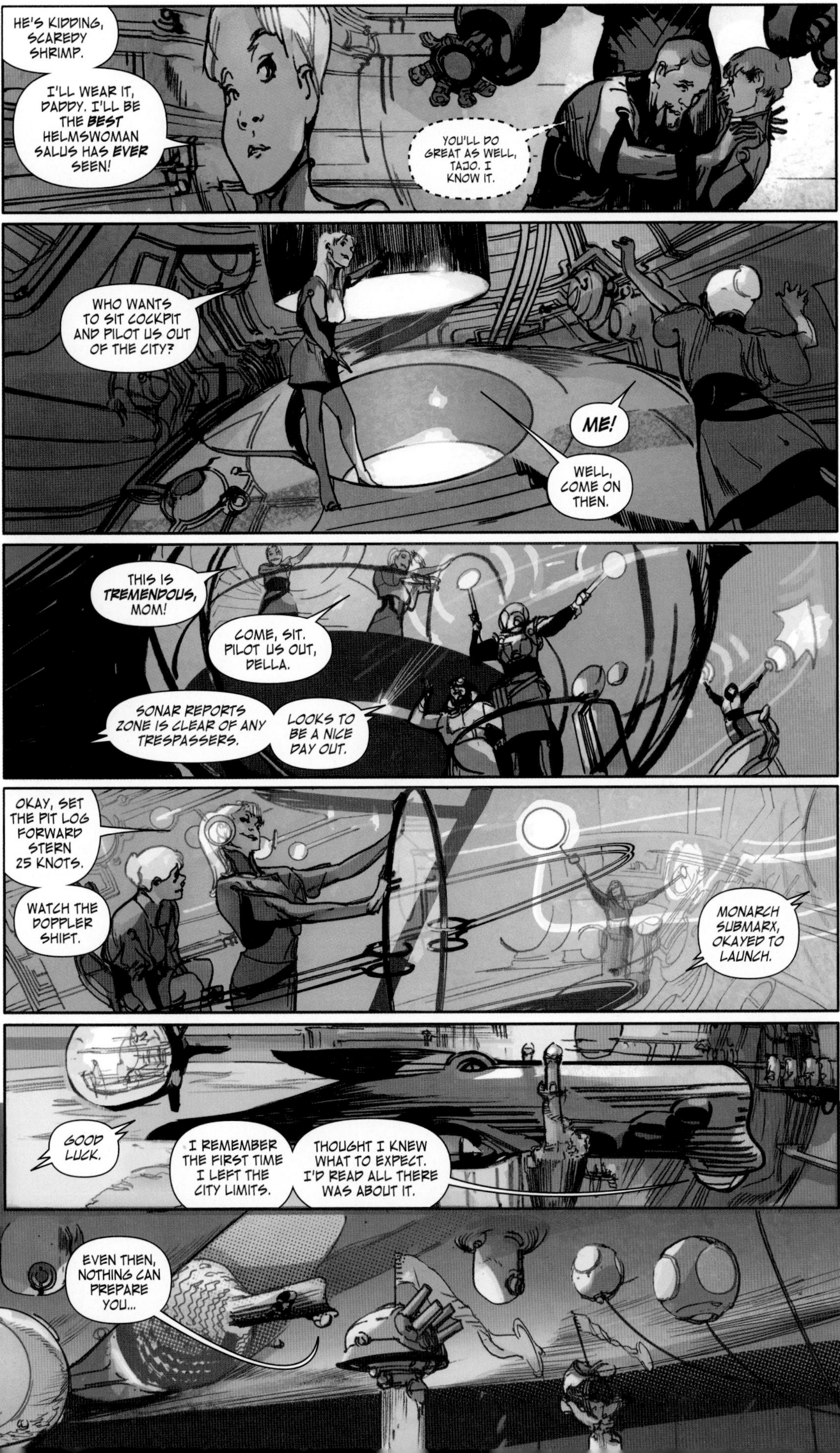
HE'S KIDDING, SCAREDY SHRIMP.
I'LL WEAR IT, DADDY. I'LL BE THE BEST HELMSWOMAN SALUS HAS EVER SEEN!
YOU'LL DO GREAT AS WELL, TAJO. I KNOW IT.
WHO WANTS TO SIT COCKPIT AND PILOT US OUT OF THE CITY?
ME!
WELL, COME ON THEN.
THIS IS TREMENDOUS, MOM!
COME, SIT. PILOT US OUT, DELLA.
SONAR REPORTS ZONE IS CLEAR OF ANY TRESPASSERS.
LOOKS TO BE A NICE DAY OUT.
OKAY, SET THE PIT LOG FORWARD STERN 25 KNOTS.
WATCH THE DOPPLER SHIFT.
MONARCH SUBMARX, OKAYED TO LAUNCH.
GOOD LUCK.
I REMEMBER THE FIRST TIME I LEFT THE CITY LIMITS.
THOUGHT I KNEW WHAT TO EXPECT. I'D READ ALL THERE WAS ABOUT IT.
EVEN THEN, NOTHING CAN PREPARE YOU...

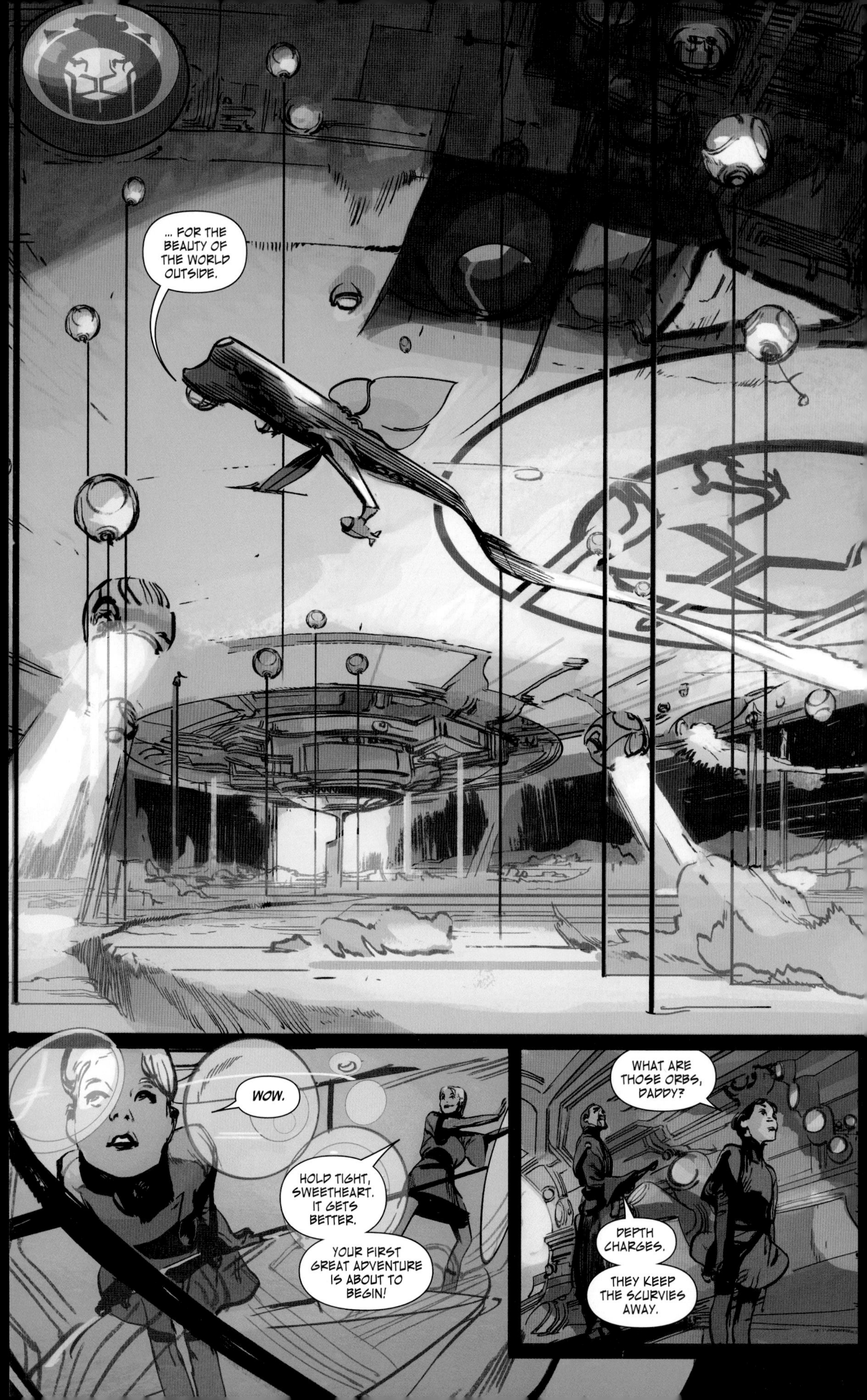
... FOR THE BEAUTY OF THE WORLD OUTSIDE.
WOW.
HOLD TIGHT, SWEETHEART. IT GETS BETTER.
YOUR FIRST GREAT ADVENTURE IS ABOUT TO BEGIN!
WHAT ARE THOSE ORBS, DADDY?
DEPTH CHARGES.
THEY KEEP THE SCURVIES AWAY.

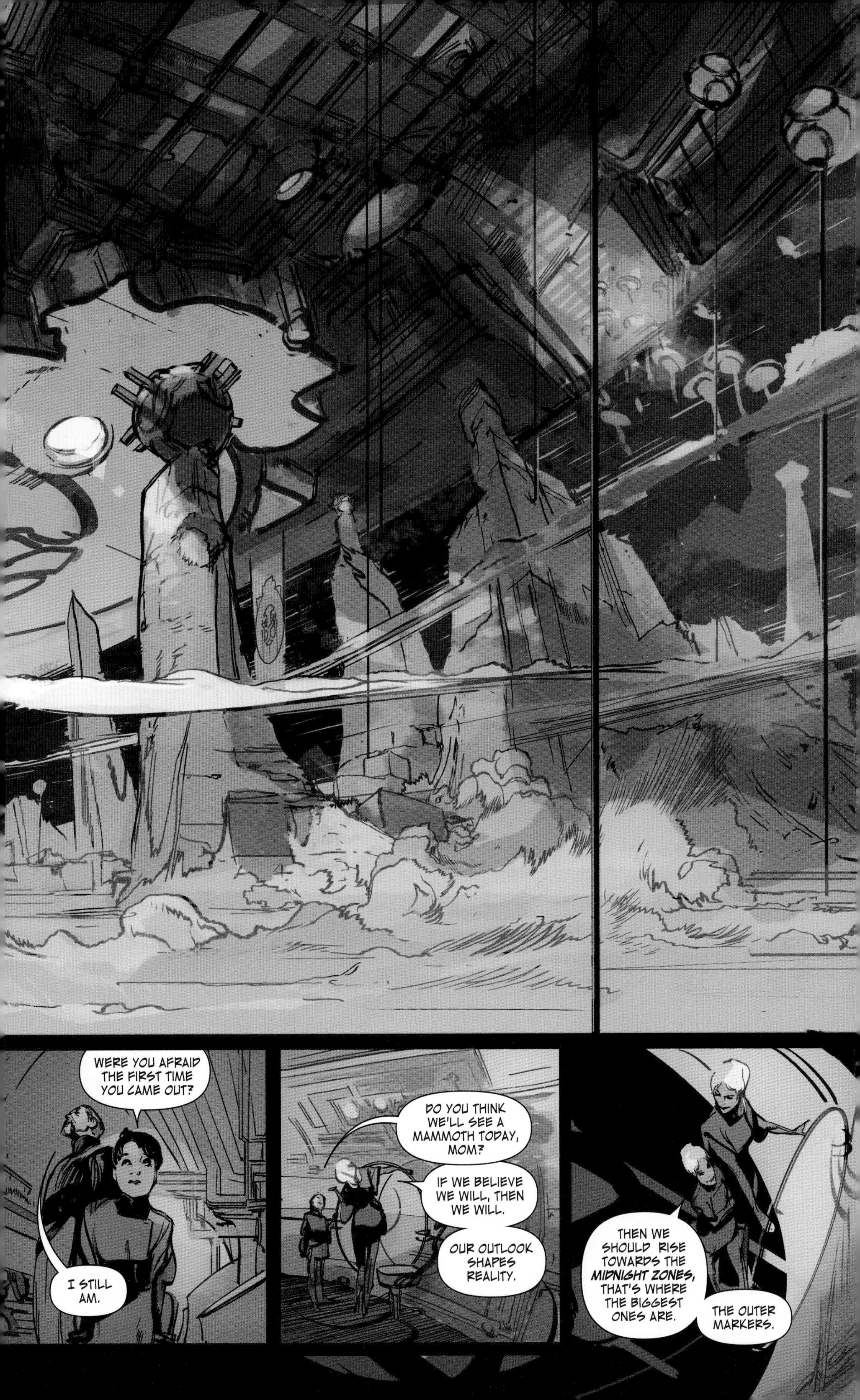
WERE YOU AFRAID THE FIRST TIME YOU CAME OUT?
I STILL AM.
DO YOU THINK WE'LL SEE A MAMMOTH TODAY, MOM?
IF WE BELIEVE WE WILL, THEN WE WILL.
OUR OUTLOOK SHAPES REALITY.
THEN WE SHOULD RISE TOWARDS THE *MIDNIGHT ZONES,* THAT'S WHERE THE BIGGEST ONES ARE.
THE OUTER MARKERS.

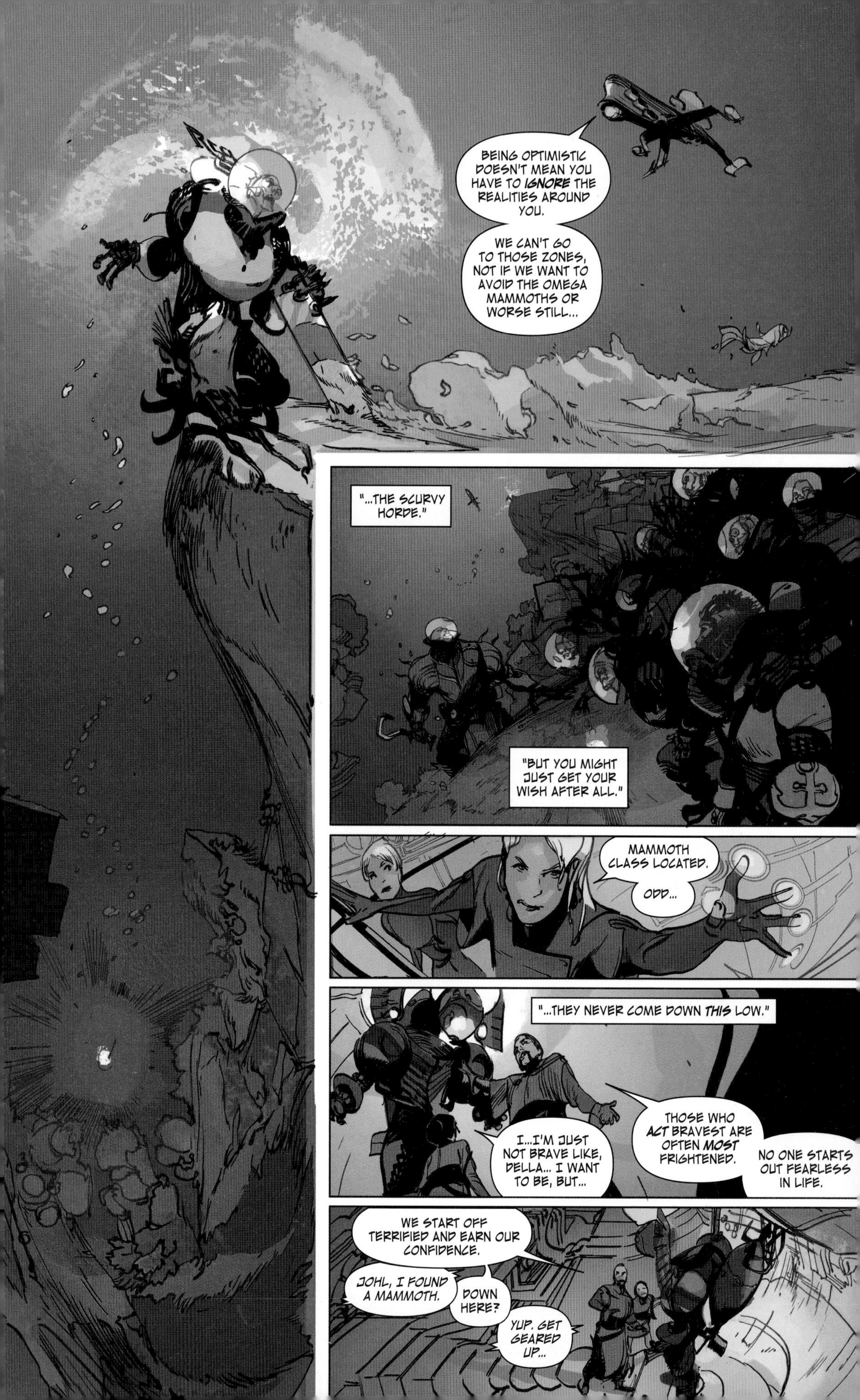
BEING OPTIMISTIC DOESN'T MEAN YOU HAVE TO IGNORE THE REALITIES AROUND YOU.
WE CAN'T GO TO THOSE ZONES, NOT IF WE WANT TO AVOID THE OMEGA MAMMOTHS OR WORSE STILL...
"...THE SCURVY HORDE."
"BUT YOU MIGHT JUST GET YOUR WISH AFTER ALL."
MAMMOTH CLASS LOCATED.
ODD...
"...THEY NEVER COME DOWN THIS LOW."
I...I'M JUST NOT BRAVE LIKE, DELLA... I WANT TO BE, BUT...
THOSE WHO ACT BRAVEST ARE OFTEN MOST FRIGHTENED.
NO ONE STARTS OUT FEARLESS IN LIFE.
WE START OFF TERRIFIED AND EARN OUR CONFIDENCE.
JOHL, I FOUND A MAMMOTH.
DOWN HERE?
YUP. GET GEARED UP...

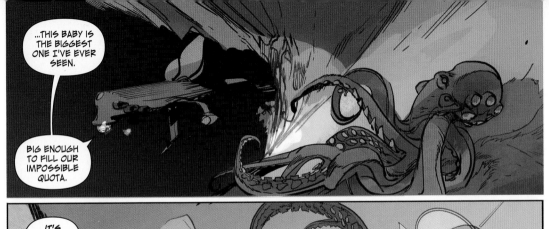

...THIS BABY IS THE BIGGEST ONE I'VE EVER SEEN.

BIG ENOUGH TO FILL OUR IMPOSSIBLE QUOTA.

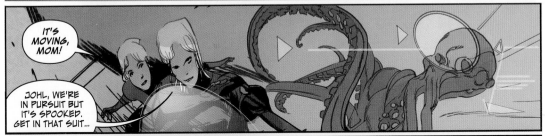

IT'S MOVING, MOM!

JOHL, WE'RE IN PURSUIT BUT IT'S SPOOKED. GET IN THAT SUIT...

...BE READY TO LAUNCH!

HOLD ON-- IT INKED!

I'M LOST, READOUTS ARE DEAD--NEVER SEEN INK LIKE THIS--

BIO-MAGNETIC CLOAKING!

NEVER SEEN ONE SO DELIBERATE.

SO CALCULATED.

WHY ARE WE STOPPING?

HANG ONTO SOMETHING, JOHL. WE'RE MAKING A HARD REVERSE--

WHY?! STEL, WHAT'S GOING ON UP THERE?

WHAT IS IT?!

LIGHTS PRESERVE US...

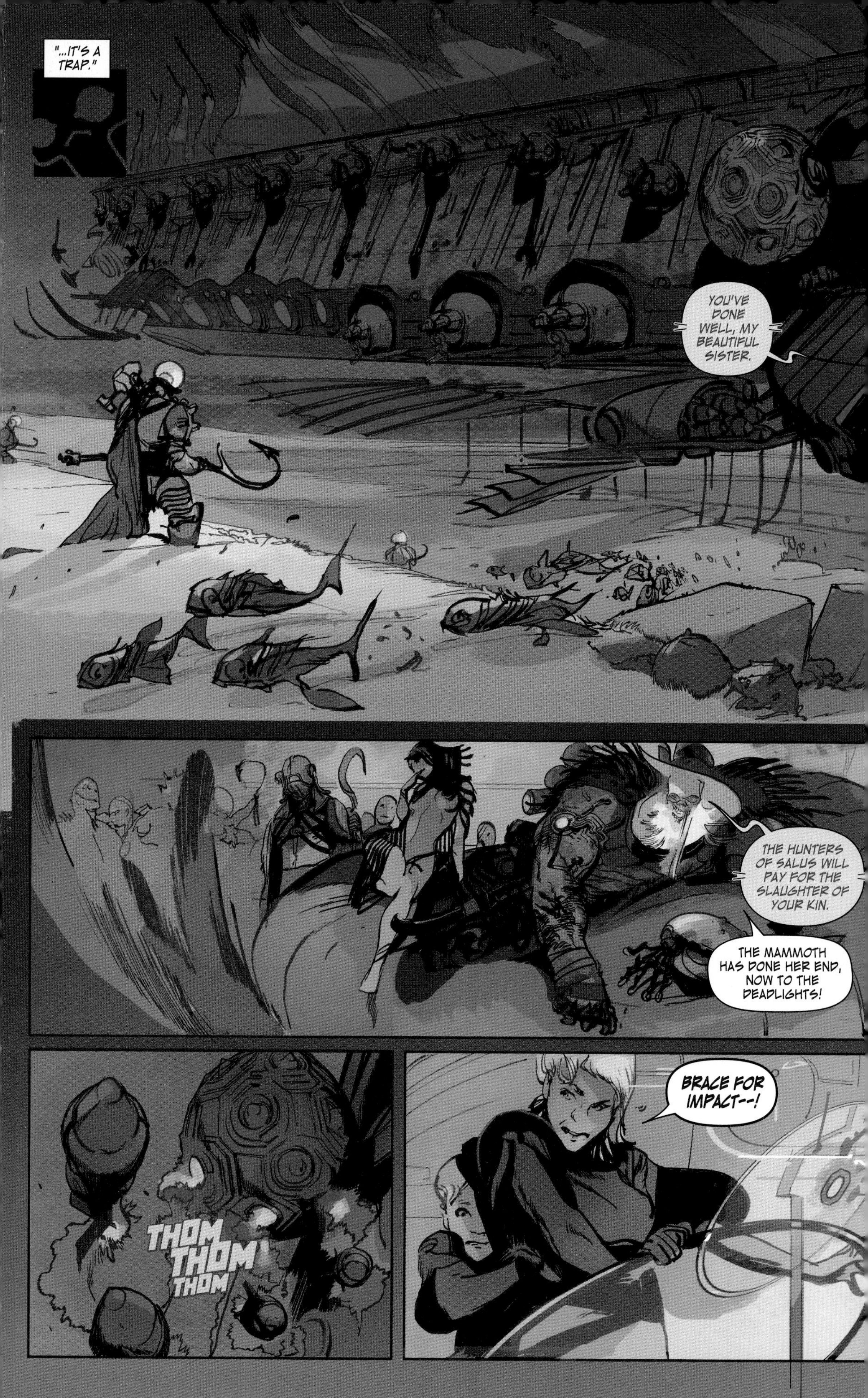
"...IT'S A TRAP."
YOU'VE DONE WELL, MY BEAUTIFUL SISTER.
THE HUNTERS OF SALUS WILL PAY FOR THE SLAUGHTER OF YOUR KIN.
THE MAMMOTH HAS DONE HER END, NOW TO THE DEADLIGHTS!
THOM THOM THOM
BRACE FOR IMPACT--!

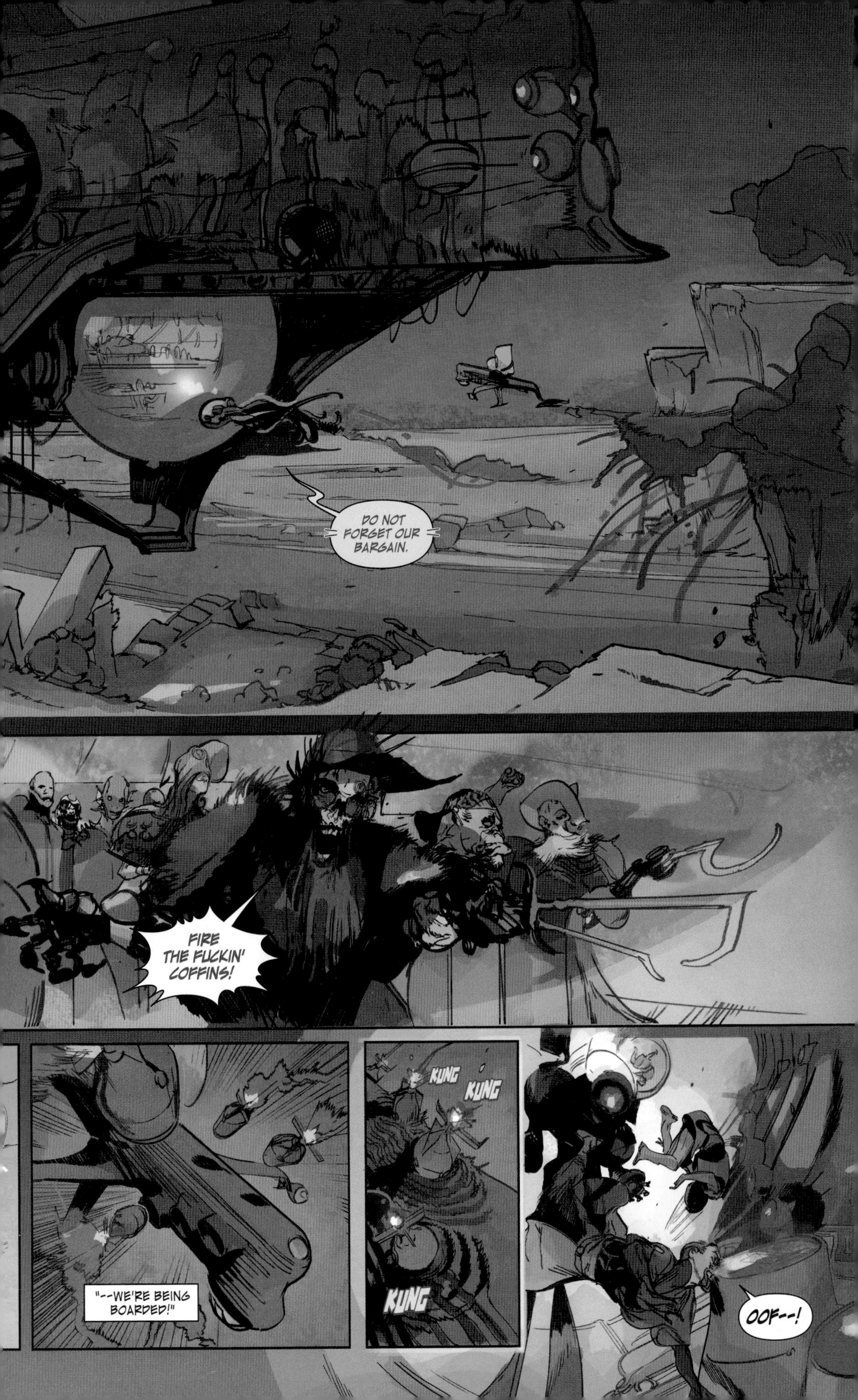
DO NOT FORGET OUR BARGAIN.
FIRE THE FUCKIN' COFFINS!
"--WE'RE BEING BOARDED!"
KUNG
KUNG
KUNG
OOF--!

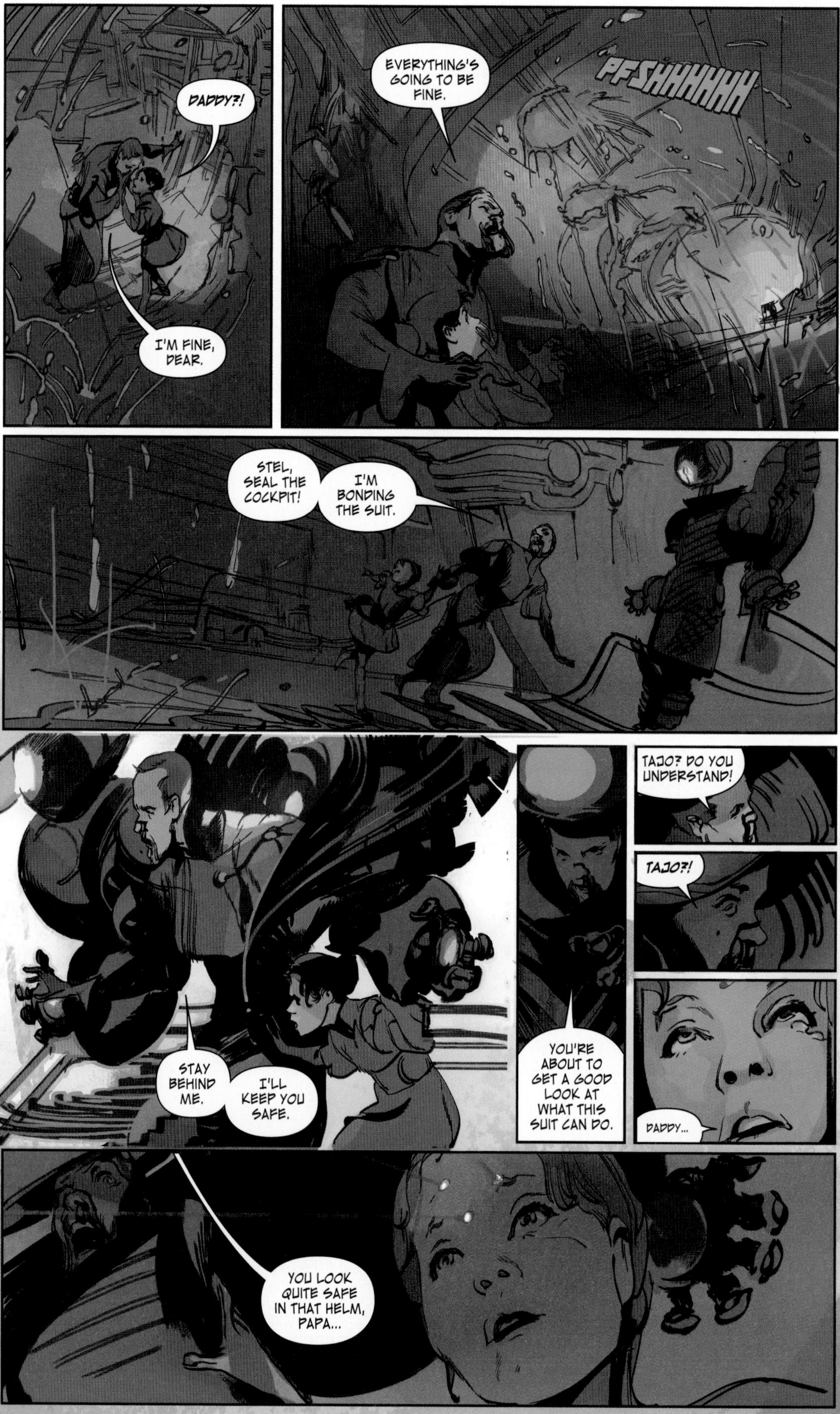
DADDY?!
I'M FINE, DEAR.
EVERYTHING'S GOING TO BE FINE.
PFSHHHHHH
STEL, SEAL THE COCKPIT!
I'M BONDING THE SUIT.
STAY BEHIND ME.
I'LL KEEP YOU SAFE.
YOU'RE ABOUT TO GET A GOOD LOOK AT WHAT THIS SUIT CAN DO.
TAJO? DO YOU UNDERSTAND!
TAJO?!
DADDY...
YOU LOOK QUITE SAFE IN THAT HELM, PAPA...

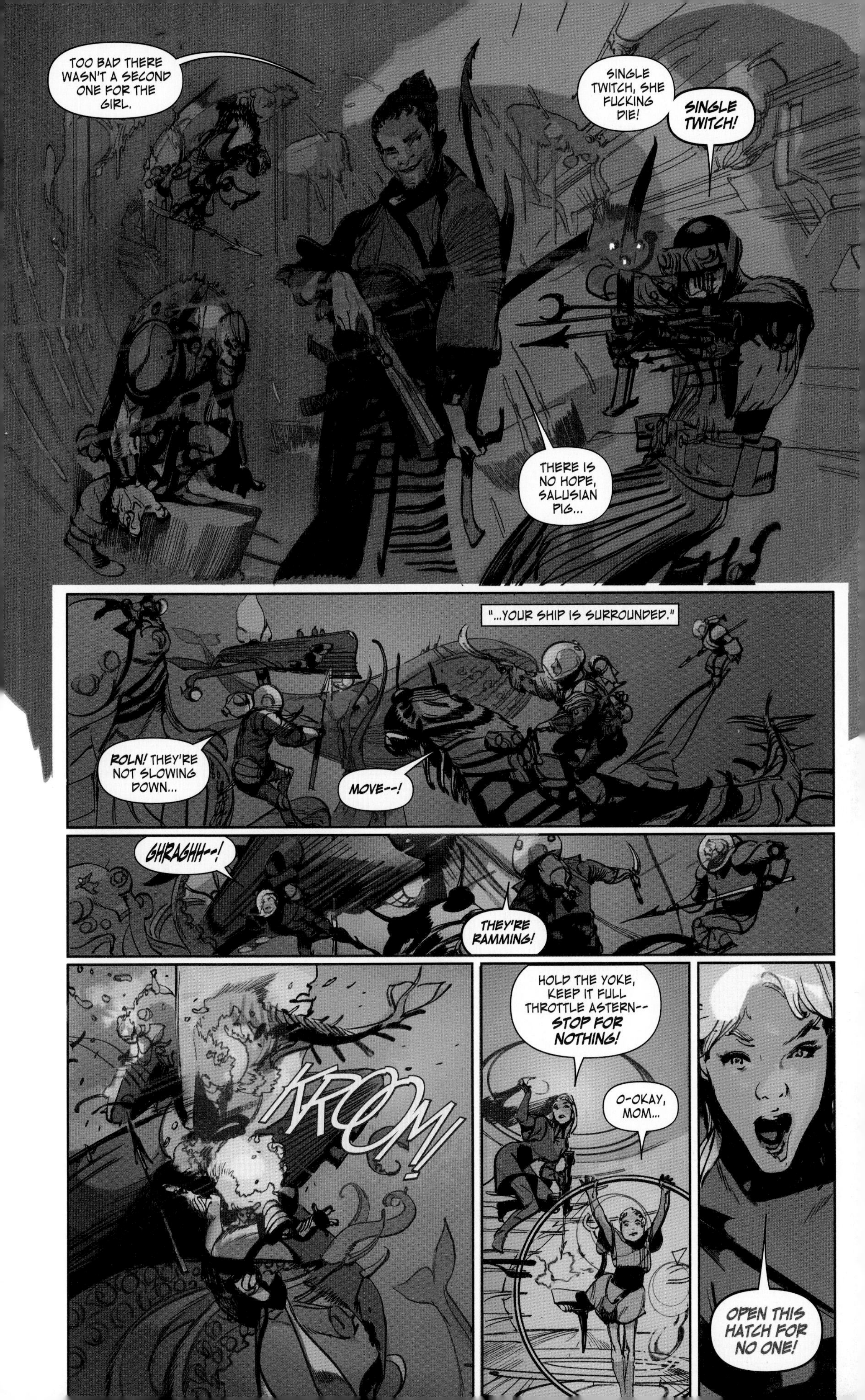
TOO BAD THERE WASN'T A SECOND ONE FOR THE GIRL.
SINGLE TWITCH, SHE FUCKING DIE!
SINGLE TWITCH!
THERE IS NO HOPE, SALUSIAN PIG...
"...YOUR SHIP IS SURROUNDED."
ROLN! THEY'RE NOT SLOWING DOWN...
MOVE--!
GHRAGHH--!
THEY'RE RAMMING!
KROOM!
HOLD THE YOKE, KEEP IT FULL THROTTLE ASTERN-- STOP FOR NOTHING!
O-OKAY, MOM...
OPEN THIS HATCH FOR NO ONE!

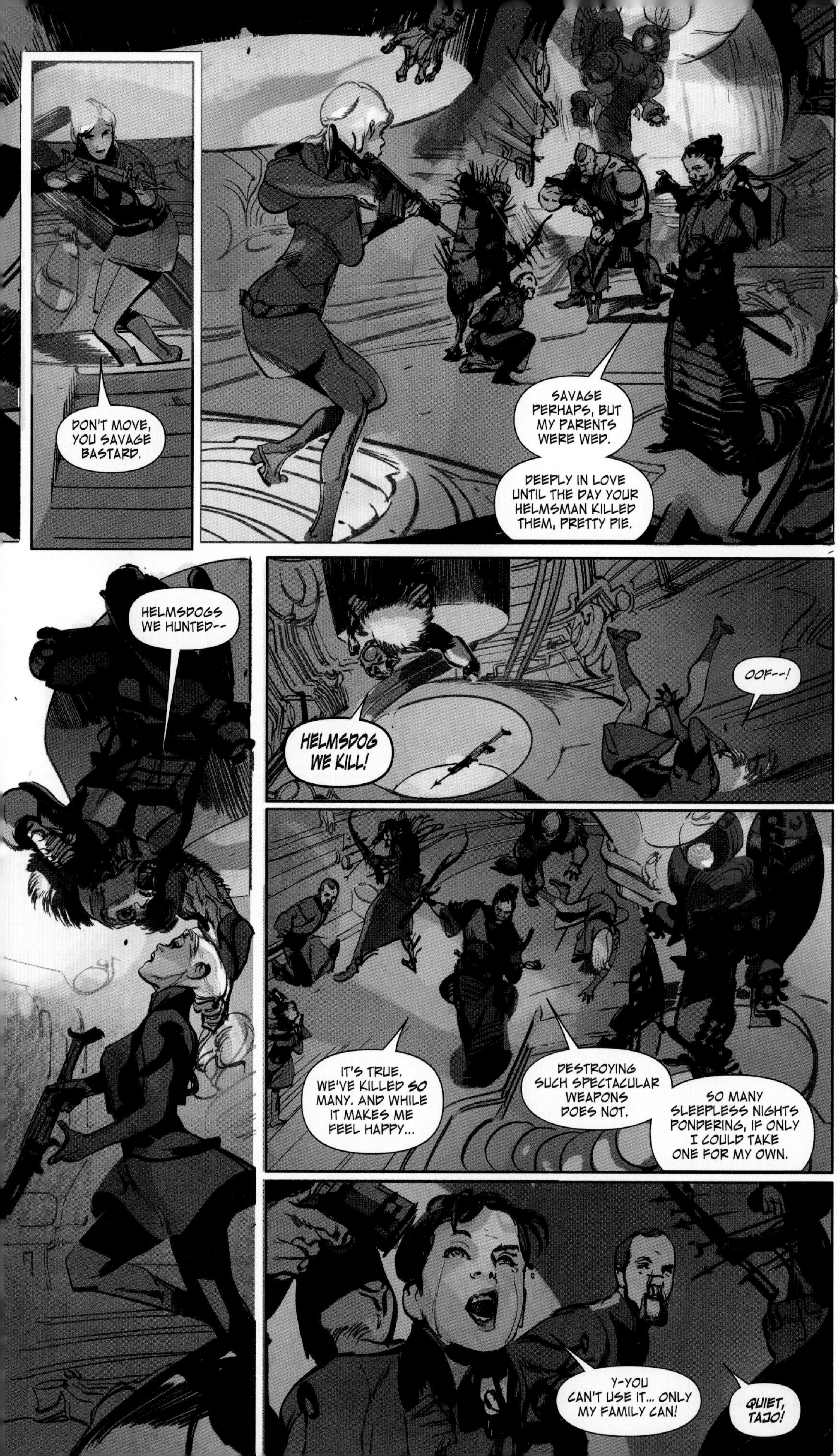
DON'T MOVE, YOU SAVAGE BASTARD.
SAVAGE PERHAPS, BUT MY PARENTS WERE WED.
DEEPLY IN LOVE UNTIL THE DAY YOUR HELMSMAN KILLED THEM, PRETTY PIE.
HELMSDOGS WE HUNTED--
HELMSDOG WE KILL!
OOF--!
IT'S TRUE. WE'VE KILLED SO MANY. AND WHILE IT MAKES ME FEEL HAPPY...
DESTROYING SUCH SPECTACULAR WEAPONS DOES NOT.
SO MANY SLEEPLESS NIGHTS PONDERING, IF ONLY I COULD TAKE ONE FOR MY OWN.
Y-YOU CAN'T USE IT... ONLY MY FAMILY CAN!
QUIET, TAJO!

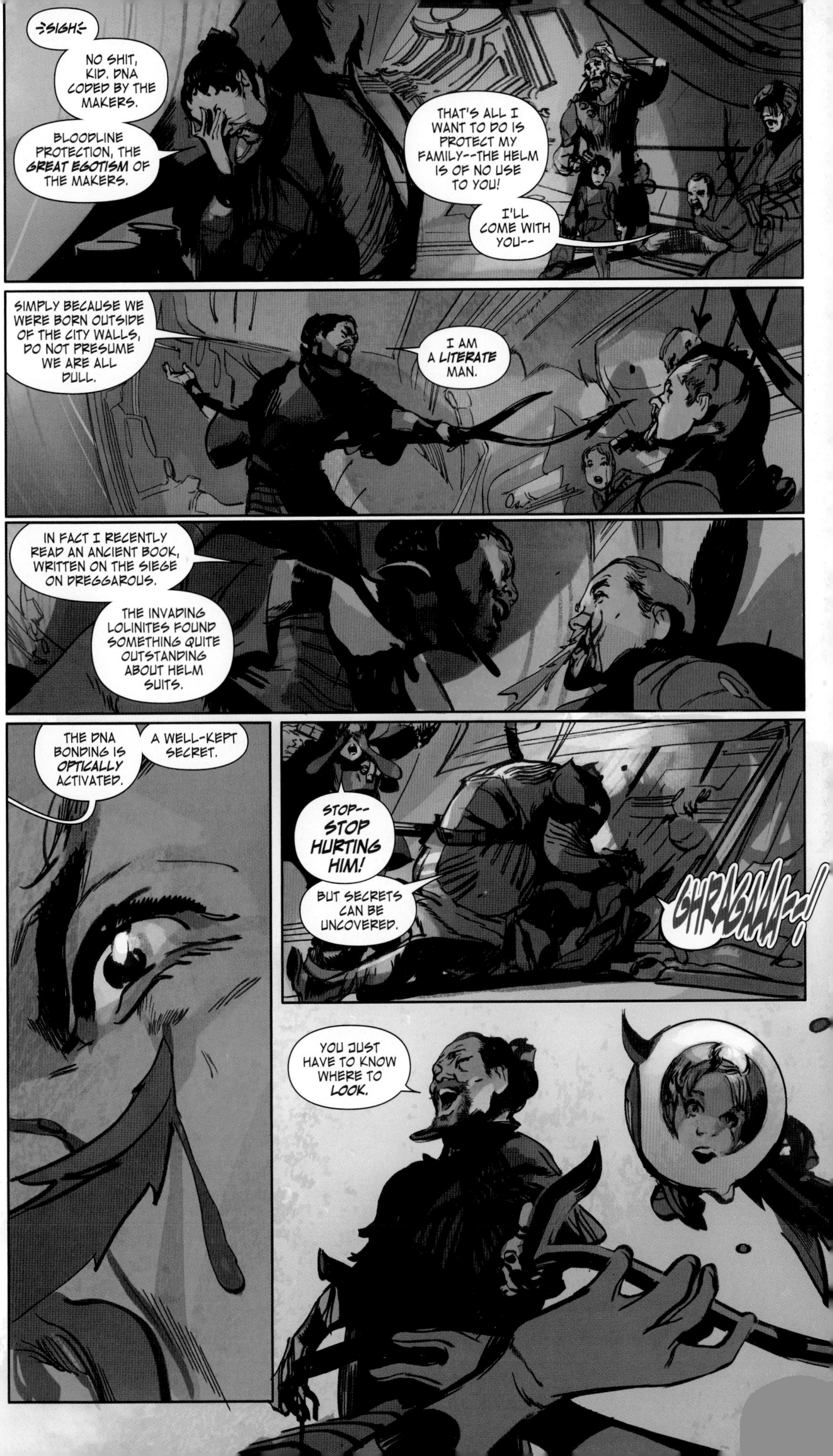
-SIGH-
NO SHIT, KID. DNA CODED BY THE MAKERS.
BLOODLINE PROTECTION, THE **GREAT EGOTISM** OF THE MAKERS.
THAT'S ALL I WANT TO DO IS PROTECT MY FAMILY--THE HELM IS OF NO USE TO YOU!
I'LL COME WITH YOU--
SIMPLY BECAUSE WE WERE BORN OUTSIDE OF THE CITY WALLS, DO NOT PRESUME WE ARE ALL DULL.
I AM A **LITERATE** MAN.
IN FACT I RECENTLY READ AN ANCIENT BOOK, WRITTEN ON THE SIEGE ON DREGGAROUS.
THE INVADING LOLINITES FOUND SOMETHING QUITE OUTSTANDING ABOUT HELM SUITS.
THE DNA BONDING IS **OPTICALLY** ACTIVATED.
A WELL-KEPT SECRET.
STOP-- **STOP HURTING HIM!**
BUT SECRETS CAN BE UNCOVERED.
GHRAGAAA--!
YOU JUST HAVE TO KNOW WHERE TO **LOOK**.

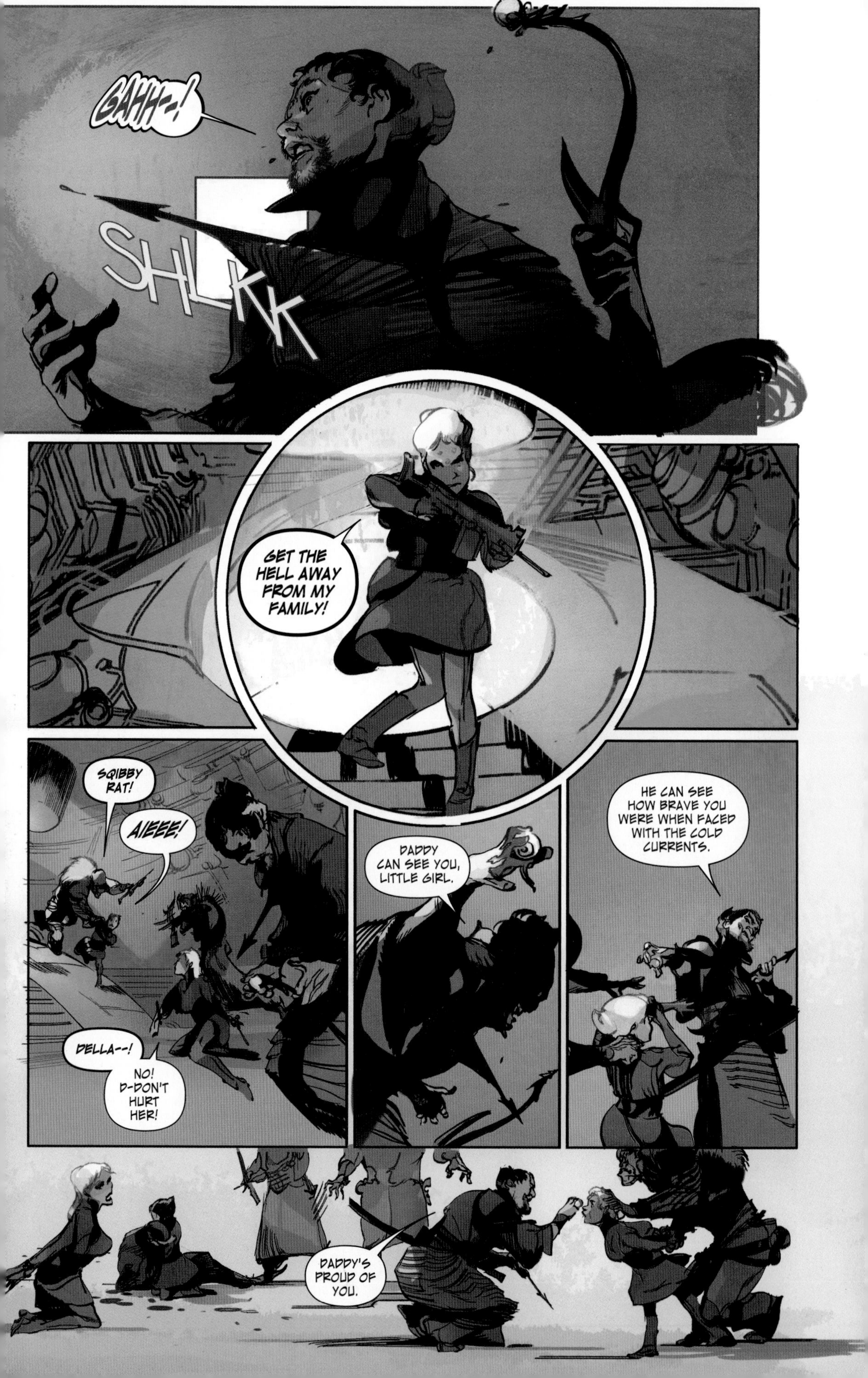
GAHH--!
SHLKK
GET THE HELL AWAY FROM MY FAMILY!
SQIBBY RAT!
AIEEE!
DELLA--!
NO! D-DON'T HURT HER!
DADDY CAN SEE YOU, LITTLE GIRL.
HE CAN SEE HOW BRAVE YOU WERE WHEN FACED WITH THE COLD CURRENTS.
DADDY'S PROUD OF YOU.

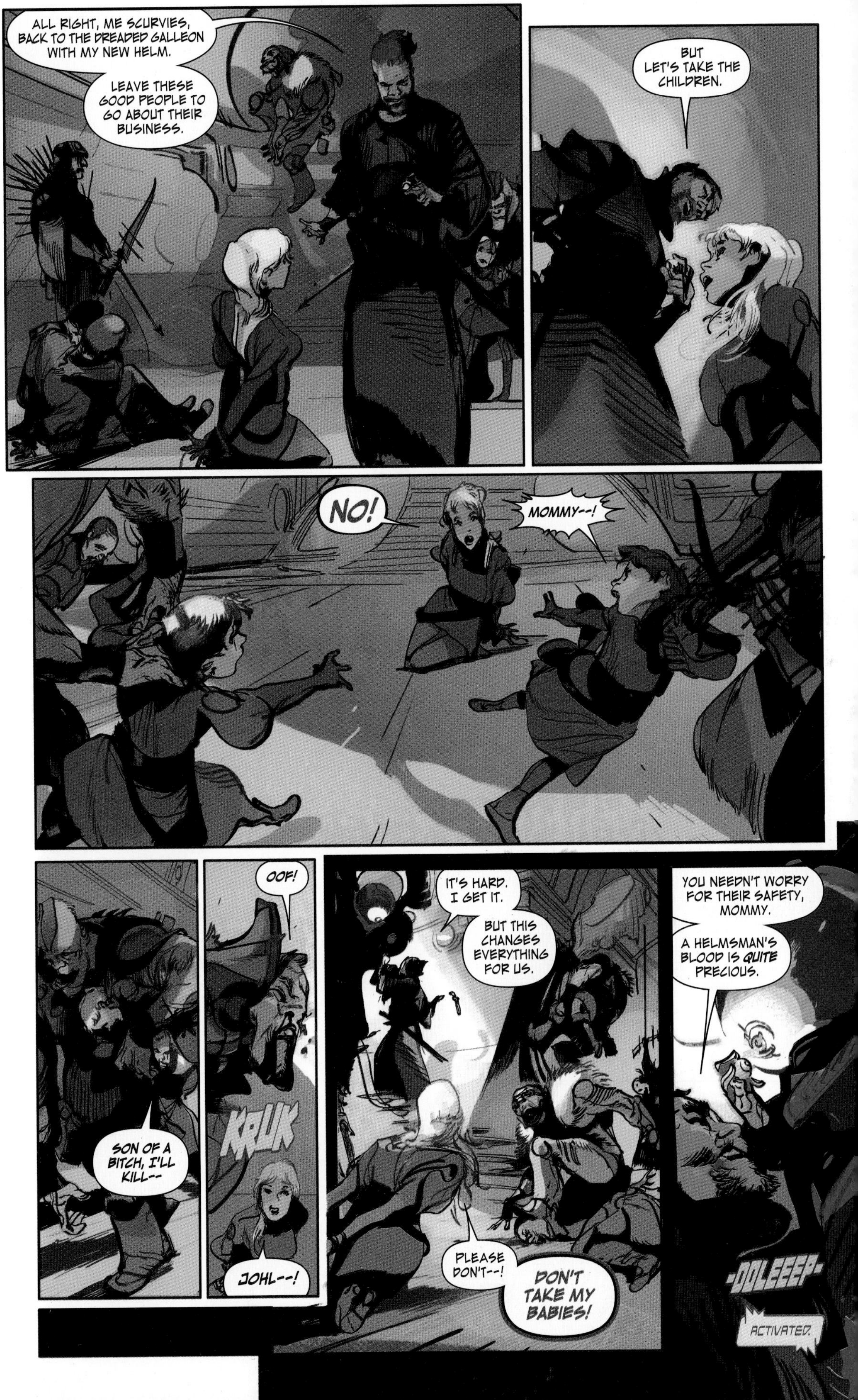
ALL RIGHT, ME SCURVIES, BACK TO THE DREADED GALLEON WITH MY NEW HELM.
LEAVE THESE GOOD PEOPLE TO GO ABOUT THEIR BUSINESS.
BUT LET'S TAKE THE CHILDREN.
NO!
MOMMY--!
SON OF A BITCH, I'LL KILL--
OOF!
KRUK
JOHL--!
IT'S HARD. I GET IT.
BUT THIS CHANGES EVERYTHING FOR US.
PLEASE DON'T--!
DON'T TAKE MY BABIES!
YOU NEEDN'T WORRY FOR THEIR SAFETY, MOMMY.
A HELMSMAN'S BLOOD IS QUITE PRECIOUS.
-DOLEEEP-
ACTIVATED.

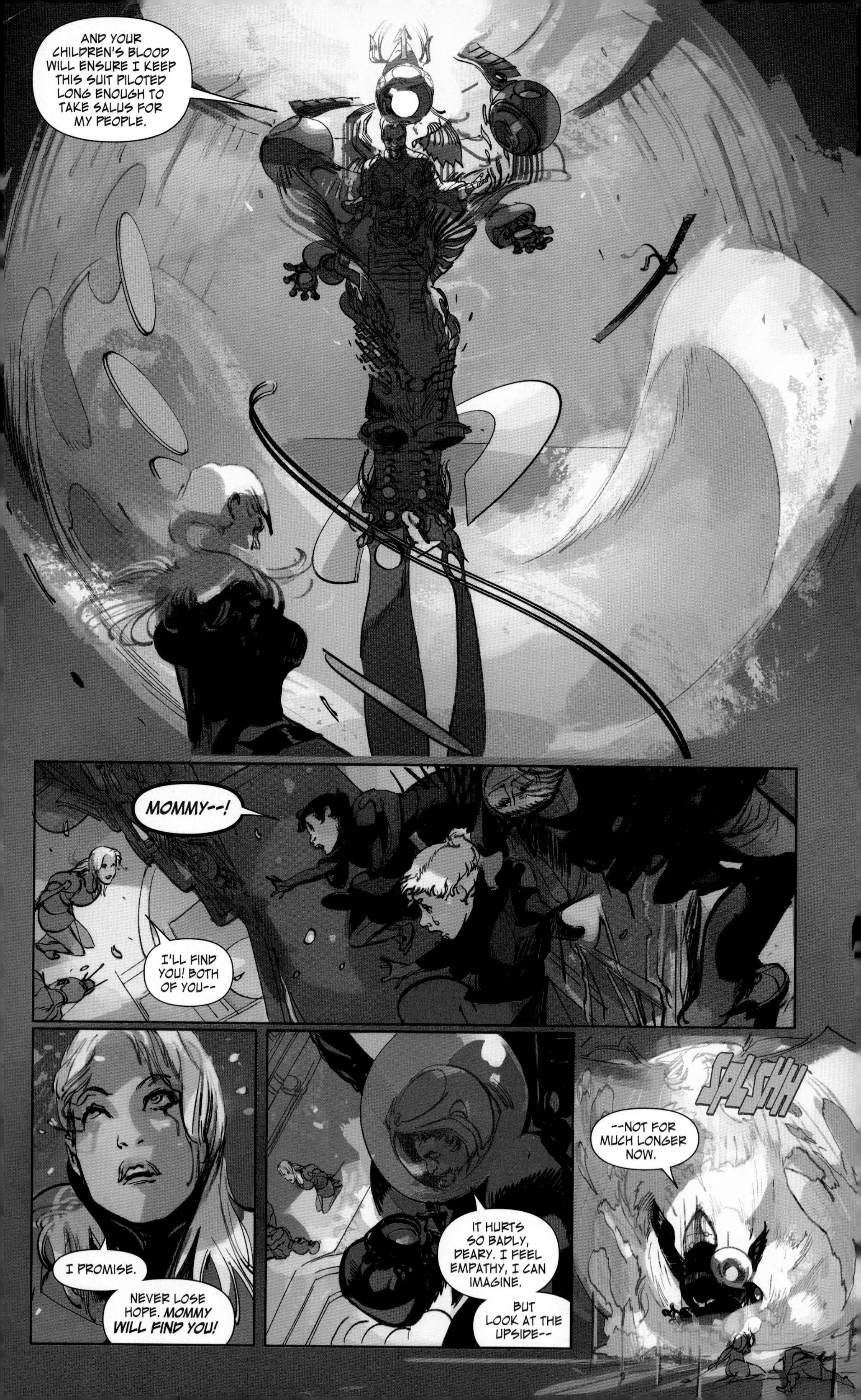
AND YOUR CHILDREN'S BLOOD WILL ENSURE I KEEP THIS SUIT PILOTED LONG ENOUGH TO TAKE SALUS FOR MY PEOPLE.
MOMMY--!
I'LL FIND YOU! BOTH OF YOU--
I PROMISE.
NEVER LOSE HOPE. MOMMY WILL FIND YOU!
IT HURTS SO BADLY, DEARY. I FEEL EMPATHY, I CAN IMAGINE.
BUT LOOK AT THE UPSIDE--
SPLSHH
--NOT FOR MUCH LONGER NOW.

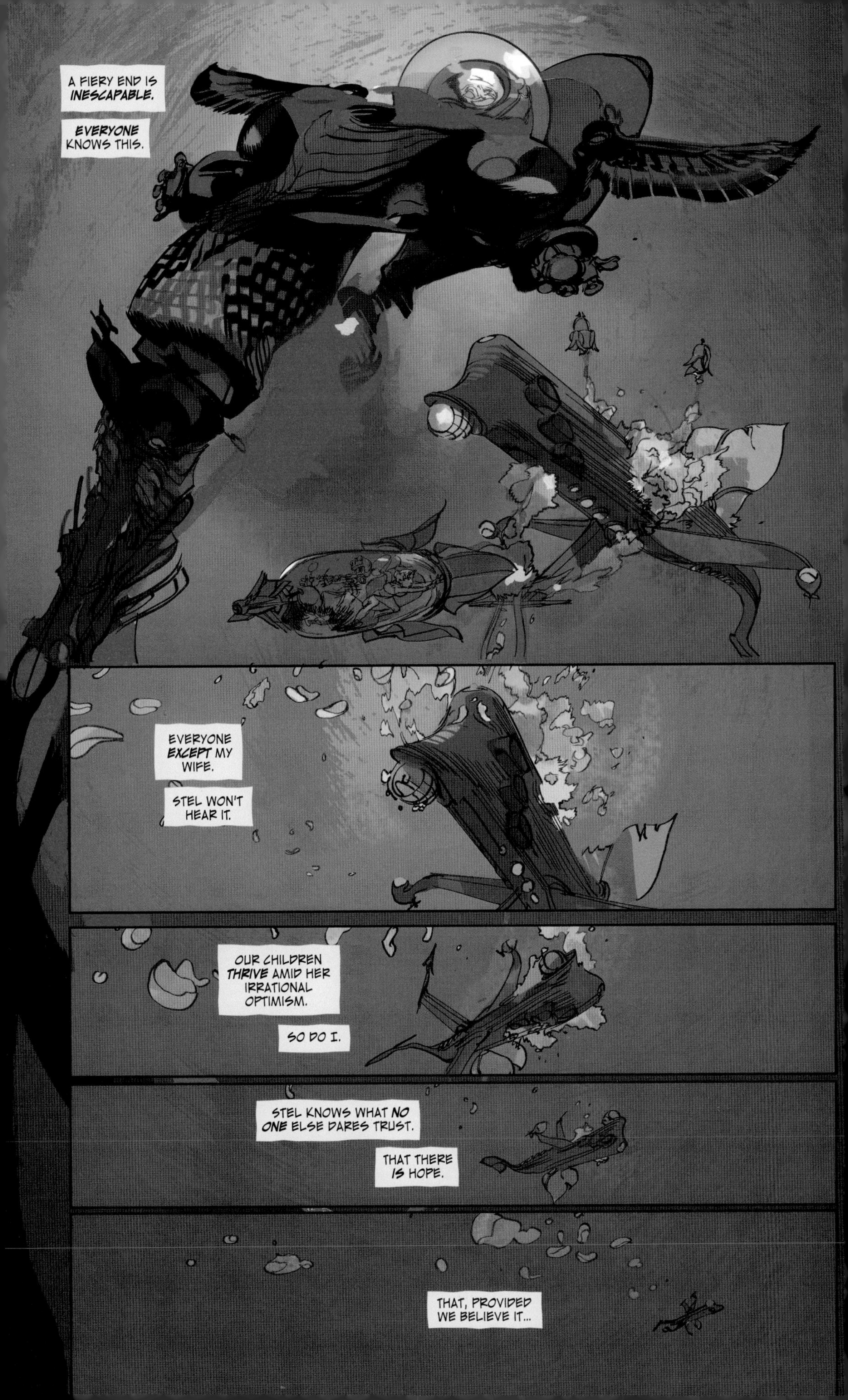
A FIERY END IS INESCAPABLE.
EVERYONE KNOWS THIS.
EVERYONE EXCEPT MY WIFE.
STEL WON'T HEAR IT.
OUR CHILDREN THRIVE AMID HER IRRATIONAL OPTIMISM.
SO DO I.
STEL KNOWS WHAT NO ONE ELSE DARES TRUST.
THAT THERE IS HOPE.
THAT, PROVIDED WE BELIEVE IT...

...WE WILL RISE AGAIN.

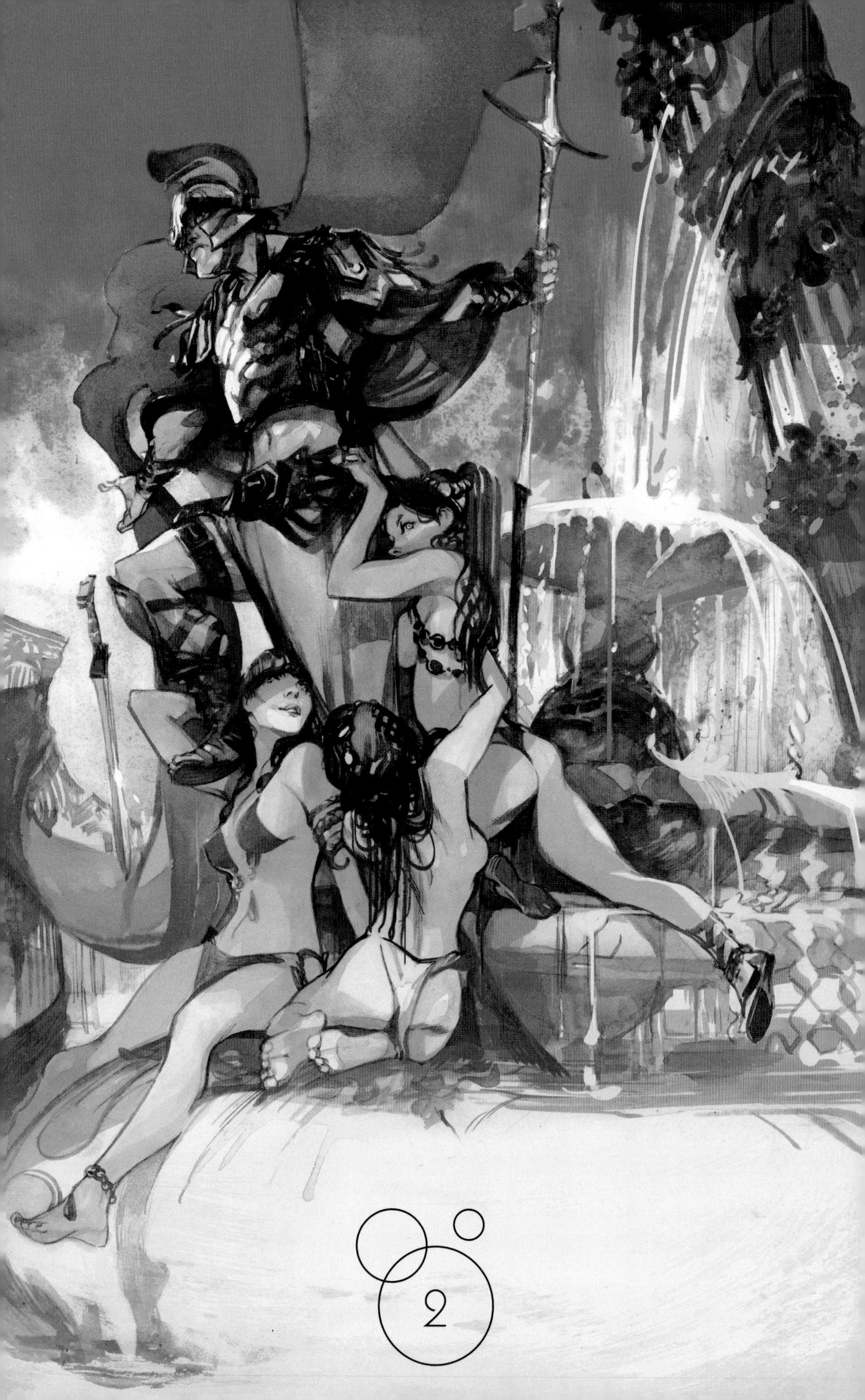
2

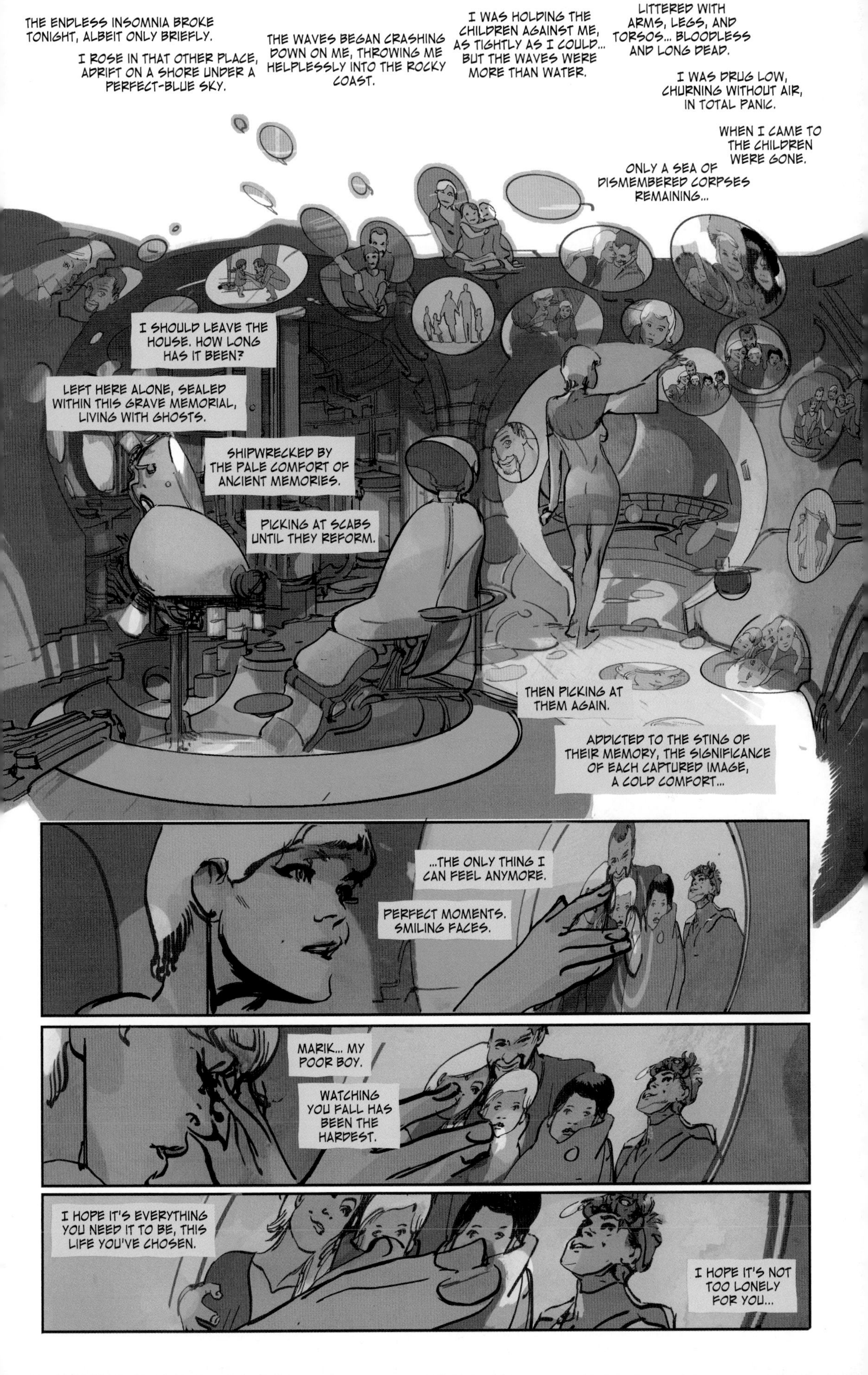
THE ENDLESS INSOMNIA BROKE TONIGHT, ALBEIT ONLY BRIEFLY.
I ROSE IN THAT OTHER PLACE, ADRIFT ON A SHORE UNDER A PERFECT-BLUE SKY.
THE WAVES BEGAN CRASHING DOWN ON ME, THROWING ME HELPLESSLY INTO THE ROCKY COAST.
I WAS HOLDING THE CHILDREN AGAINST ME, AS TIGHTLY AS I COULD... BUT THE WAVES WERE MORE THAN WATER.
LITTERED WITH ARMS, LEGS, AND TORSOS... BLOODLESS AND LONG DEAD.
I WAS DRUG LOW, CHURNING WITHOUT AIR, IN TOTAL PANIC.
WHEN I CAME TO THE CHILDREN WERE GONE.
ONLY A SEA OF DISMEMBERED CORPSES REMAINING...
I SHOULD LEAVE THE HOUSE. HOW LONG HAS IT BEEN?
LEFT HERE ALONE, SEALED WITHIN THIS GRAVE MEMORIAL, LIVING WITH GHOSTS.
SHIPWRECKED BY THE PALE COMFORT OF ANCIENT MEMORIES.
PICKING AT SCABS UNTIL THEY REFORM.
THEN PICKING AT THEM AGAIN.
ADDICTED TO THE STING OF THEIR MEMORY, THE SIGNIFICANCE OF EACH CAPTURED IMAGE, A COLD COMFORT...
...THE ONLY THING I CAN FEEL ANYMORE.
PERFECT MOMENTS. SMILING FACES.
MARIK... MY POOR BOY.
WATCHING YOU FALL HAS BEEN THE HARDEST.
I HOPE IT'S EVERYTHING YOU NEED IT TO BE, THIS LIFE YOU'VE CHOSEN.
I HOPE IT'S NOT TOO LONELY FOR YOU...

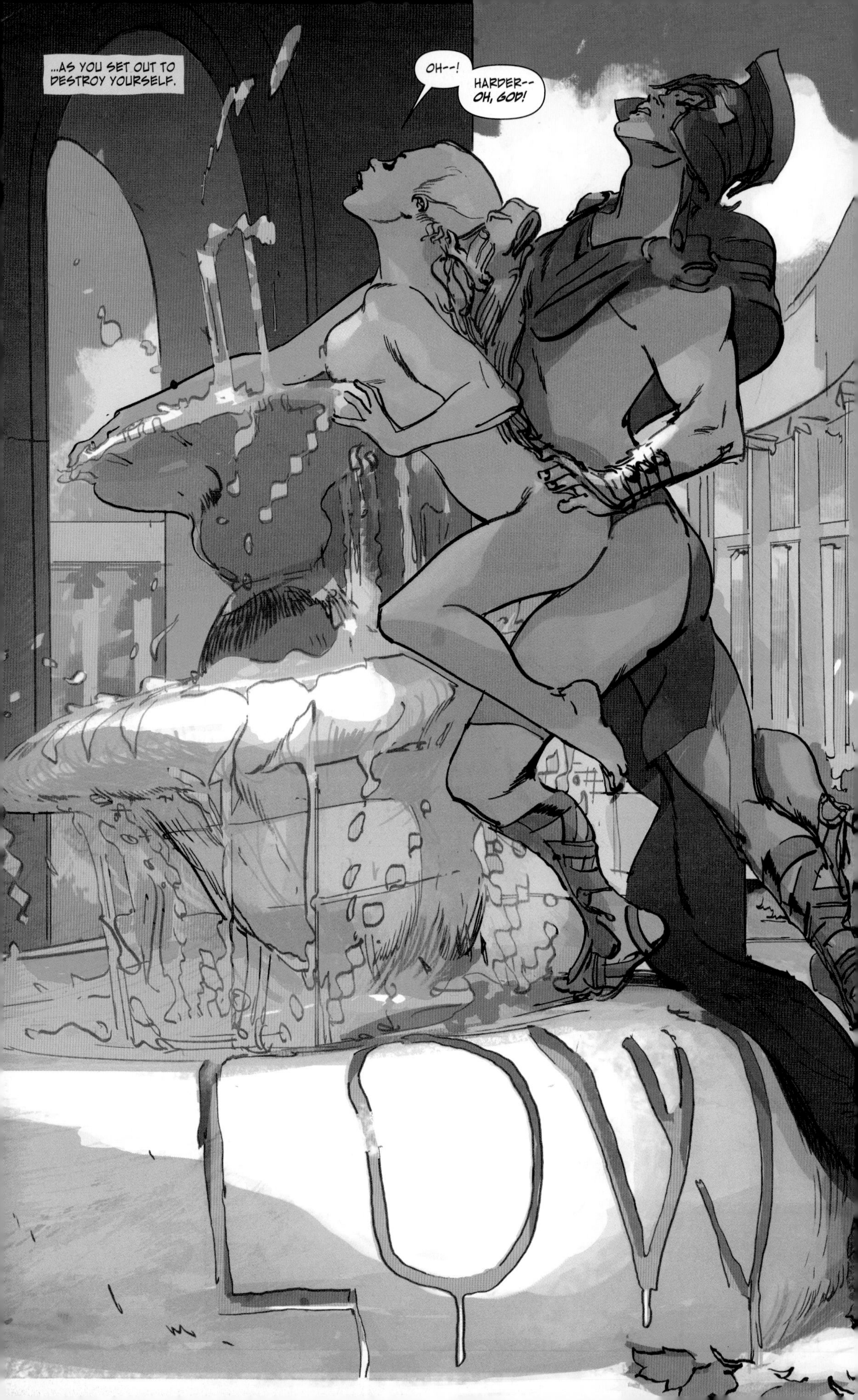
...AS YOU SET OUT TO DESTROY YOURSELF.
OH--! HARDER-- OH, GOD!

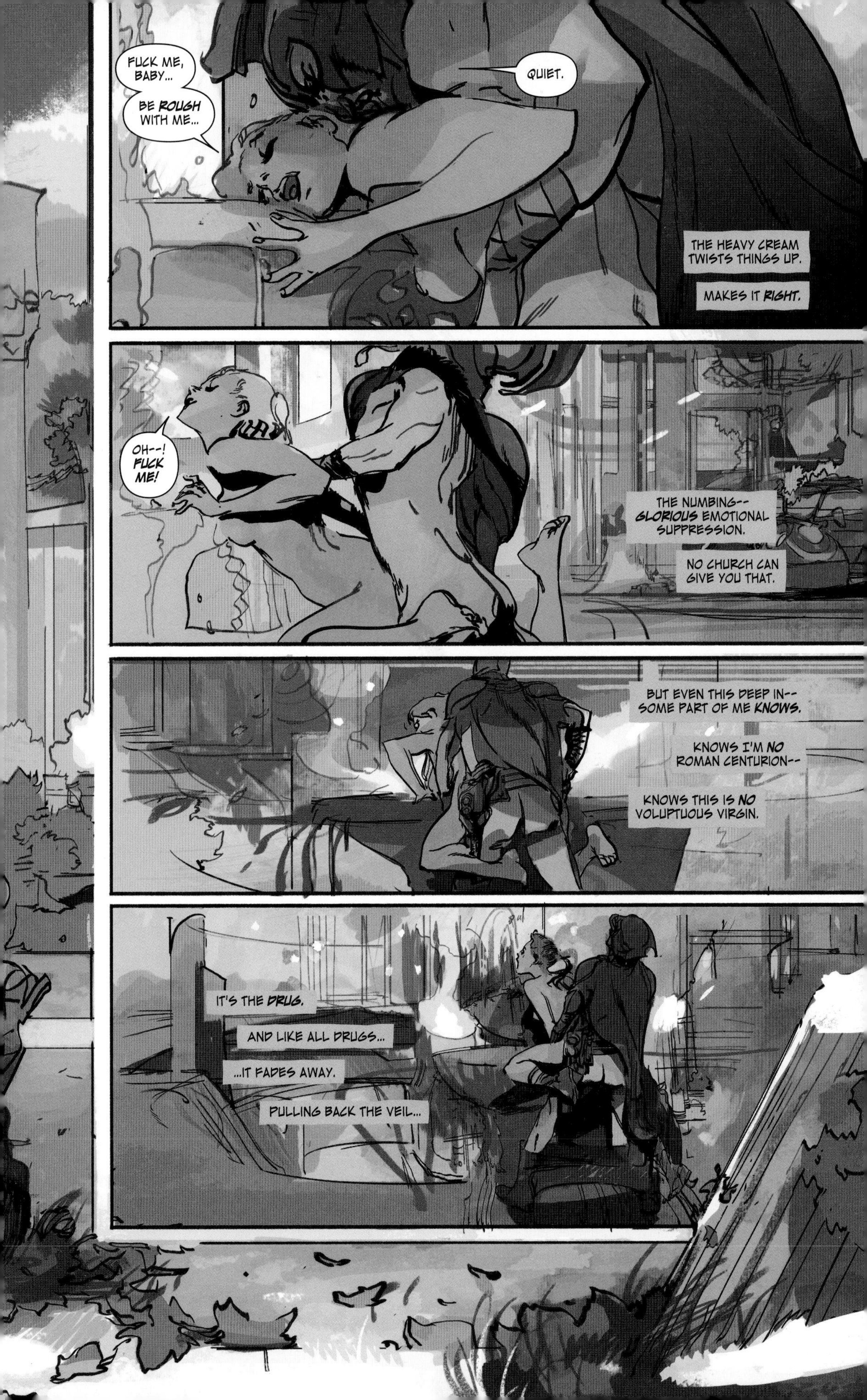

FUCK ME, BABY...
BE ROUGH WITH ME...
QUIET.
THE HEAVY CREAM TWISTS THINGS UP.
MAKES IT RIGHT.
OH--! FUCK ME!
THE NUMBING-- GLORIOUS EMOTIONAL SUPPRESSION.
NO CHURCH CAN GIVE YOU THAT.
BUT EVEN THIS DEEP IN-- SOME PART OF ME KNOWS.
KNOWS I'M NO ROMAN CENTURION--
KNOWS THIS IS NO VOLUPTUOUS VIRGIN.
IT'S THE DRUG.
AND LIKE ALL DRUGS...
...IT FADES AWAY.
PULLING BACK THE VEIL...

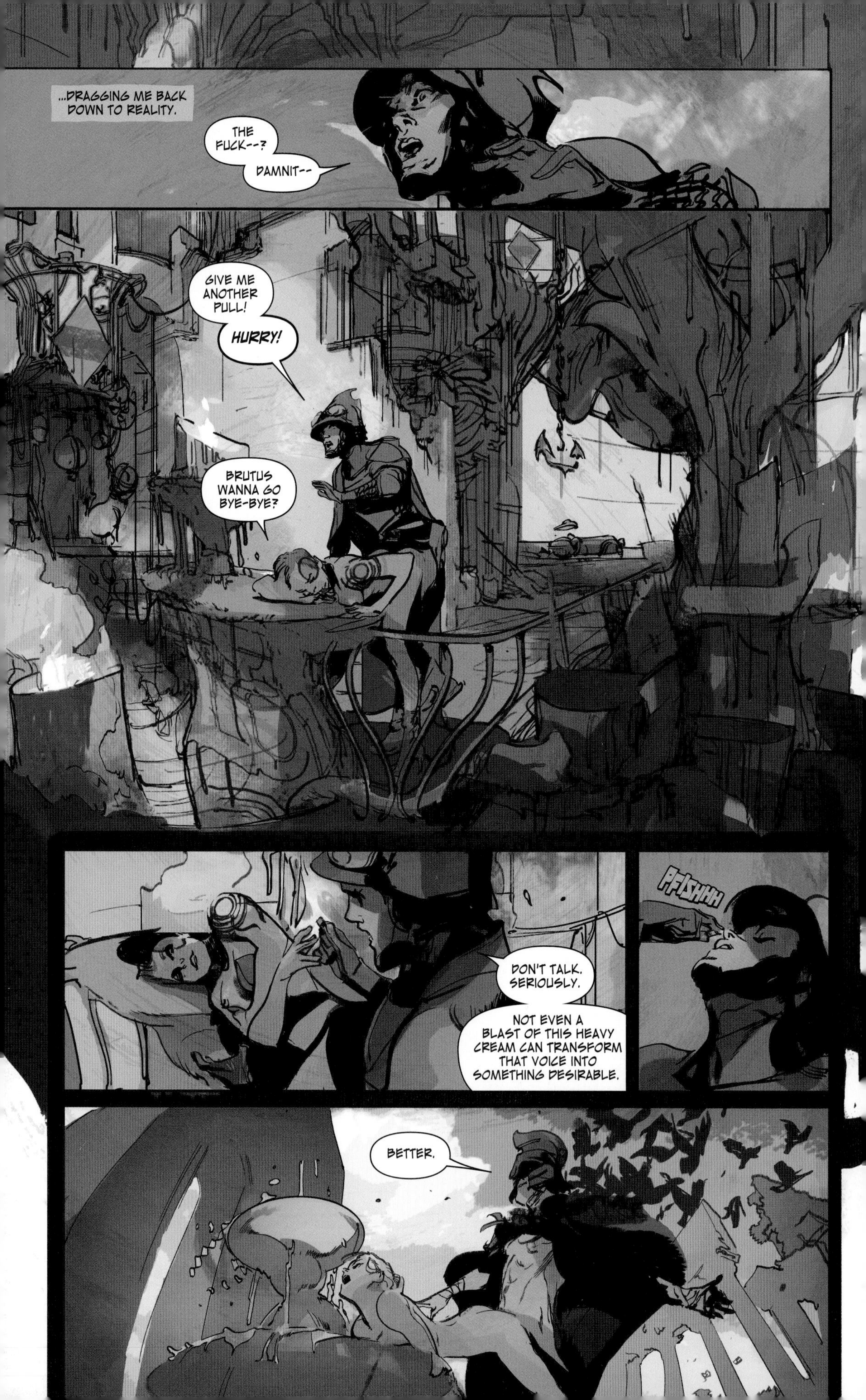
...DRAGGING ME BACK DOWN TO REALITY.
THE FUCK--?
DAMNIT--
GIVE ME ANOTHER PULL!
HURRY!
BRUTUS WANNA GO BYE-BYE?
DON'T TALK. SERIOUSLY.
NOT EVEN A BLAST OF THIS HEAVY CREAM CAN TRANSFORM THAT VOICE INTO SOMETHING DESIRABLE.
PFISHHH
BETTER.

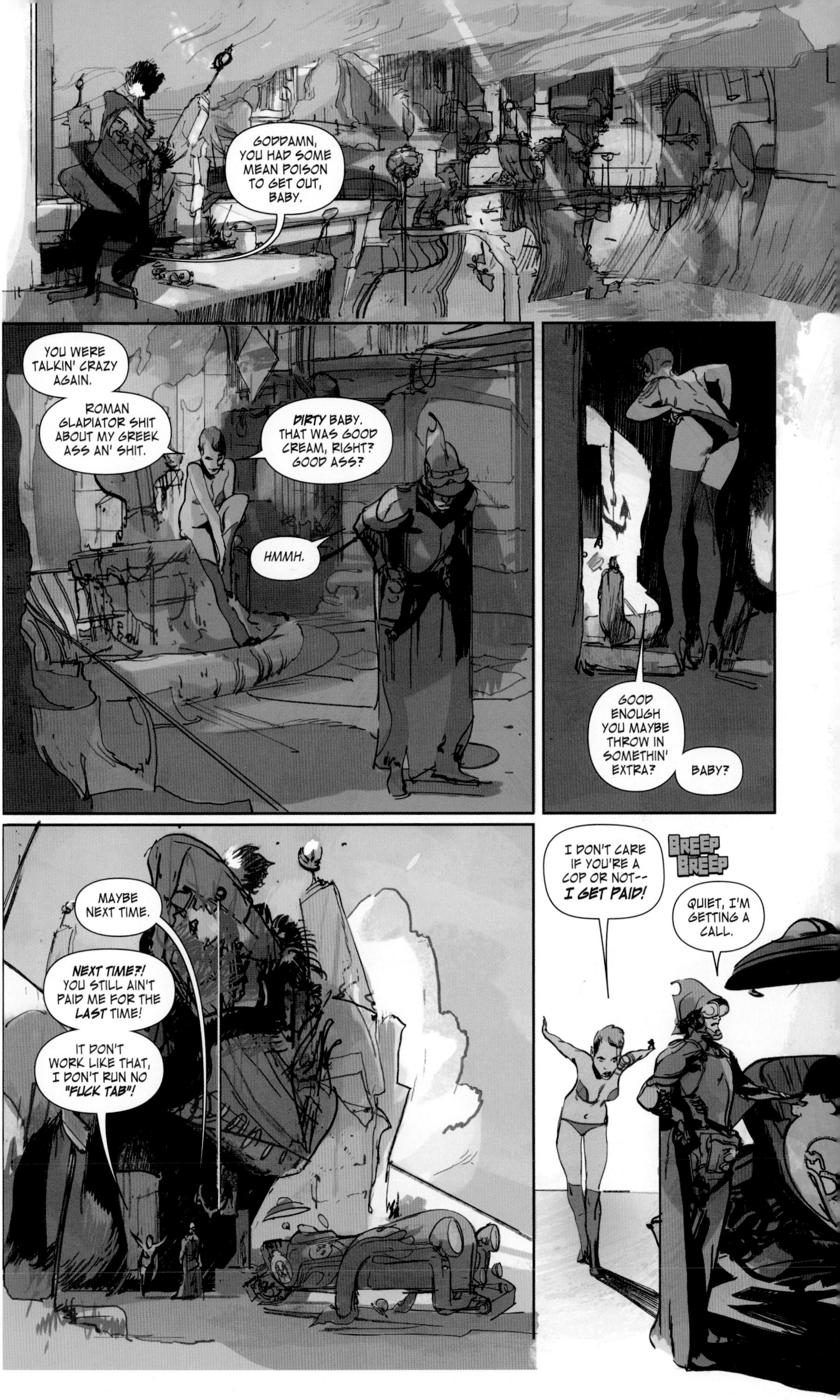
GODDAMN, YOU HAD SOME MEAN POISON TO GET OUT, BABY.
YOU WERE TALKIN' CRAZY AGAIN.
ROMAN GLADIATOR SHIT ABOUT MY GREEK ASS AN' SHIT.
DIRTY BABY. THAT WAS GOOD CREAM, RIGHT? GOOD ASS?
HMMH.
GOOD ENOUGH YOU MAYBE THROW IN SOMETHIN' EXTRA?
BABY?
MAYBE NEXT TIME.
NEXT TIME?! YOU STILL AIN'T PAID ME FOR THE LAST TIME!
IT DON'T WORK LIKE THAT, I DON'T RUN NO "FUCK TAB"!
I DON'T CARE IF YOU'RE A COP OR NOT-- I GET PAID!
BREEP BREEP
QUIET, I'M GETTING A CALL.

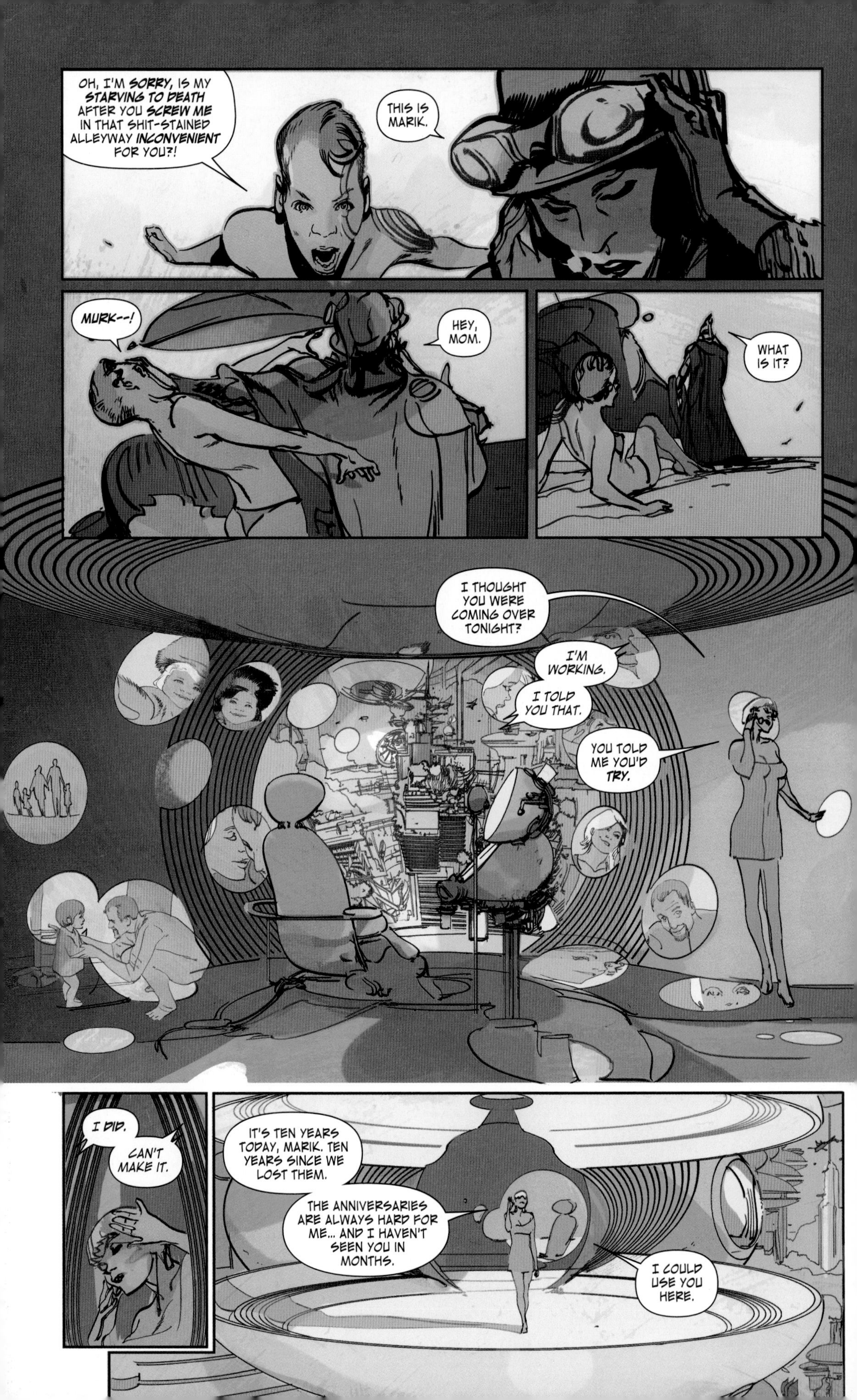
OH, I'M SORRY, IS MY STARVING TO DEATH AFTER YOU SCREW ME IN THAT SHIT-STAINED ALLEYWAY INCONVENIENT FOR YOU?!
THIS IS MARIK.
MURK--!
HEY, MOM.
WHAT IS IT?
I THOUGHT YOU WERE COMING OVER TONIGHT?
I'M WORKING.
I TOLD YOU THAT.
YOU TOLD ME YOU'D TRY.
I DID.
CAN'T MAKE IT.
IT'S TEN YEARS TODAY, MARIK. TEN YEARS SINCE WE LOST THEM.
THE ANNIVERSARIES ARE ALWAYS HARD FOR ME... AND I HAVEN'T SEEN YOU IN MONTHS.
I COULD USE YOU HERE.

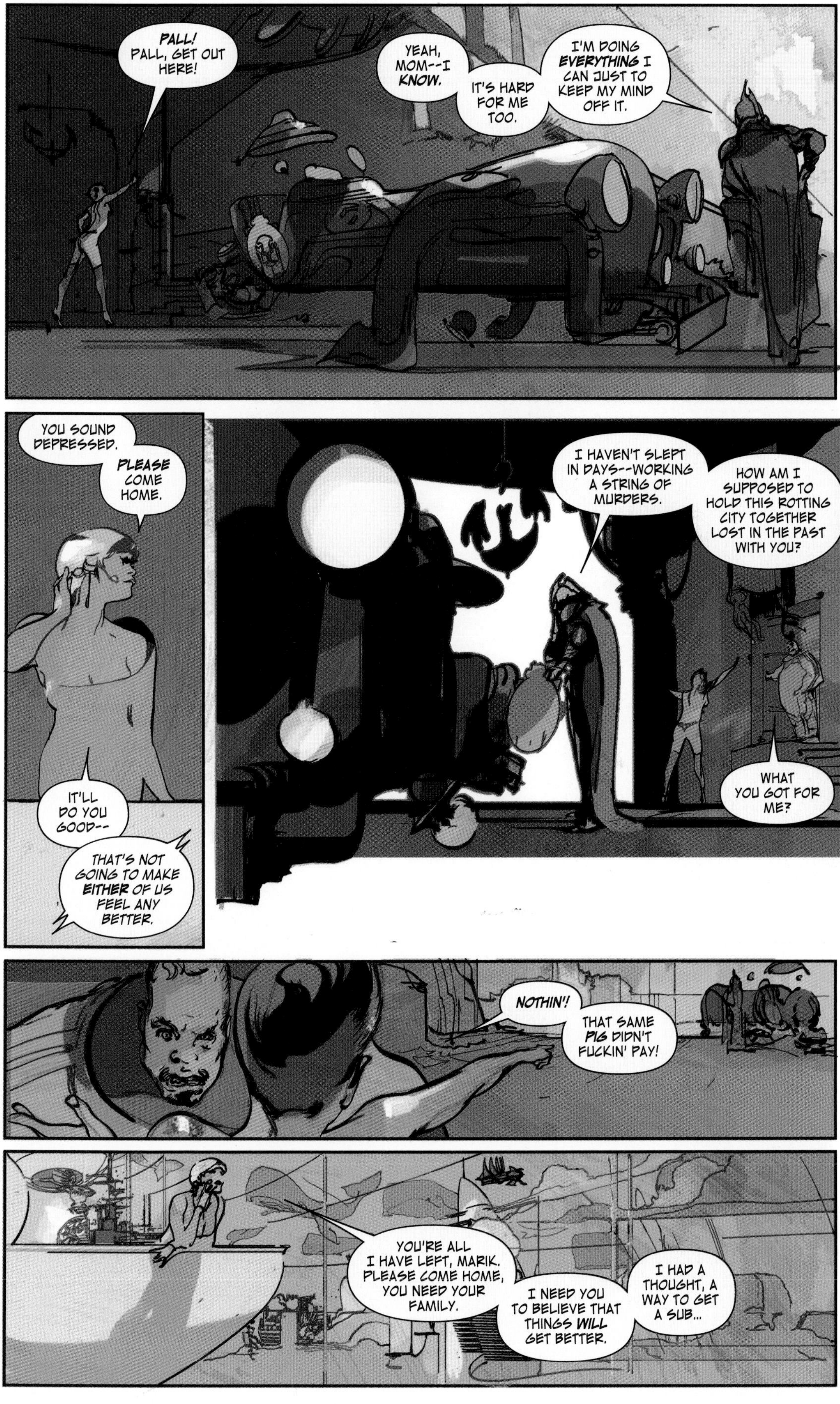
PALL! PALL, GET OUT HERE!
YEAH, MOM--I KNOW.
IT'S HARD FOR ME TOO.
I'M DOING EVERYTHING I CAN JUST TO KEEP MY MIND OFF IT.
YOU SOUND DEPRESSED.
PLEASE COME HOME.
IT'LL DO YOU GOOD--
THAT'S NOT GOING TO MAKE EITHER OF US FEEL ANY BETTER.
I HAVEN'T SLEPT IN DAYS--WORKING A STRING OF MURDERS.
HOW AM I SUPPOSED TO HOLD THIS ROTTING CITY TOGETHER LOST IN THE PAST WITH YOU?
WHAT YOU GOT FOR ME?
NOTHIN'!
THAT SAME PIG DIDN'T FUCKIN' PAY!
YOU'RE ALL I HAVE LEFT, MARIK. PLEASE COME HOME, YOU NEED YOUR FAMILY.
I NEED YOU TO BELIEVE THAT THINGS WILL GET BETTER.
I HAD A THOUGHT, A WAY TO GET A SUB...

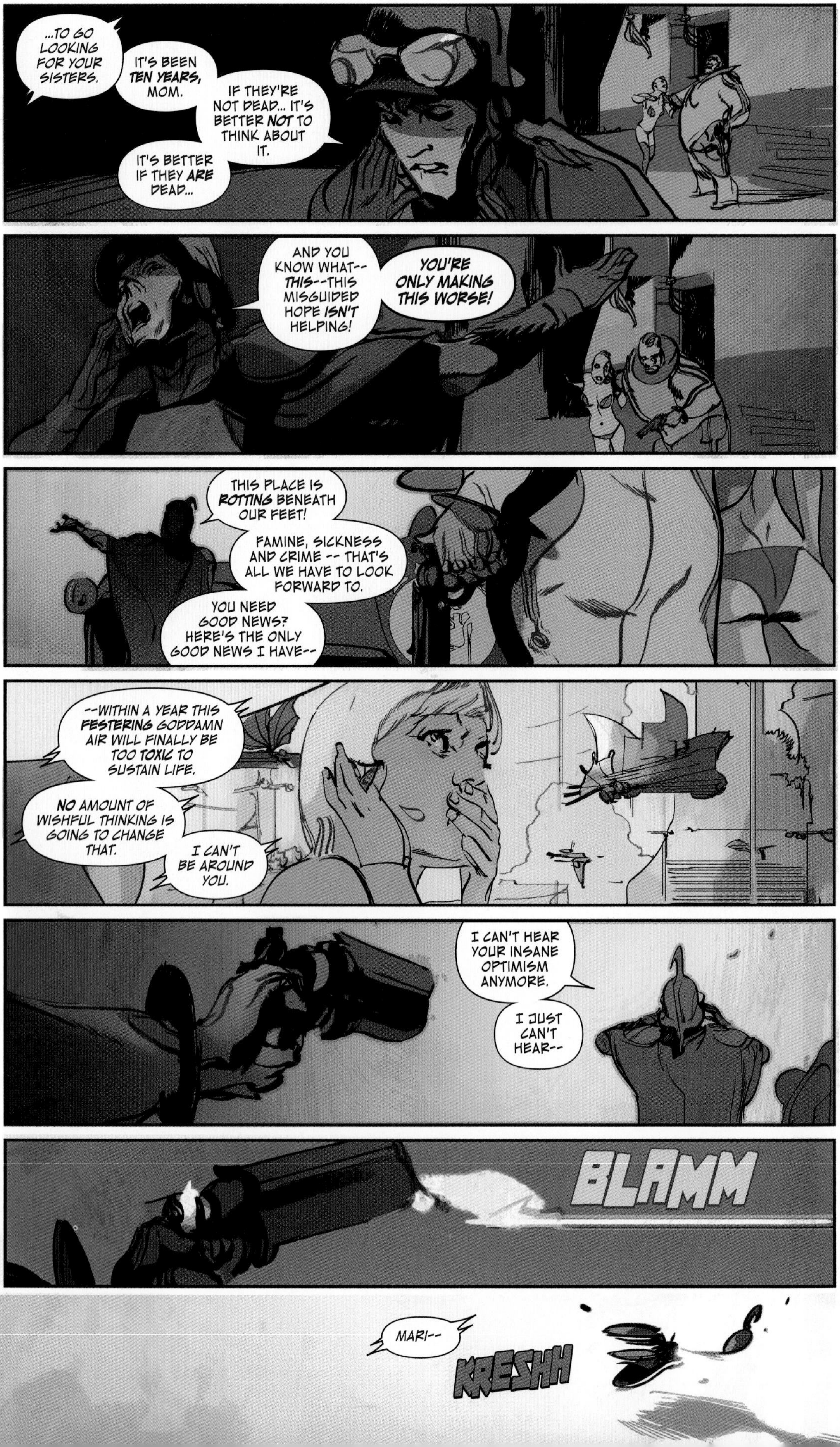
...TO GO LOOKING FOR YOUR SISTERS.
IT'S BEEN TEN YEARS, MOM.
IF THEY'RE NOT DEAD... IT'S BETTER NOT TO THINK ABOUT IT.
IT'S BETTER IF THEY ARE DEAD...
AND YOU KNOW WHAT--THIS--THIS MISGUIDED HOPE ISN'T HELPING!
YOU'RE ONLY MAKING THIS WORSE!
THIS PLACE IS ROTTING BENEATH OUR FEET!
FAMINE, SICKNESS AND CRIME -- THAT'S ALL WE HAVE TO LOOK FORWARD TO.
YOU NEED GOOD NEWS? HERE'S THE ONLY GOOD NEWS I HAVE--
--WITHIN A YEAR THIS FESTERING GODDAMN AIR WILL FINALLY BE TOO TOXIC TO SUSTAIN LIFE.
NO AMOUNT OF WISHFUL THINKING IS GOING TO CHANGE THAT.
I CAN'T BE AROUND YOU.
I CAN'T HEAR YOUR INSANE OPTIMISM ANYMORE.
I JUST CAN'T HEAR--
BLAMM
MARI--
KRESHH

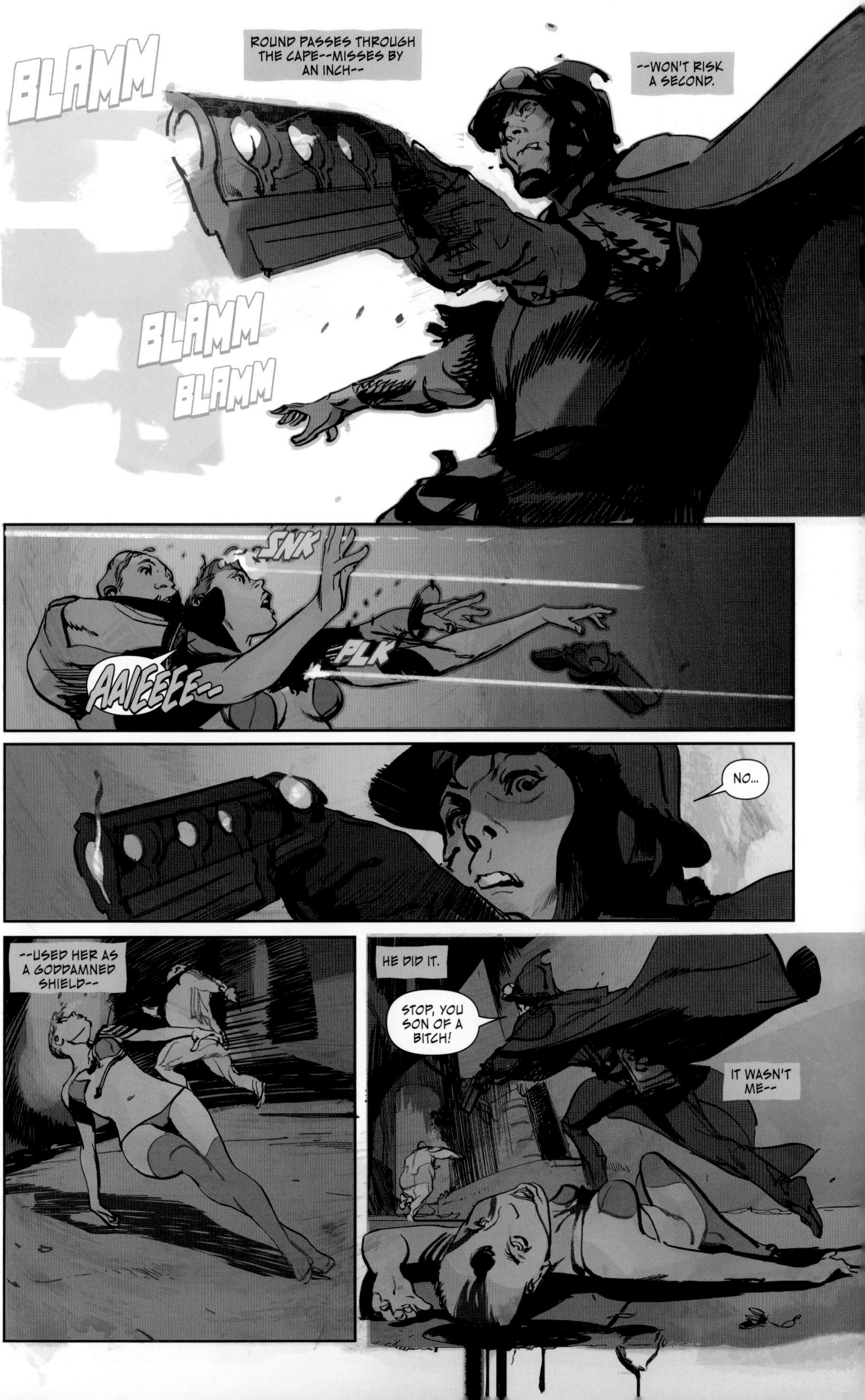
BLAMM
ROUND PASSES THROUGH THE CAPE--MISSES BY AN INCH--
--WON'T RISK A SECOND.
BLAMM
BLAMM
SNK
PLK
AAIEEEE--
NO...
--USED HER AS A GODDAMNED SHIELD--
HE DID IT.
STOP, YOU SON OF A BITCH!
IT WASN'T ME--

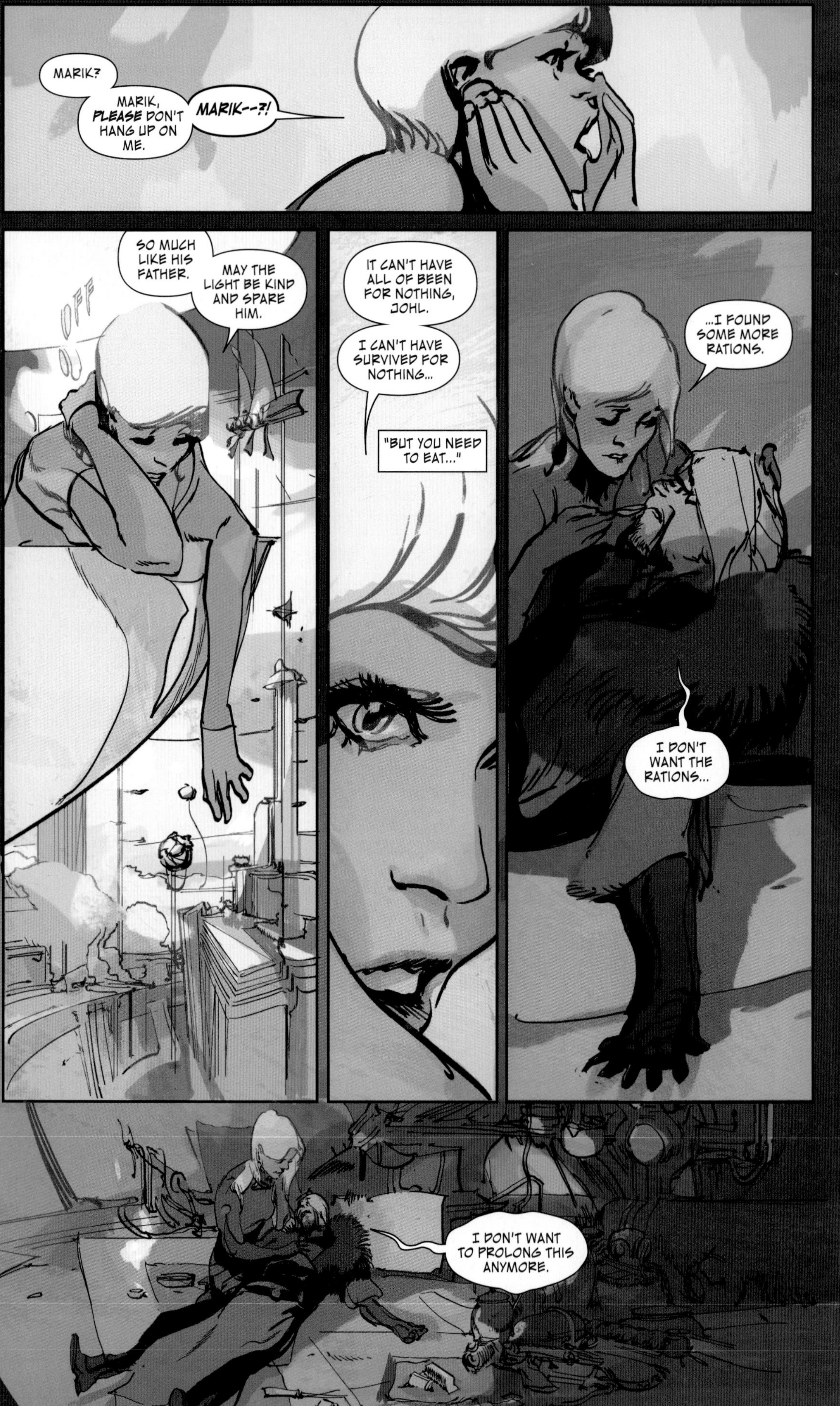
MARIK?
MARIK, PLEASE DON'T HANG UP ON ME.
MARIK--?!
SO MUCH LIKE HIS FATHER.
MAY THE LIGHT BE KIND AND SPARE HIM.
IT CAN'T HAVE ALL OF BEEN FOR NOTHING, JOHL.
I CAN'T HAVE SURVIVED FOR NOTHING...
"BUT YOU NEED TO EAT..."
...I FOUND SOME MORE RATIONS.
I DON'T WANT THE RATIONS...
I DON'T WANT TO PROLONG THIS ANYMORE.

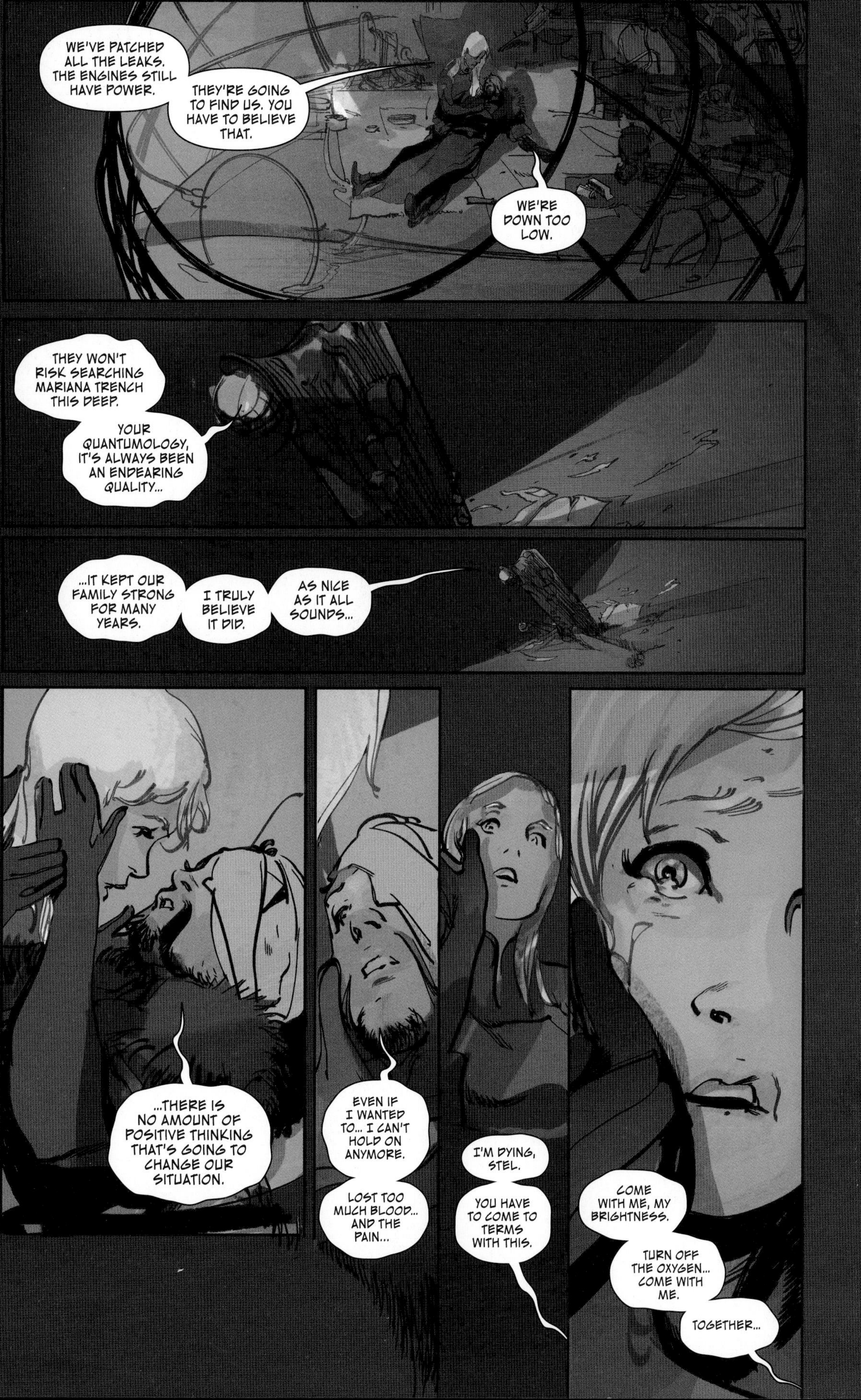

WE'VE PATCHED ALL THE LEAKS. THE ENGINES STILL HAVE POWER.
THEY'RE GOING TO FIND US. YOU HAVE TO BELIEVE THAT.
WE'RE DOWN TOO LOW.
THEY WON'T RISK SEARCHING MARIANA TRENCH THIS DEEP.
YOUR QUANTUMOLOGY, IT'S ALWAYS BEEN AN ENDEARING QUALITY...
...IT KEPT OUR FAMILY STRONG FOR MANY YEARS.
I TRULY BELIEVE IT DID.
AS NICE AS IT ALL SOUNDS...
...THERE IS NO AMOUNT OF POSITIVE THINKING THAT'S GOING TO CHANGE OUR SITUATION.
EVEN IF I WANTED TO... I CAN'T HOLD ON ANYMORE.
LOST TOO MUCH BLOOD... AND THE PAIN...
I'M DYING, STEL.
YOU HAVE TO COME TO TERMS WITH THIS.
COME WITH ME, MY BRIGHTNESS.
TURN OFF THE OXYGEN... COME WITH ME.
TOGETHER...

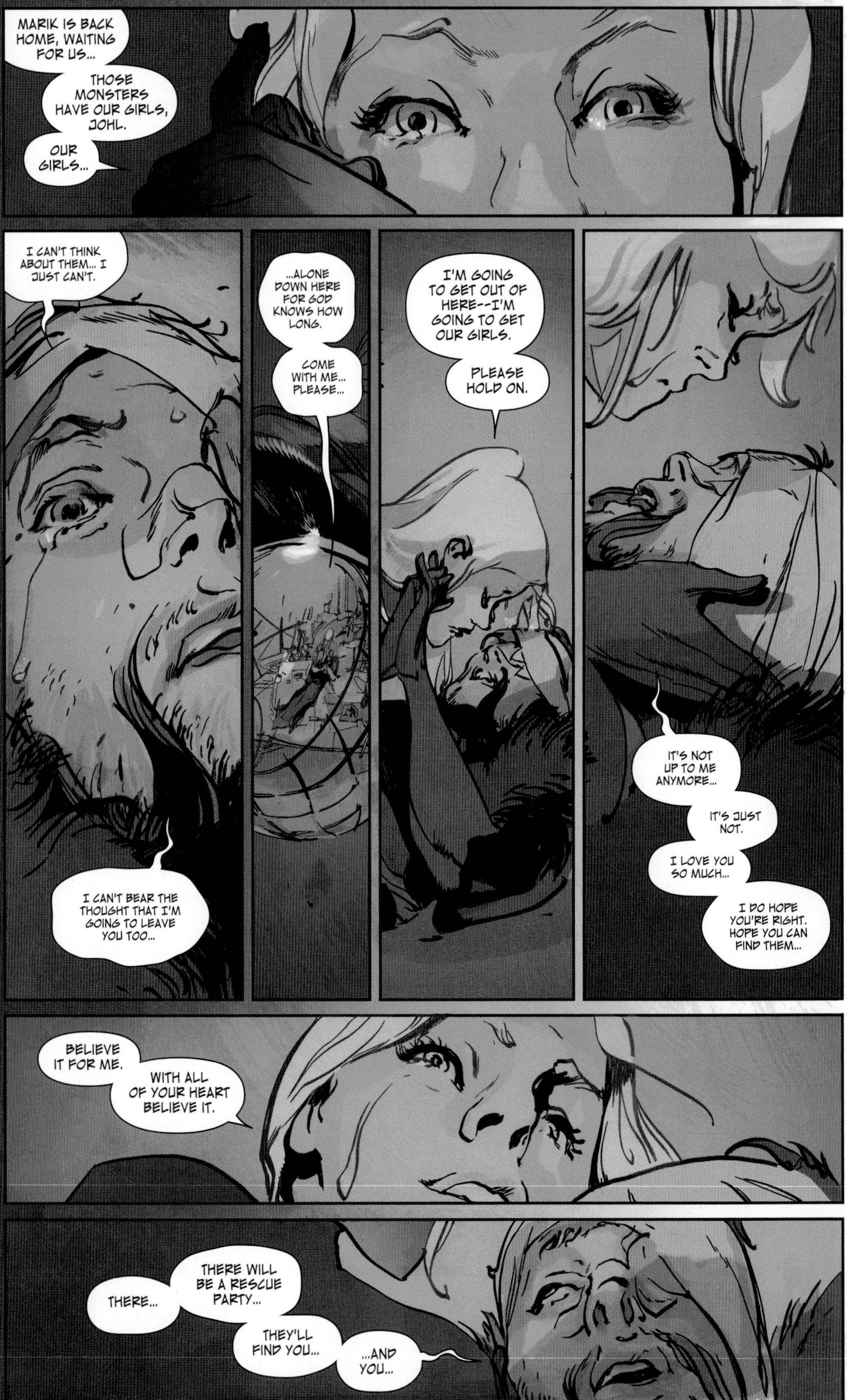
MARIK IS BACK HOME, WAITING FOR US...
THOSE MONSTERS HAVE OUR GIRLS, JOHL.
OUR GIRLS...
I CAN'T THINK ABOUT THEM... I JUST CAN'T.
I CAN'T BEAR THE THOUGHT THAT I'M GOING TO LEAVE YOU TOO...
...ALONE DOWN HERE FOR GOD KNOWS HOW LONG.
COME WITH ME... PLEASE...
I'M GOING TO GET OUT OF HERE--I'M GOING TO GET OUR GIRLS.
PLEASE HOLD ON.
IT'S NOT UP TO ME ANYMORE...
IT'S JUST NOT.
I LOVE YOU SO MUCH...
I DO HOPE YOU'RE RIGHT. HOPE YOU CAN FIND THEM...
BELIEVE IT FOR ME.
WITH ALL OF YOUR HEART BELIEVE IT.
THERE...
THERE WILL BE A RESCUE PARTY...
THEY'LL FIND YOU...
...AND YOU...

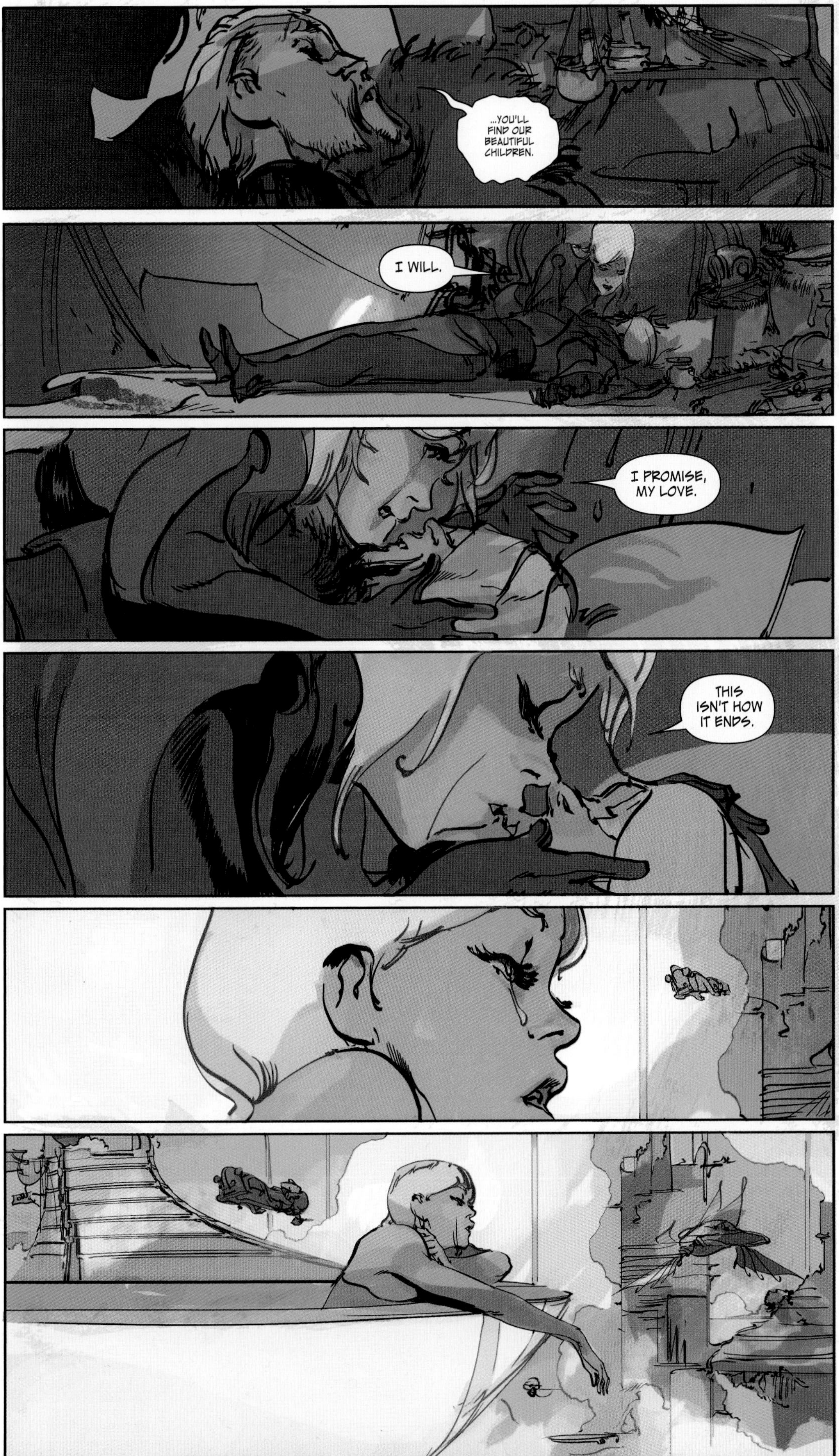
...YOU'LL FIND OUR BEAUTIFUL CHILDREN.
I WILL.
I PROMISE, MY LOVE.
THIS ISN'T HOW IT ENDS.

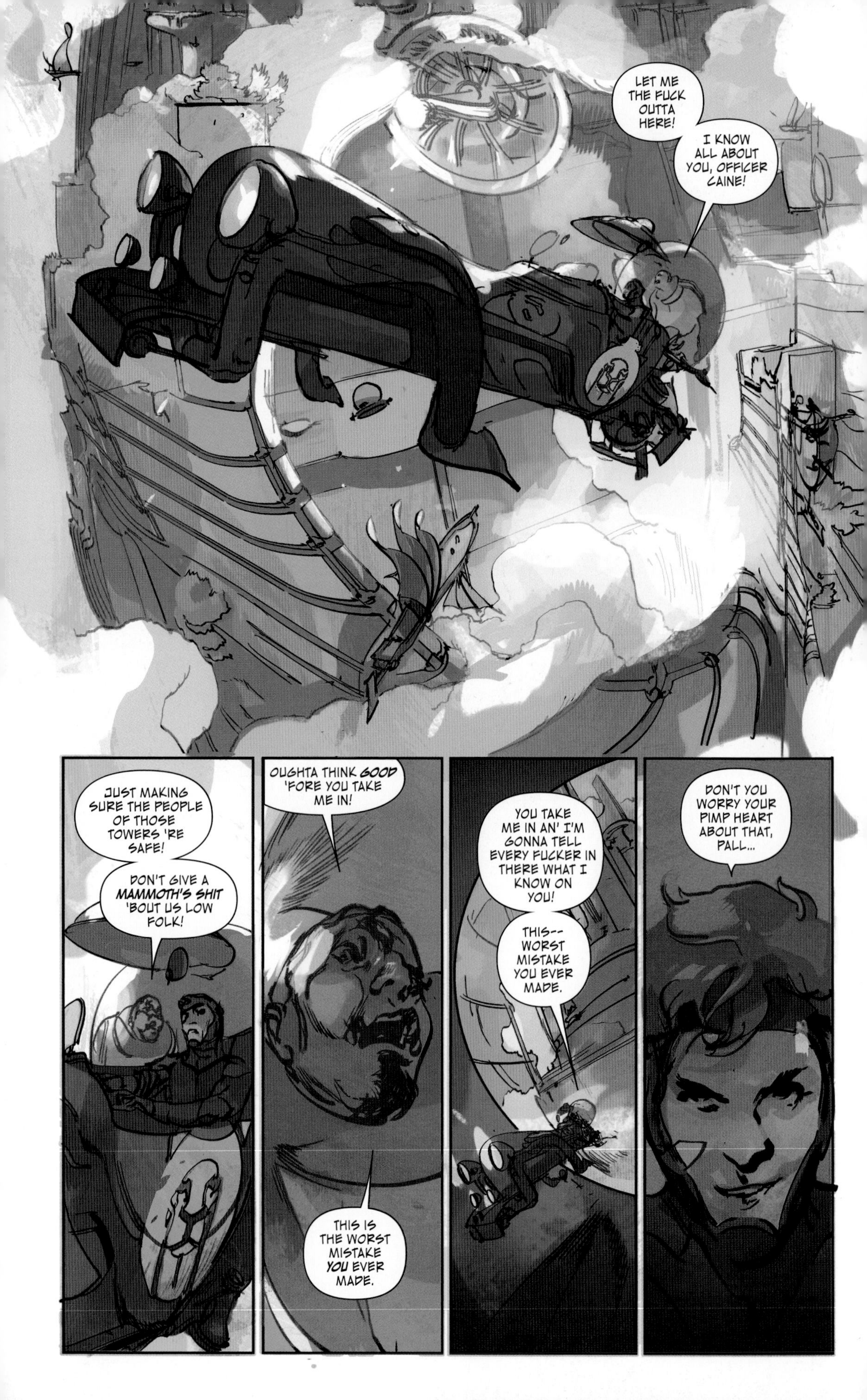
LET ME THE FUCK OUTTA HERE!
I KNOW ALL ABOUT YOU, OFFICER CAINE!
JUST MAKING SURE THE PEOPLE OF THOSE TOWERS 'RE SAFE!
DON'T GIVE A **MAMMOTH'S SHIT** 'BOUT US LOW FOLK!
OUGHTA THINK **GOOD** 'FORE YOU TAKE ME IN!
THIS IS THE WORST MISTAKE **YOU** EVER MADE.
YOU TAKE ME IN AN' I'M GONNA TELL EVERY FUCKER IN THERE WHAT I KNOW ON YOU!
THIS-- WORST MISTAKE YOU EVER MADE.
DON'T YOU WORRY YOUR PIMP HEART ABOUT THAT, PALL...

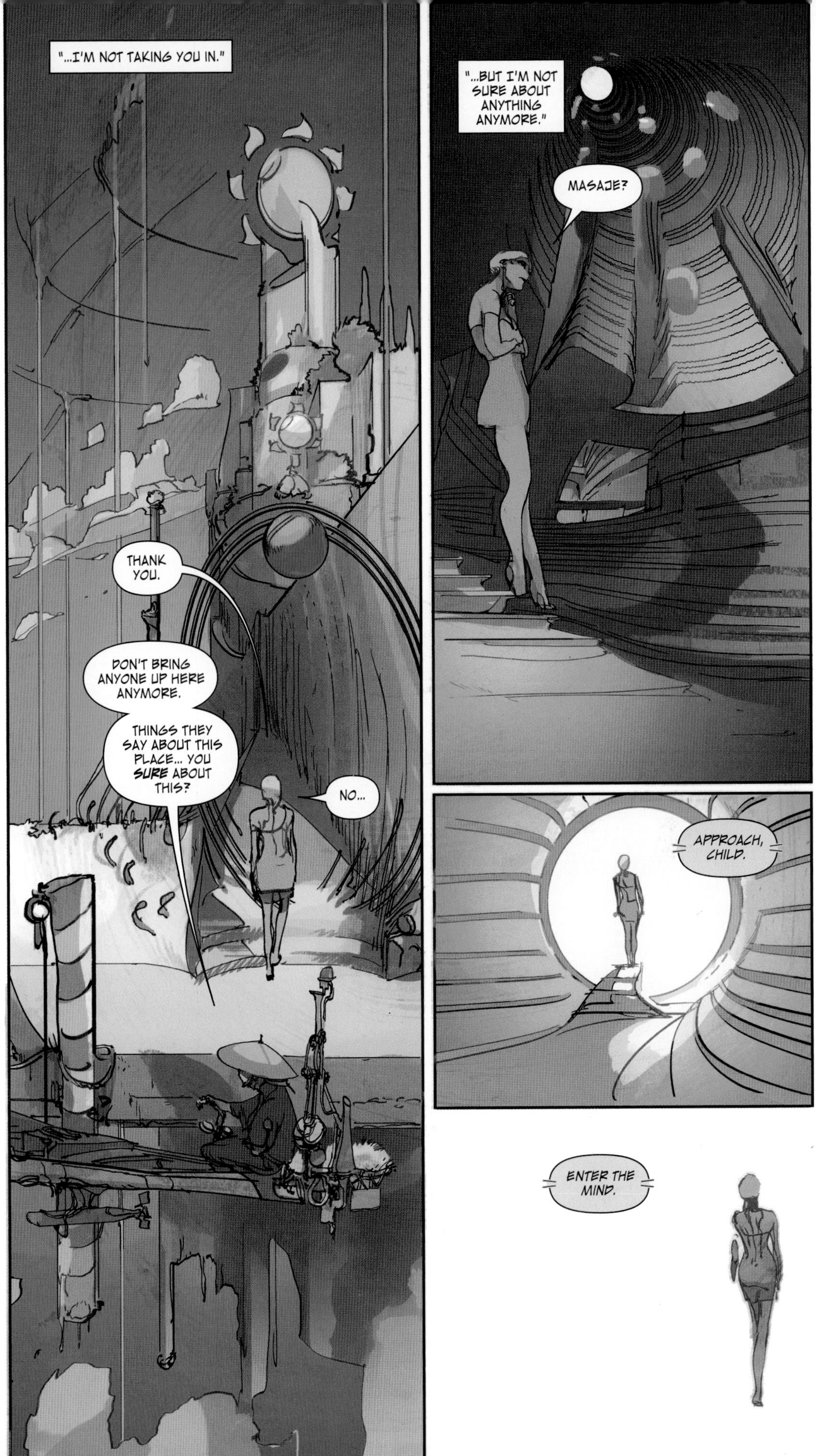
"...I'M NOT TAKING YOU IN."
THANK YOU.
DON'T BRING ANYONE UP HERE ANYMORE.
THINGS THEY SAY ABOUT THIS PLACE... YOU SURE ABOUT THIS?
NO...
"...BUT I'M NOT SURE ABOUT ANYTHING ANYMORE."
MASAJE?
APPROACH, CHILD.
ENTER THE MIND.

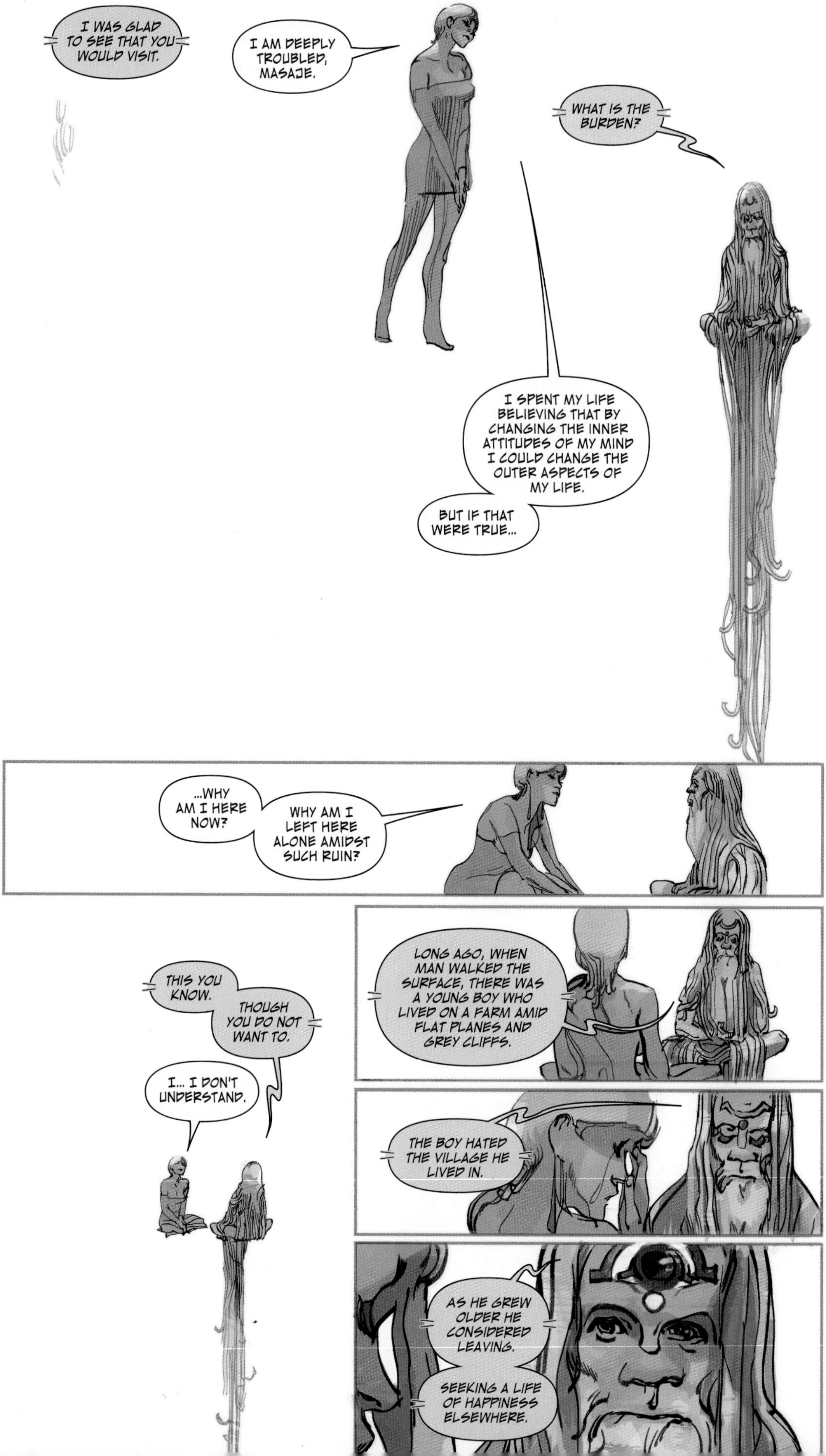
I WAS GLAD TO SEE THAT YOU WOULD VISIT.
I AM DEEPLY TROUBLED, MASAJE.
WHAT IS THE BURDEN?
I SPENT MY LIFE BELIEVING THAT BY CHANGING THE INNER ATTITUDES OF MY MIND I COULD CHANGE THE OUTER ASPECTS OF MY LIFE.
BUT IF THAT WERE TRUE...
...WHY AM I HERE NOW?
WHY AM I LEFT HERE ALONE AMIDST SUCH RUIN?
THIS YOU KNOW.
THOUGH YOU DO NOT WANT TO.
I... I DON'T UNDERSTAND.
LONG AGO, WHEN MAN WALKED THE SURFACE, THERE WAS A YOUNG BOY WHO LIVED ON A FARM AMID FLAT PLANES AND GREY CLIFFS.
THE BOY HATED THE VILLAGE HE LIVED IN.
AS HE GREW OLDER HE CONSIDERED LEAVING.
SEEKING A LIFE OF HAPPINESS ELSEWHERE.

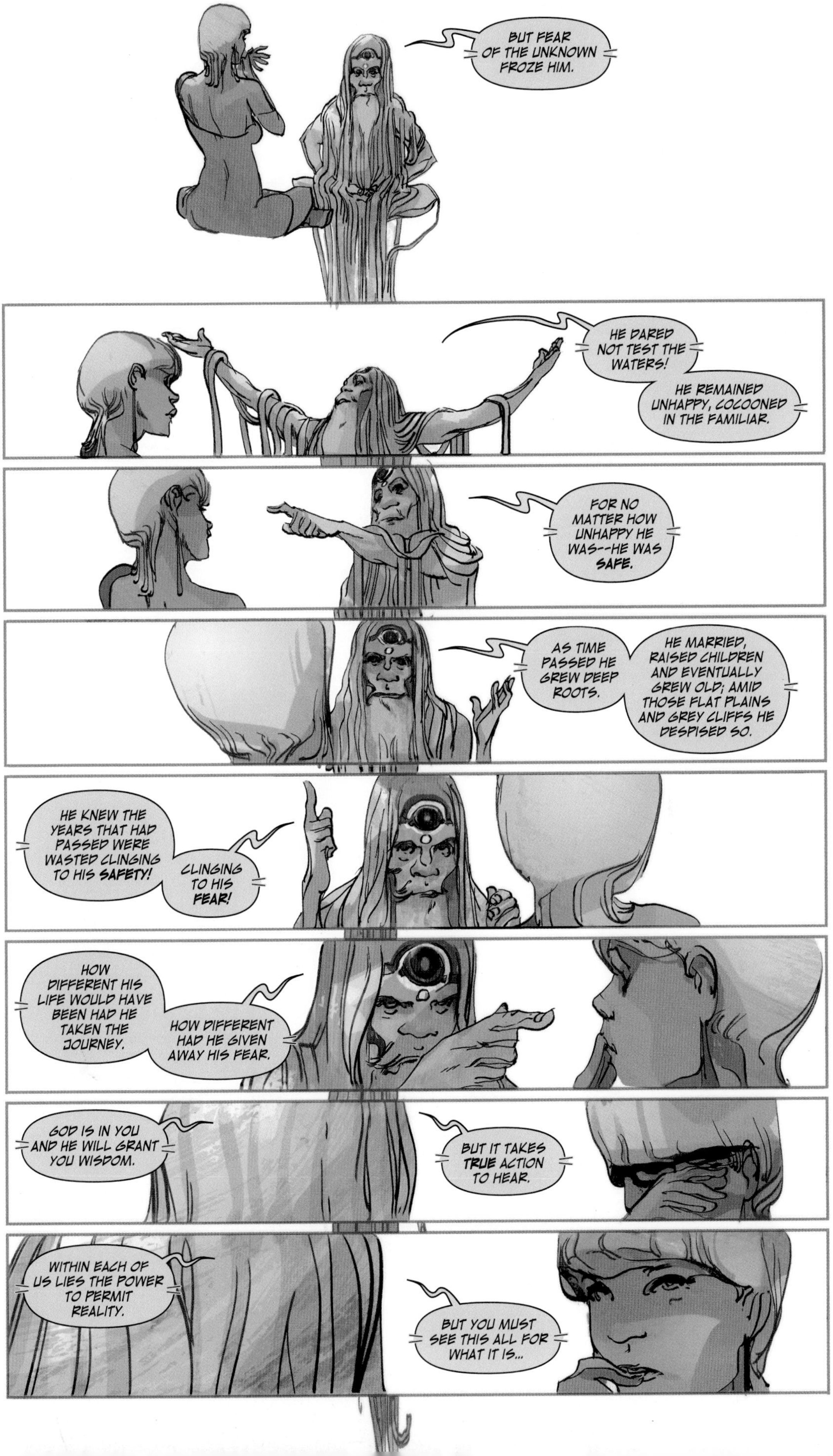
BUT FEAR OF THE UNKNOWN FROZE HIM.
HE DARED NOT TEST THE WATERS!
HE REMAINED UNHAPPY, COCOONED IN THE FAMILIAR.
FOR NO MATTER HOW UNHAPPY HE WAS--HE WAS **SAFE.**
AS TIME PASSED HE GREW DEEP ROOTS.
HE MARRIED, RAISED CHILDREN AND EVENTUALLY GREW OLD; AMID THOSE FLAT PLAINS AND GREY CLIFFS HE DESPISED SO.
HE KNEW THE YEARS THAT HAD PASSED WERE WASTED CLINGING TO HIS **SAFETY!**
CLINGING TO HIS **FEAR!**
HOW DIFFERENT HIS LIFE WOULD HAVE BEEN HAD HE TAKEN THE JOURNEY.
HOW DIFFERENT HAD HE GIVEN AWAY HIS FEAR.
GOD IS IN YOU AND HE WILL GRANT YOU WISDOM.
BUT IT TAKES **TRUE** ACTION TO HEAR.
WITHIN EACH OF US LIES THE POWER TO PERMIT REALITY.
BUT YOU MUST SEE THIS ALL FOR WHAT IT IS...

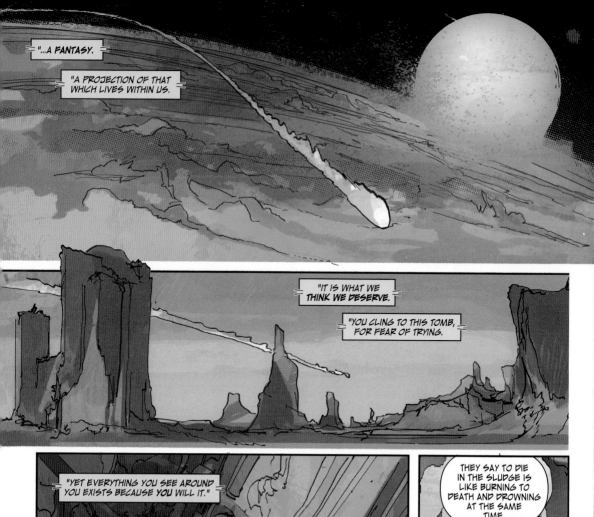

"...A FANTASY.

"A PROJECTION OF THAT WHICH LIVES WITHIN US.

"IT IS WHAT WE THINK WE DESERVE.

"YOU CLING TO THIS TOMB, FOR FEAR OF TRYING.

"YET EVERYTHING YOU SEE AROUND YOU EXISTS BECAUSE YOU WILL IT."

DON'T-- PLEASE!

PLEASE DON'T DO THIS!

THEY SAY TO DIE IN THE SLUDGE IS LIKE BURNING TO DEATH AND DROWNING AT THE SAME TIME.

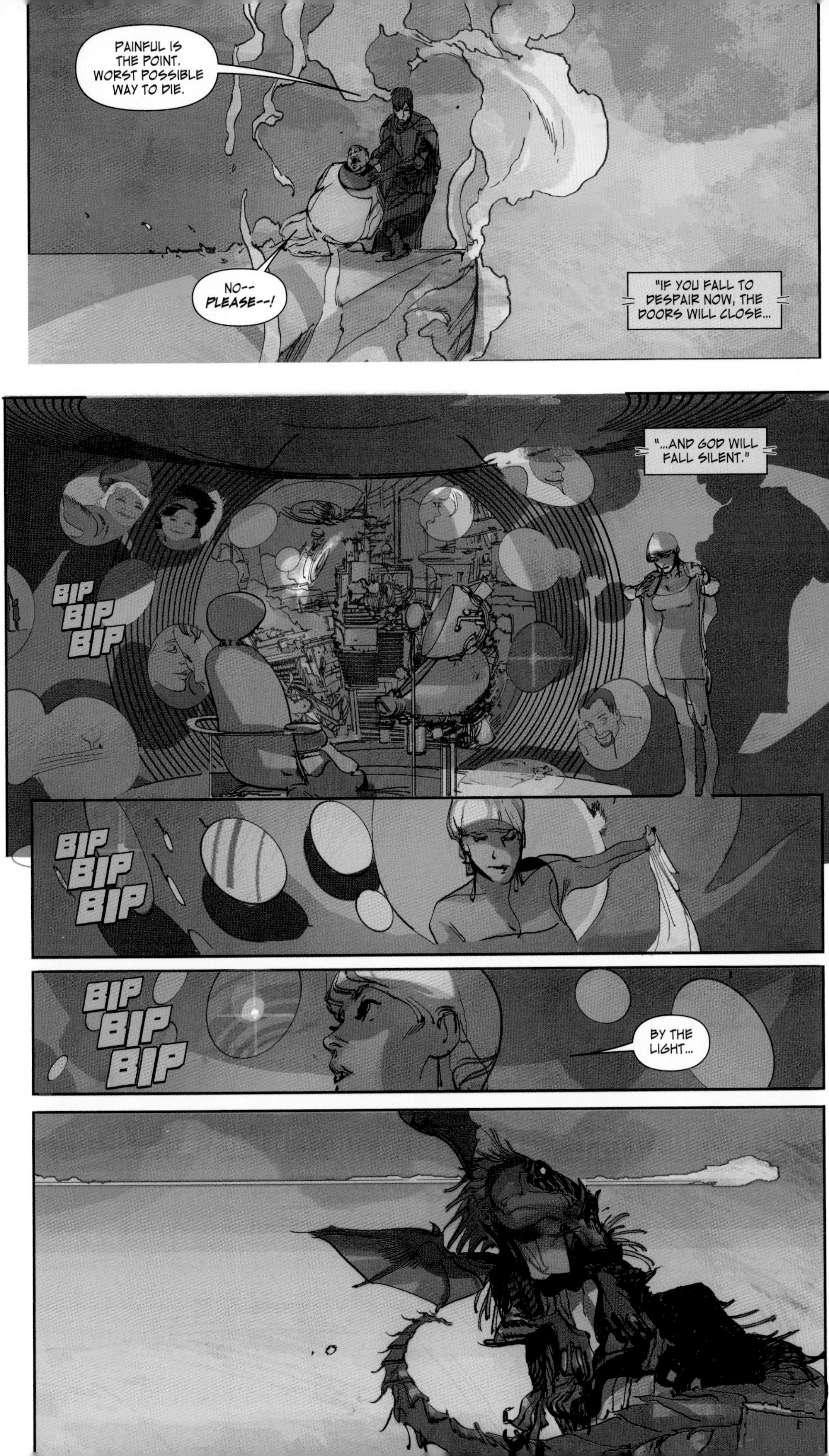
PAINFUL IS THE POINT. WORST POSSIBLE WAY TO DIE.
NO-- PLEASE--!
"IF YOU FALL TO DESPAIR NOW, THE DOORS WILL CLOSE...
"...AND GOD WILL FALL SILENT."
BIP BIP BIP
BIP BIP BIP
BIP BIP BIP
BY THE LIGHT...

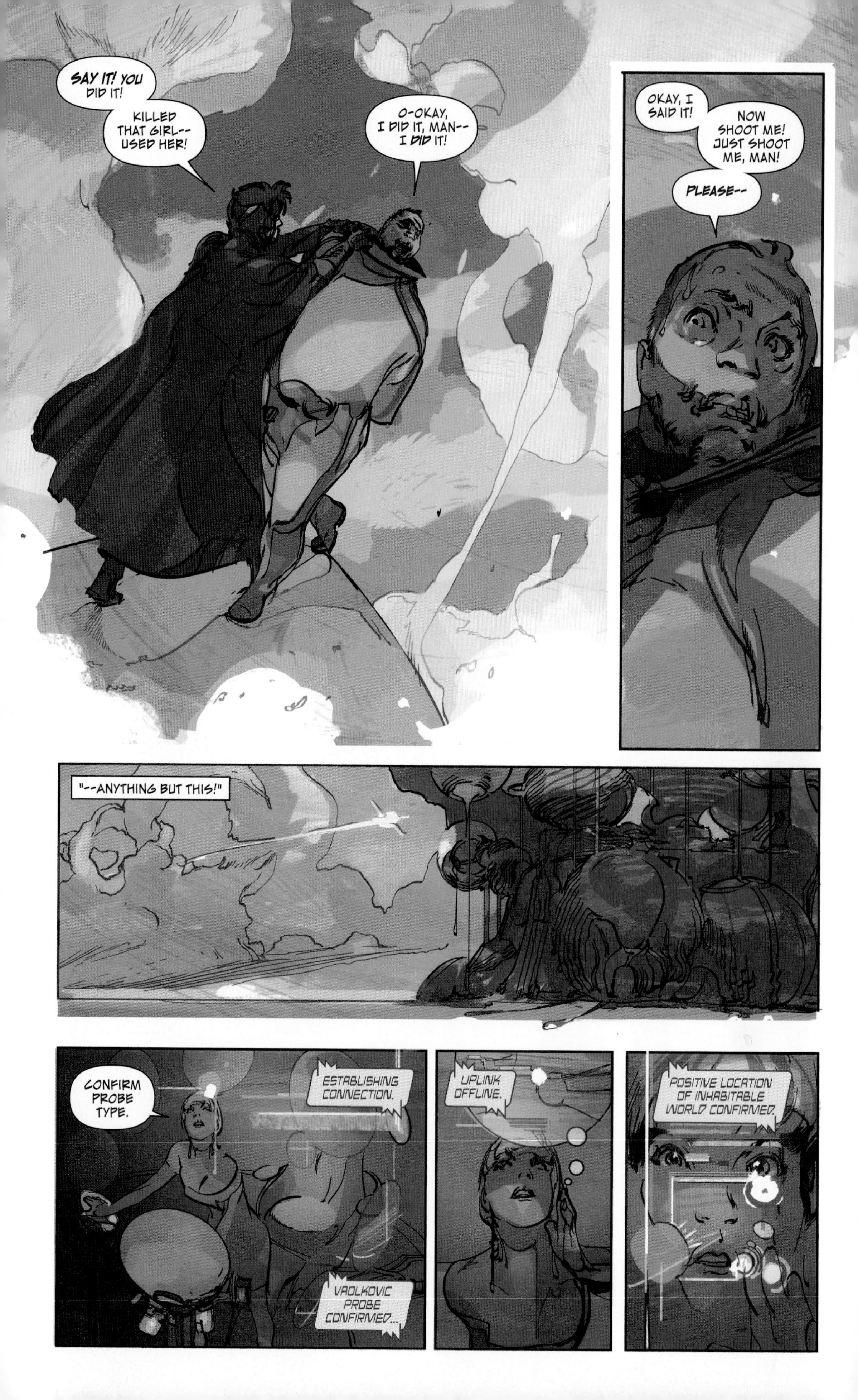

SAY IT! YOU DID IT!
KILLED THAT GIRL-- USED HER!
O-OKAY, I DID IT, MAN-- I DID IT!
OKAY, I SAID IT!
NOW SHOOT ME! JUST SHOOT ME, MAN!
PLEASE--
"--ANYTHING BUT THIS!"
CONFIRM PROBE TYPE.
ESTABLISHING CONNECTION.
VADLKOVIC PROBE CONFIRMED...
UPLINK OFFLINE.
POSITIVE LOCATION OF INHABITABLE WORLD CONFIRMED.

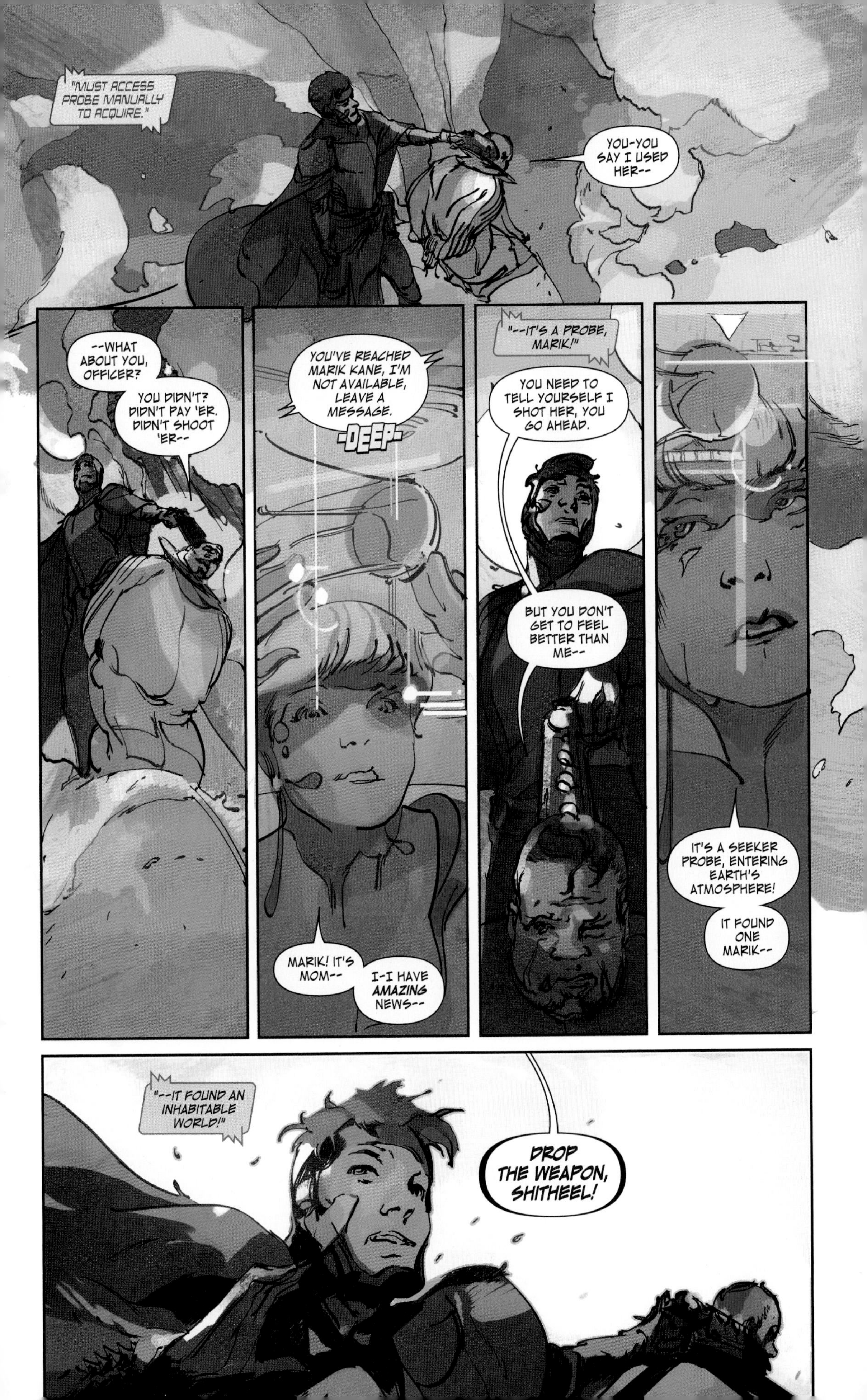
"MUST ACCESS PROBE MANUALLY TO ACQUIRE."
YOU-YOU SAY I USED HER--
--WHAT ABOUT YOU, OFFICER?
YOU DIDN'T? DIDN'T PAY 'ER. DIDN'T SHOOT 'ER--
YOU'VE REACHED MARIK KANE, I'M NOT AVAILABLE, LEAVE A MESSAGE.
-BEEP-
MARIK! IT'S MOM--
I-I HAVE AMAZING NEWS--
"--IT'S A PROBE, MARIK!"
YOU NEED TO TELL YOURSELF I SHOT HER, YOU GO AHEAD.
BUT YOU DON'T GET TO FEEL BETTER THAN ME--
IT'S A SEEKER PROBE, ENTERING EARTH'S ATMOSPHERE!
IT FOUND ONE MARIK--
"--IT FOUND AN INHABITABLE WORLD!"
DROP THE WEAPON, SHITHEEL!

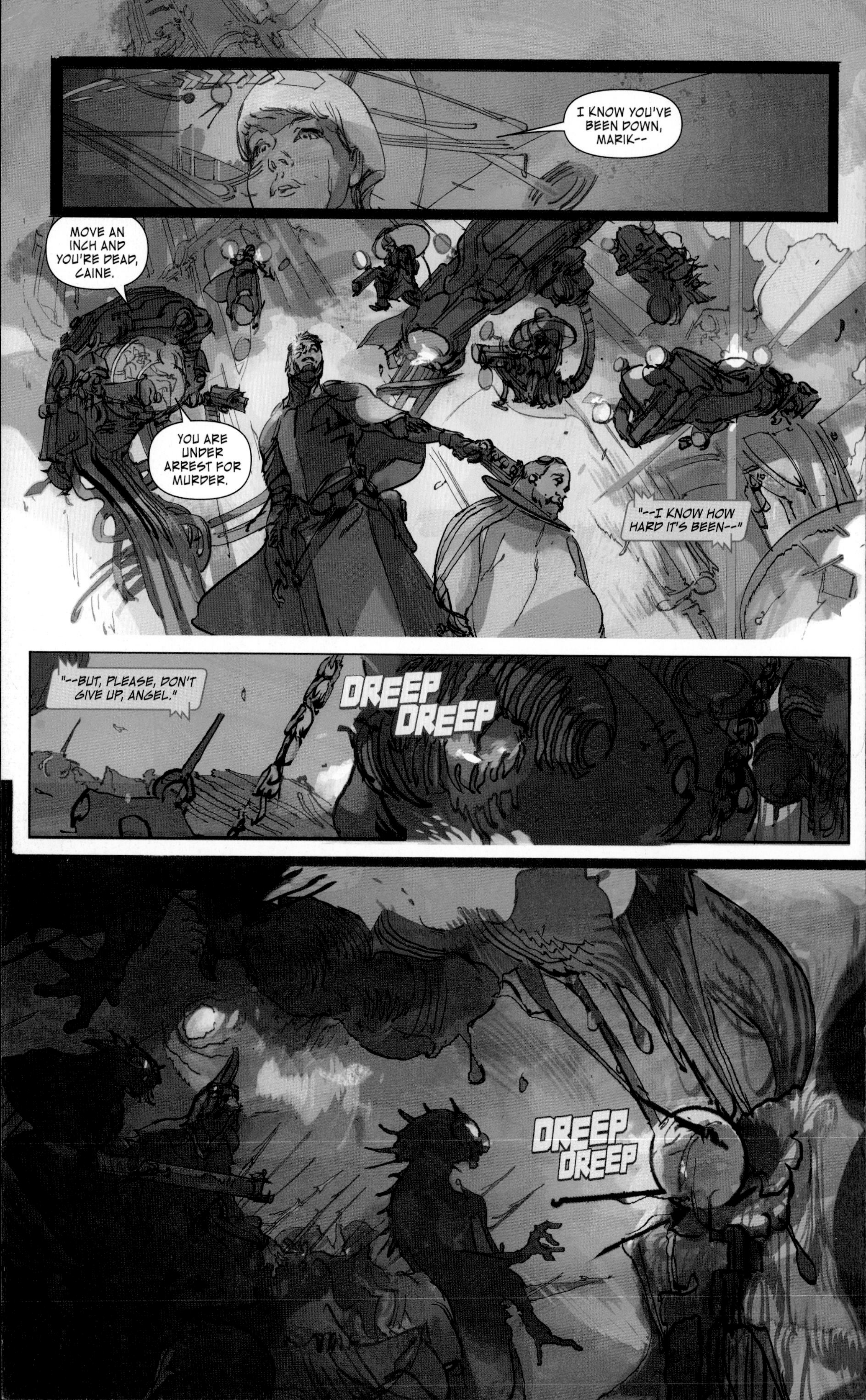
I KNOW YOU'VE BEEN DOWN, MARIK--
MOVE AN INCH AND YOU'RE DEAD, CAINE.
YOU ARE UNDER ARREST FOR MURDER.
"--I KNOW HOW HARD IT'S BEEN--"
"--BUT, PLEASE, DON'T GIVE UP, ANGEL."
DREEP DREEP
DREEP DREEP

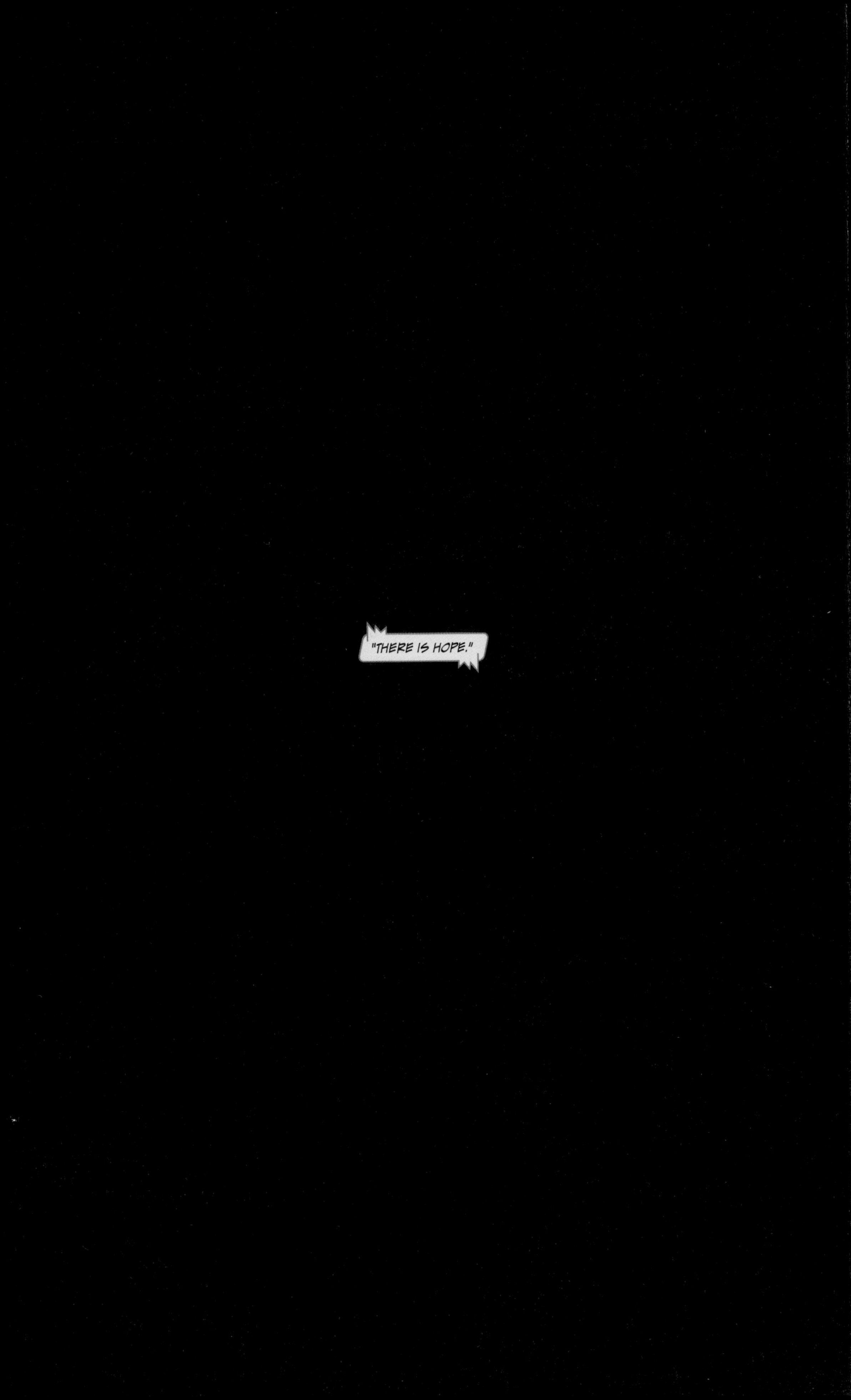
"THERE IS HOPE."

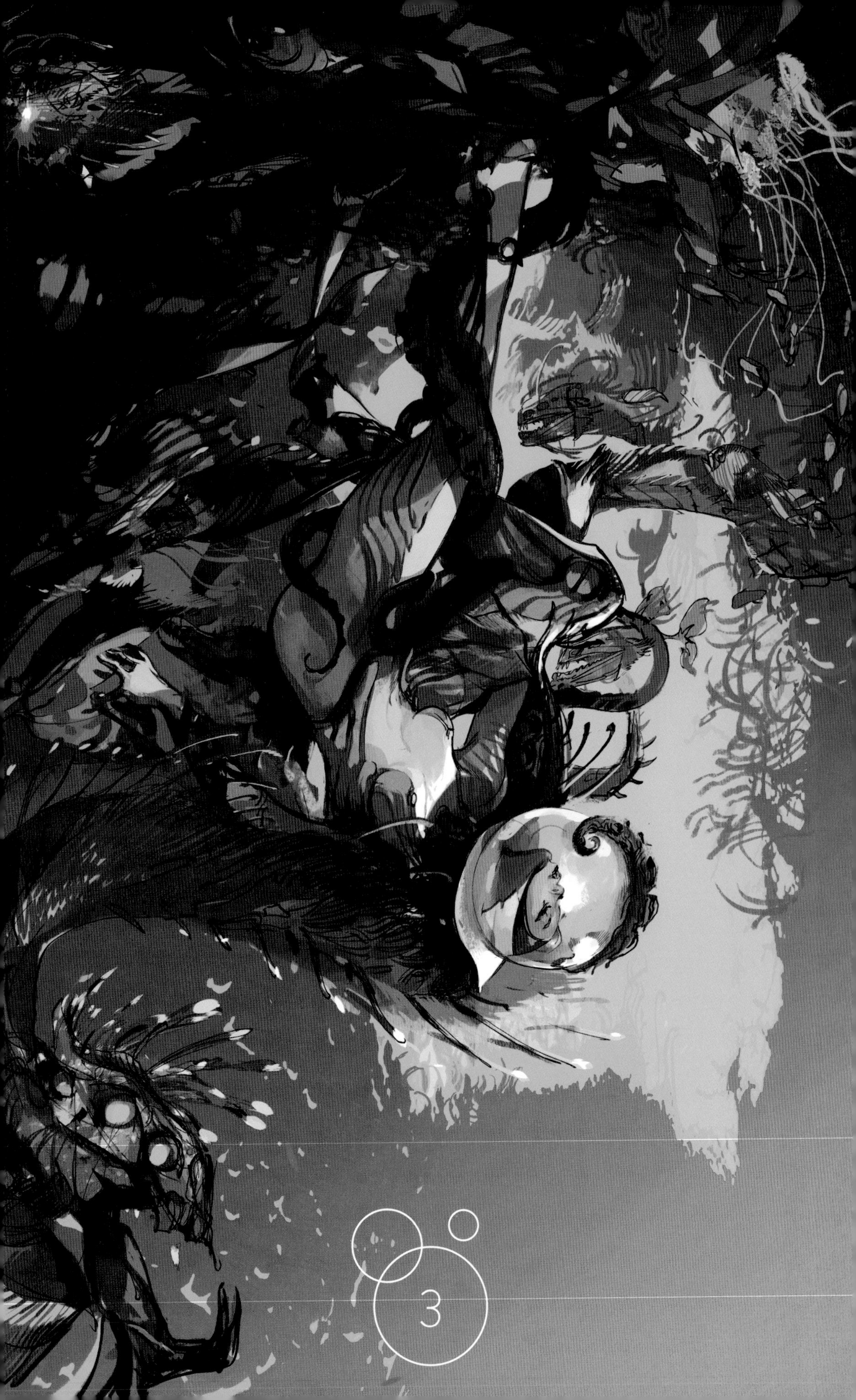

# 3

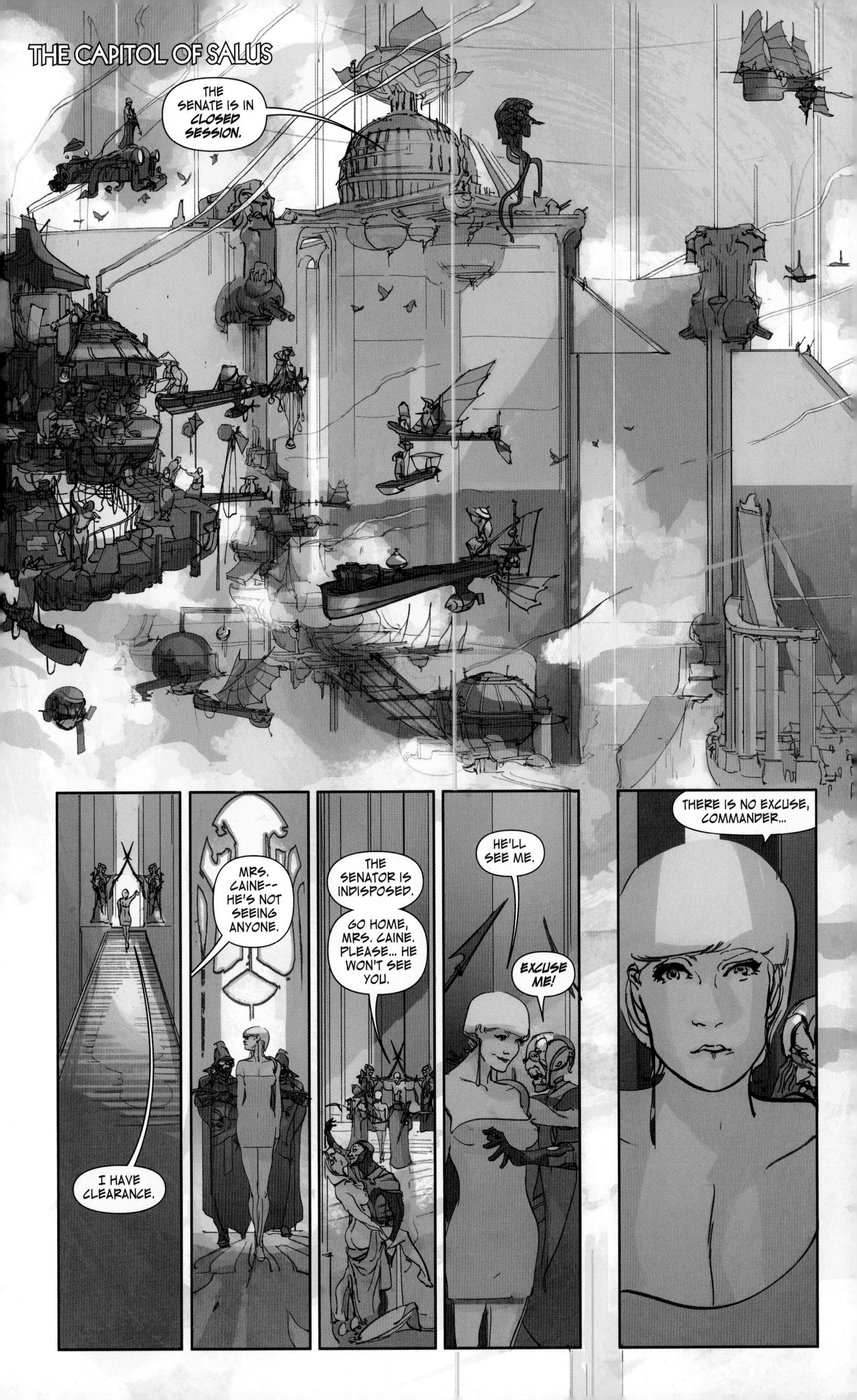
THE CAPITOL OF SALUS
THE SENATE IS IN CLOSED SESSION.
I HAVE CLEARANCE.
MRS. CAINE-- HE'S NOT SEEING ANYONE.
THE SENATOR IS INDISPOSED.
GO HOME, MRS. CAINE. PLEASE... HE WON'T SEE YOU.
HE'LL SEE ME.
EXCUSE ME!
THERE IS NO EXCUSE, COMMANDER...

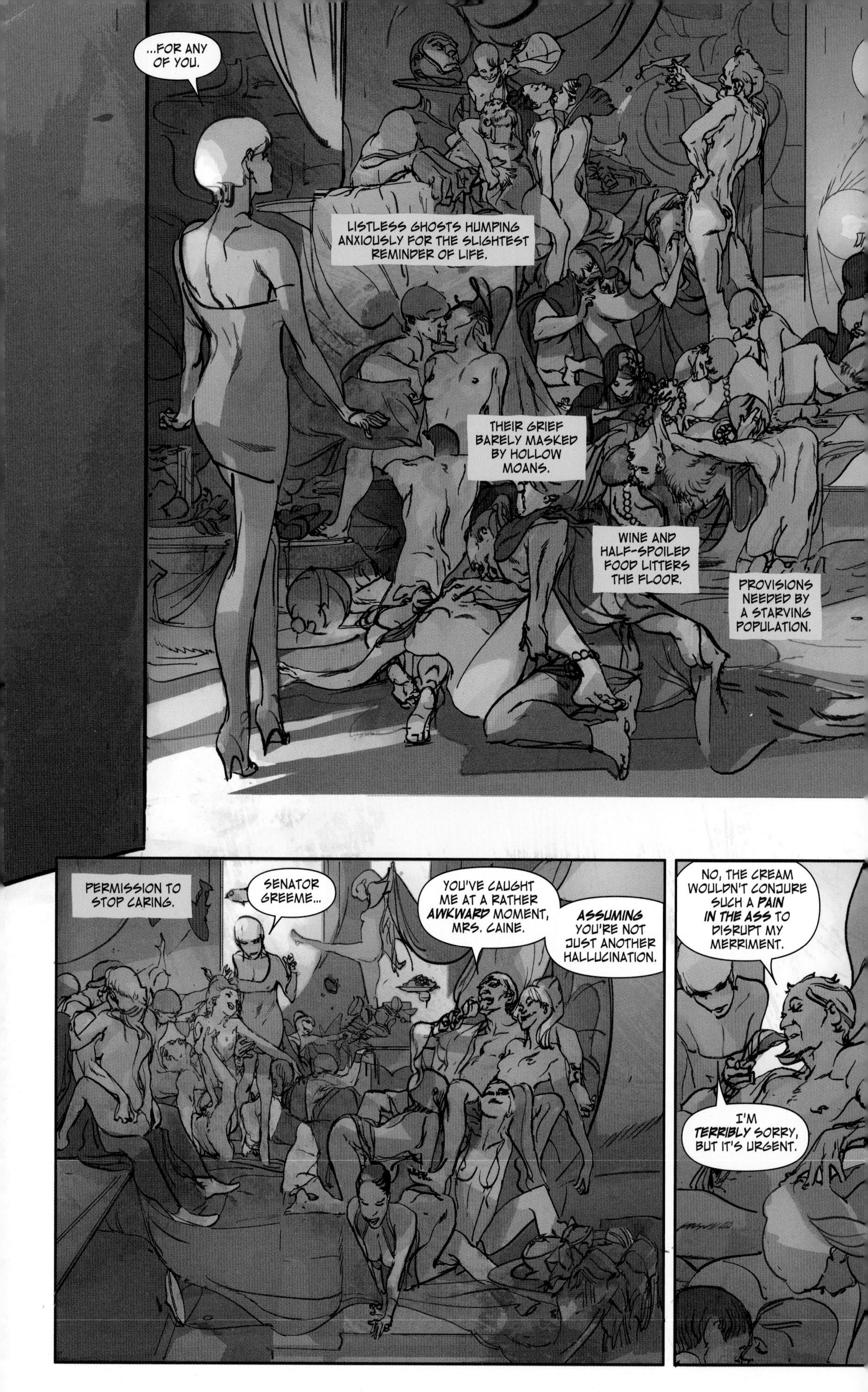
...FOR ANY OF YOU.
LISTLESS GHOSTS HUMPING ANXIOUSLY FOR THE SLIGHTEST REMINDER OF LIFE.
THEIR GRIEF BARELY MASKED BY HOLLOW MOANS.
WINE AND HALF-SPOILED FOOD LITTERS THE FLOOR.
PROVISIONS NEEDED BY A STARVING POPULATION.
PERMISSION TO STOP CARING.
SENATOR GREEME...
YOU'VE CAUGHT ME AT A RATHER **AWKWARD** MOMENT, MRS. CAINE.
**ASSUMING** YOU'RE NOT JUST ANOTHER HALLUCINATION.
NO, THE CREAM WOULDN'T CONJURE SUCH A **PAIN IN THE ASS** TO DISRUPT MY MERRIMENT.
I'M **TERRIBLY** SORRY, BUT IT'S URGENT.

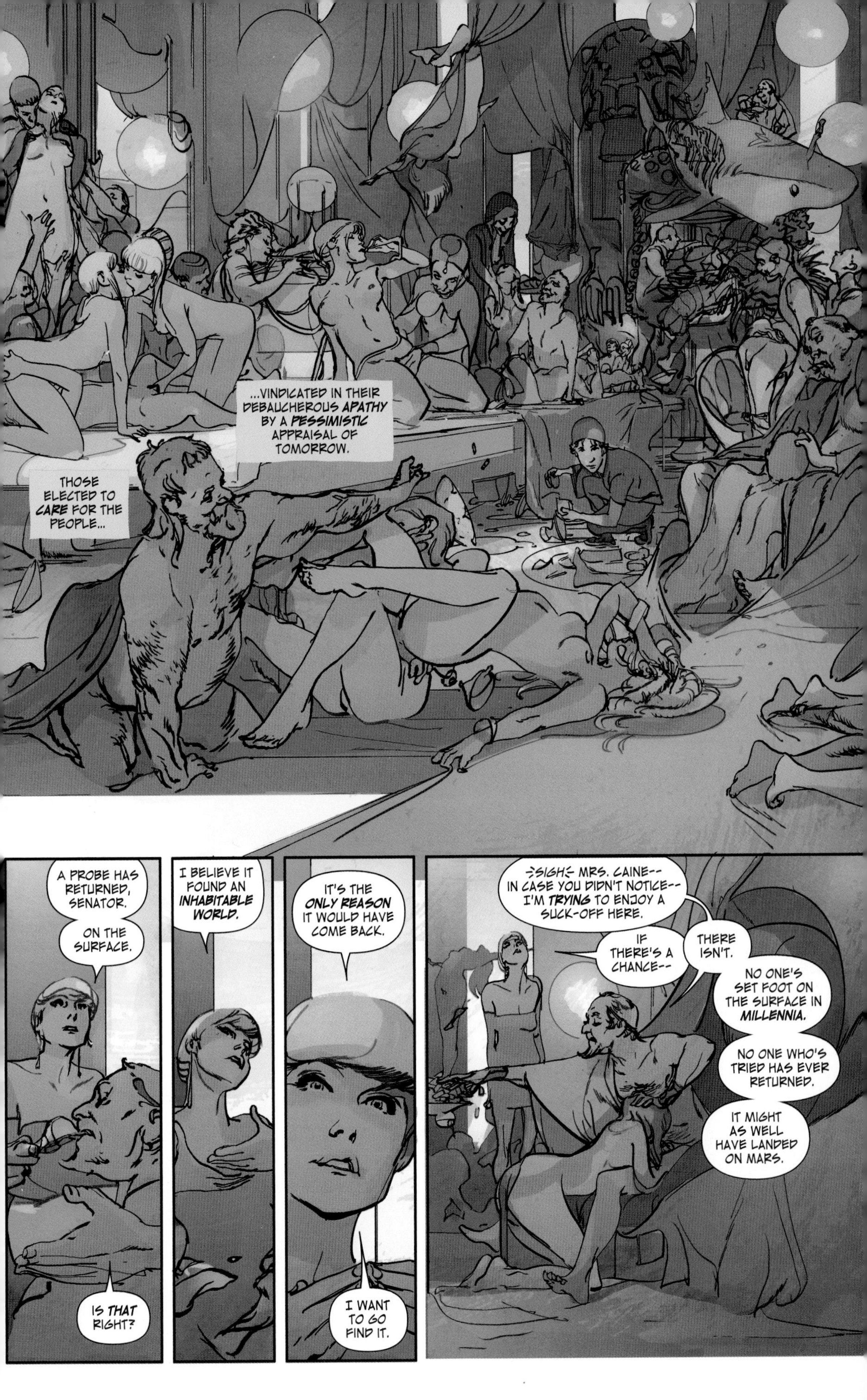
...VINDICATED IN THEIR DEBAUCHEROUS APATHY BY A PESSIMISTIC APPRAISAL OF TOMORROW.
THOSE ELECTED TO CARE FOR THE PEOPLE...
A PROBE HAS RETURNED, SENATOR.
ON THE SURFACE.
IS THAT RIGHT?
I BELIEVE IT FOUND AN INHABITABLE WORLD.
IT'S THE ONLY REASON IT WOULD HAVE COME BACK.
I WANT TO GO FIND IT.
-SIGH- MRS. CAINE-- IN CASE YOU DIDN'T NOTICE-- I'M TRYING TO ENJOY A SUCK-OFF HERE.
IF THERE'S A CHANCE--
THERE ISN'T.
NO ONE'S SET FOOT ON THE SURFACE IN MILLENNIA.
NO ONE WHO'S TRIED HAS EVER RETURNED.
IT MIGHT AS WELL HAVE LANDED ON MARS.

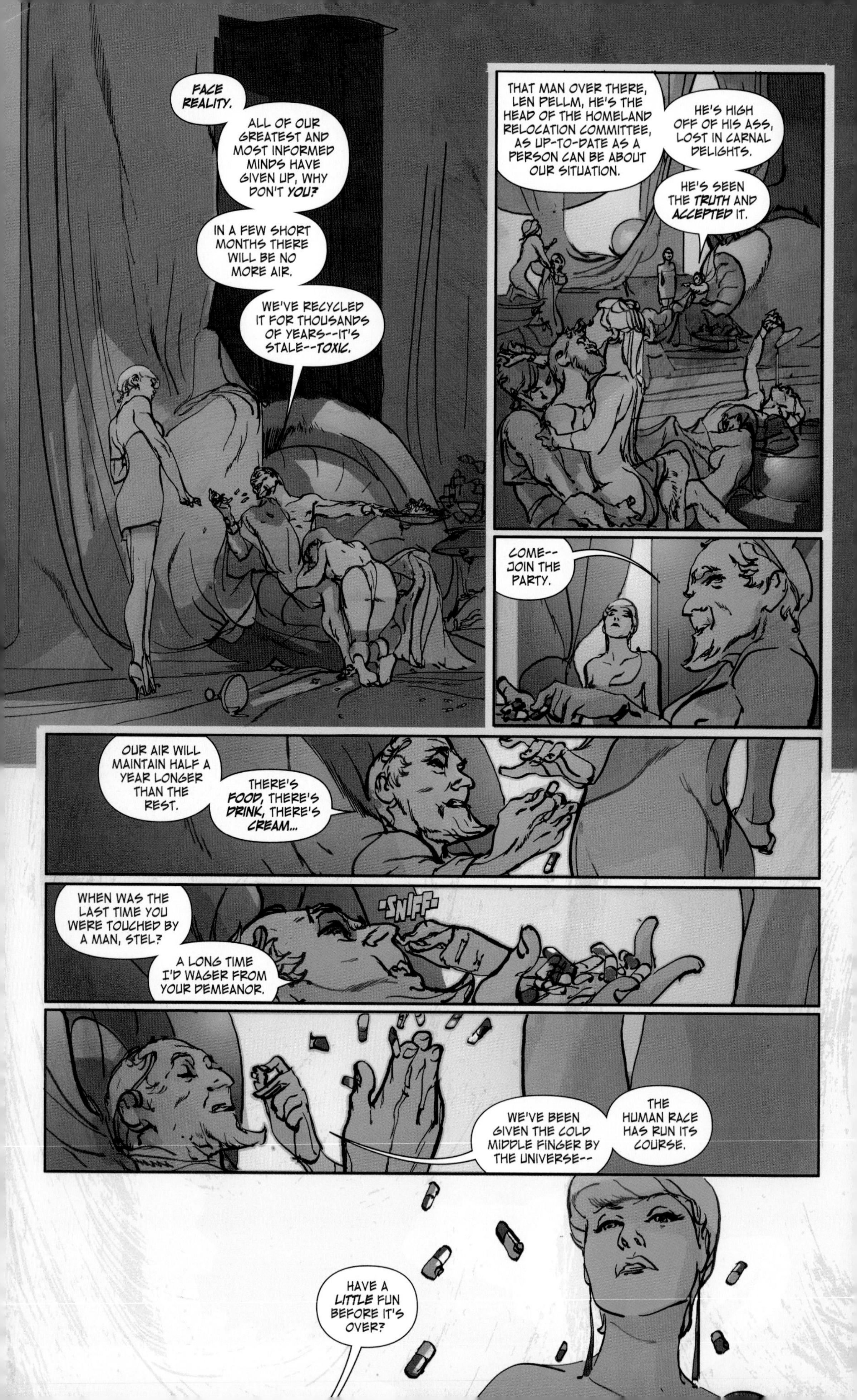
FACE REALITY.
ALL OF OUR GREATEST AND MOST INFORMED MINDS HAVE GIVEN UP, WHY DON'T YOU?
IN A FEW SHORT MONTHS THERE WILL BE NO MORE AIR.
WE'VE RECYCLED IT FOR THOUSANDS OF YEARS--IT'S STALE--TOXIC.
THAT MAN OVER THERE, LEN PELLM, HE'S THE HEAD OF THE HOMELAND RELOCATION COMMITTEE, AS UP-TO-DATE AS A PERSON CAN BE ABOUT OUR SITUATION.
HE'S HIGH OFF OF HIS ASS, LOST IN CARNAL DELIGHTS.
HE'S SEEN THE TRUTH AND ACCEPTED IT.
COME--JOIN THE PARTY.
OUR AIR WILL MAINTAIN HALF A YEAR LONGER THAN THE REST.
THERE'S FOOD, THERE'S DRINK, THERE'S CREAM...
WHEN WAS THE LAST TIME YOU WERE TOUCHED BY A MAN, STEL?
-SNIFF-
A LONG TIME I'D WAGER FROM YOUR DEMEANOR.
THE HUMAN RACE HAS RUN ITS COURSE.
WE'VE BEEN GIVEN THE COLD MIDDLE FINGER BY THE UNIVERSE--
HAVE A LITTLE FUN BEFORE IT'S OVER?

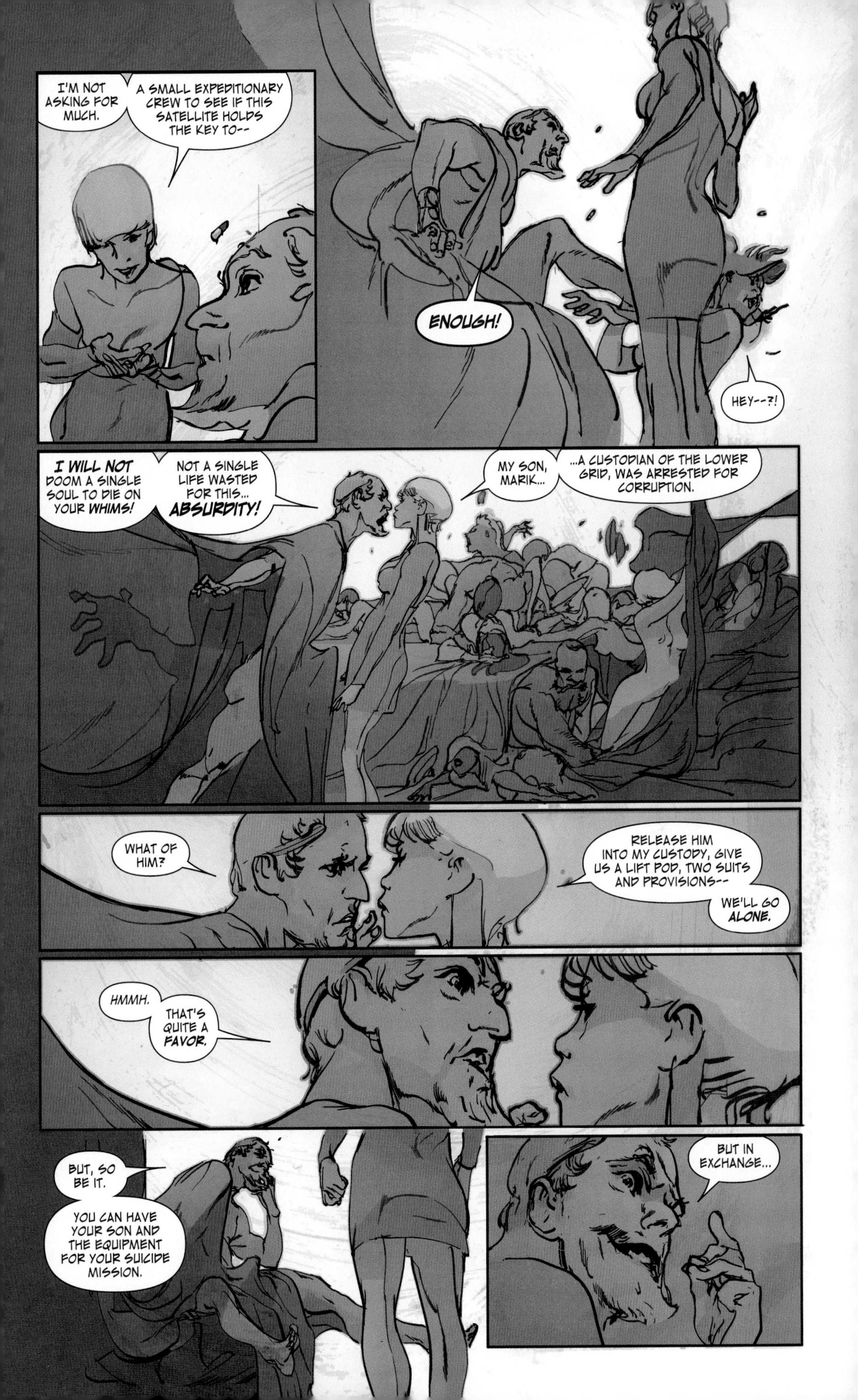
I'M NOT ASKING FOR MUCH.
A SMALL EXPEDITIONARY CREW TO SEE IF THIS SATELLITE HOLDS THE KEY TO--
ENOUGH!
HEY--?!
I WILL NOT DOOM A SINGLE SOUL TO DIE ON YOUR WHIMS!
NOT A SINGLE LIFE WASTED FOR THIS... ABSURDITY!
MY SON, MARIK...
...A CUSTODIAN OF THE LOWER GRID, WAS ARRESTED FOR CORRUPTION.
WHAT OF HIM?
RELEASE HIM INTO MY CUSTODY, GIVE US A LIFT POD, TWO SUITS AND PROVISIONS--
WE'LL GO ALONE.
HMMH.
THAT'S QUITE A FAVOR.
BUT, SO BE IT.
YOU CAN HAVE YOUR SON AND THE EQUIPMENT FOR YOUR SUICIDE MISSION.
BUT IN EXCHANGE...

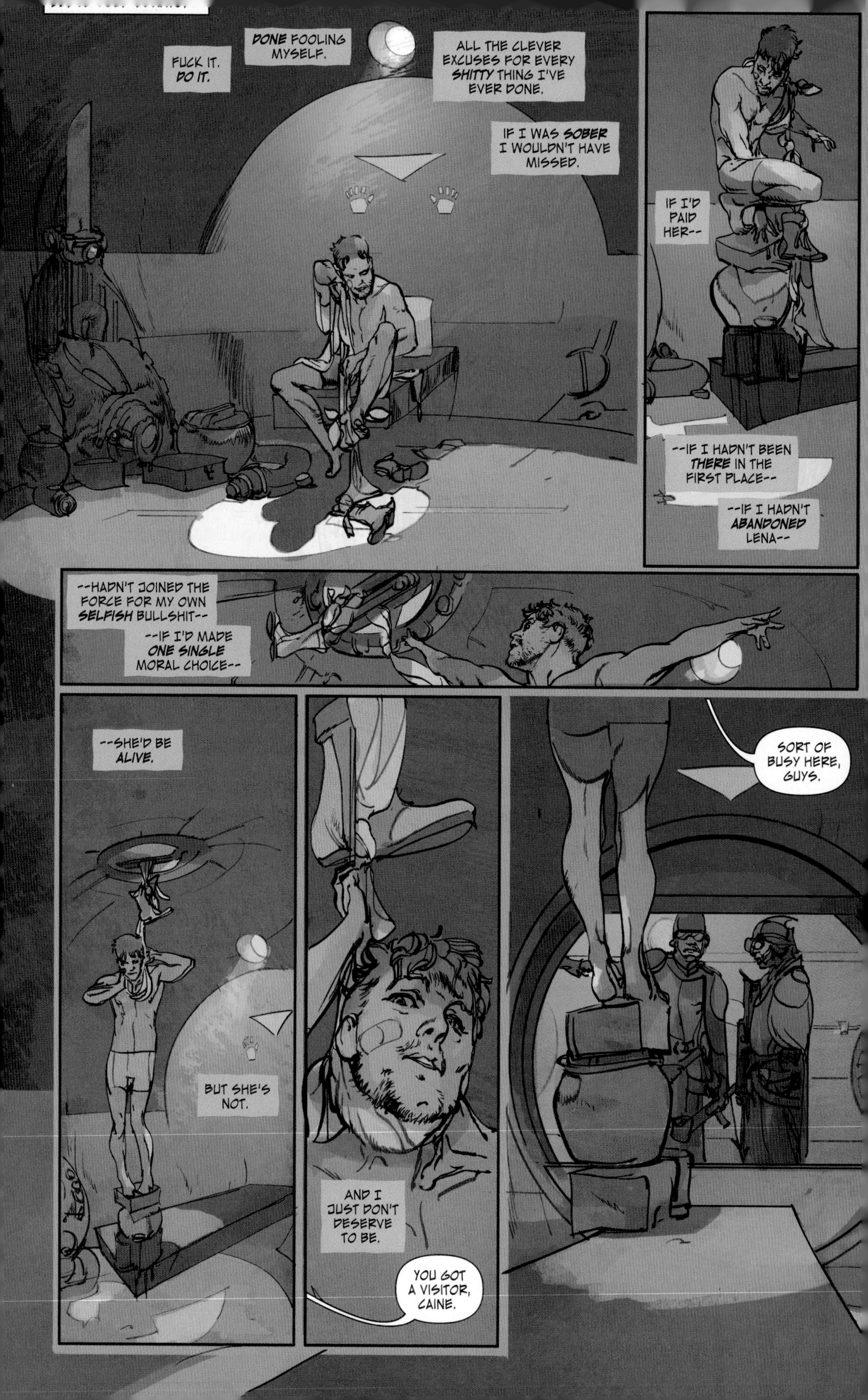
FUCK IT. DO IT.
DONE FOOLING MYSELF.
ALL THE CLEVER EXCUSES FOR EVERY SHITTY THING I'VE EVER DONE.
IF I WAS SOBER I WOULDN'T HAVE MISSED.
IF I'D PAID HER--
--IF I HADN'T BEEN THERE IN THE FIRST PLACE--
--IF I HADN'T ABANDONED LENA--
--HADN'T JOINED THE FORCE FOR MY OWN SELFISH BULLSHIT--
--IF I'D MADE ONE SINGLE MORAL CHOICE--
--SHE'D BE ALIVE.
BUT SHE'S NOT.
AND I JUST DON'T DESERVE TO BE.
YOU GOT A VISITOR, CAINE.
SORT OF BUSY HERE, GUYS.

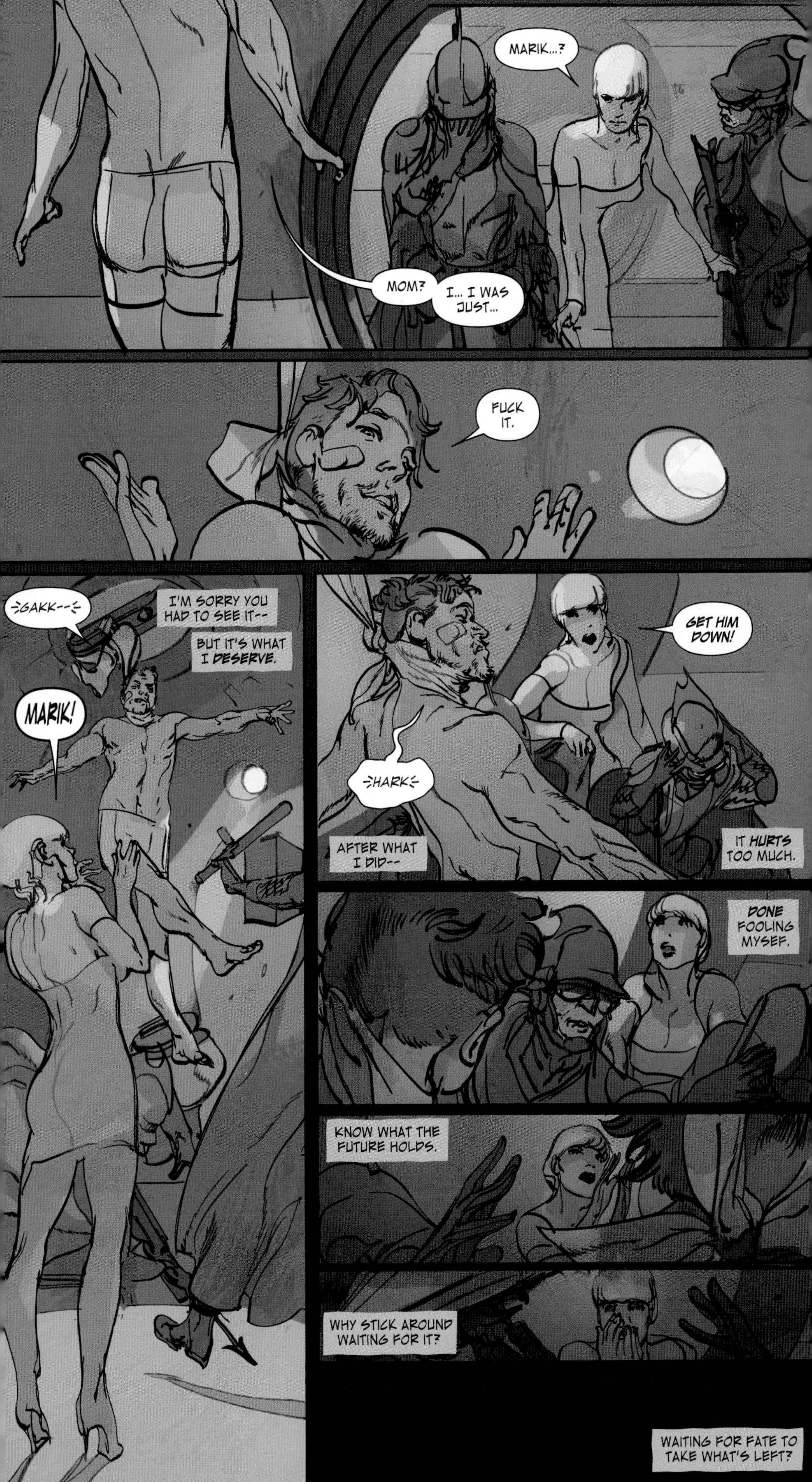
MARIK...?
MOM?
I... I WAS JUST...
FUCK IT.
-GAKK--
I'M SORRY YOU HAD TO SEE IT--
BUT IT'S WHAT I DESERVE.
MARIK!
GET HIM DOWN!
-HARK-
AFTER WHAT I DID--
IT HURTS TOO MUCH.
DONE FOOLING MYSEF.
KNOW WHAT THE FUTURE HOLDS.
WHY STICK AROUND WAITING FOR IT?
WAITING FOR FATE TO TAKE WHAT'S LEFT?

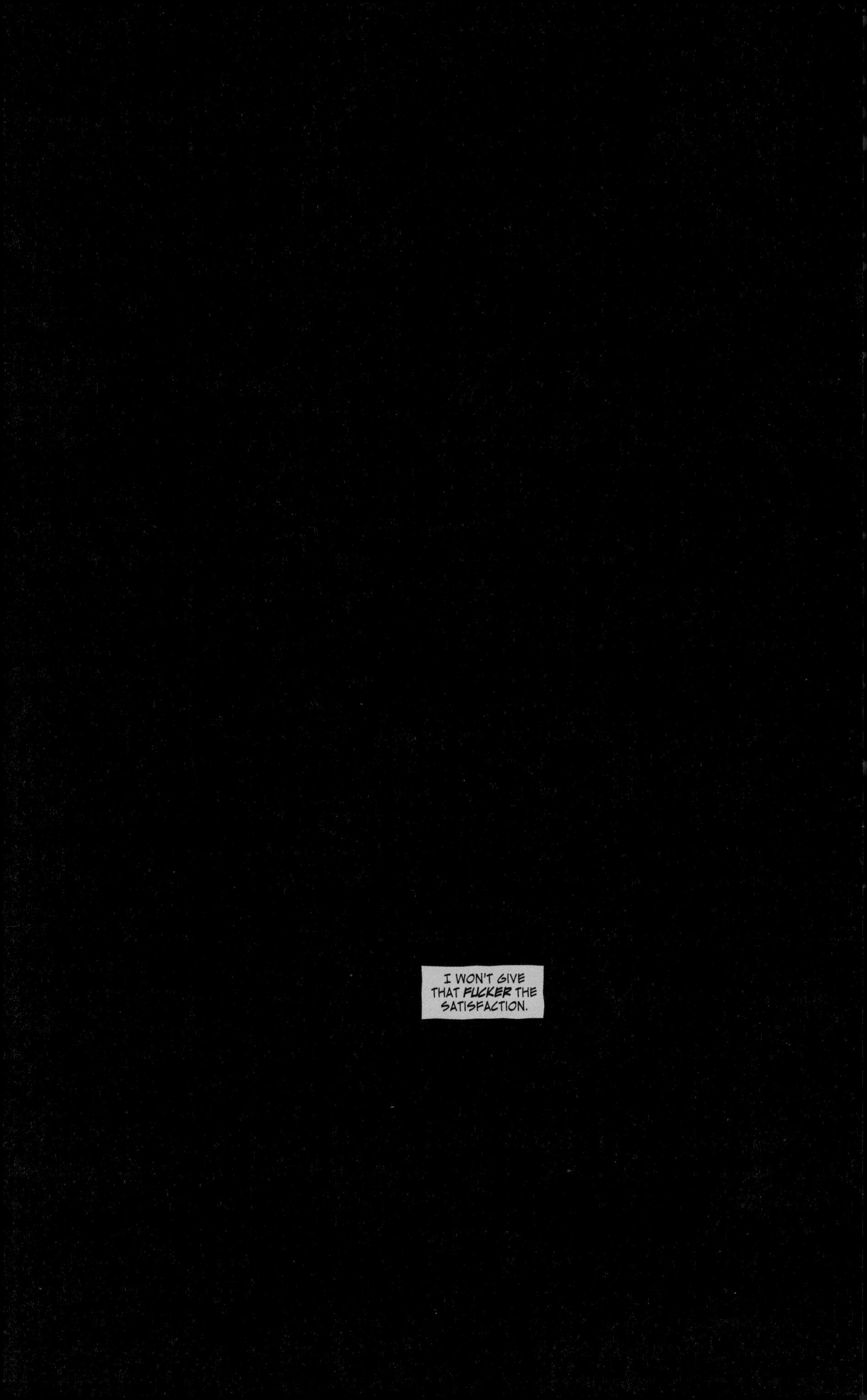
I WON'T GIVE THAT FUCKER THE SATISFACTION.

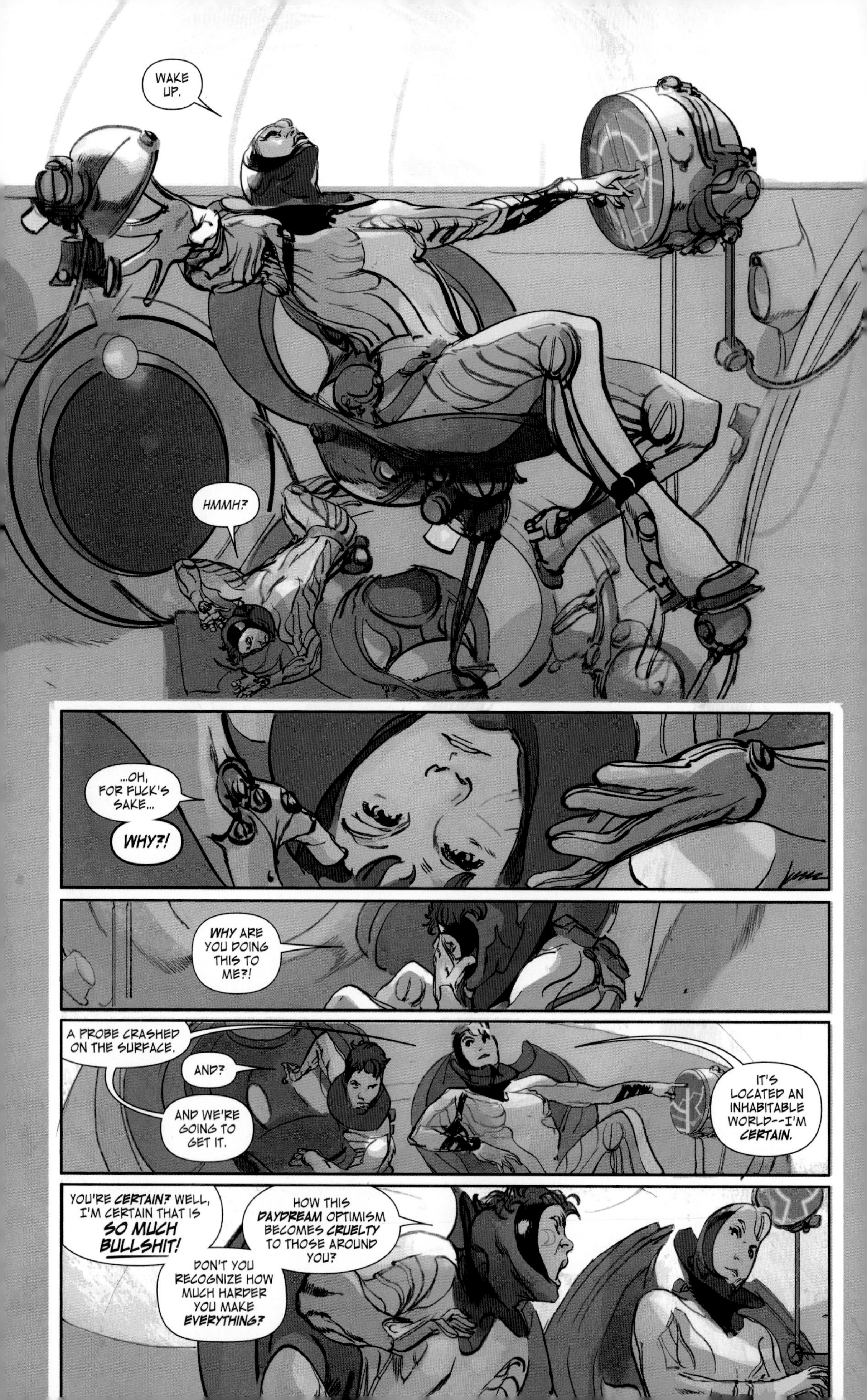

WAKE UP.
HMMH?
...OH, FOR FUCK'S SAKE...
WHY?!
WHY ARE YOU DOING THIS TO ME?!
A PROBE CRASHED ON THE SURFACE.
AND?
AND WE'RE GOING TO GET IT.
IT'S LOCATED AN INHABITABLE WORLD--I'M CERTAIN.
YOU'RE CERTAIN? WELL, I'M CERTAIN THAT IS SO MUCH BULLSHIT!
DON'T YOU RECOGNIZE HOW MUCH HARDER YOU MAKE EVERYTHING?
HOW THIS DAYDREAM OPTIMISM BECOMES CRUELTY TO THOSE AROUND YOU?

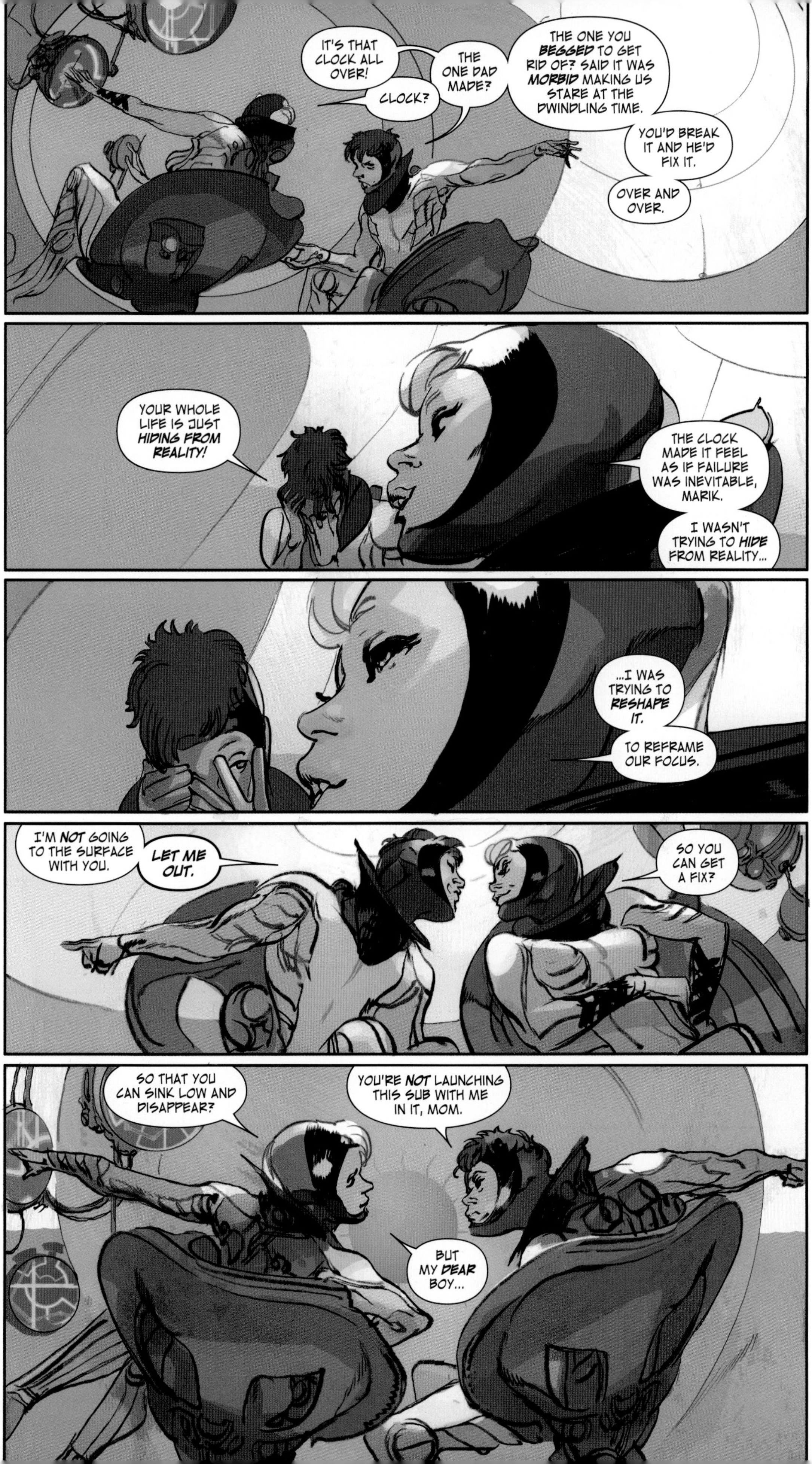
IT'S THAT CLOCK ALL OVER!
CLOCK?
THE ONE DAD MADE?
THE ONE YOU **BEGGED** TO GET RID OF? SAID IT WAS **MORBID** MAKING US STARE AT THE DWINDLING TIME.
YOU'D BREAK IT AND HE'D FIX IT.
OVER AND OVER.
YOUR WHOLE LIFE IS JUST **HIDING FROM REALITY!**
THE CLOCK MADE IT FEEL AS IF FAILURE WAS INEVITABLE, MARIK.
I WASN'T TRYING TO **HIDE** FROM REALITY...
...I WAS TRYING TO **RESHAPE IT.**
TO REFRAME OUR FOCUS.
I'M **NOT** GOING TO THE SURFACE WITH YOU.
**LET ME OUT.**
SO YOU CAN GET A FIX?
SO THAT YOU CAN SINK LOW AND DISAPPEAR?
YOU'RE **NOT** LAUNCHING THIS SUB WITH ME IN IT, MOM.
BUT MY **DEAR** BOY...

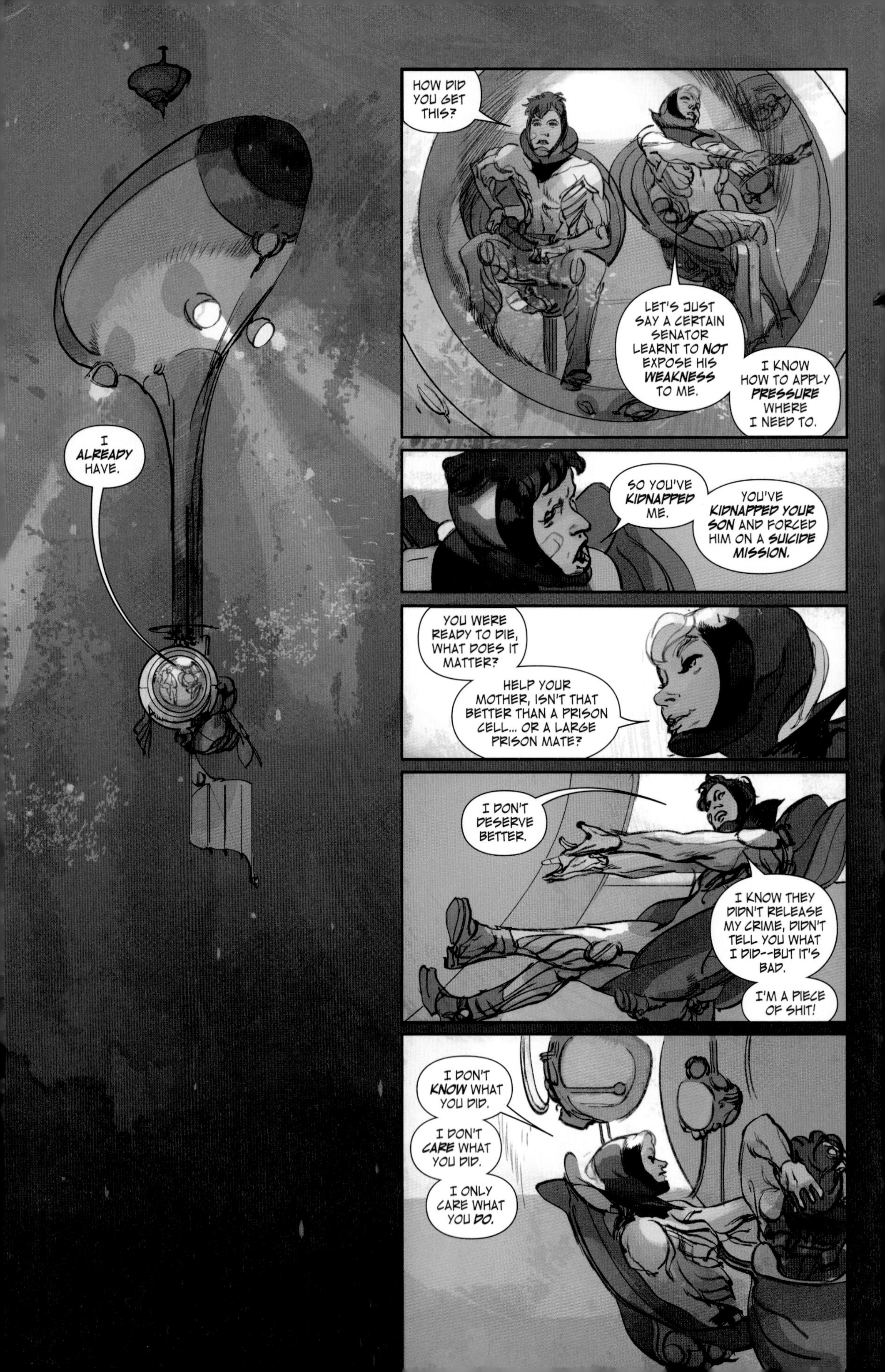
I ALREADY HAVE.
HOW DID YOU GET THIS?
LET'S JUST SAY A CERTAIN SENATOR LEARNT TO NOT EXPOSE HIS WEAKNESS TO ME.
I KNOW HOW TO APPLY PRESSURE WHERE I NEED TO.
SO YOU'VE KIDNAPPED ME.
YOU'VE KIDNAPPED YOUR SON AND FORCED HIM ON A SUICIDE MISSION.
YOU WERE READY TO DIE, WHAT DOES IT MATTER?
HELP YOUR MOTHER, ISN'T THAT BETTER THAN A PRISON CELL... OR A LARGE PRISON MATE?
I DON'T DESERVE BETTER.
I KNOW THEY DIDN'T RELEASE MY CRIME, DIDN'T TELL YOU WHAT I DID--BUT IT'S BAD.
I'M A PIECE OF SHIT!
I DON'T KNOW WHAT YOU DID.
I DON'T CARE WHAT YOU DID.
I ONLY CARE WHAT YOU DO.

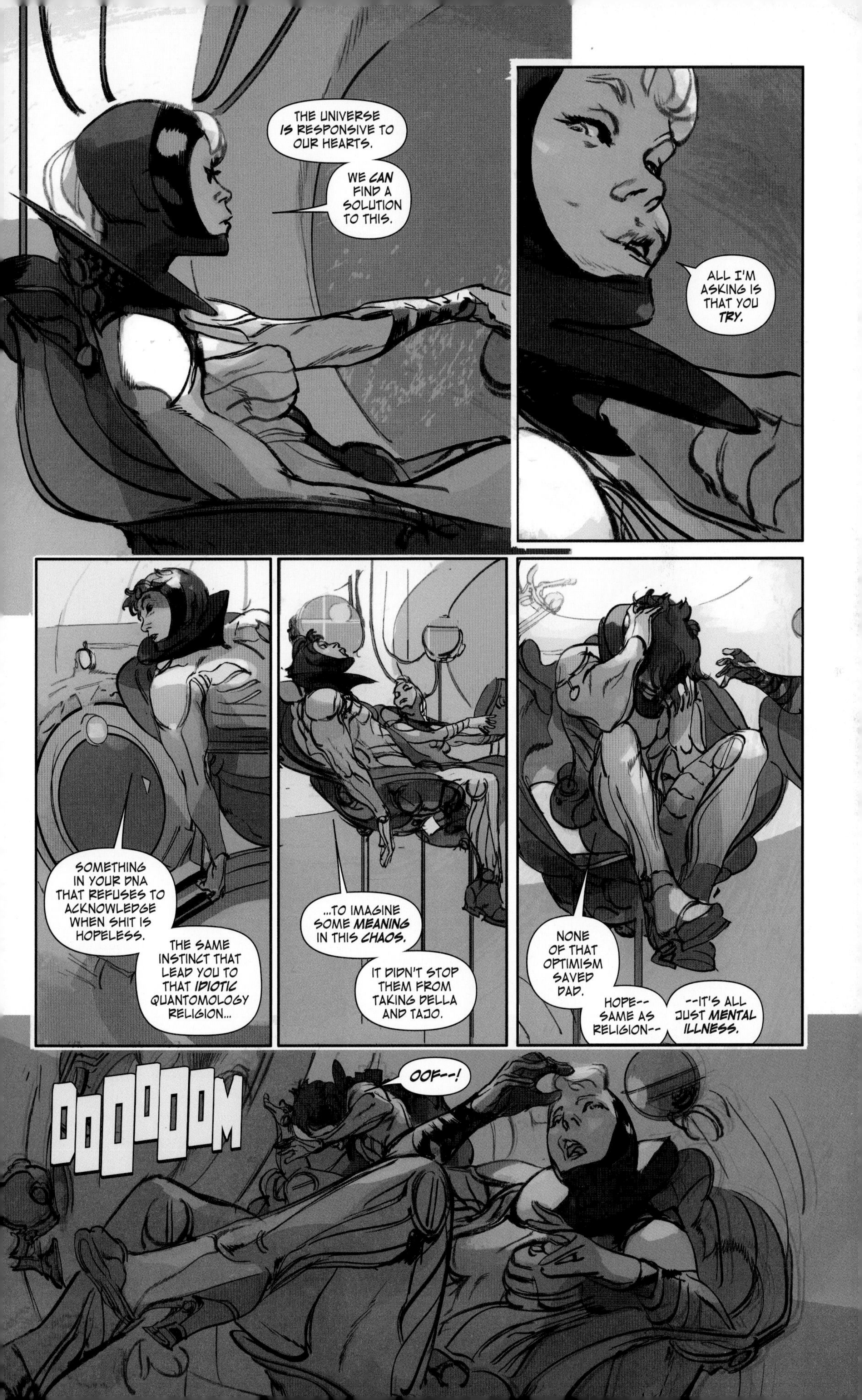
THE UNIVERSE IS RESPONSIVE TO OUR HEARTS.
WE CAN FIND A SOLUTION TO THIS.
ALL I'M ASKING IS THAT YOU TRY.
SOMETHING IN YOUR DNA THAT REFUSES TO ACKNOWLEDGE WHEN SHIT IS HOPELESS.
THE SAME INSTINCT THAT LEAD YOU TO THAT IDIOTIC QUANTOMOLOGY RELIGION...
...TO IMAGINE SOME MEANING IN THIS CHAOS.
IT DIDN'T STOP THEM FROM TAKING DELLA AND TAJO.
NONE OF THAT OPTIMISM SAVED DAD.
HOPE-- SAME AS RELIGION--
--IT'S ALL JUST MENTAL ILLNESS.
DOOOOOM
OOF--!

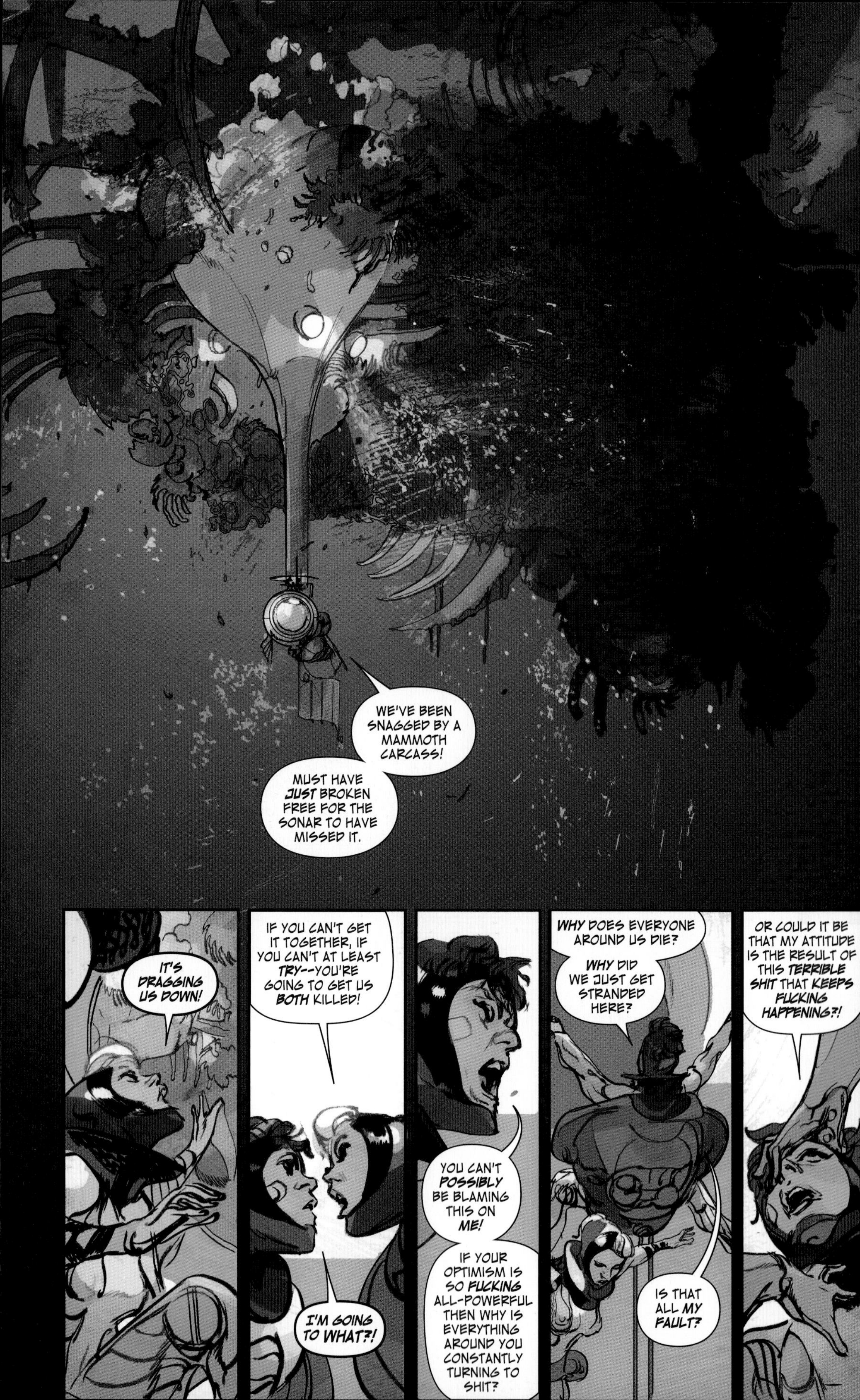

WE'VE BEEN SNAGGED BY A MAMMOTH CARCASS!
MUST HAVE JUST BROKEN FREE FOR THE SONAR TO HAVE MISSED IT.
IT'S DRAGGING US DOWN!
IF YOU CAN'T GET IT TOGETHER, IF YOU CAN'T AT LEAST TRY--YOU'RE GOING TO GET US BOTH KILLED!
I'M GOING TO WHAT?!
YOU CAN'T POSSIBLY BE BLAMING THIS ON ME!
IF YOUR OPTIMISM IS SO FUCKING ALL-POWERFUL THEN WHY IS EVERYTHING AROUND YOU CONSTANTLY TURNING TO SHIT?
WHY DOES EVERYONE AROUND US DIE?
WHY DID WE JUST GET STRANDED HERE?
IS THAT ALL MY FAULT?
OR COULD IT BE THAT MY ATTITUDE IS THE RESULT OF THIS TERRIBLE SHIT THAT KEEPS FUCKING HAPPENING?!

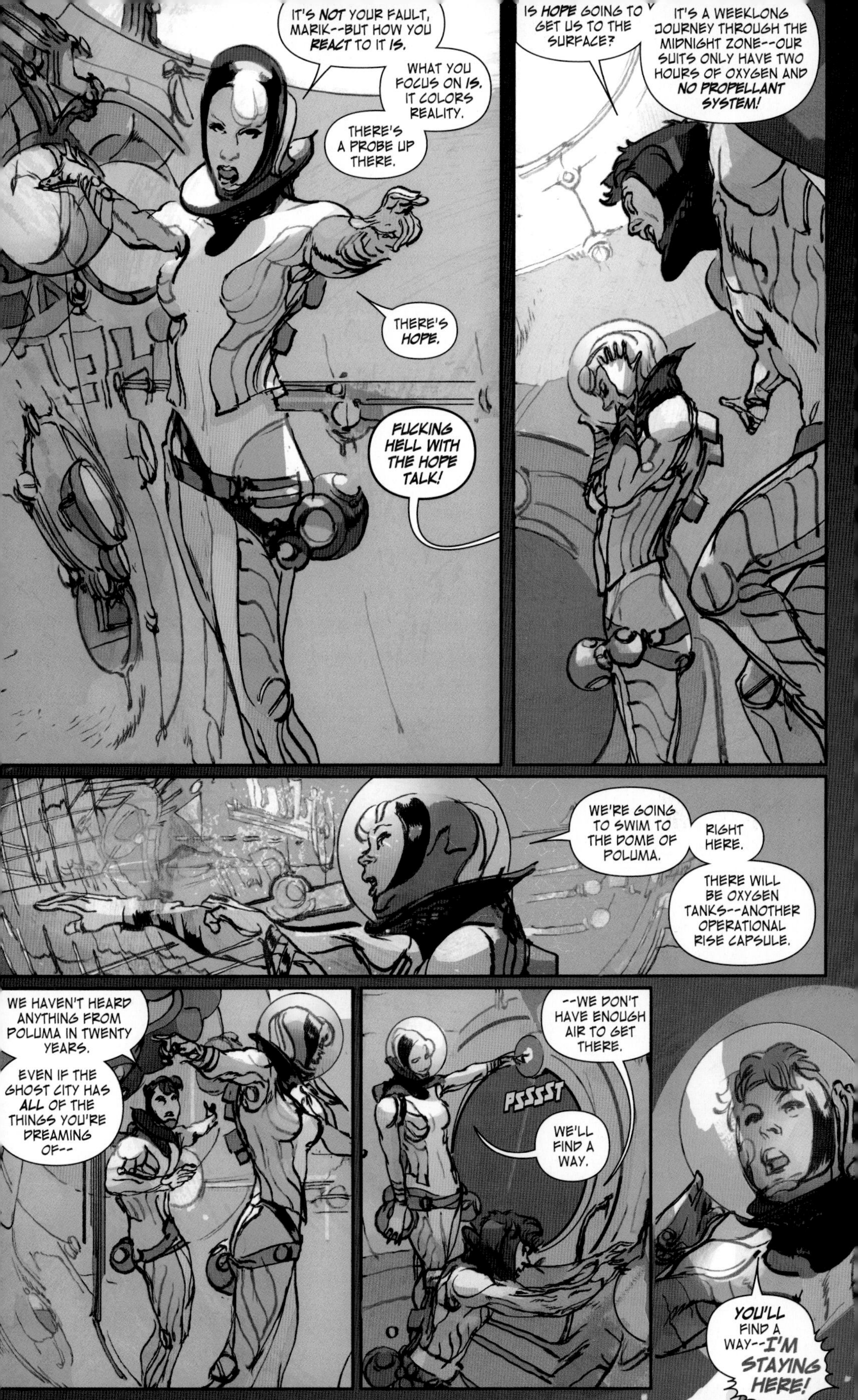
IT'S NOT YOUR FAULT, MARIK--BUT HOW YOU REACT TO IT IS.
WHAT YOU FOCUS ON IS. IT COLORS REALITY.
THERE'S A PROBE UP THERE.
THERE'S HOPE.
FUCKING HELL WITH THE HOPE TALK!
IS HOPE GOING TO GET US TO THE SURFACE?
IT'S A WEEKLONG JOURNEY THROUGH THE MIDNIGHT ZONE--OUR SUITS ONLY HAVE TWO HOURS OF OXYGEN AND NO PROPELLANT SYSTEM!
WE'RE GOING TO SWIM TO THE DOME OF POLUMA.
RIGHT HERE.
THERE WILL BE OXYGEN TANKS--ANOTHER OPERATIONAL RISE CAPSULE.
WE HAVEN'T HEARD ANYTHING FROM POLUMA IN TWENTY YEARS.
EVEN IF THE GHOST CITY HAS ALL OF THE THINGS YOU'RE DREAMING OF--
--WE DON'T HAVE ENOUGH AIR TO GET THERE.
PSSSST
WE'LL FIND A WAY.
YOU'LL FIND A WAY--I'M STAYING HERE!

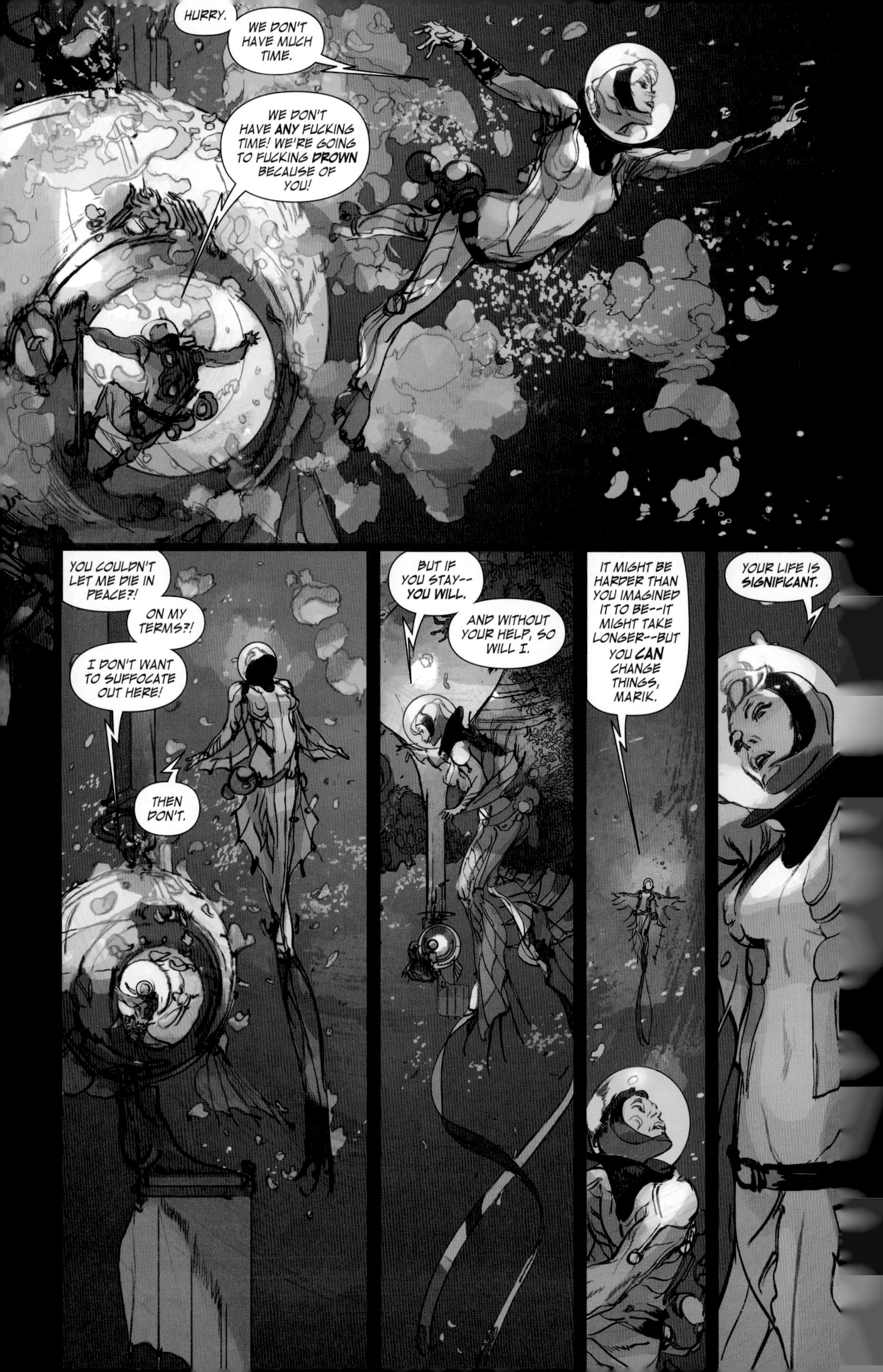
HURRY.
WE DON'T HAVE MUCH TIME.
WE DON'T HAVE **ANY** FUCKING TIME! WE'RE GOING TO FUCKING **DROWN** BECAUSE OF YOU!
YOU COULDN'T LET ME DIE IN PEACE?!
ON MY TERMS?!
I DON'T WANT TO SUFFOCATE OUT HERE!
THEN DON'T.
BUT IF YOU STAY-- **YOU WILL.**
AND WITHOUT YOUR HELP, SO WILL I.
IT MIGHT BE HARDER THAN YOU IMAGINED IT TO BE--IT MIGHT TAKE LONGER--BUT YOU **CAN** CHANGE THINGS, MARIK.
YOUR LIFE IS **SIGNIFICANT.**

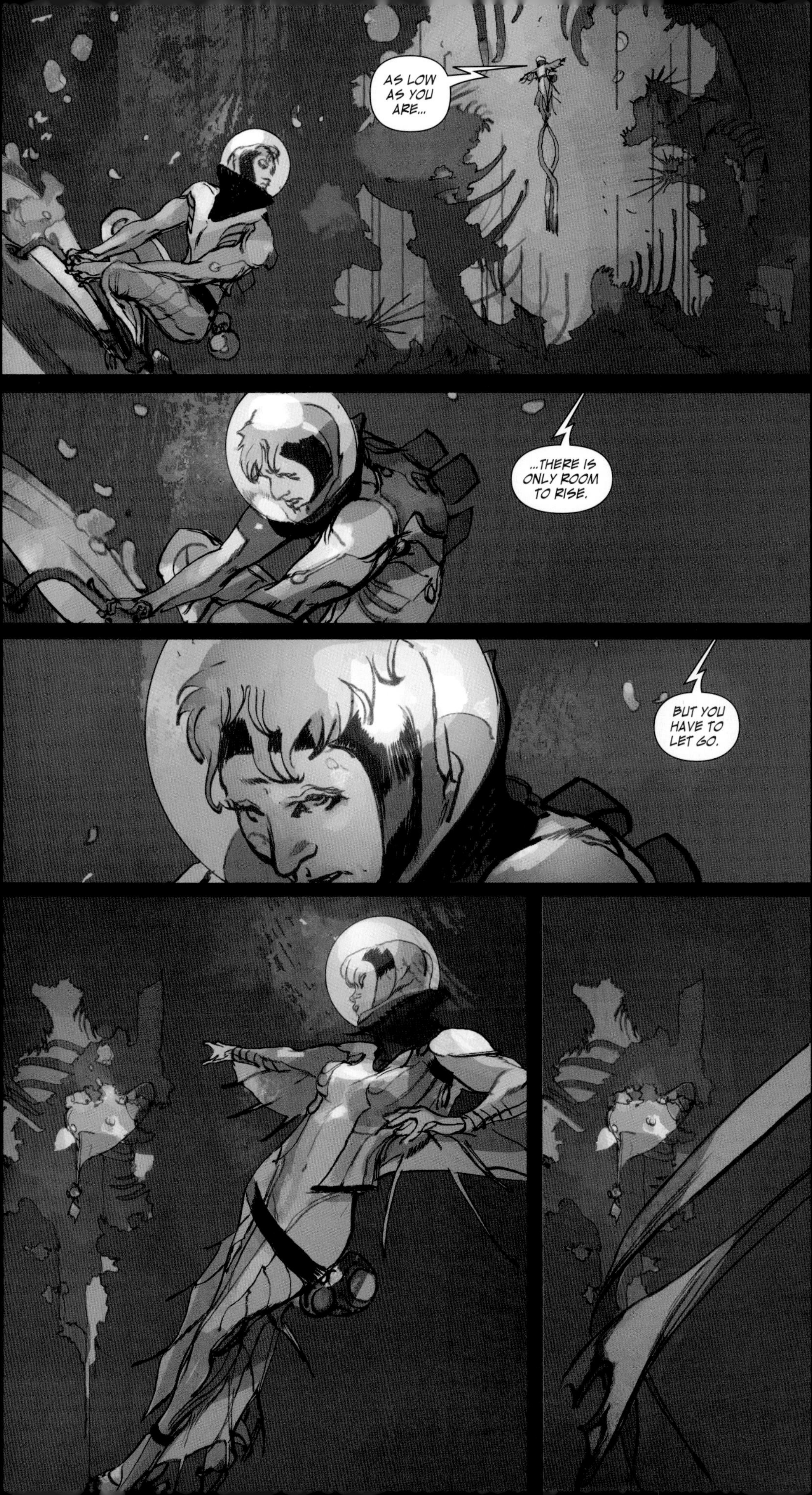
AS LOW AS YOU ARE...
...THERE IS ONLY ROOM TO RISE.
BUT YOU HAVE TO LET GO.

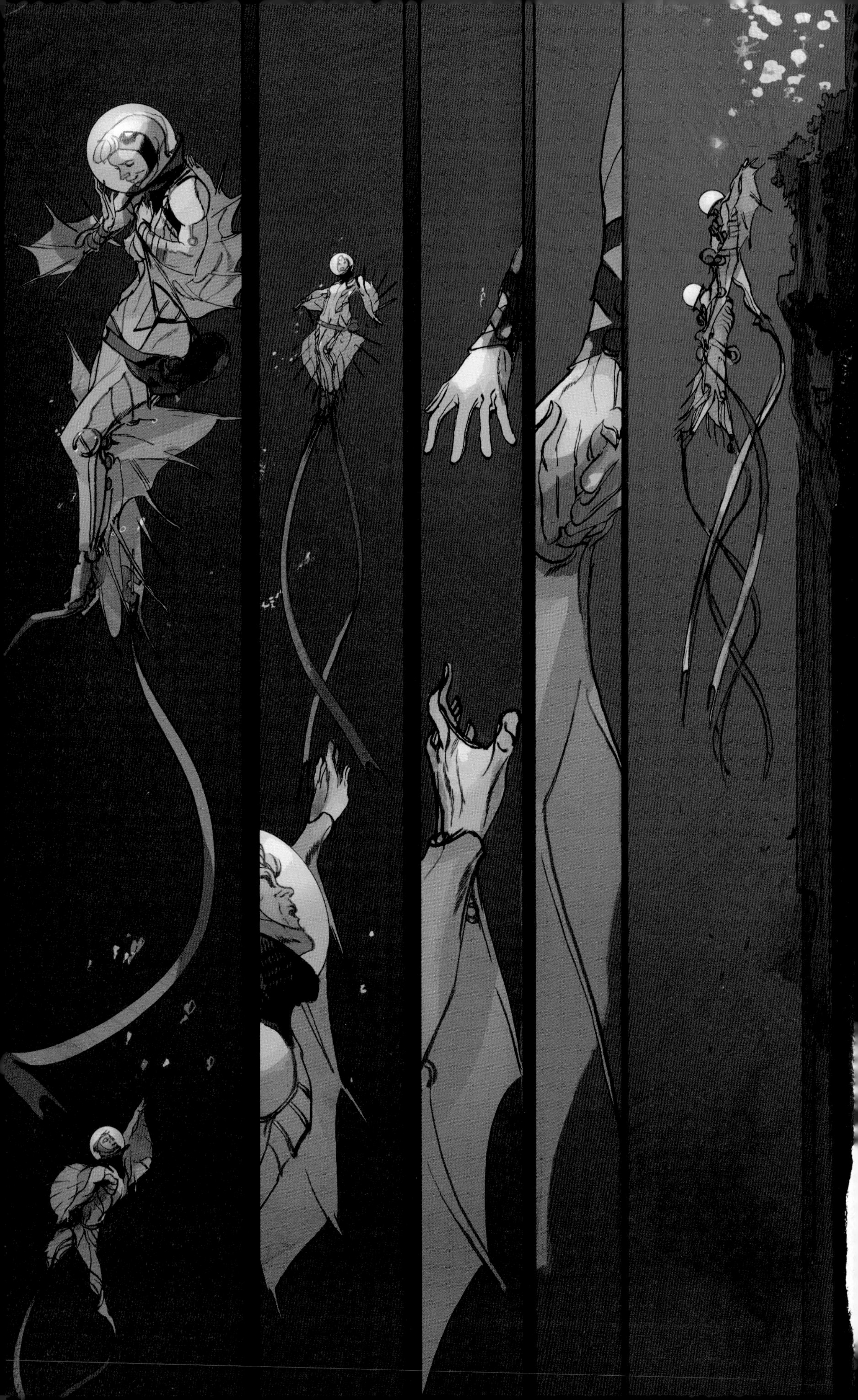

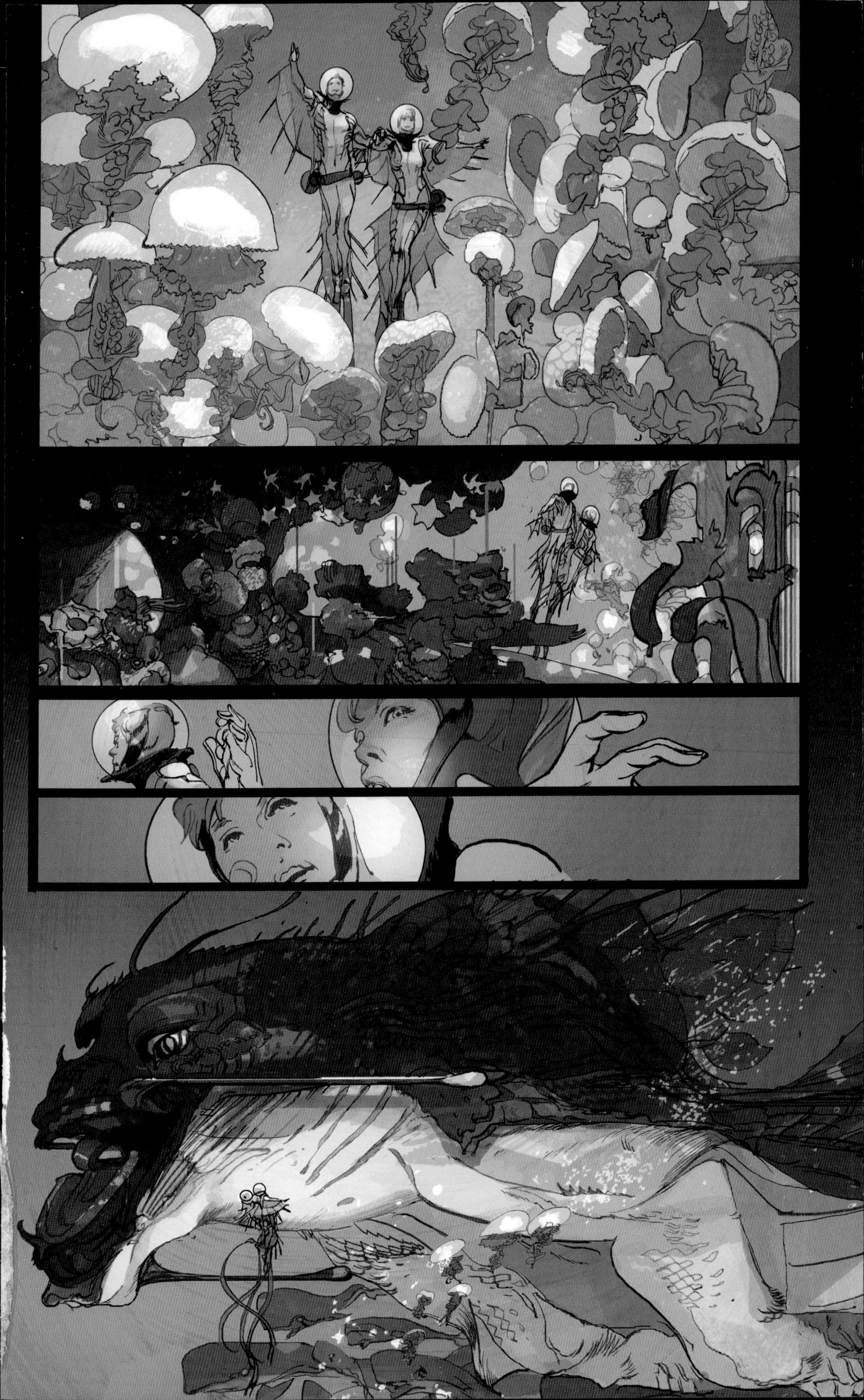

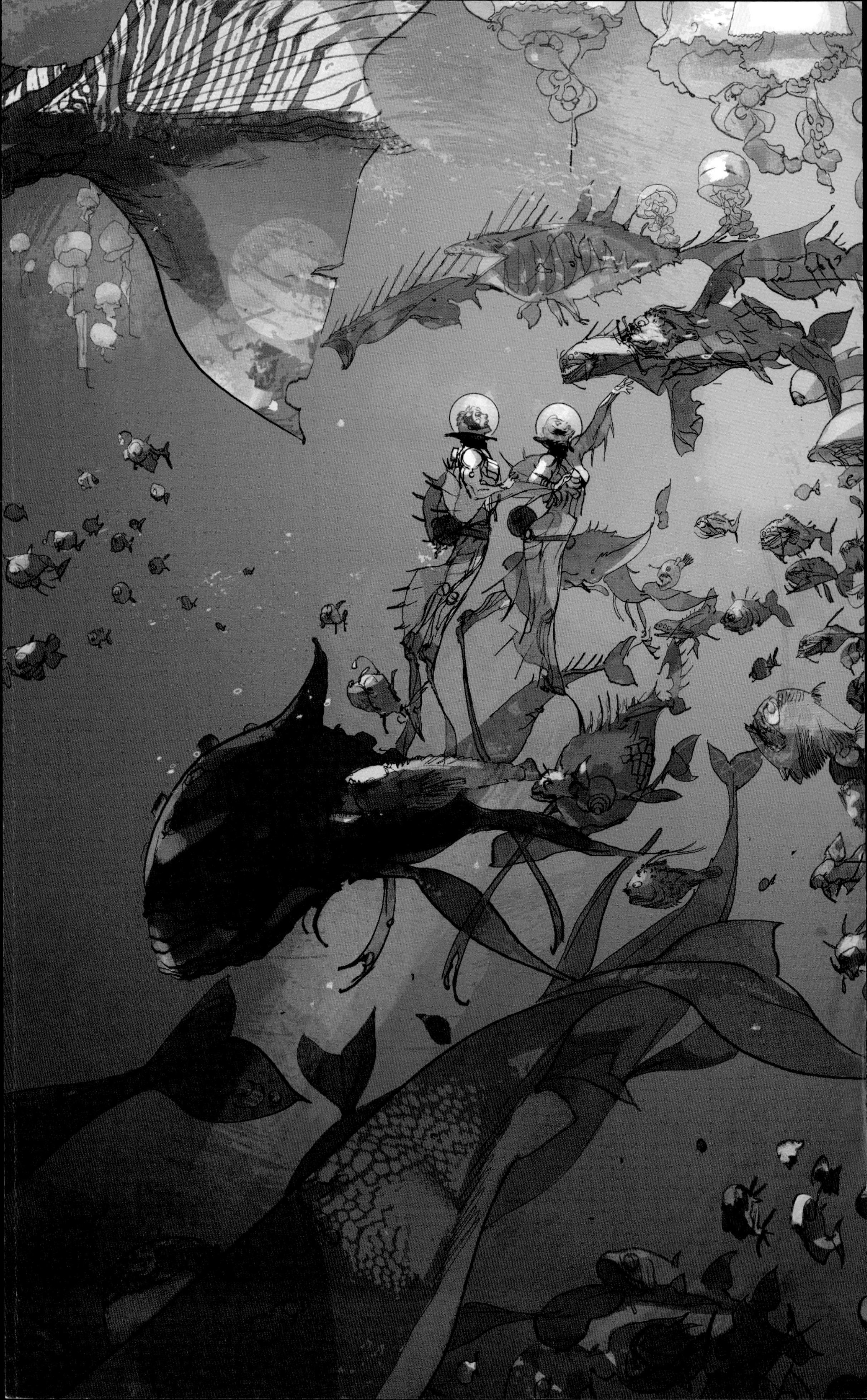

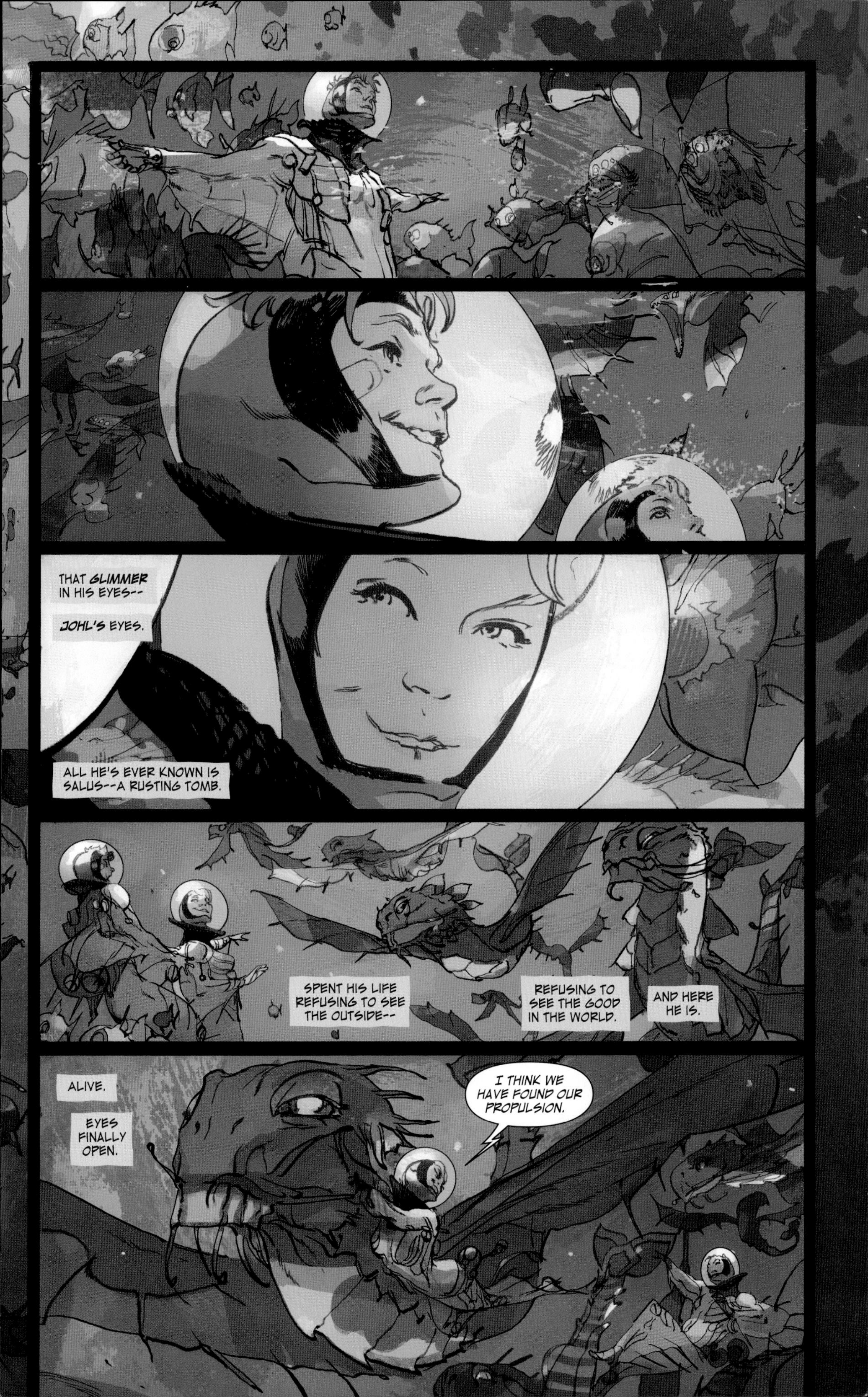
THAT GLIMMER IN HIS EYES--
JOHL'S EYES.
ALL HE'S EVER KNOWN IS SALUS--A RUSTING TOMB.
SPENT HIS LIFE REFUSING TO SEE THE OUTSIDE--
REFUSING TO SEE THE GOOD IN THE WORLD.
AND HERE HE IS.
ALIVE.
EYES FINALLY OPEN.
I THINK WE HAVE FOUND OUR PROPULSION.

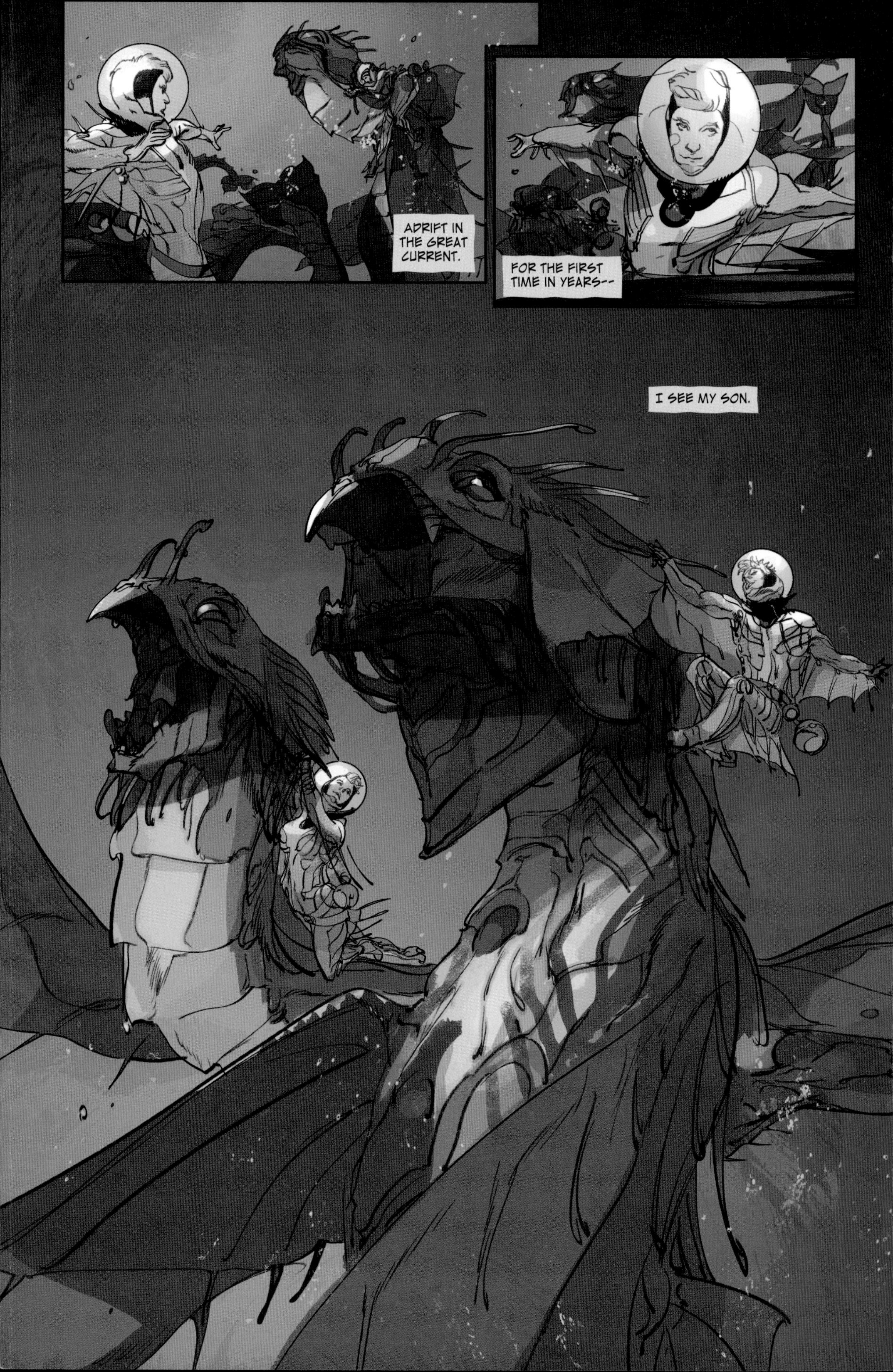
ADRIFT IN THE GREAT CURRENT.
FOR THE FIRST TIME IN YEARS--
I SEE MY SON.

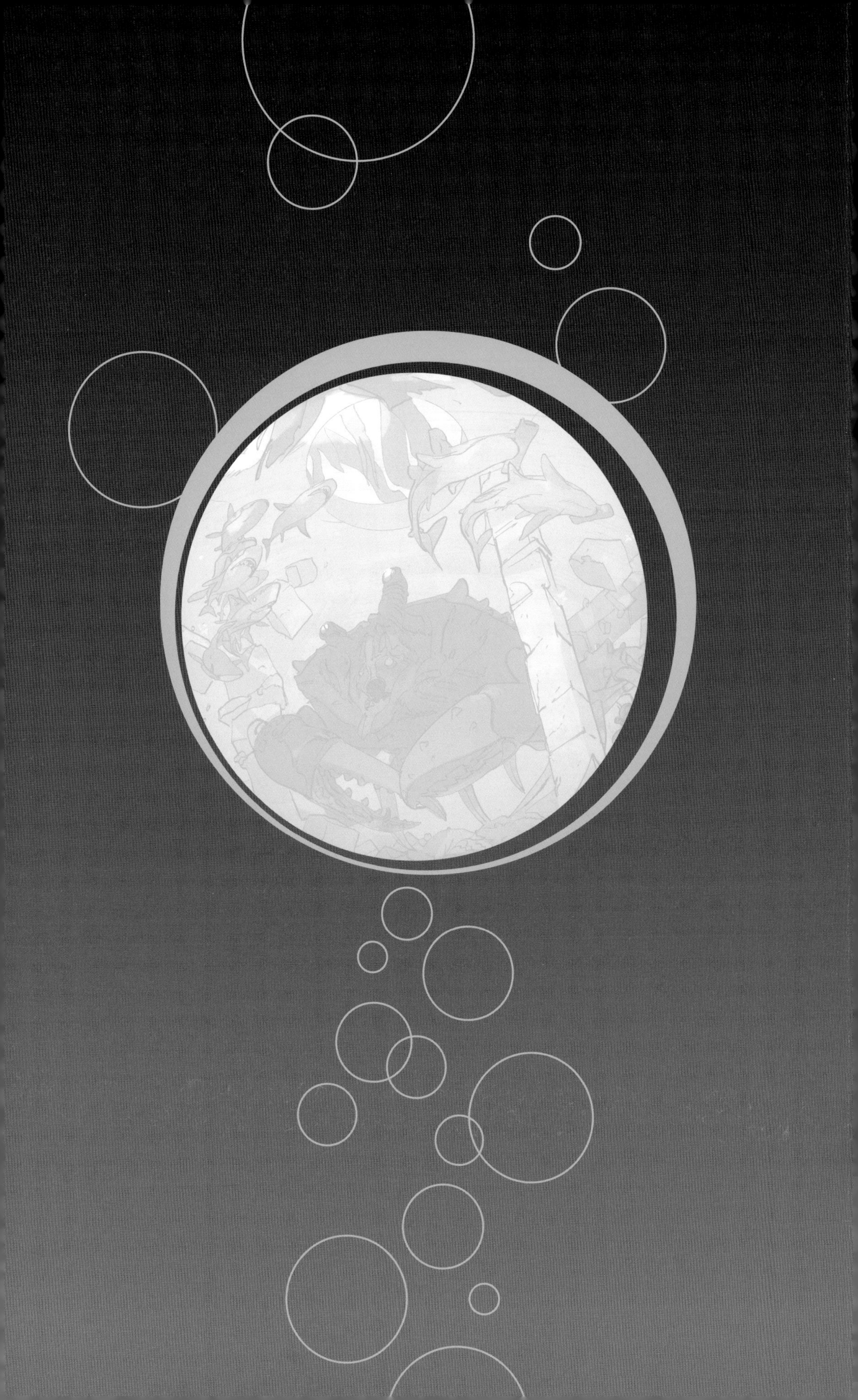

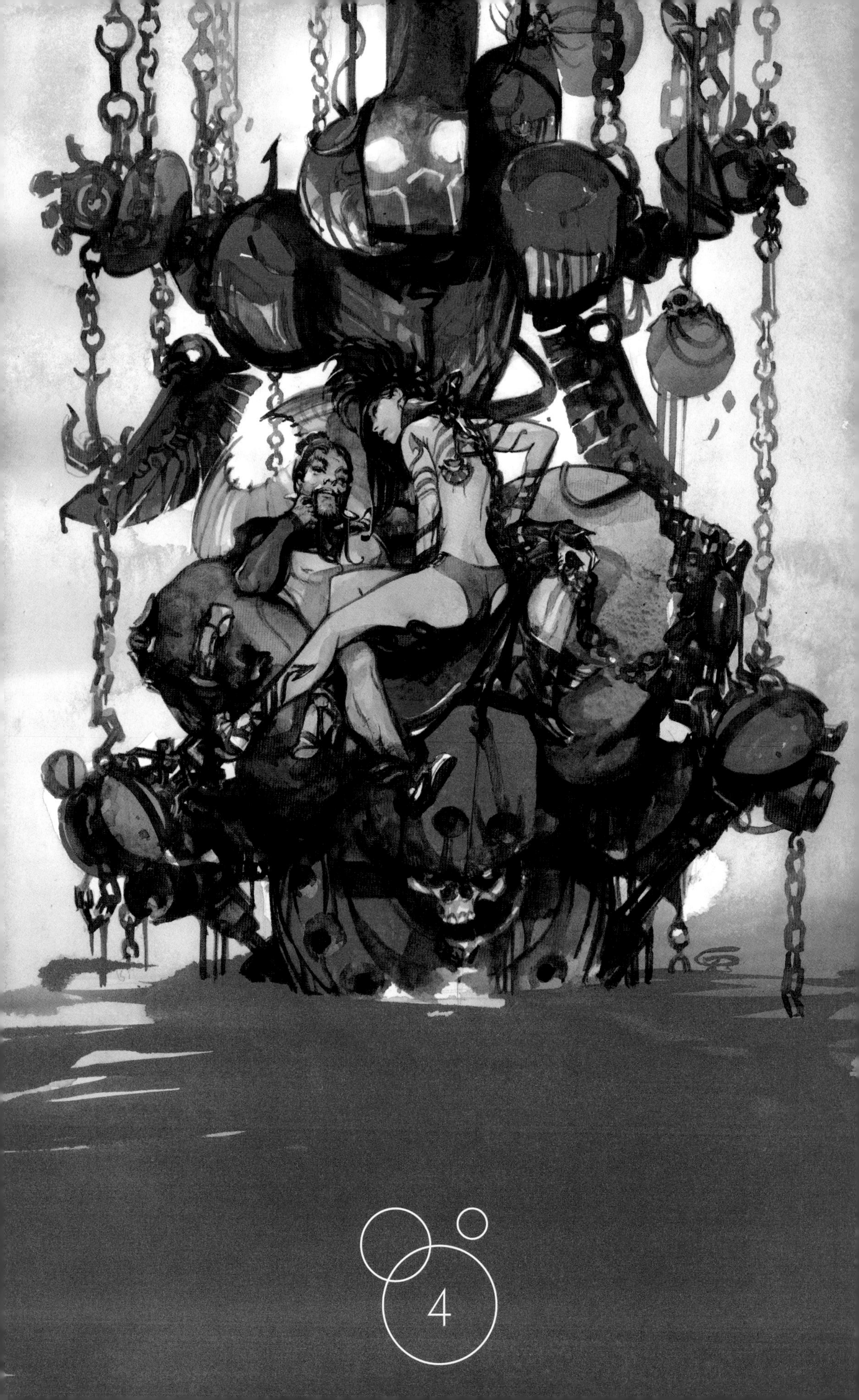

# 4

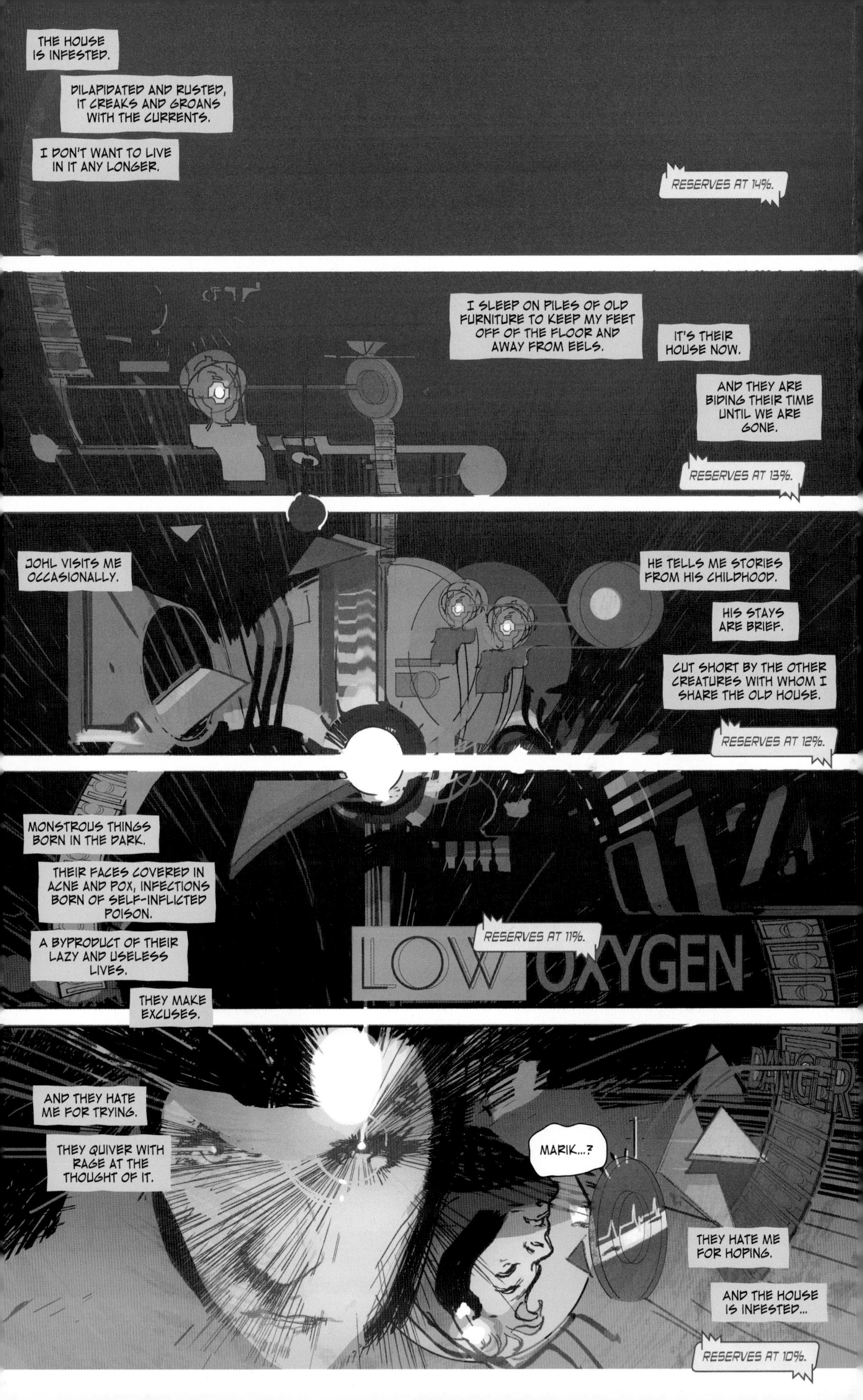
THE HOUSE IS INFESTED.
DILAPIDATED AND RUSTED, IT CREAKS AND GROANS WITH THE CURRENTS.
I DON'T WANT TO LIVE IN IT ANY LONGER.
RESERVES AT 14%.
I SLEEP ON PILES OF OLD FURNITURE TO KEEP MY FEET OFF OF THE FLOOR AND AWAY FROM EELS.
IT'S THEIR HOUSE NOW.
AND THEY ARE BIDING THEIR TIME UNTIL WE ARE GONE.
RESERVES AT 13%.
JOHL VISITS ME OCCASIONALLY.
HE TELLS ME STORIES FROM HIS CHILDHOOD.
HIS STAYS ARE BRIEF.
CUT SHORT BY THE OTHER CREATURES WITH WHOM I SHARE THE OLD HOUSE.
RESERVES AT 12%.
MONSTROUS THINGS BORN IN THE DARK.
THEIR FACES COVERED IN ACNE AND POX, INFECTIONS BORN OF SELF-INFLICTED POISON.
A BYPRODUCT OF THEIR LAZY AND USELESS LIVES.
THEY MAKE EXCUSES.
RESERVES AT 11%.
LOW OXYGEN
AND THEY HATE ME FOR TRYING.
THEY QUIVER WITH RAGE AT THE THOUGHT OF IT.
MARIK...?
THEY HATE ME FOR HOPING.
AND THE HOUSE IS INFESTED...
RESERVES AT 10%.

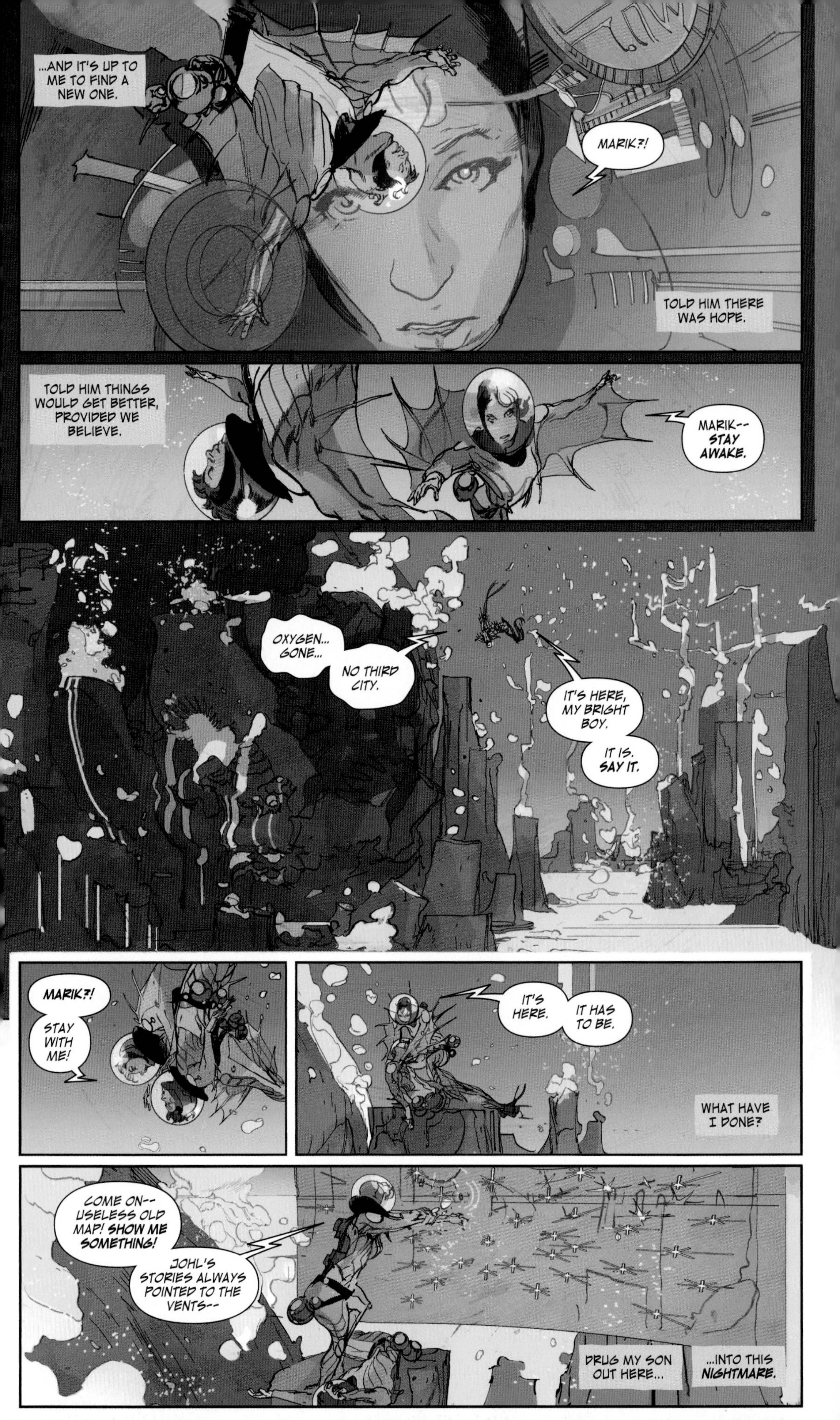
...AND IT'S UP TO ME TO FIND A NEW ONE.
MARIK?!
TOLD HIM THERE WAS HOPE.
TOLD HIM THINGS WOULD GET BETTER, PROVIDED WE BELIEVE.
MARIK-- STAY AWAKE.
OXYGEN... GONE...
NO THIRD CITY.
IT'S HERE, MY BRIGHT BOY.
IT IS. SAY IT.
MARIK?!
STAY WITH ME!
IT'S HERE.
IT HAS TO BE.
WHAT HAVE I DONE?
COME ON-- USELESS OLD MAP! SHOW ME SOMETHING!
JOHL'S STORIES ALWAYS POINTED TO THE VENTS--
DRUG MY SON OUT HERE...
...INTO THIS NIGHTMARE.

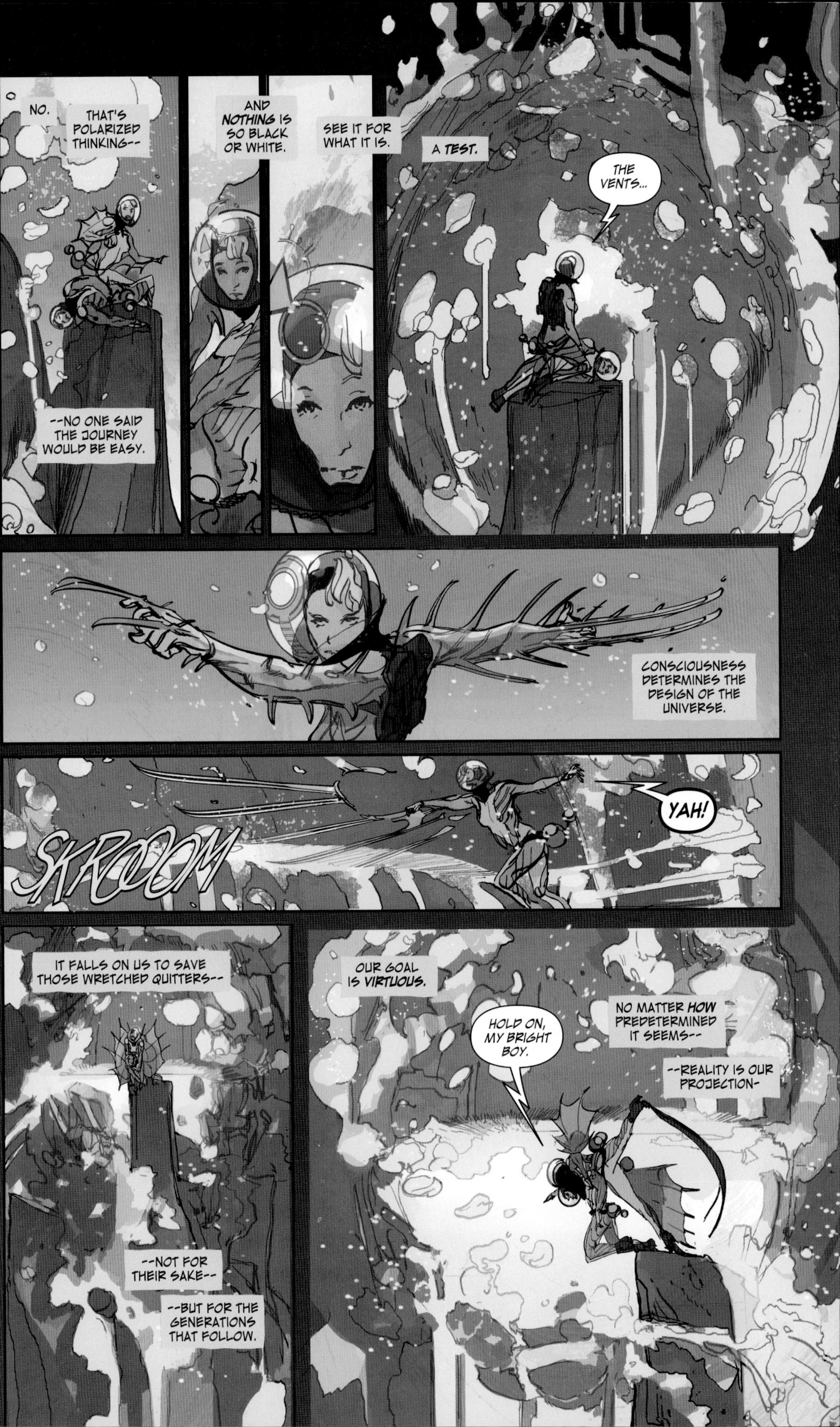
NO.
THAT'S POLARIZED THINKING--
--NO ONE SAID THE JOURNEY WOULD BE EASY.
AND NOTHING IS SO BLACK OR WHITE.
SEE IT FOR WHAT IT IS.
A TEST.
THE VENTS...
CONSCIOUSNESS DETERMINES THE DESIGN OF THE UNIVERSE.
SKROOOM
YAH!
IT FALLS ON US TO SAVE THOSE WRETCHED QUITTERS--
--NOT FOR THEIR SAKE--
--BUT FOR THE GENERATIONS THAT FOLLOW.
OUR GOAL IS VIRTUOUS.
HOLD ON, MY BRIGHT BOY.
NO MATTER HOW PREDETERMINED IT SEEMS--
--REALITY IS OUR PROJECTION-

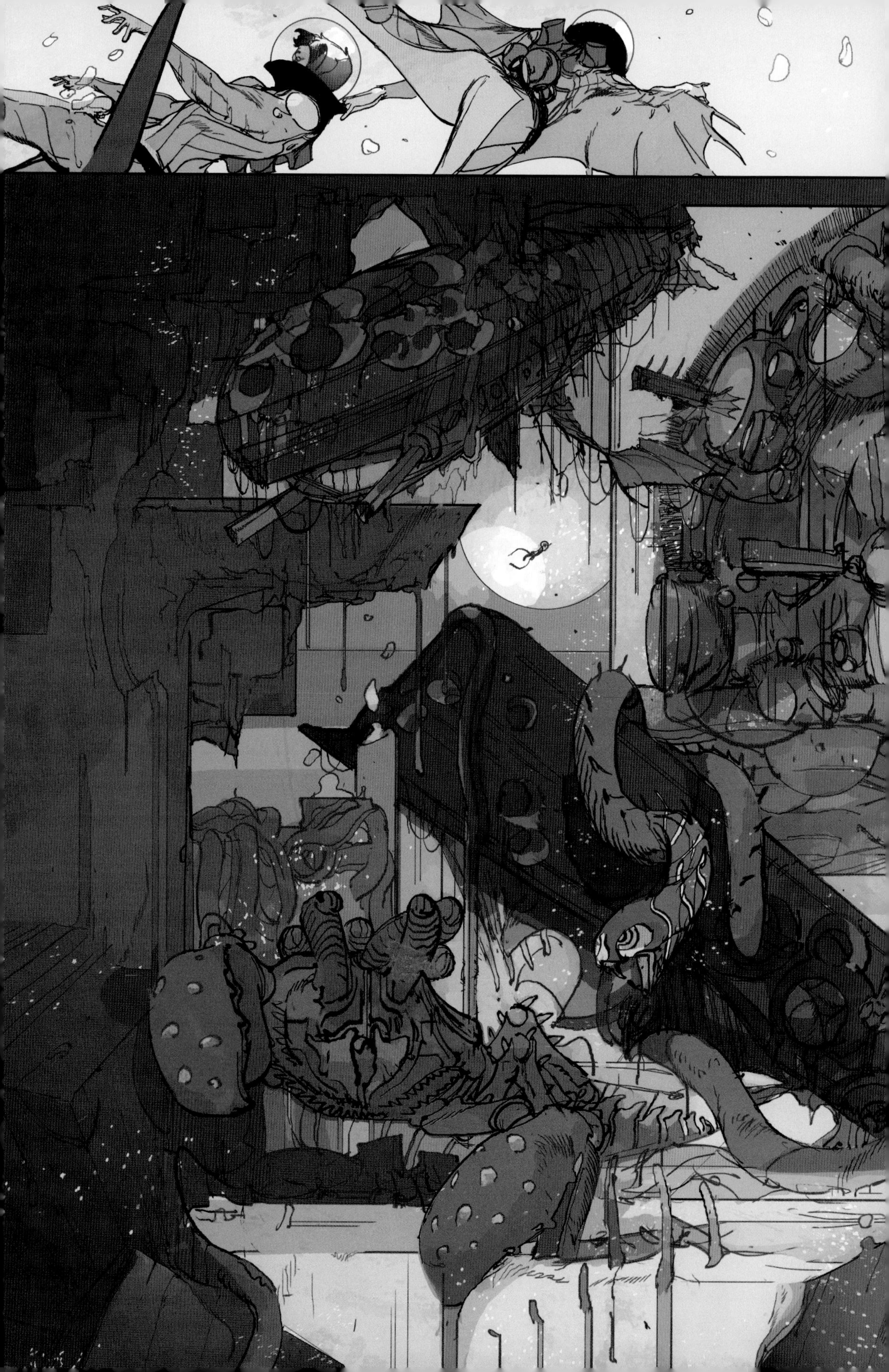

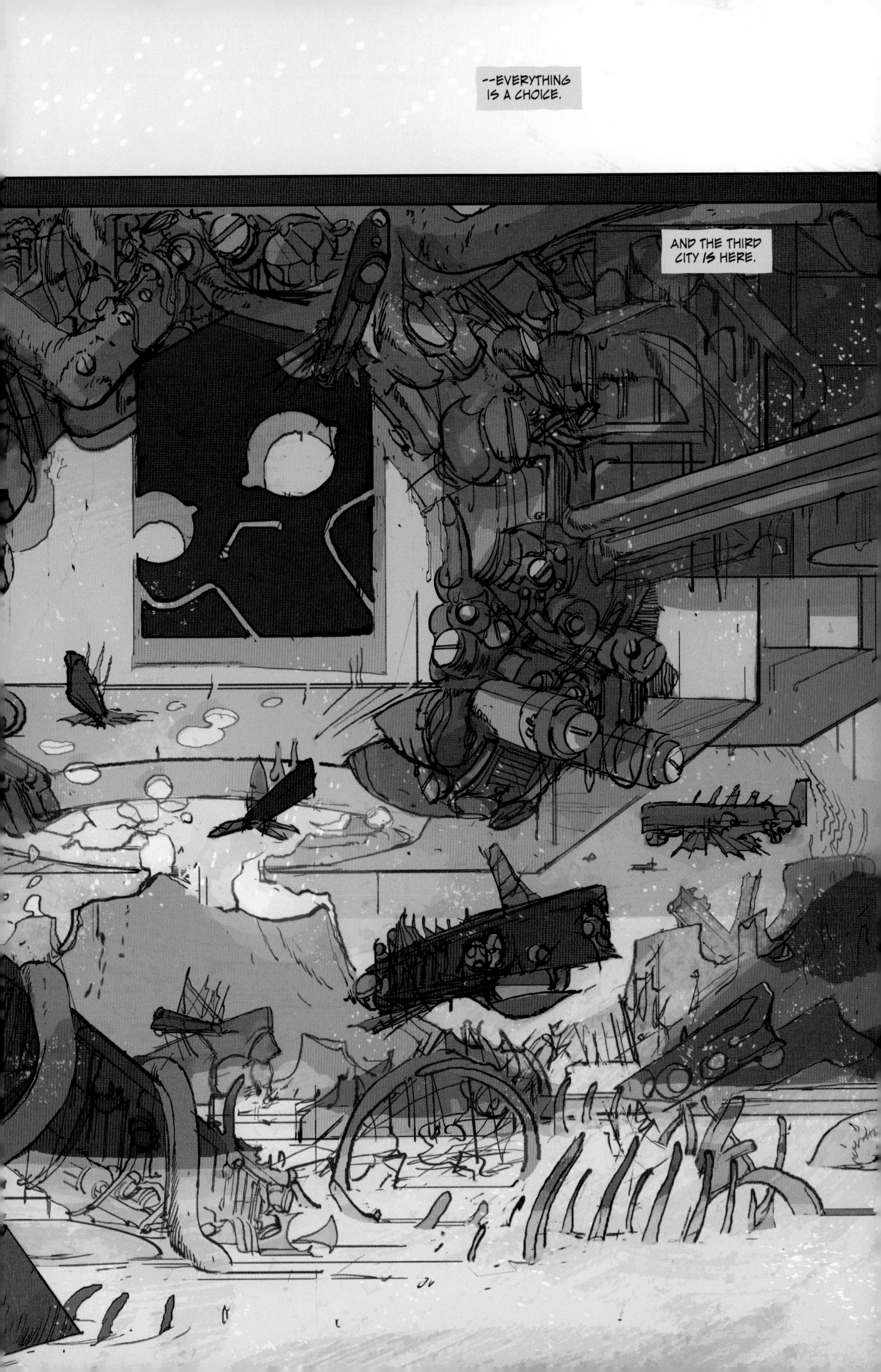
--EVERYTHING IS A CHOICE.
AND THE THIRD CITY IS HERE.

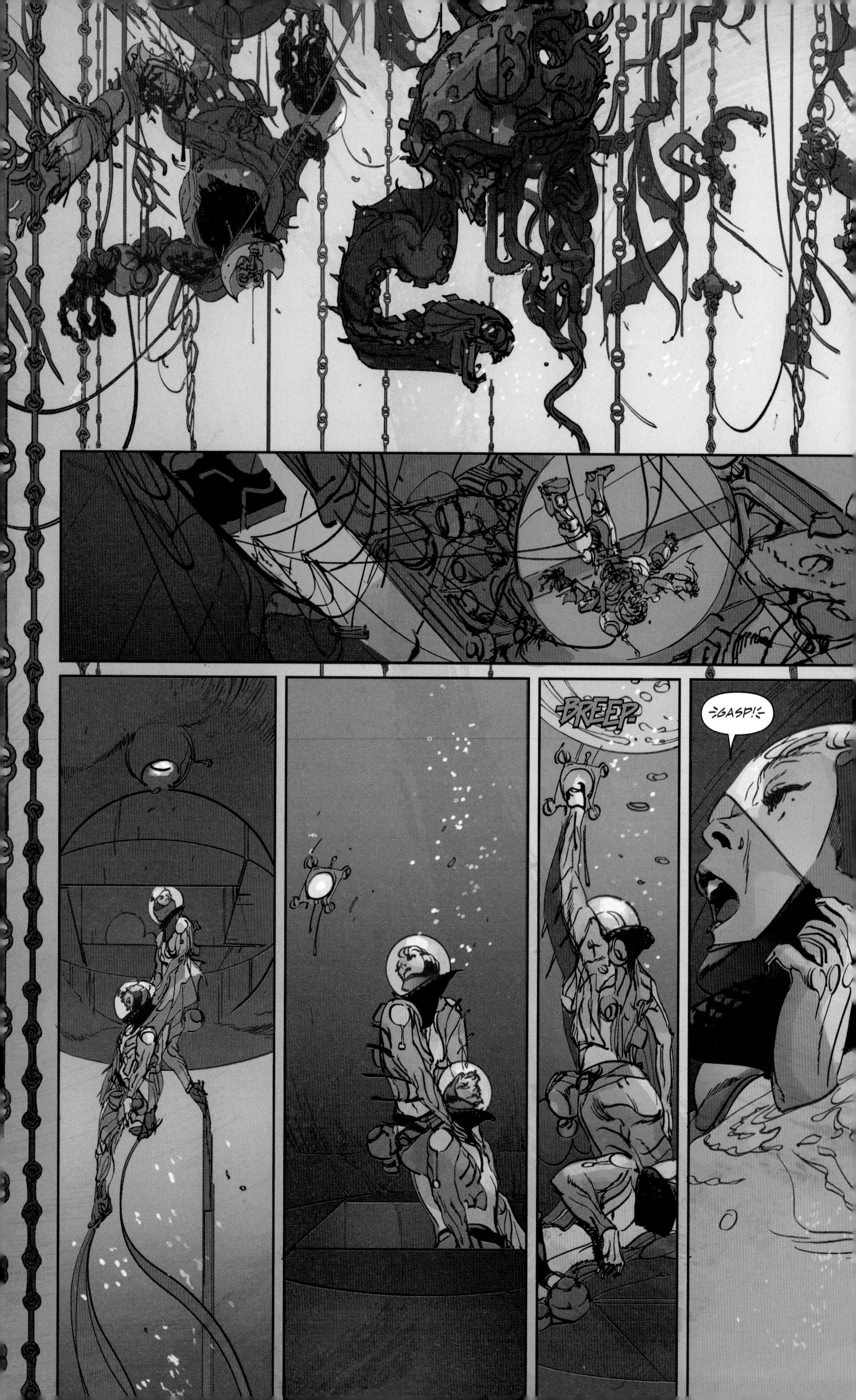
BREEP
GASP!

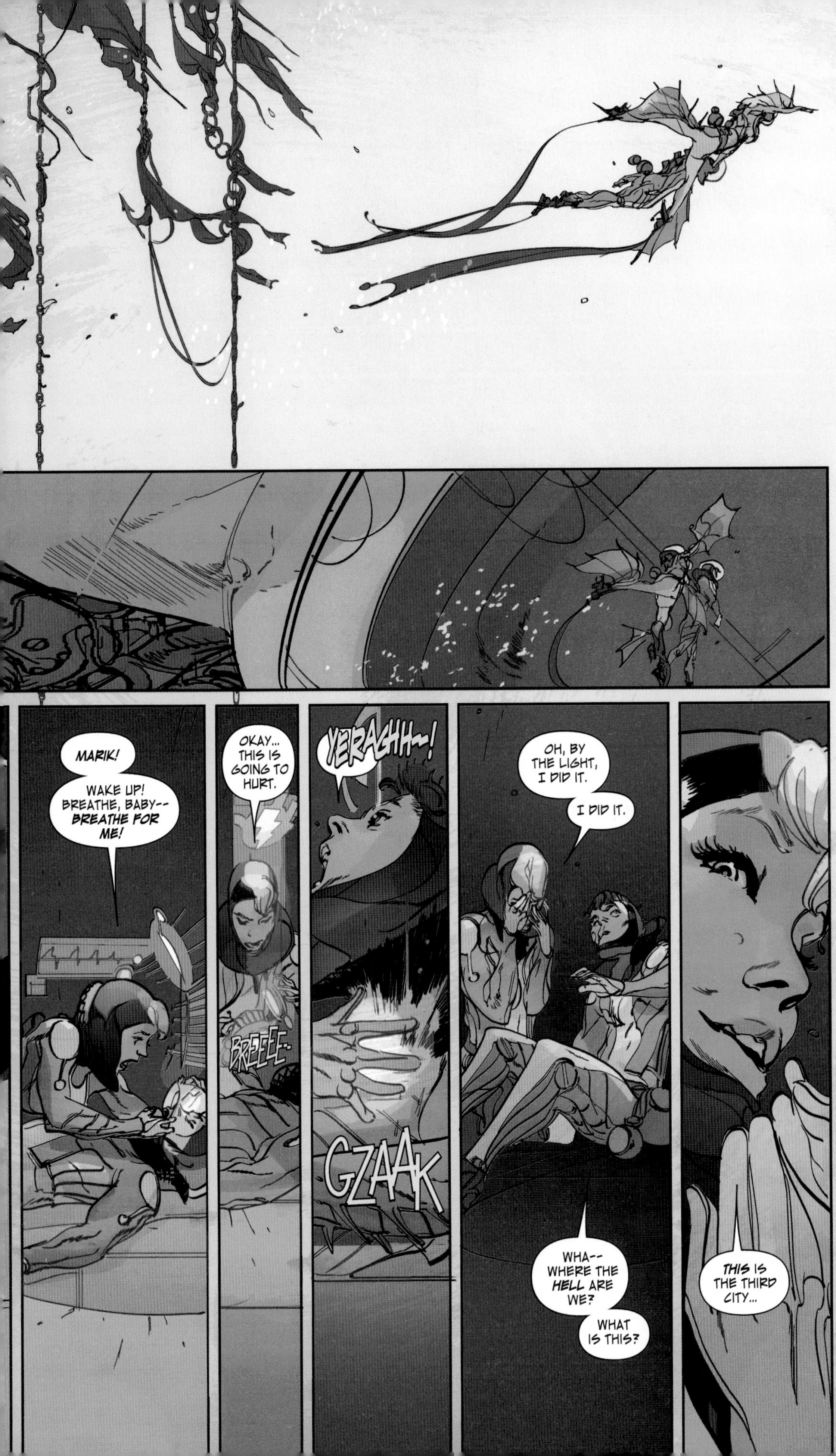
MARIK!
WAKE UP! BREATHE, BABY-- BREATHE FOR ME!
OKAY... THIS IS GOING TO HURT.
BREEEE--
YEEAGHH--!
GZAAK
OH, BY THE LIGHT, I DID IT.
I DID IT.
WHA-- WHERE THE HELL ARE WE?
WHAT IS THIS?
THIS IS THE THIRD CITY...

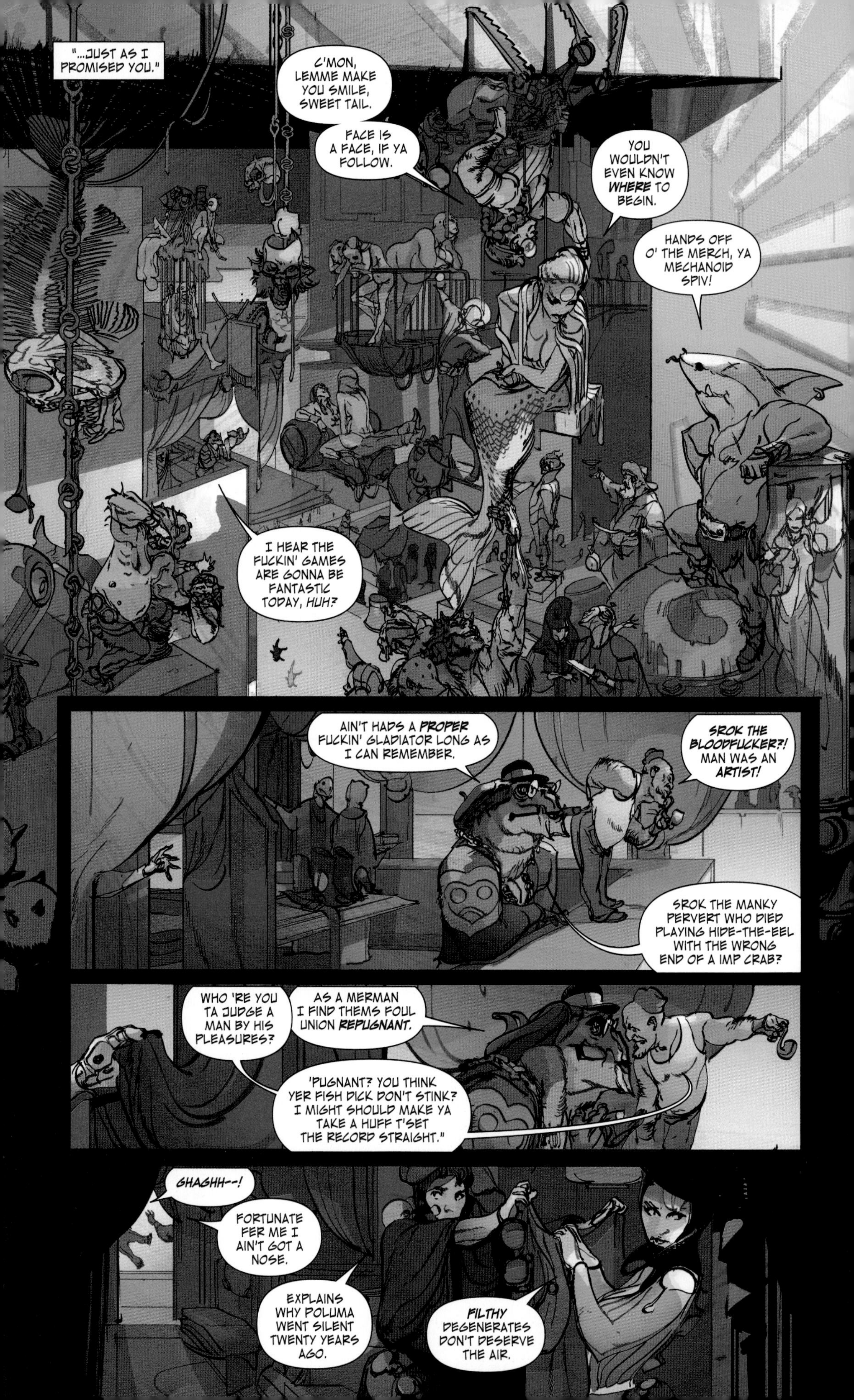
"...JUST AS I PROMISED YOU."
C'MON, LEMME MAKE YOU SMILE, SWEET TAIL.
FACE IS A FACE, IF YA FOLLOW.
YOU WOULDN'T EVEN KNOW WHERE TO BEGIN.
HANDS OFF O' THE MERCH, YA MECHANOID SPIV!
I HEAR THE FUCKIN' GAMES ARE GONNA BE FANTASTIC TODAY, HUH?
AIN'T HADS A PROPER FUCKIN' GLADIATOR LONG AS I CAN REMEMBER.
SROK THE BLOODFUCKER?! MAN WAS AN ARTIST!
SROK THE MANKY PERVERT WHO DIED PLAYING HIDE-THE-EEL WITH THE WRONG END OF A IMP CRAB?
WHO 'RE YOU TA JUDGE A MAN BY HIS PLEASURES?
AS A MERMAN I FIND THEMS FOUL UNION REPUGNANT.
'PUGNANT? YOU THINK YER FISH DICK DON'T STINK? I MIGHT SHOULD MAKE YA TAKE A HUFF T'SET THE RECORD STRAIGHT."
GHAGHH--!
FORTUNATE FER ME I AIN'T GOT A NOSE.
EXPLAINS WHY POLUMA WENT SILENT TWENTY YEARS AGO.
FILTHY DEGENERATES DON'T DESERVE THE AIR.

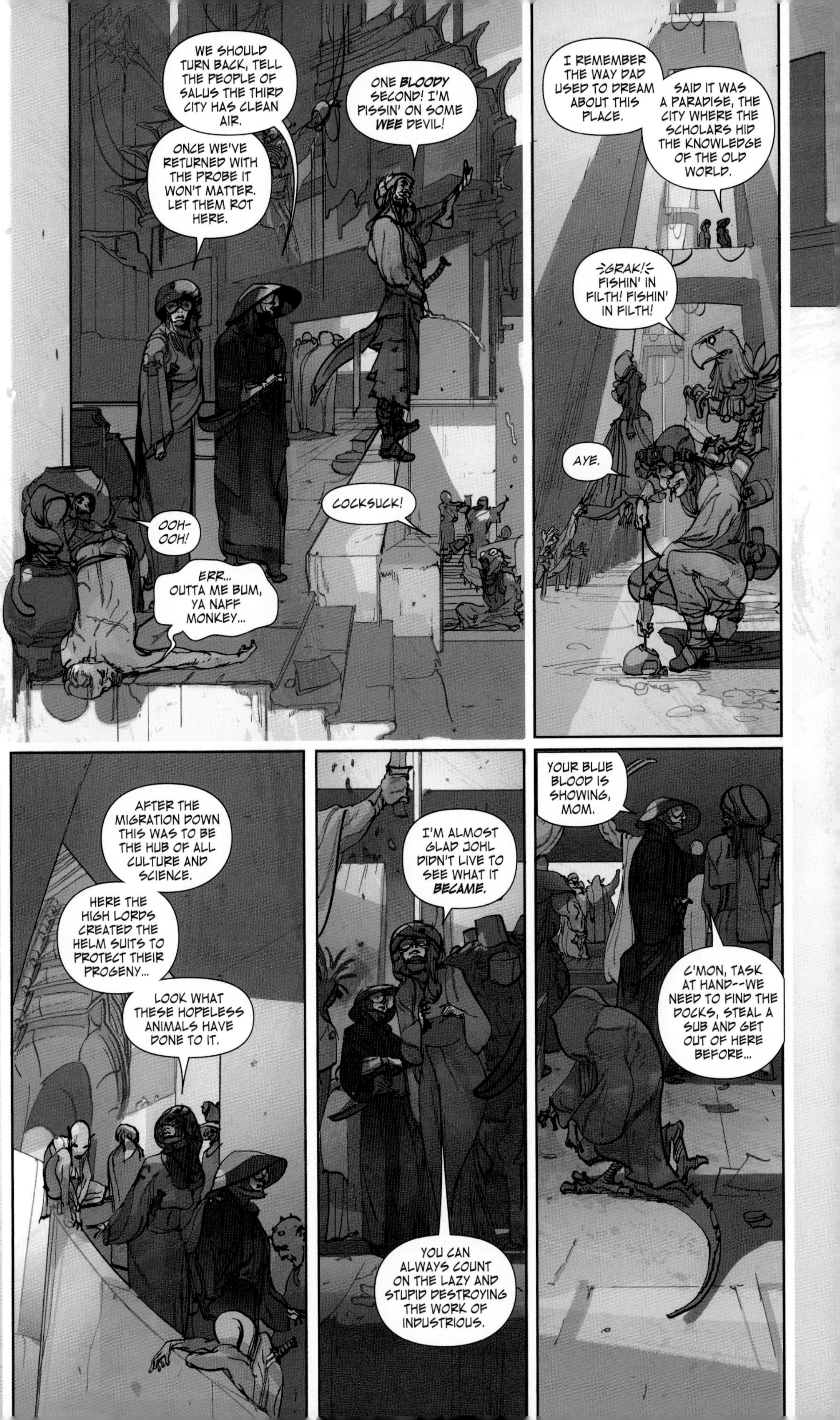
WE SHOULD TURN BACK, TELL THE PEOPLE OF SALUS THE THIRD CITY HAS CLEAN AIR.
ONCE WE'VE RETURNED WITH THE PROBE IT WON'T MATTER. LET THEM ROT HERE.
ONE BLOODY SECOND! I'M PISSIN' ON SOME WEE DEVIL!
OOH-OOH!
ERR... OUTTA ME BUM, YA NAFF MONKEY...
COCKSUCK!
I REMEMBER THE WAY DAD USED TO DREAM ABOUT THIS PLACE.
SAID IT WAS A PARADISE, THE CITY WHERE THE SCHOLARS HID THE KNOWLEDGE OF THE OLD WORLD.
GRAK! FISHIN' IN FILTH! FISHIN' IN FILTH!
AYE.
AFTER THE MIGRATION DOWN THIS WAS TO BE THE HUB OF ALL CULTURE AND SCIENCE.
HERE THE HIGH LORDS CREATED THE HELM SUITS TO PROTECT THEIR PROGENY...
LOOK WHAT THESE HOPELESS ANIMALS HAVE DONE TO IT.
I'M ALMOST GLAD JOHL DIDN'T LIVE TO SEE WHAT IT BECAME.
YOU CAN ALWAYS COUNT ON THE LAZY AND STUPID DESTROYING THE WORK OF INDUSTRIOUS.
YOUR BLUE BLOOD IS SHOWING, MOM.
C'MON, TASK AT HAND--WE NEED TO FIND THE DOCKS, STEAL A SUB AND GET OUT OF HERE BEFORE...

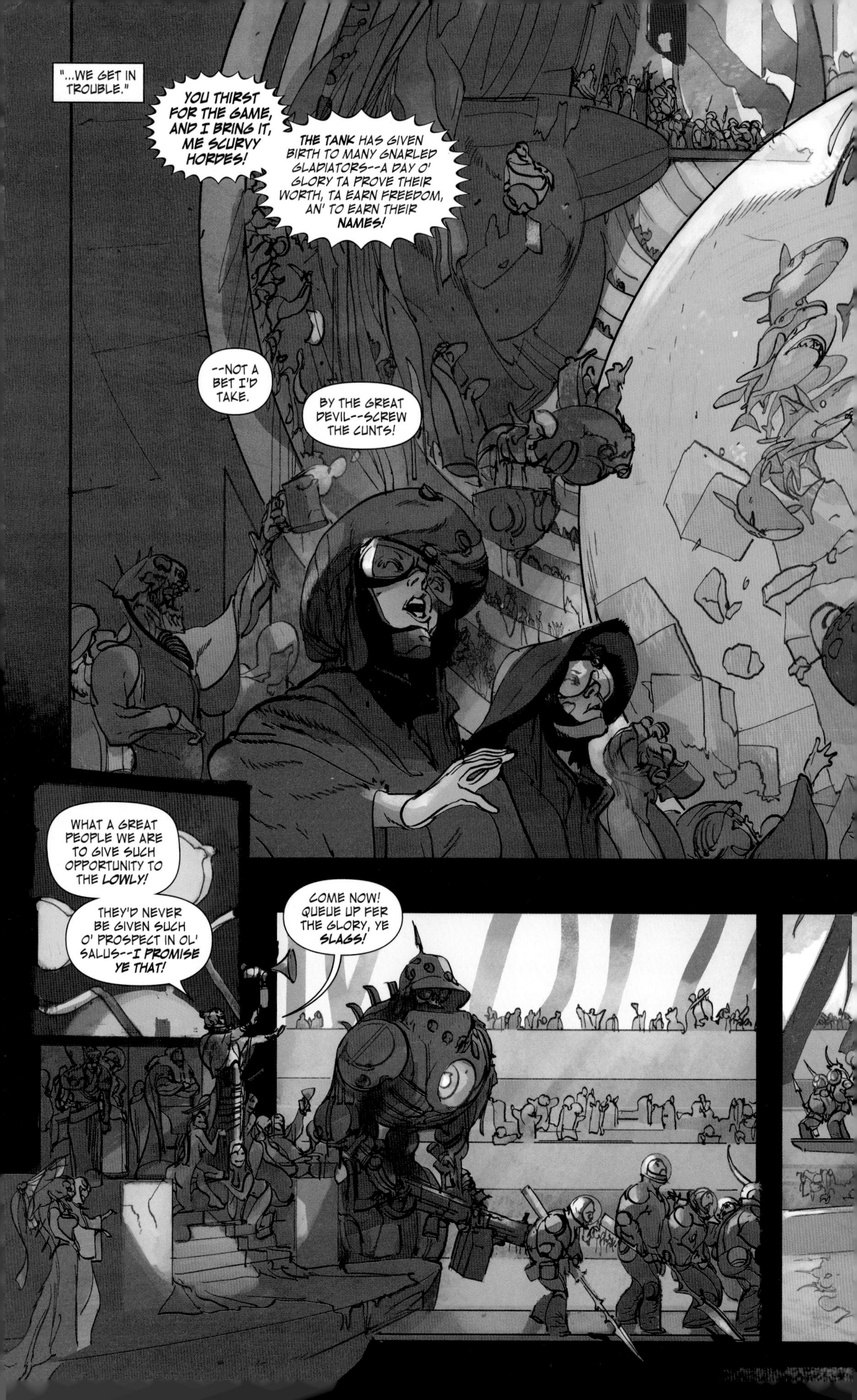
"...WE GET IN TROUBLE."
YOU THIRST FOR THE GAME, AND I BRING IT, ME SCURVY HORDES!
THE TANK HAS GIVEN BIRTH TO MANY GNARLED GLADIATORS--A DAY O' GLORY TA PROVE THEIR WORTH, TA EARN FREEDOM, AN' TO EARN THEIR NAMES!
--NOT A BET I'D TAKE.
BY THE GREAT DEVIL--SCREW THE CUNTS!
WHAT A GREAT PEOPLE WE ARE TO GIVE SUCH OPPORTUNITY TO THE LOWLY!
THEY'D NEVER BE GIVEN SUCH O' PROSPECT IN OL' SALUS--I PROMISE YE THAT!
COME NOW! QUEUE UP FER THE GLORY, YE SLAGS!

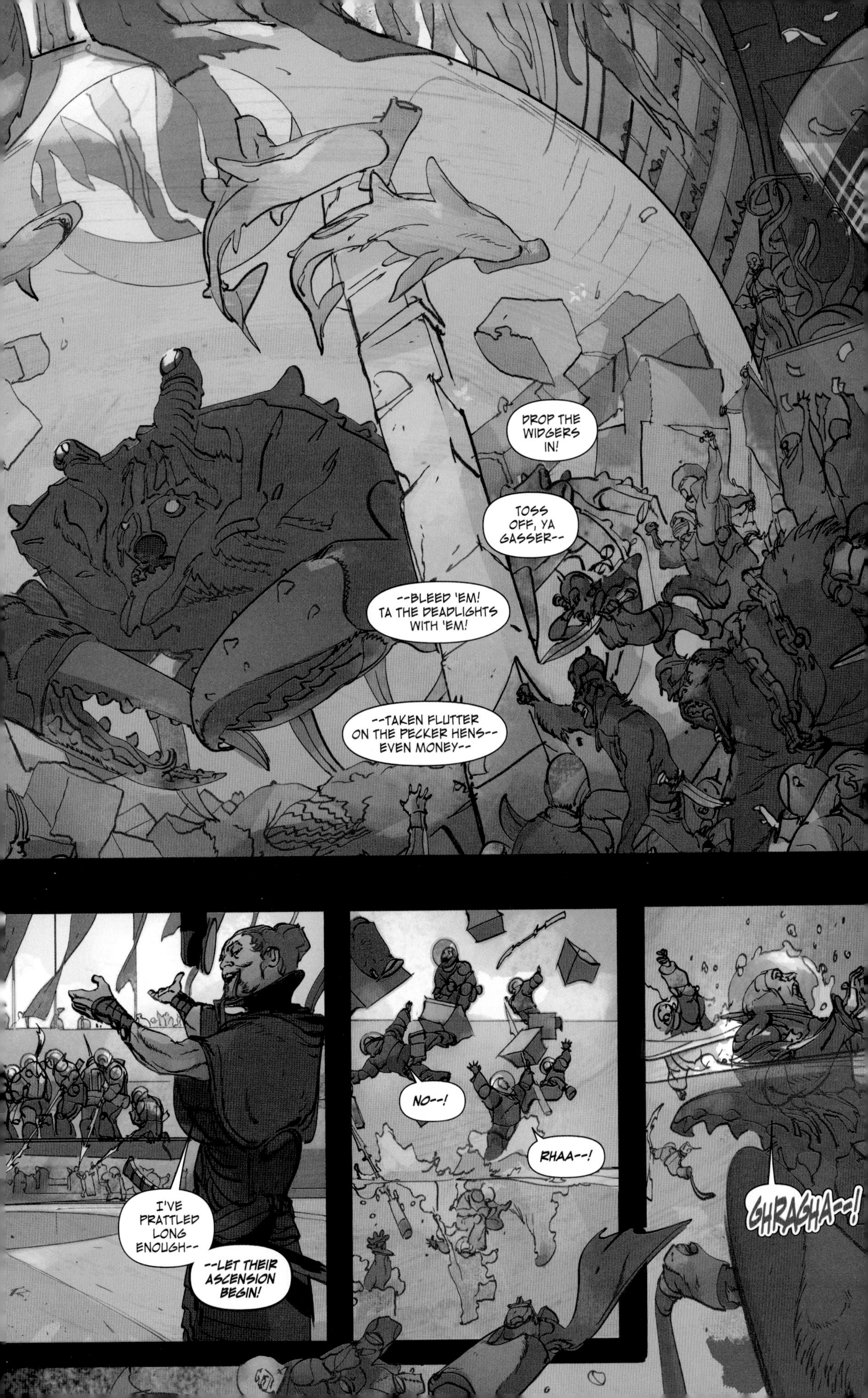
DROP THE WIDGERS IN!
TOSS OFF, YA GASSER--
--BLEED 'EM! TA THE DEADLIGHTS WITH 'EM!
--TAKEN FLUTTER ON THE PECKER HENS-- EVEN MONEY--
I'VE PRATTLED LONG ENOUGH--
--LET THEIR ASCENSION BEGIN!
NO--!
RHAA--!
GHRASHA--!

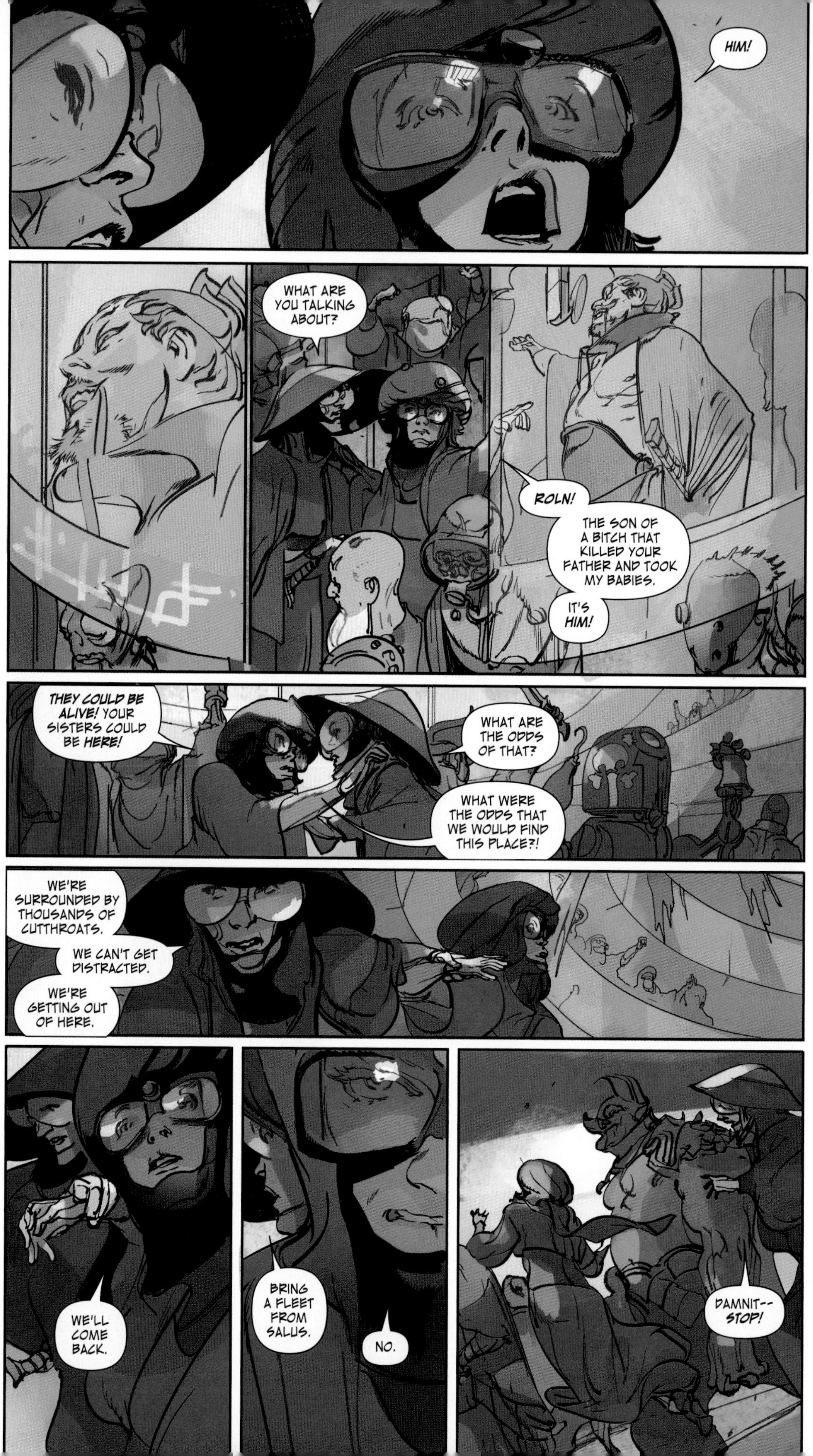
HIM!
WHAT ARE YOU TALKING ABOUT?
ROLN!
THE SON OF A BITCH THAT KILLED YOUR FATHER AND TOOK MY BABIES.
IT'S HIM!
THEY COULD BE ALIVE! YOUR SISTERS COULD BE HERE!
WHAT ARE THE ODDS OF THAT?
WHAT WERE THE ODDS THAT WE WOULD FIND THIS PLACE?!
WE'RE SURROUNDED BY THOUSANDS OF CUTTHROATS.
WE CAN'T GET DISTRACTED.
WE'RE GETTING OUT OF HERE.
WE'LL COME BACK.
BRING A FLEET FROM SALUS.
NO.
DAMNIT--STOP!

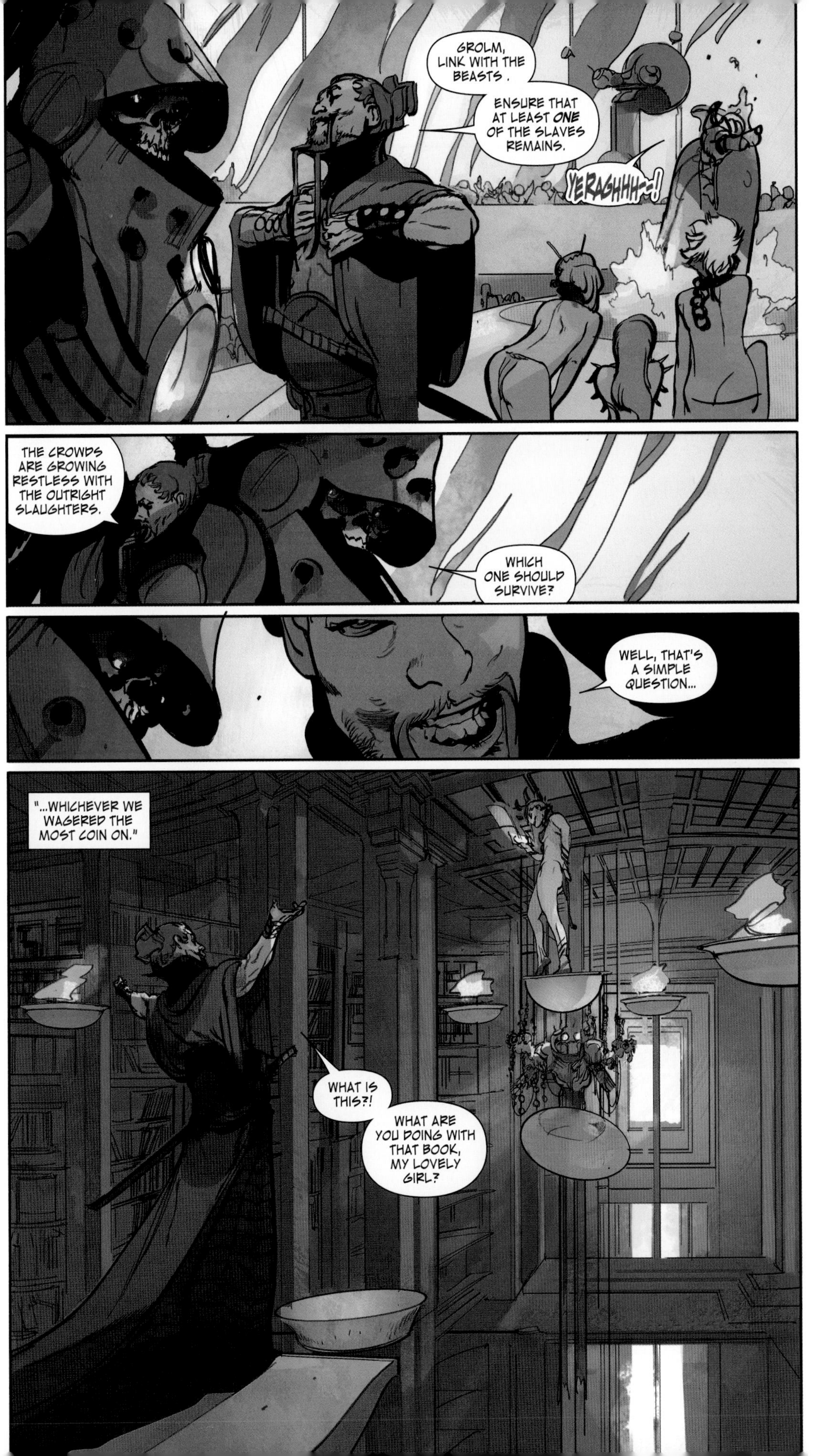
GROLM, LINK WITH THE BEASTS .
ENSURE THAT AT LEAST ONE OF THE SLAVES REMAINS.
YERAGHHH--!
THE CROWDS ARE GROWING RESTLESS WITH THE OUTRIGHT SLAUGHTERS.
WHICH ONE SHOULD SURVIVE?
WELL, THAT'S A SIMPLE QUESTION...
"...WHICHEVER WE WAGERED THE MOST COIN ON."
WHAT IS THIS?!
WHAT ARE YOU DOING WITH THAT BOOK, MY LOVELY GIRL?

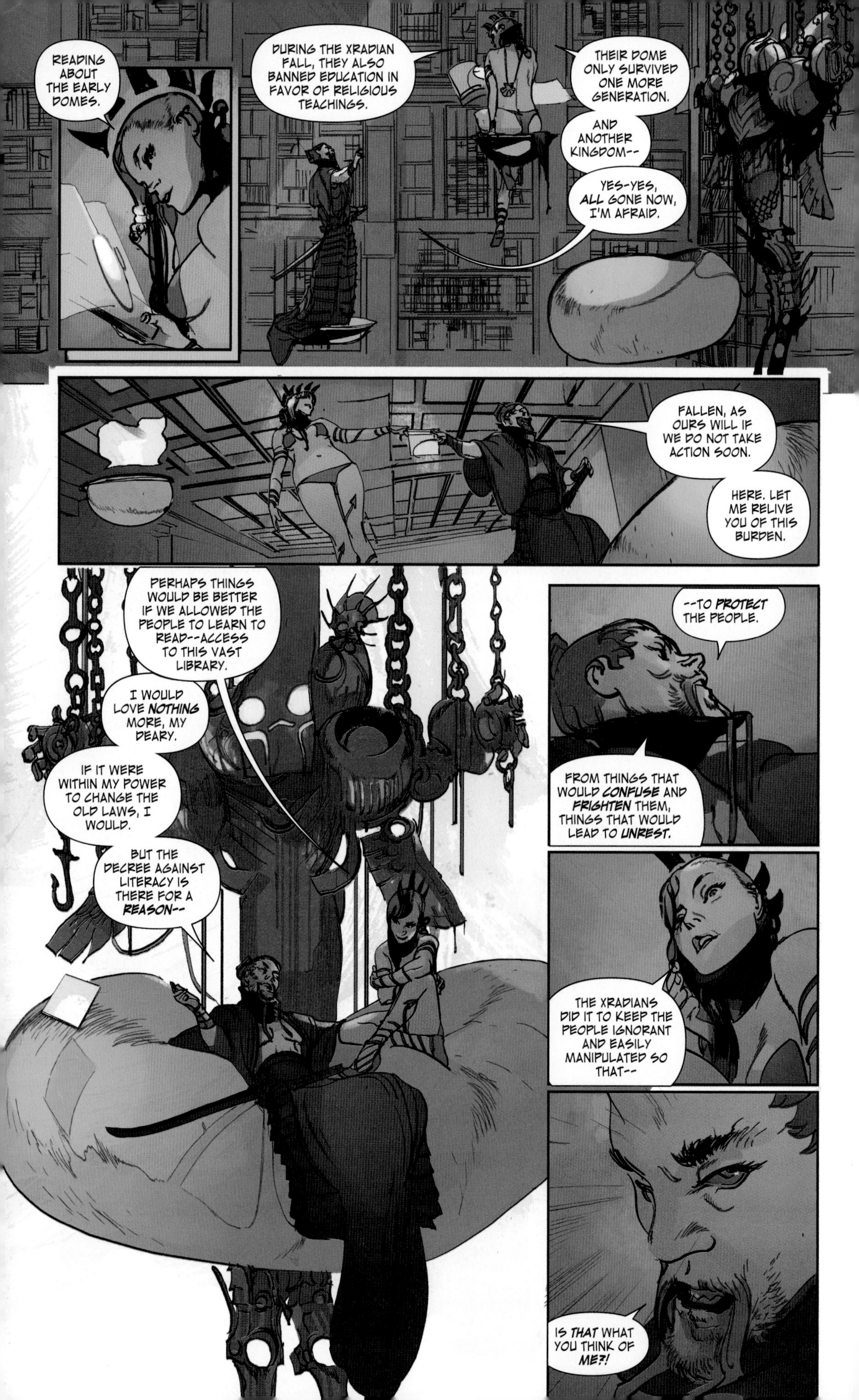
READING ABOUT THE EARLY DOMES.
DURING THE XRADIAN FALL, THEY ALSO BANNED EDUCATION IN FAVOR OF RELIGIOUS TEACHINGS.
THEIR DOME ONLY SURVIVED ONE MORE GENERATION.
AND ANOTHER KINGDOM--
YES-YES, ALL GONE NOW, I'M AFRAID.
FALLEN, AS OURS WILL IF WE DO NOT TAKE ACTION SOON.
HERE. LET ME RELIVE YOU OF THIS BURDEN.
PERHAPS THINGS WOULD BE BETTER IF WE ALLOWED THE PEOPLE TO LEARN TO READ--ACCESS TO THIS VAST LIBRARY.
I WOULD LOVE NOTHING MORE, MY DEARY.
IF IT WERE WITHIN MY POWER TO CHANGE THE OLD LAWS, I WOULD.
BUT THE DECREE AGAINST LITERACY IS THERE FOR A REASON--
--TO PROTECT THE PEOPLE.
FROM THINGS THAT WOULD CONFUSE AND FRIGHTEN THEM, THINGS THAT WOULD LEAD TO UNREST.
THE XRADIANS DID IT TO KEEP THE PEOPLE IGNORANT AND EASILY MANIPULATED SO THAT--
IS THAT WHAT YOU THINK OF ME?!

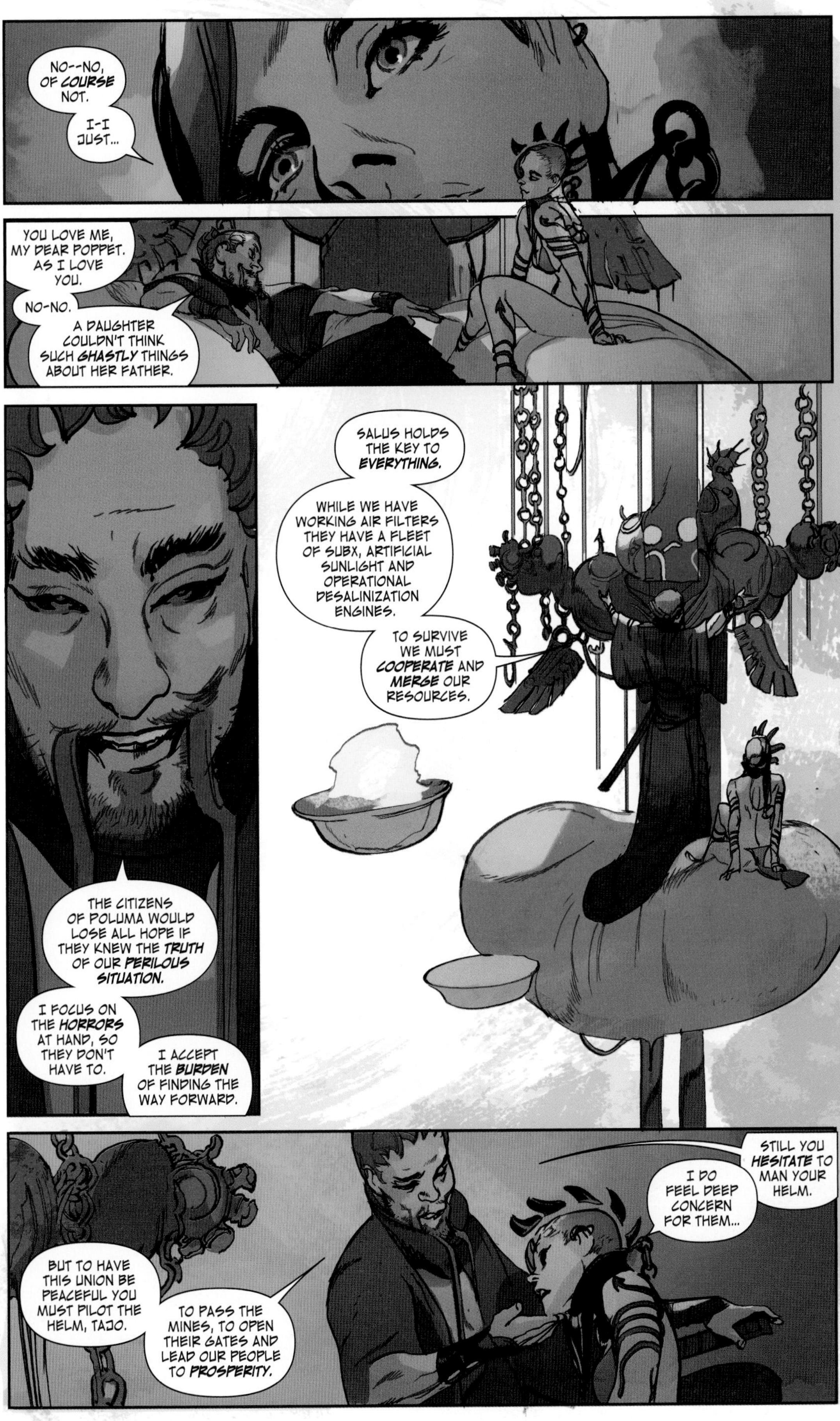
NO--NO, OF COURSE NOT.
I-I JUST...
YOU LOVE ME, MY DEAR POPPET. AS I LOVE YOU.
NO-NO.
A DAUGHTER COULDN'T THINK SUCH GHASTLY THINGS ABOUT HER FATHER.
SALUS HOLDS THE KEY TO EVERYTHING.
WHILE WE HAVE WORKING AIR FILTERS THEY HAVE A FLEET OF SUBX, ARTIFICIAL SUNLIGHT AND OPERATIONAL DESALINIZATION ENGINES.
TO SURVIVE WE MUST COOPERATE AND MERGE OUR RESOURCES.
THE CITIZENS OF POLUMA WOULD LOSE ALL HOPE IF THEY KNEW THE TRUTH OF OUR PERILOUS SITUATION.
I FOCUS ON THE HORRORS AT HAND, SO THEY DON'T HAVE TO.
I ACCEPT THE BURDEN OF FINDING THE WAY FORWARD.
STILL YOU HESITATE TO MAN YOUR HELM.
I DO FEEL DEEP CONCERN FOR THEM...
BUT TO HAVE THIS UNION BE PEACEFUL YOU MUST PILOT THE HELM, TAJO.
TO PASS THE MINES, TO OPEN THEIR GATES AND LEAD OUR PEOPLE TO PROSPERITY.

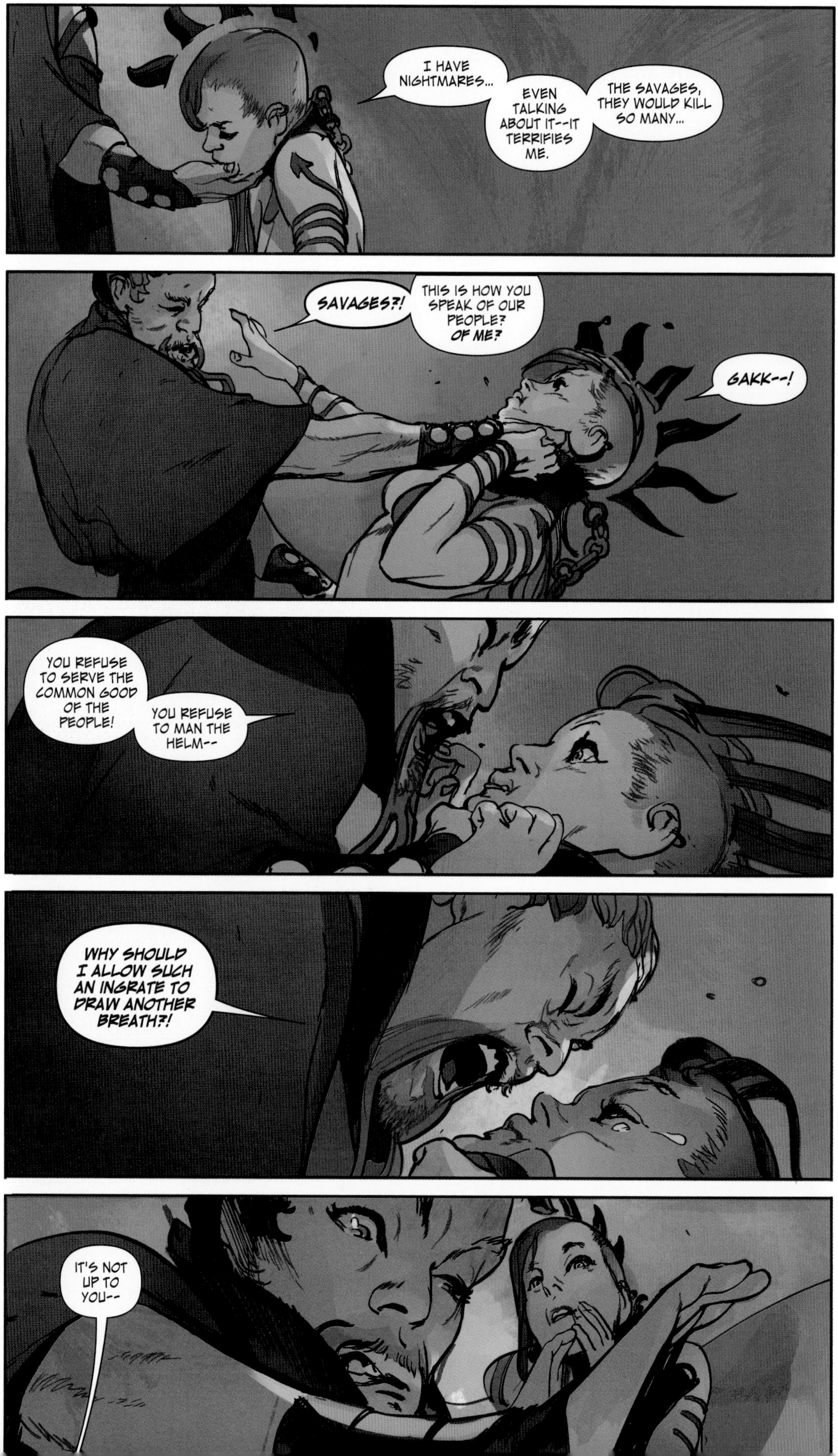
I HAVE NIGHTMARES...
EVEN TALKING ABOUT IT--IT TERRIFIES ME.
THE SAVAGES, THEY WOULD KILL SO MANY...
SAVAGES?!
THIS IS HOW YOU SPEAK OF OUR PEOPLE? OF ME?
GAKK--!
YOU REFUSE TO SERVE THE COMMON GOOD OF THE PEOPLE!
YOU REFUSE TO MAN THE HELM--
WHY SHOULD I ALLOW SUCH AN INGRATE TO DRAW ANOTHER BREATH?!
IT'S NOT UP TO YOU--

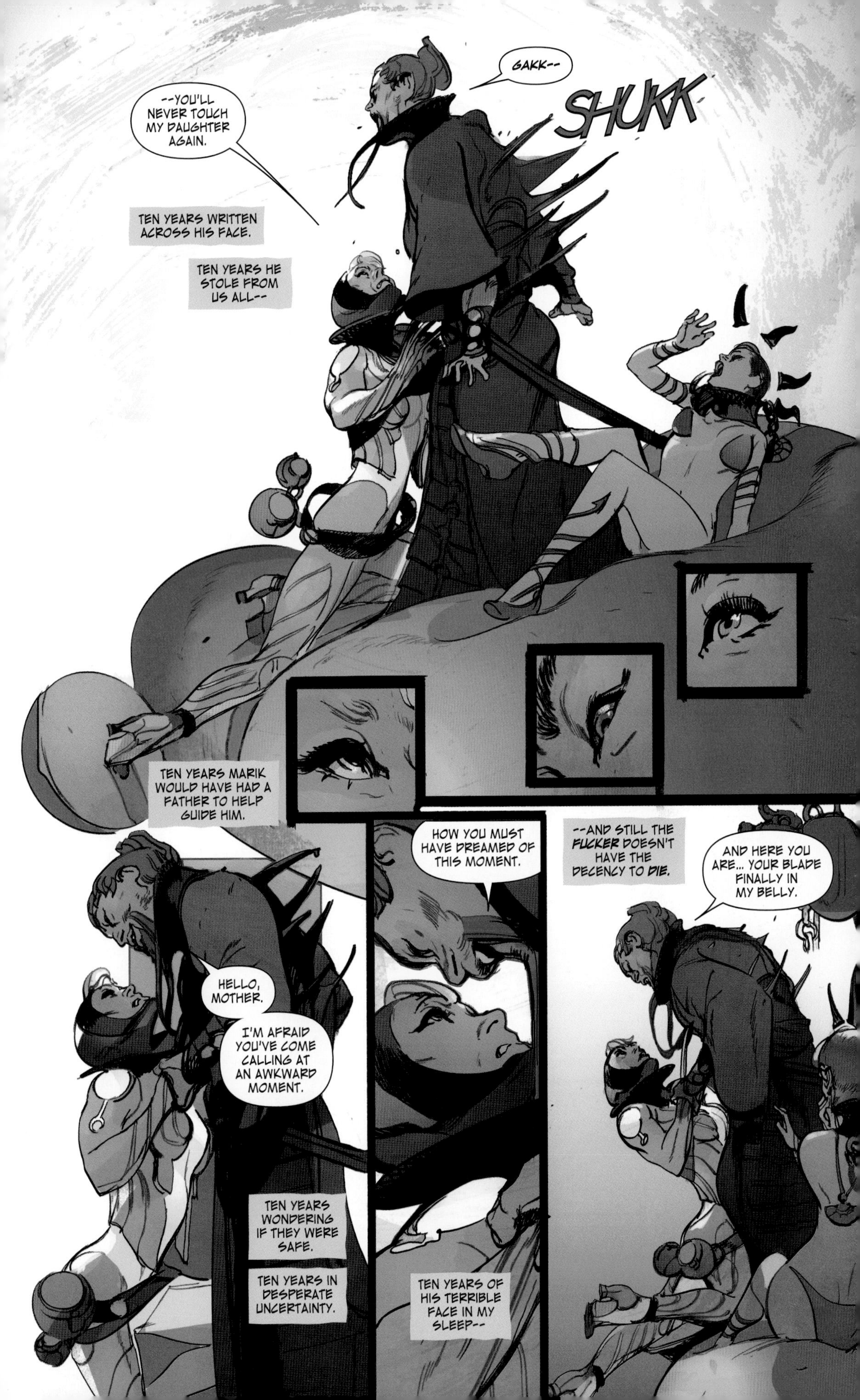
--YOU'LL NEVER TOUCH MY DAUGHTER AGAIN.
GAKK--
SHUKK
TEN YEARS WRITTEN ACROSS HIS FACE.
TEN YEARS HE STOLE FROM US ALL--
TEN YEARS MARIK WOULD HAVE HAD A FATHER TO HELP GUIDE HIM.
HELLO, MOTHER.
I'M AFRAID YOU'VE COME CALLING AT AN AWKWARD MOMENT.
TEN YEARS WONDERING IF THEY WERE SAFE.
TEN YEARS IN DESPERATE UNCERTAINTY.
HOW YOU MUST HAVE DREAMED OF THIS MOMENT.
TEN YEARS OF HIS TERRIBLE FACE IN MY SLEEP--
--AND STILL THE FUCKER DOESN'T HAVE THE DECENCY TO DIE.
AND HERE YOU ARE... YOUR BLADE FINALLY IN MY BELLY.

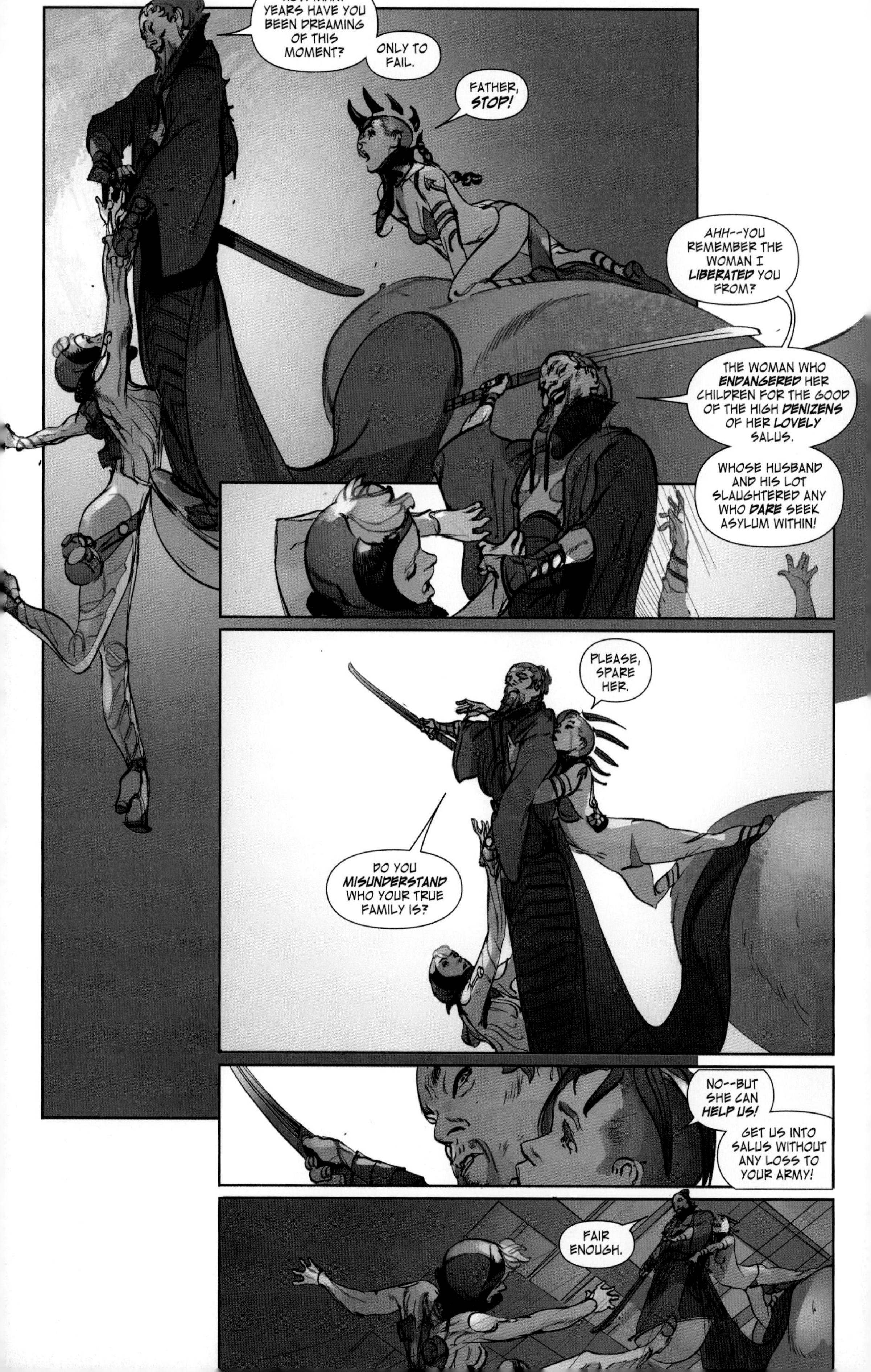

HOW MANY YEARS HAVE YOU BEEN DREAMING OF THIS MOMENT?
ONLY TO FAIL.
FATHER, STOP!
AHH--YOU REMEMBER THE WOMAN I LIBERATED YOU FROM?
THE WOMAN WHO ENDANGERED HER CHILDREN FOR THE GOOD OF THE HIGH DENIZENS OF HER LOVELY SALUS.
WHOSE HUSBAND AND HIS LOT SLAUGHTERED ANY WHO DARE SEEK ASYLUM WITHIN!
PLEASE, SPARE HER.
DO YOU MISUNDERSTAND WHO YOUR TRUE FAMILY IS?
NO--BUT SHE CAN HELP US!
GET US INTO SALUS WITHOUT ANY LOSS TO YOUR ARMY!
FAIR ENOUGH.

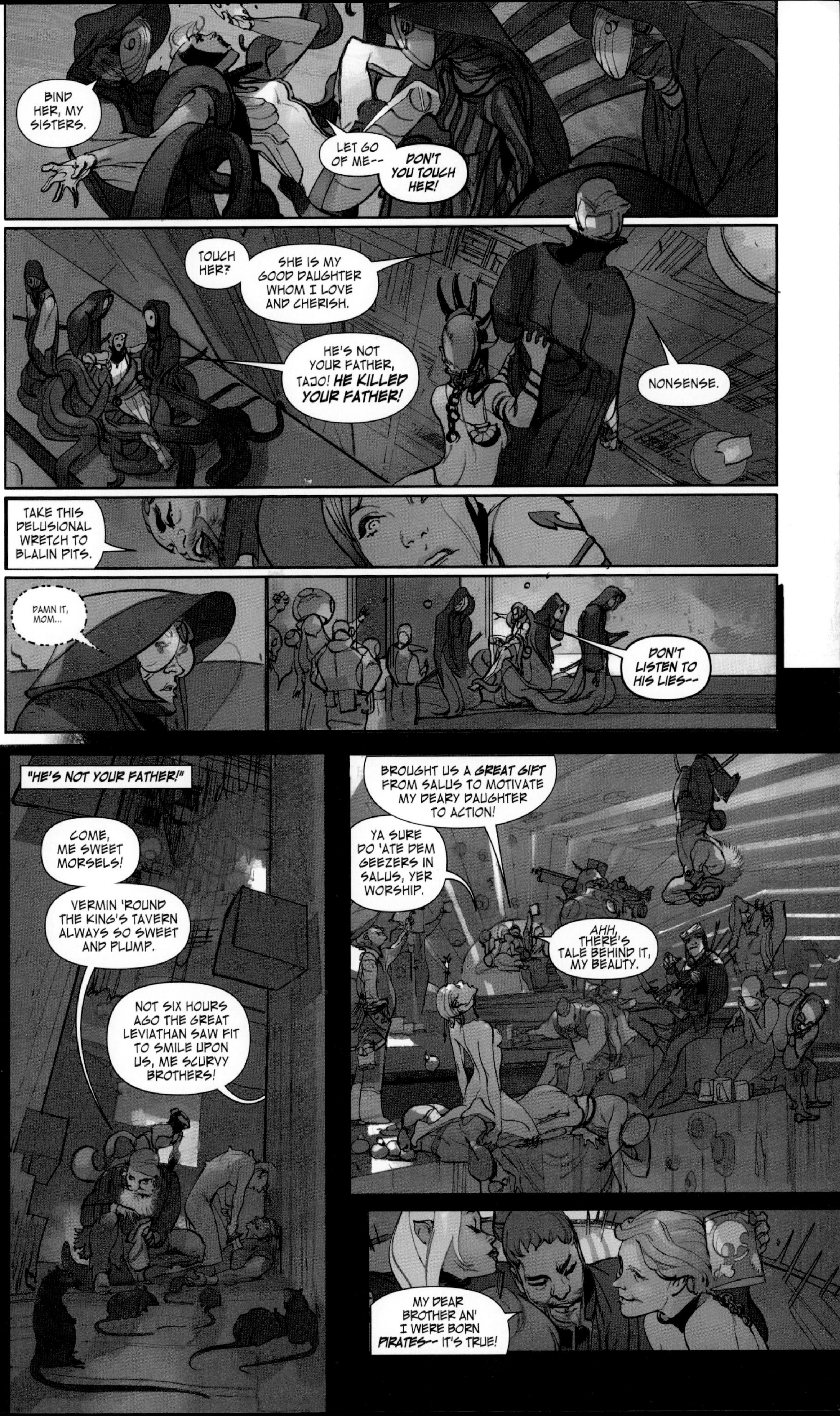
BIND HER, MY SISTERS.
LET GO OF ME--
DON'T YOU TOUCH HER!
TOUCH HER?
SHE IS MY GOOD DAUGHTER WHOM I LOVE AND CHERISH.
HE'S NOT YOUR FATHER, TAJO! HE KILLED YOUR FATHER!
NONSENSE.
TAKE THIS DELUSIONAL WRETCH TO BLALIN PITS.
DAMN IT, MOM...
DON'T LISTEN TO HIS LIES--
"HE'S NOT YOUR FATHER!"
COME, ME SWEET MORSELS!
VERMIN 'ROUND THE KING'S TAVERN ALWAYS SO SWEET AND PLUMP.
NOT SIX HOURS AGO THE GREAT LEVIATHAN SAW FIT TO SMILE UPON US, ME SCURVY BROTHERS!
BROUGHT US A GREAT GIFT FROM SALUS TO MOTIVATE MY DEARY DAUGHTER TO ACTION!
YA SURE DO 'ATE DEM GEEZERS IN SALUS, YER WORSHIP.
AHH, THERE'S TALE BEHIND IT, MY BEAUTY.
MY DEAR BROTHER AN' I WERE BORN PIRATES-- IT'S TRUE!

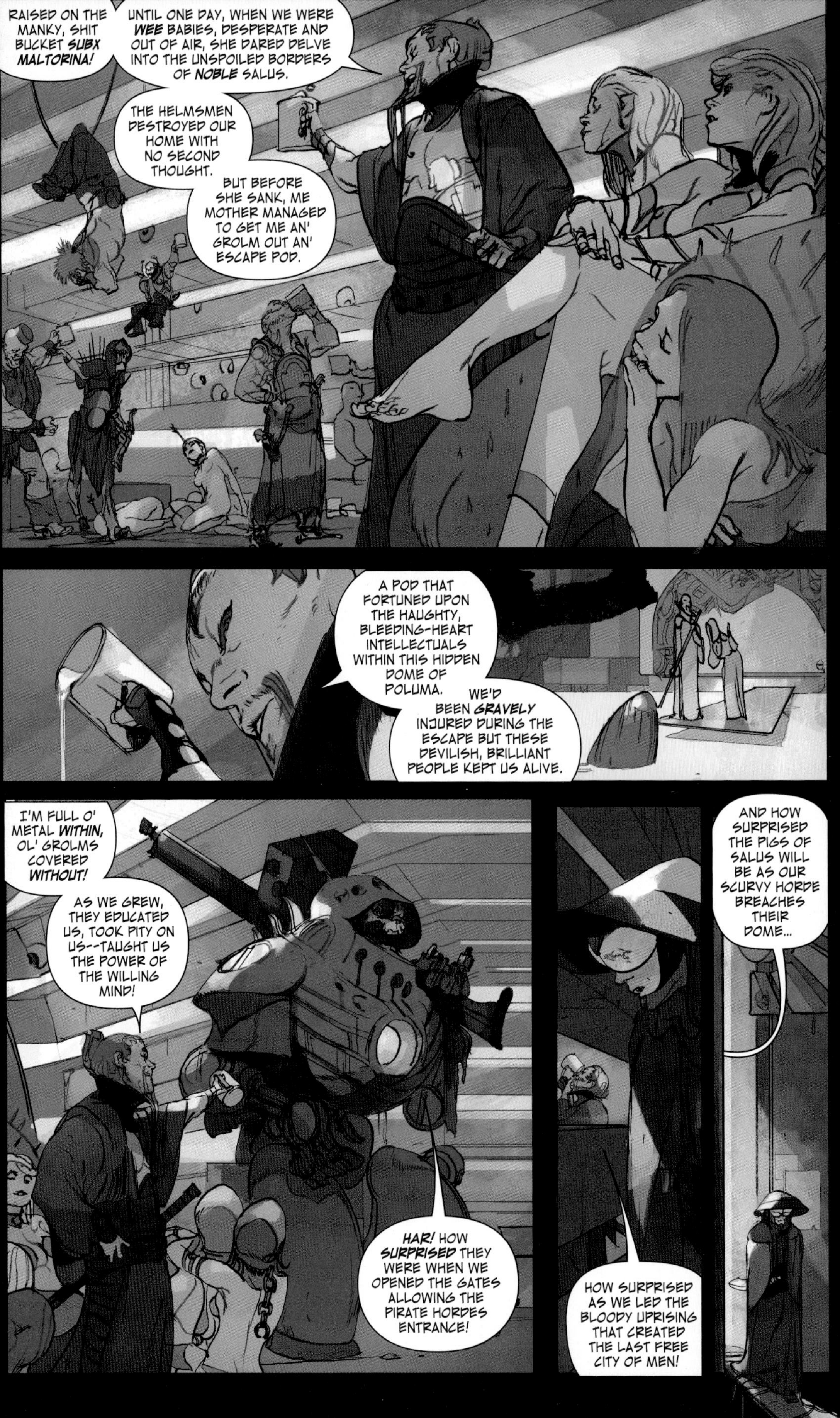
RAISED ON THE MANKY, SHIT BUCKET SUBX MALTORINA!
UNTIL ONE DAY, WHEN WE WERE WEE BABIES, DESPERATE AND OUT OF AIR, SHE DARED DELVE INTO THE UNSPOILED BORDERS OF NOBLE SALUS.
THE HELMSMEN DESTROYED OUR HOME WITH NO SECOND THOUGHT.
BUT BEFORE SHE SANK, ME MOTHER MANAGED TO GET ME AN' GROLM OUT AN' ESCAPE POD.
A POD THAT FORTUNED UPON THE HAUGHTY, BLEEDING-HEART INTELLECTUALS WITHIN THIS HIDDEN DOME OF POLUMA.
WE'D BEEN GRAVELY INJURED DURING THE ESCAPE BUT THESE DEVILISH, BRILLIANT PEOPLE KEPT US ALIVE.
I'M FULL O' METAL WITHIN, OL' GROLMS COVERED WITHOUT!
AS WE GREW, THEY EDUCATED US, TOOK PITY ON US--TAUGHT US THE POWER OF THE WILLING MIND!
HAR! HOW SURPRISED THEY WERE WHEN WE OPENED THE GATES ALLOWING THE PIRATE HORDES ENTRANCE!
AND HOW SURPRISED THE PIGS OF SALUS WILL BE AS OUR SCURVY HORDE BREACHES THEIR DOME...
HOW SURPRISED AS WE LED THE BLOODY UPRISING THAT CREATED THE LAST FREE CITY OF MEN!

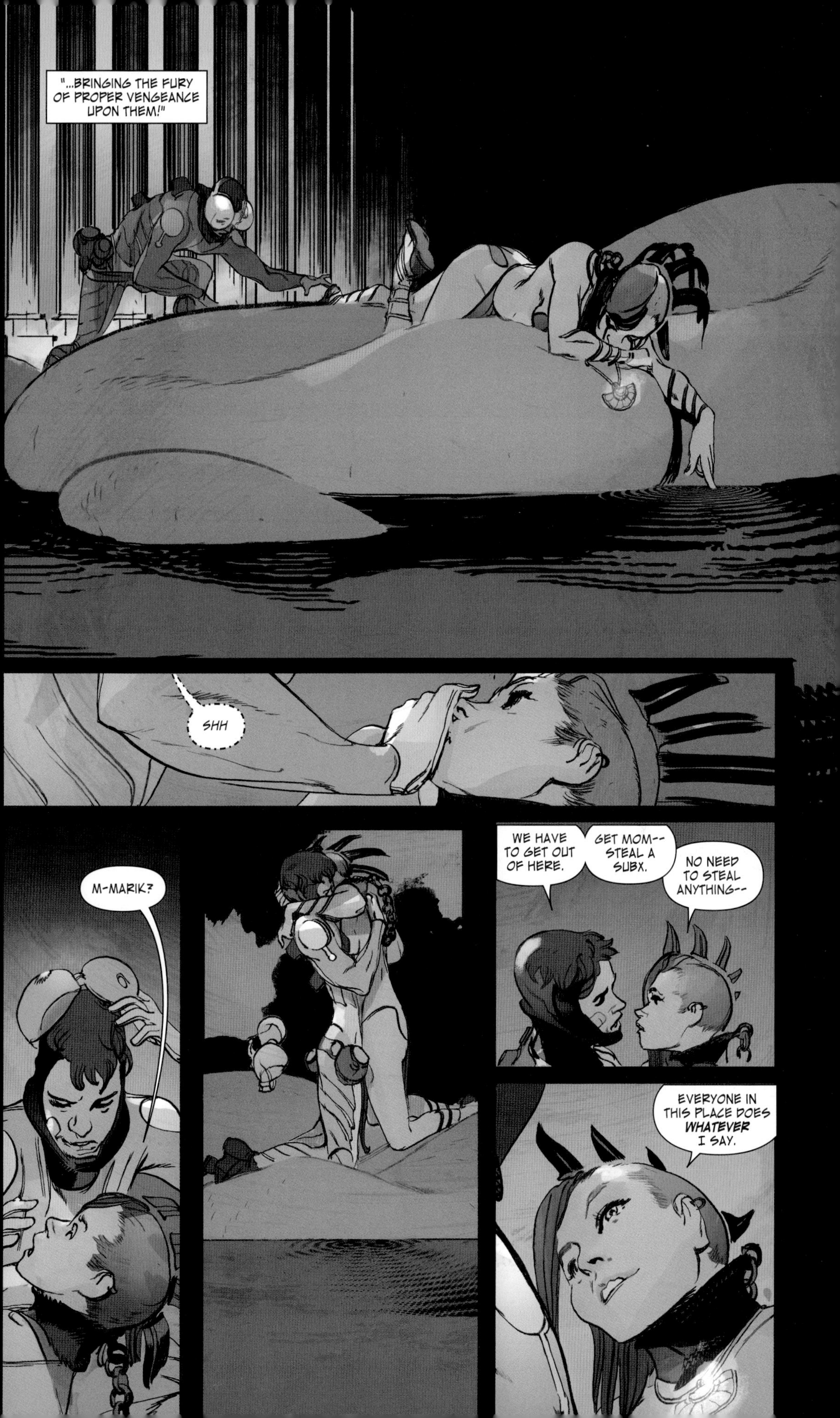
"...BRINGING THE FURY OF PROPER VENGEANCE UPON THEM!"
SHH
M-MARIK?
WE HAVE TO GET OUT OF HERE.
GET MOM-- STEAL A SUBX.
NO NEED TO STEAL ANYTHING--
EVERYONE IN THIS PLACE DOES WHATEVER I SAY.

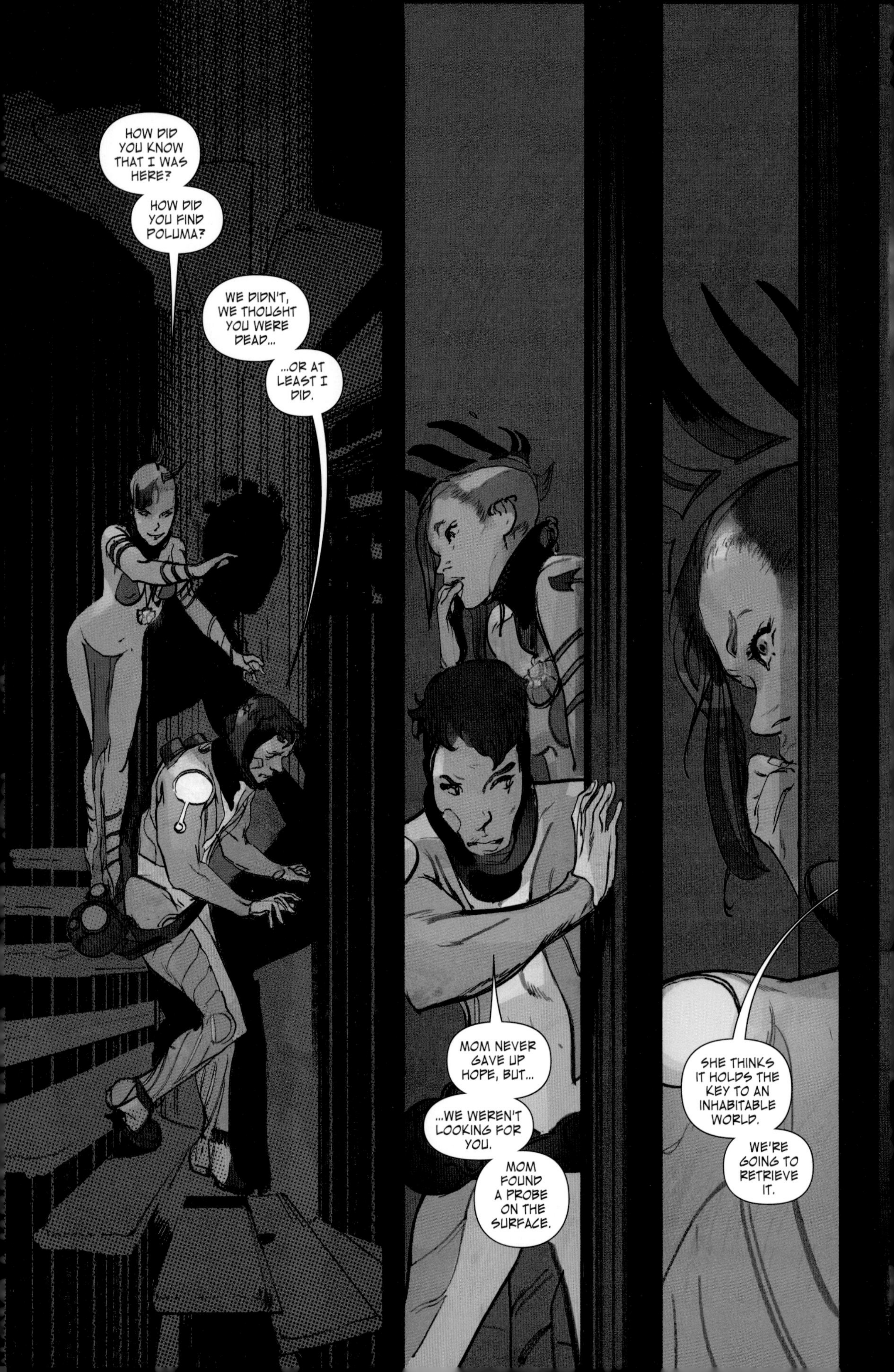
HOW DID YOU KNOW THAT I WAS HERE?
HOW DID YOU FIND POLUMA?
WE DIDN'T, WE THOUGHT YOU WERE DEAD...
...OR AT LEAST I DID.
MOM NEVER GAVE UP HOPE, BUT...
...WE WEREN'T LOOKING FOR YOU.
MOM FOUND A PROBE ON THE SURFACE.
SHE THINKS IT HOLDS THE KEY TO AN INHABITABLE WORLD.
WE'RE GOING TO RETRIEVE IT.

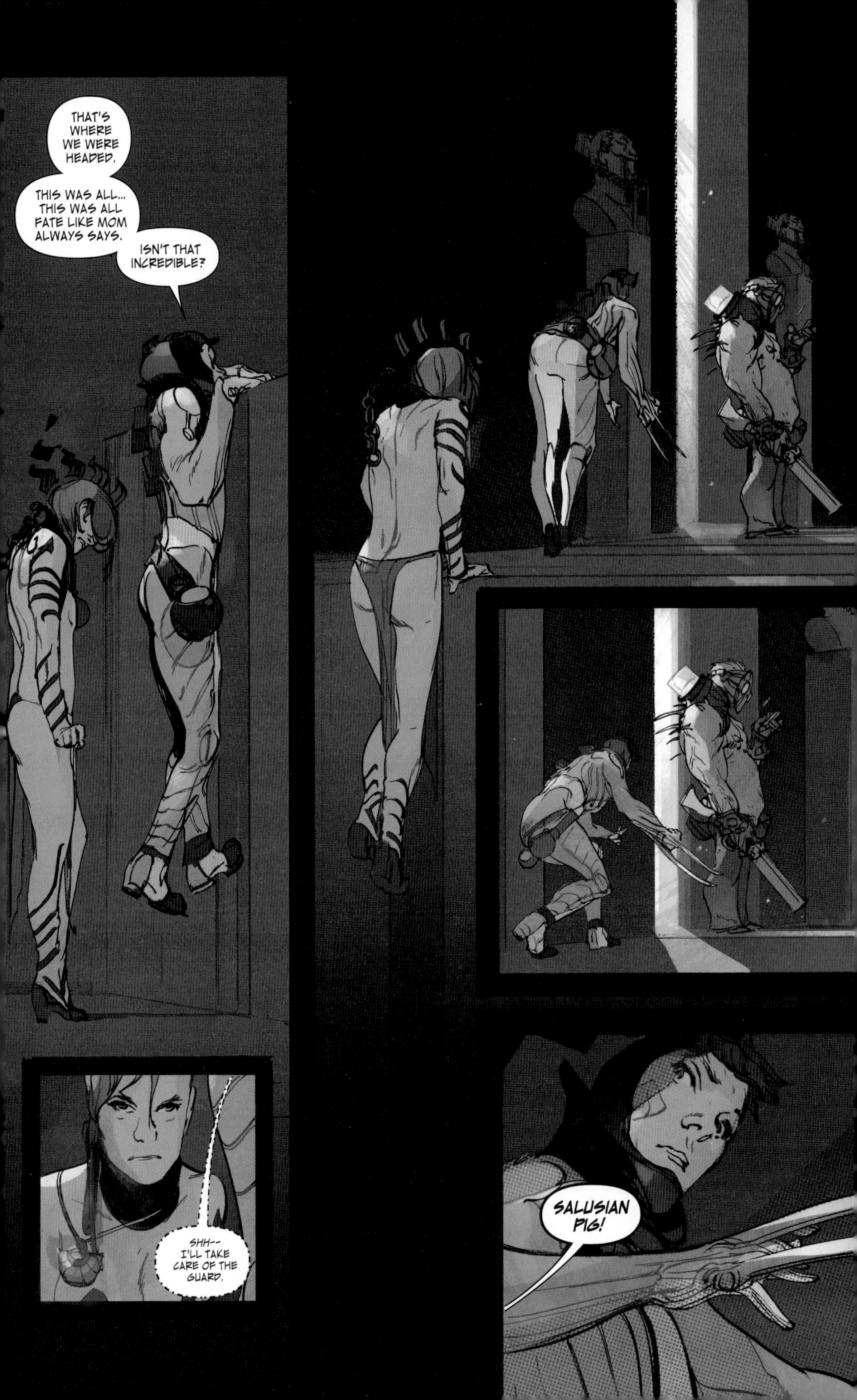
THAT'S WHERE WE WERE HEADED.
THIS WAS ALL... THIS WAS ALL FATE LIKE MOM ALWAYS SAYS.
ISN'T THAT INCREDIBLE?
SHH-- I'LL TAKE CARE OF THE GUARD.
SALUSIAN PIG!

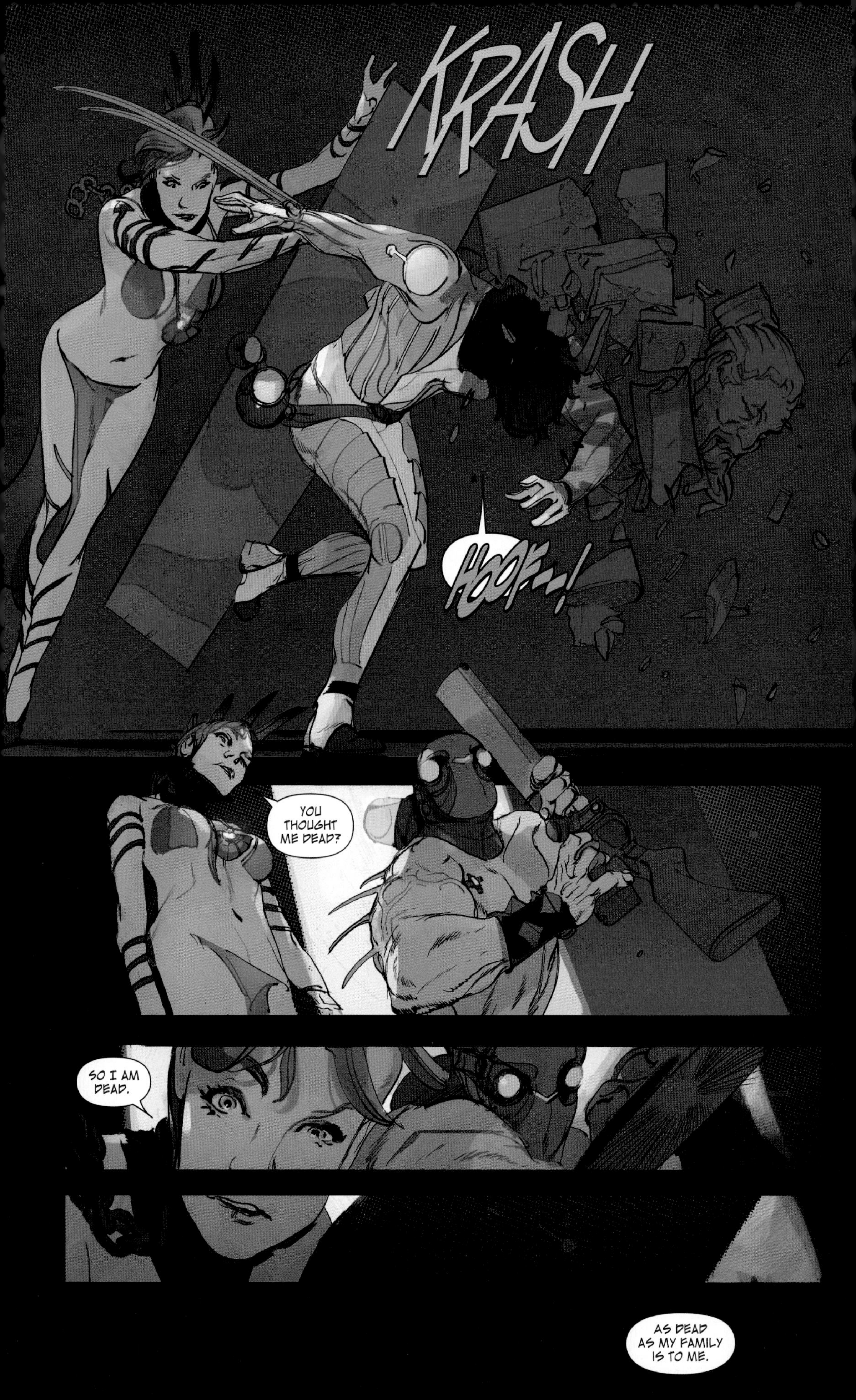
KRASH
HOOF--!
YOU THOUGHT ME DEAD?
SO I AM DEAD.
AS DEAD AS MY FAMILY IS TO ME.

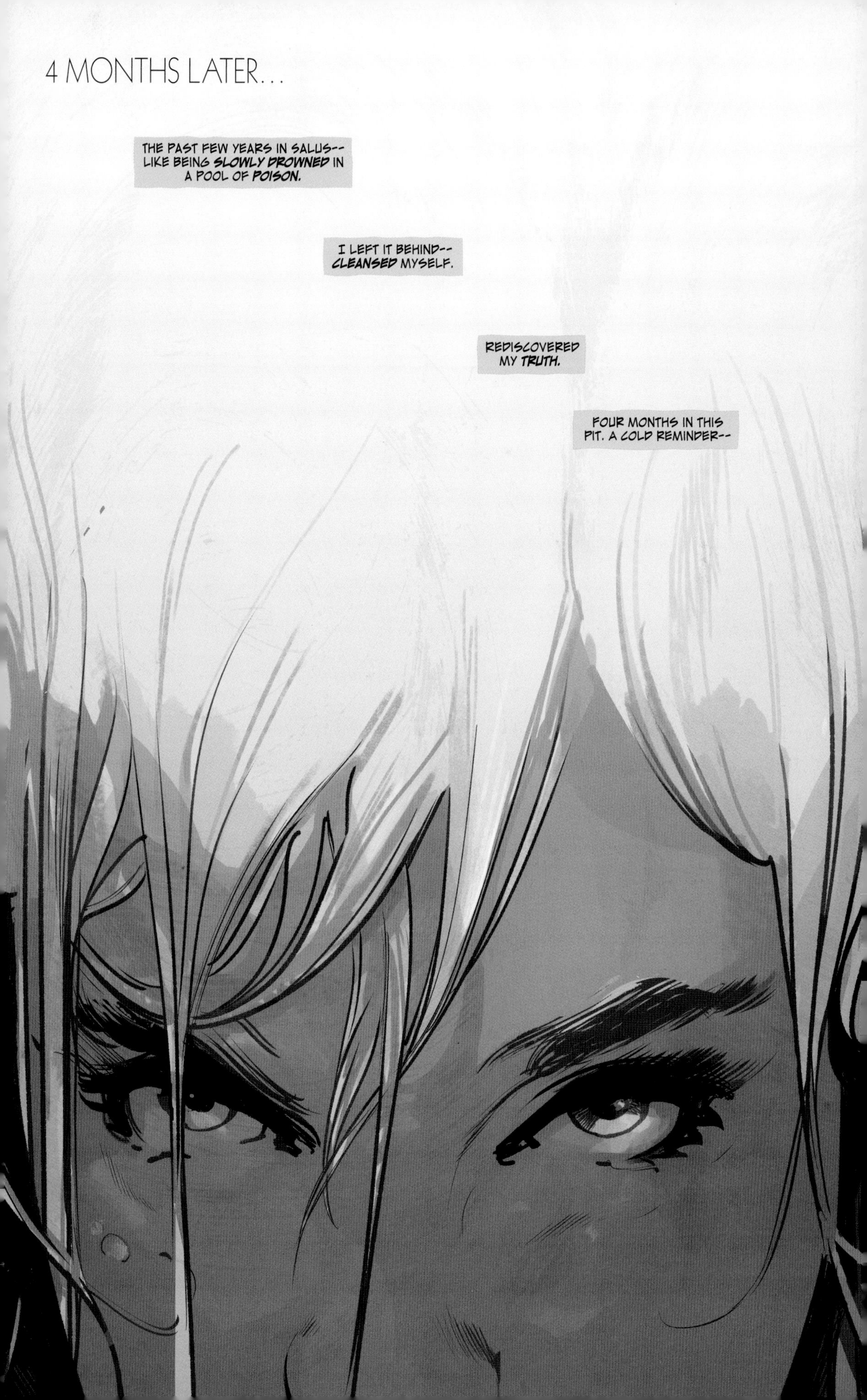
4 MONTHS LATER...
THE PAST FEW YEARS IN SALUS-- LIKE BEING SLOWLY DROWNED IN A POOL OF POISON.
I LEFT IT BEHIND-- CLEANSED MYSELF.
REDISCOVERED MY TRUTH.
FOUR MONTHS IN THIS PIT. A COLD REMINDER--

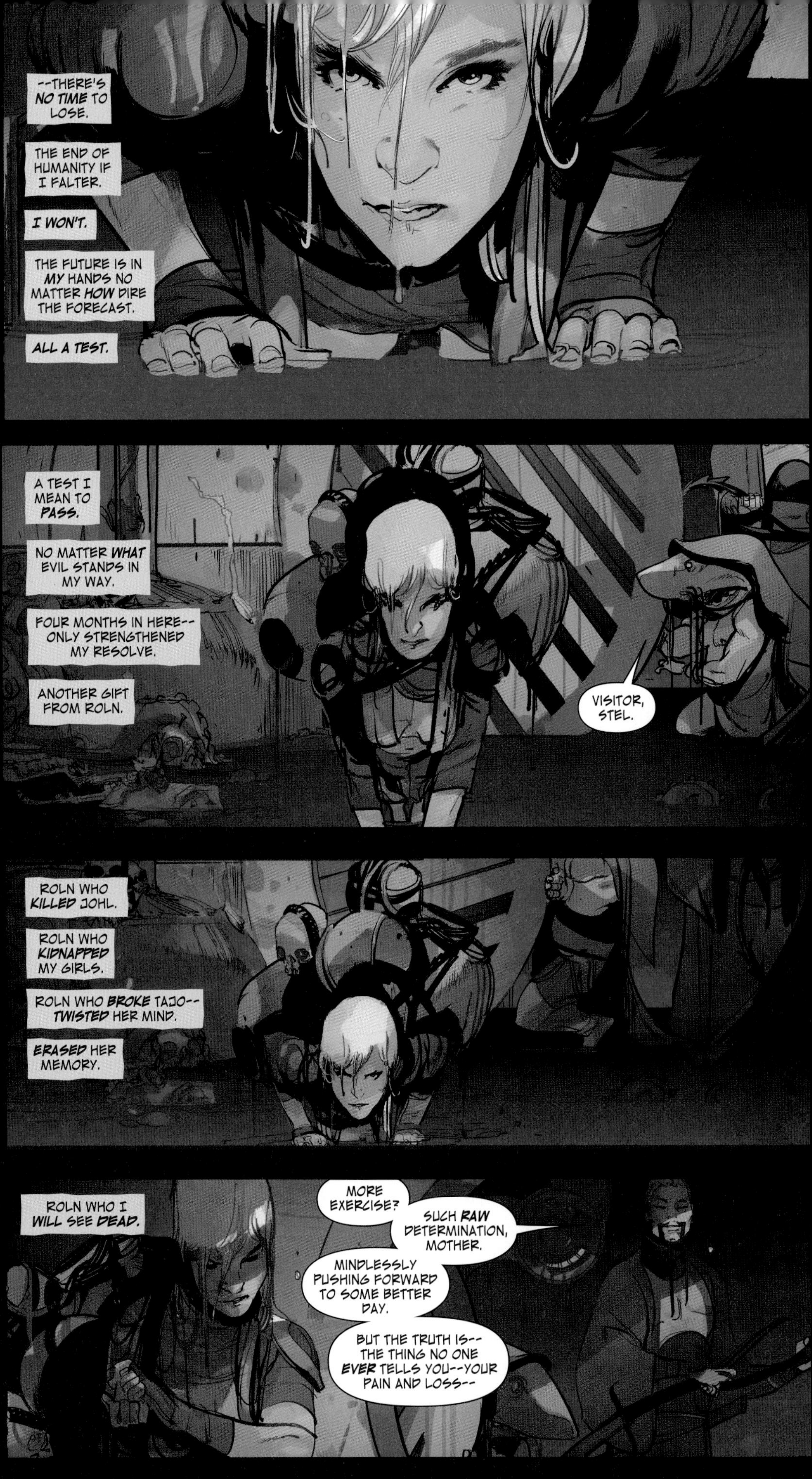

--THERE'S NO TIME TO LOSE.
THE END OF HUMANITY IF I FALTER.
I WON'T.
THE FUTURE IS IN MY HANDS NO MATTER HOW DIRE THE FORECAST.
ALL A TEST.
A TEST I MEAN TO PASS.
NO MATTER WHAT EVIL STANDS IN MY WAY.
FOUR MONTHS IN HERE-- ONLY STRENGTHENED MY RESOLVE.
ANOTHER GIFT FROM ROLN.
VISITOR, STEL.
ROLN WHO KILLED JOHL.
ROLN WHO KIDNAPPED MY GIRLS.
ROLN WHO BROKE TAJO-- TWISTED HER MIND.
ERASED HER MEMORY.
ROLN WHO I WILL SEE DEAD.
MORE EXERCISE?
SUCH RAW DETERMINATION, MOTHER.
MINDLESSLY PUSHING FORWARD TO SOME BETTER DAY.
BUT THE TRUTH IS-- THE THING NO ONE EVER TELLS YOU--YOUR PAIN AND LOSS--

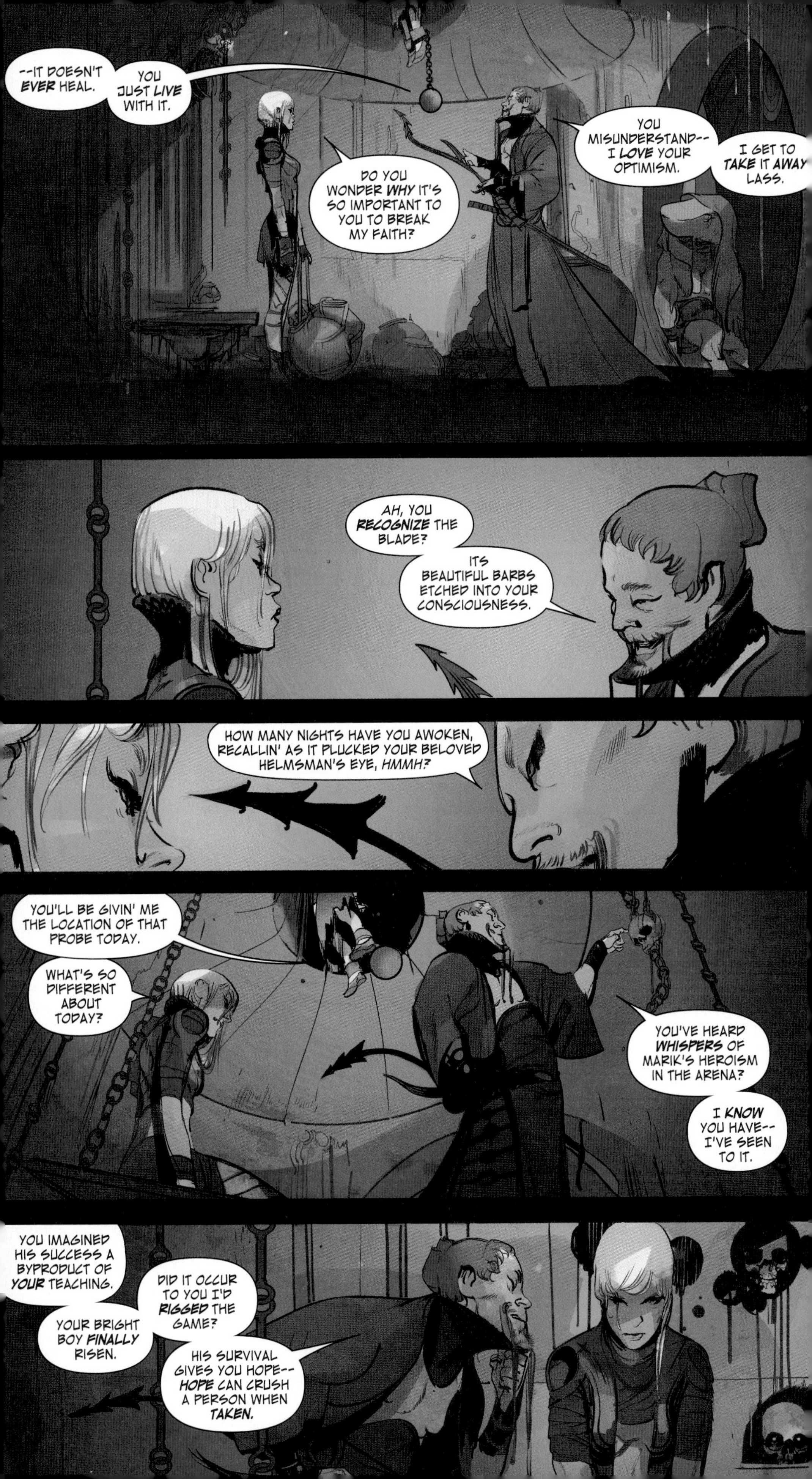
--IT DOESN'T EVER HEAL.
YOU JUST LIVE WITH IT.
DO YOU WONDER WHY IT'S SO IMPORTANT TO YOU TO BREAK MY FAITH?
YOU MISUNDERSTAND-- I LOVE YOUR OPTIMISM.
I GET TO TAKE IT AWAY LASS.
AH, YOU RECOGNIZE THE BLADE?
ITS BEAUTIFUL BARBS ETCHED INTO YOUR CONSCIOUSNESS.
HOW MANY NIGHTS HAVE YOU AWOKEN, RECALLIN' AS IT PLUCKED YOUR BELOVED HELMSMAN'S EYE, HMMH?
YOU'LL BE GIVIN' ME THE LOCATION OF THAT PROBE TODAY.
WHAT'S SO DIFFERENT ABOUT TODAY?
YOU'VE HEARD WHISPERS OF MARIK'S HEROISM IN THE ARENA?
I KNOW YOU HAVE-- I'VE SEEN TO IT.
YOU IMAGINED HIS SUCCESS A BYPRODUCT OF YOUR TEACHING.
YOUR BRIGHT BOY FINALLY RISEN.
DID IT OCCUR TO YOU I'D RIGGED THE GAME?
HIS SURVIVAL GIVES YOU HOPE-- HOPE CAN CRUSH A PERSON WHEN TAKEN.

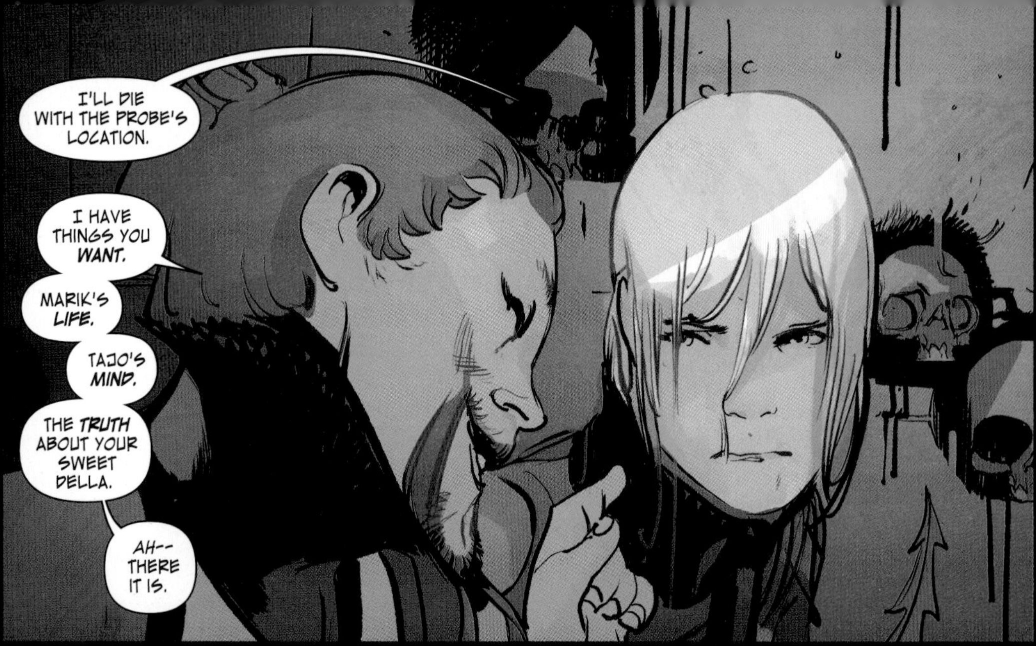
I'LL DIE WITH THE PROBE'S LOCATION.
I HAVE THINGS YOU WANT.
MARIK'S LIFE.
TAJO'S MIND.
THE TRUTH ABOUT YOUR SWEET DELLA.
AH-- THERE IT IS.

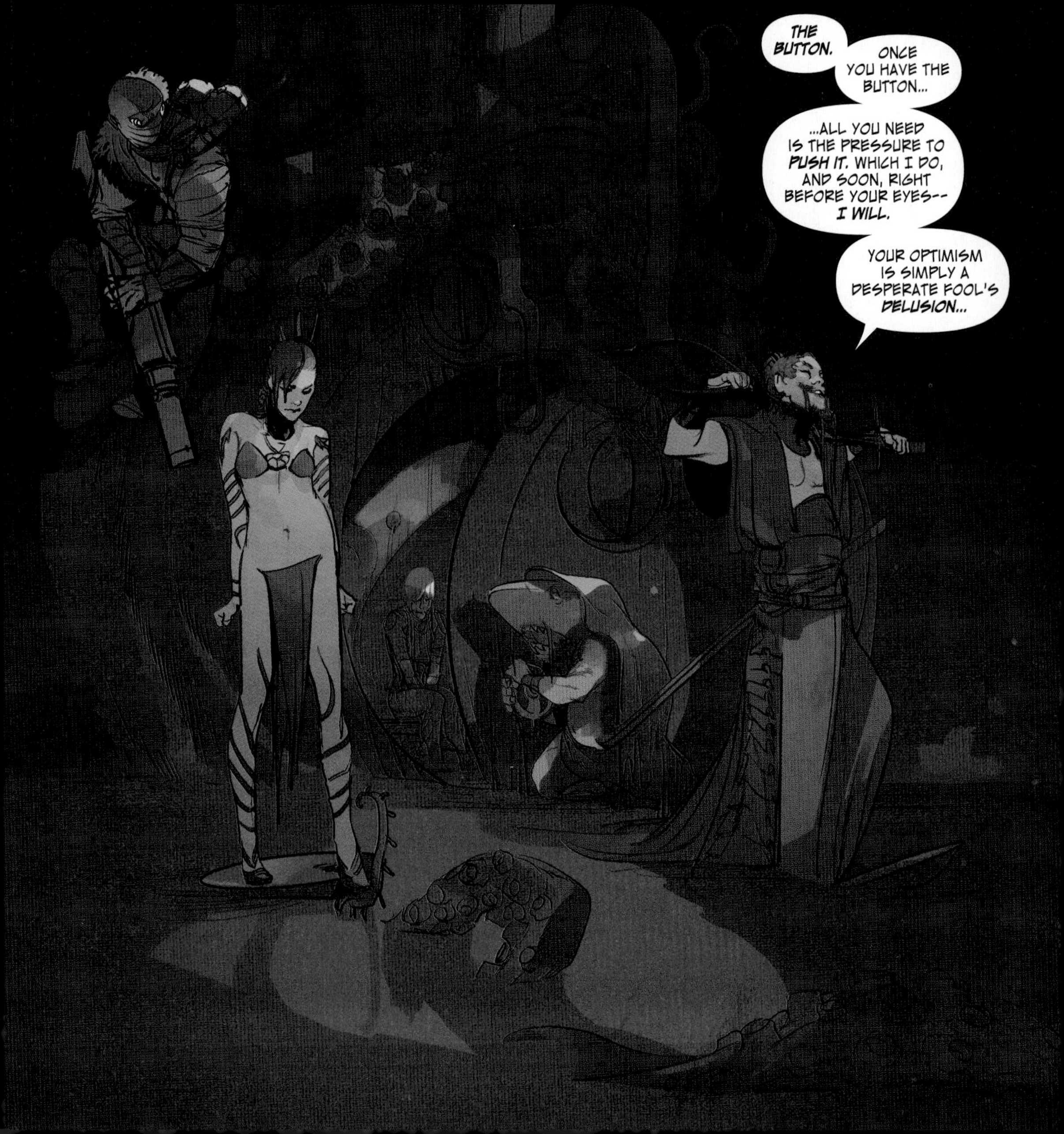
THE BUTTON.
ONCE YOU HAVE THE BUTTON...
...ALL YOU NEED IS THE PRESSURE TO PUSH IT. WHICH I DO, AND SOON, RIGHT BEFORE YOUR EYES-- I WILL.
YOUR OPTIMISM IS SIMPLY A DESPERATE FOOL'S DELUSION...

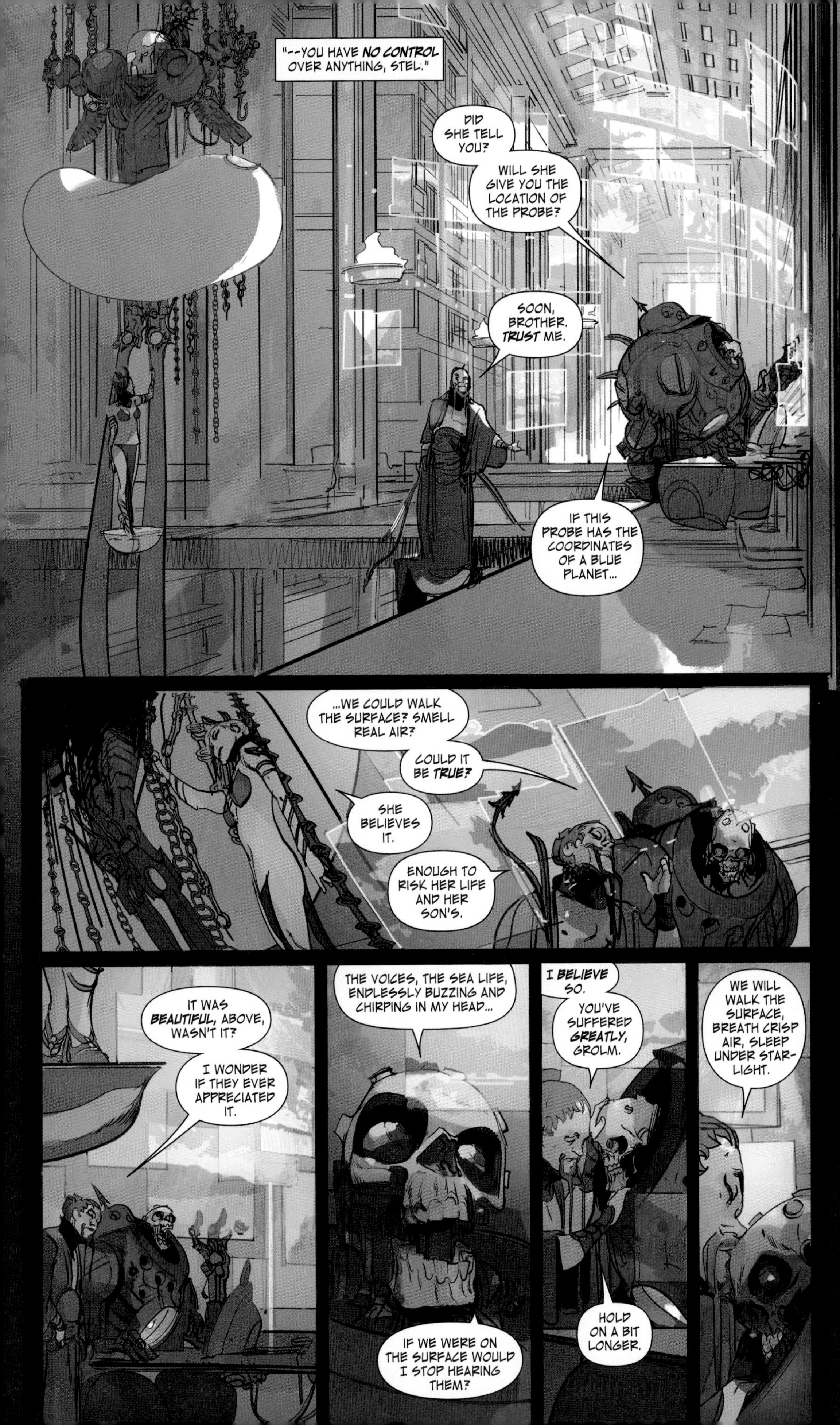
"--YOU HAVE **NO CONTROL** OVER ANYTHING, STEL."
DID SHE TELL YOU?
WILL SHE GIVE YOU THE LOCATION OF THE PROBE?
SOON, BROTHER. **TRUST** ME.
IF THIS PROBE HAS THE COORDINATES OF A BLUE PLANET...
...WE COULD WALK THE SURFACE? SMELL REAL AIR?
COULD IT BE **TRUE?**
SHE BELIEVES IT.
ENOUGH TO RISK HER LIFE AND HER SON'S.
IT WAS **BEAUTIFUL,** ABOVE, WASN'T IT?
I WONDER IF THEY EVER APPRECIATED IT.
THE VOICES, THE SEA LIFE, ENDLESSLY BUZZING AND CHIRPING IN MY HEAD...
IF WE WERE ON THE SURFACE WOULD I STOP HEARING THEM?
I **BELIEVE** SO.
YOU'VE SUFFERED **GREATLY,** GROLM.
HOLD ON A BIT LONGER.
WE WILL WALK THE SURFACE, BREATH CRISP AIR, SLEEP UNDER STAR-LIGHT.

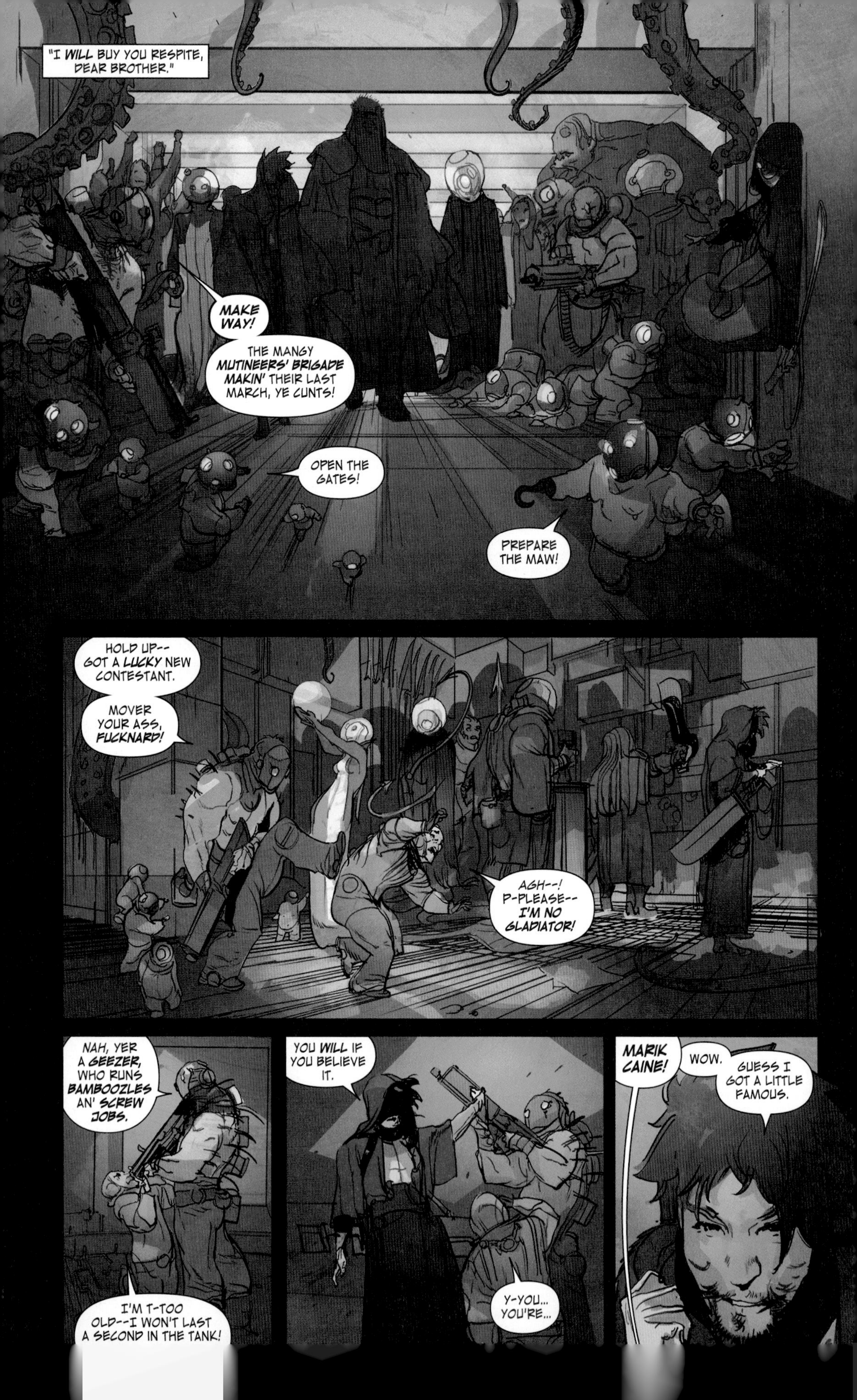
"I WILL BUY YOU RESPITE, DEAR BROTHER."
MAKE WAY!
THE MANGY MUTINEERS' BRIGADE MAKIN' THEIR LAST MARCH, YE CUNTS!
OPEN THE GATES!
PREPARE THE MAW!
HOLD UP-- GOT A LUCKY NEW CONTESTANT.
MOVER YOUR ASS, FUCKNARD!
AGH--! P-PLEASE-- I'M NO GLADIATOR!
NAH, YER A GEEZER, WHO RUNS BAMBOOZLES AN' SCREW JOBS.
I'M T-TOO OLD--I WON'T LAST A SECOND IN THE TANK!
YOU WILL IF YOU BELIEVE IT.
Y-YOU... YOU'RE...
MARIK CAINE!
WOW.
GUESS I GOT A LITTLE FAMOUS.

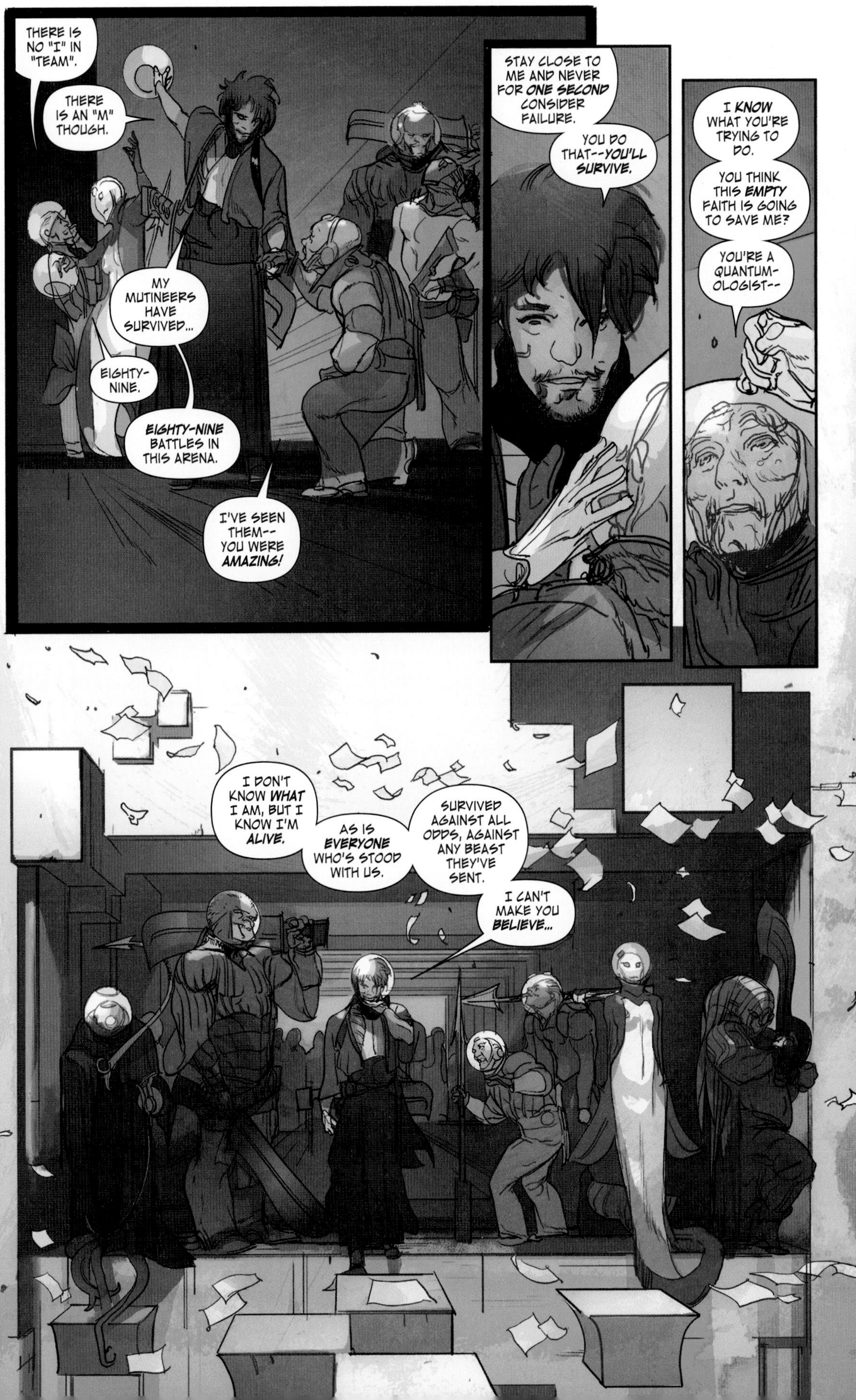
THERE IS NO "I" IN "TEAM".
THERE IS AN "M" THOUGH.
MY MUTINEERS HAVE SURVIVED...
EIGHTY-NINE.
EIGHTY-NINE BATTLES IN THIS ARENA.
I'VE SEEN THEM-- YOU WERE AMAZING!
STAY CLOSE TO ME AND NEVER FOR ONE SECOND CONSIDER FAILURE.
YOU DO THAT--YOU'LL SURVIVE.
I KNOW WHAT YOU'RE TRYING TO DO.
YOU THINK THIS EMPTY FAITH IS GOING TO SAVE ME?
YOU'RE A QUANTUM-OLOGIST--
I DON'T KNOW WHAT I AM, BUT I KNOW I'M ALIVE.
AS IS EVERYONE WHO'S STOOD WITH US.
SURVIVED AGAINST ALL ODDS, AGAINST ANY BEAST THEY'VE SENT.
I CAN'T MAKE YOU BELIEVE...

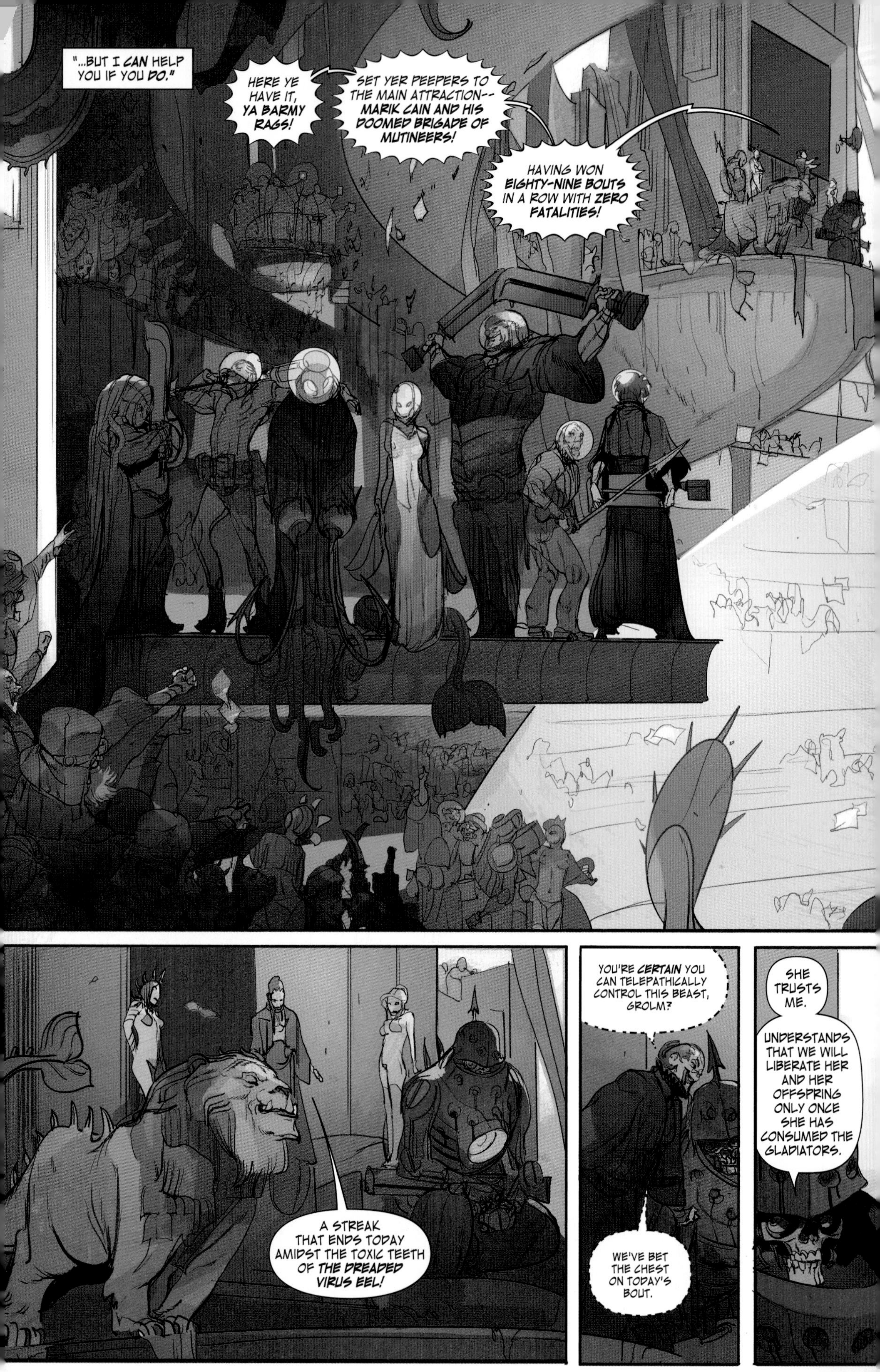
"...BUT I CAN HELP YOU IF YOU DO."
HERE YE HAVE IT, YA BARMY RAGS!
SET YER PEEPERS TO THE MAIN ATTRACTION-- MARIK CAIN AND HIS DOOMED BRIGADE OF MUTINEERS!
HAVING WON EIGHTY-NINE BOUTS IN A ROW WITH ZERO FATALITIES!
A STREAK THAT ENDS TODAY AMIDST THE TOXIC TEETH OF THE DREADED VIRUS EEL!
YOU'RE CERTAIN YOU CAN TELEPATHICALLY CONTROL THIS BEAST, GROLM?
WE'VE BET THE CHEST ON TODAY'S BOUT.
SHE TRUSTS ME.
UNDERSTANDS THAT WE WILL LIBERATE HER AND HER OFFSPRING ONLY ONCE SHE HAS CONSUMED THE GLADIATORS.

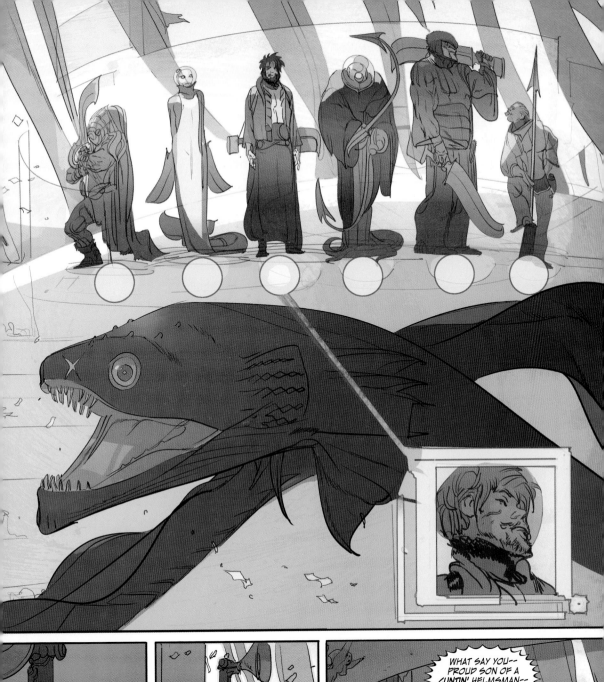

MARIK'S BELOVED STATUS AMONG THE PEOPLE ENSURES THEY WILL WAGER ON *HIS* SURVIVAL.

BUNG THIS FOR HIM AN' WE'LL BE *MINTED.*

GOOD PEOPLE OF POLUMA!

WE HAVE BEFORE US A NOBLE, BLUE-BLOODED SON OF SALUS, COME TA PERISH SPECTACULARLY FOR *YOUR* ENTERTAINMENT!

WHAT SAY YOU-- PROUD SON OF A *CUNTIN'* HELMSMAN-- ARE YE PREPARED TO *DIE?*

ANYTHING BUT ANOTHER MINUTE LISTENING TO YOU *FEIGN* THE COMMON TONGUE, YOUR "LORDSHIP".

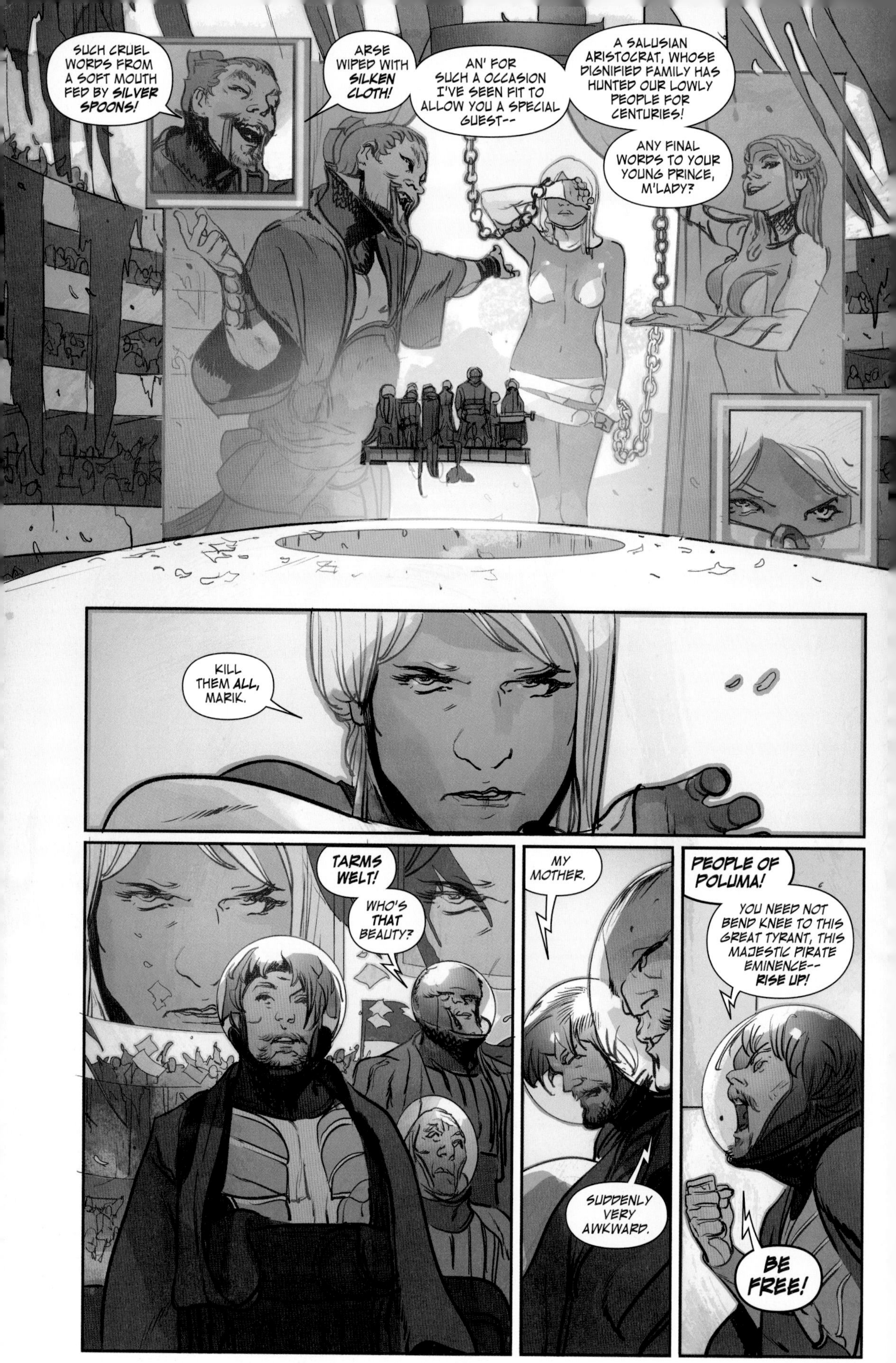
SUCH CRUEL WORDS FROM A SOFT MOUTH FED BY SILVER SPOONS!
ARSE WIPED WITH SILKEN CLOTH!
AN' FOR SUCH A OCCASION I'VE SEEN FIT TO ALLOW YOU A SPECIAL GUEST--
A SALUSIAN ARISTOCRAT, WHOSE DIGNIFIED FAMILY HAS HUNTED OUR LOWLY PEOPLE FOR CENTURIES!
ANY FINAL WORDS TO YOUR YOUNG PRINCE, M'LADY?
KILL THEM ALL, MARIK.
TARMS WELT!
WHO'S THAT BEAUTY?
MY MOTHER.
SUDDENLY VERY AWKWARD.
PEOPLE OF POLUMA!
YOU NEED NOT BEND KNEE TO THIS GREAT TYRANT, THIS MAJESTIC PIRATE EMINENCE-- RISE UP!
BE FREE!

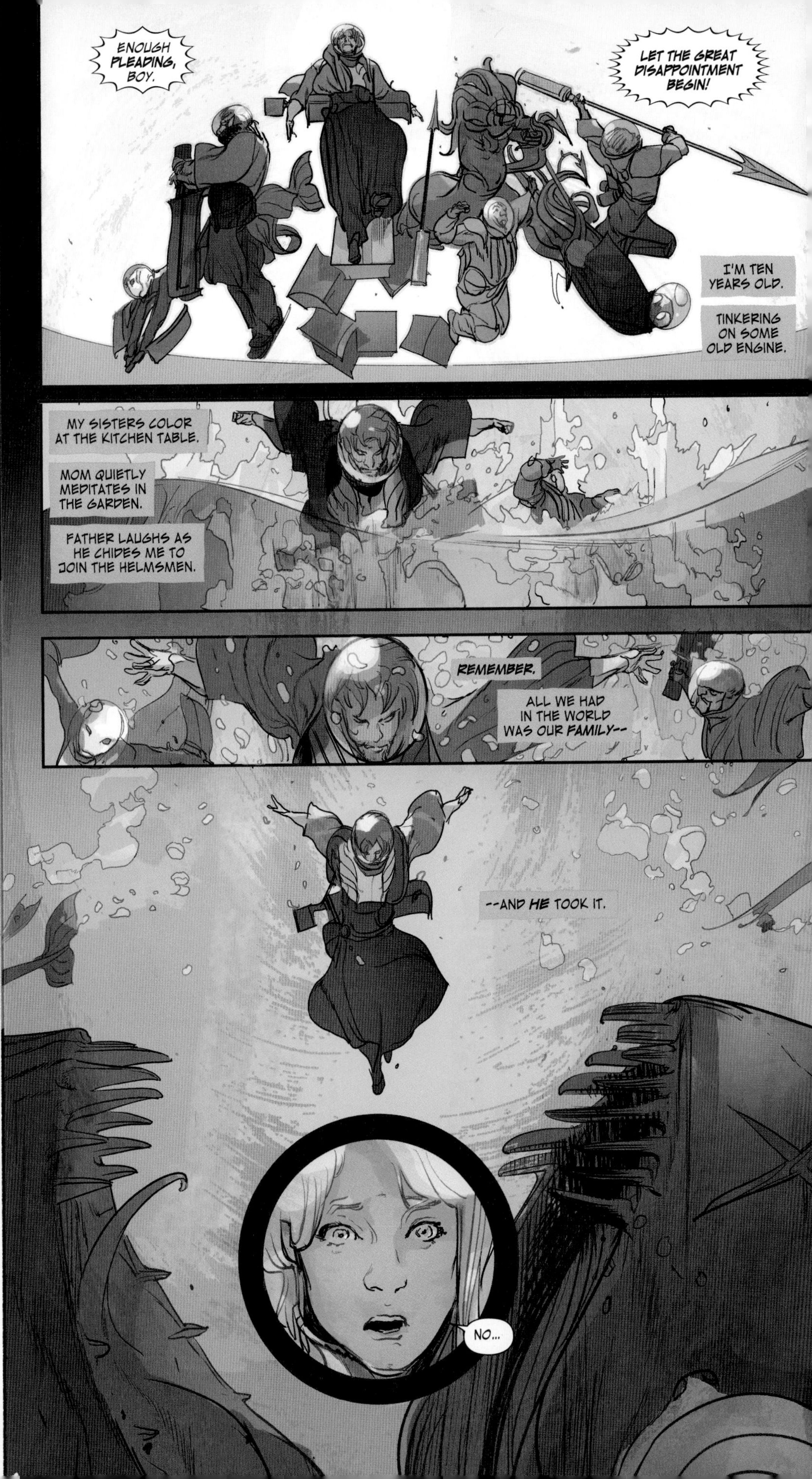
ENOUGH PLEADING, BOY.
LET THE GREAT DISAPPOINTMENT BEGIN!
I'M TEN YEARS OLD.
TINKERING ON SOME OLD ENGINE.
MY SISTERS COLOR AT THE KITCHEN TABLE.
MOM QUIETLY MEDITATES IN THE GARDEN.
FATHER LAUGHS AS HE CHIDES ME TO JOIN THE HELMSMEN.
REMEMBER.
ALL WE HAD IN THE WORLD WAS OUR FAMILY--
--AND HE TOOK IT.
NO...

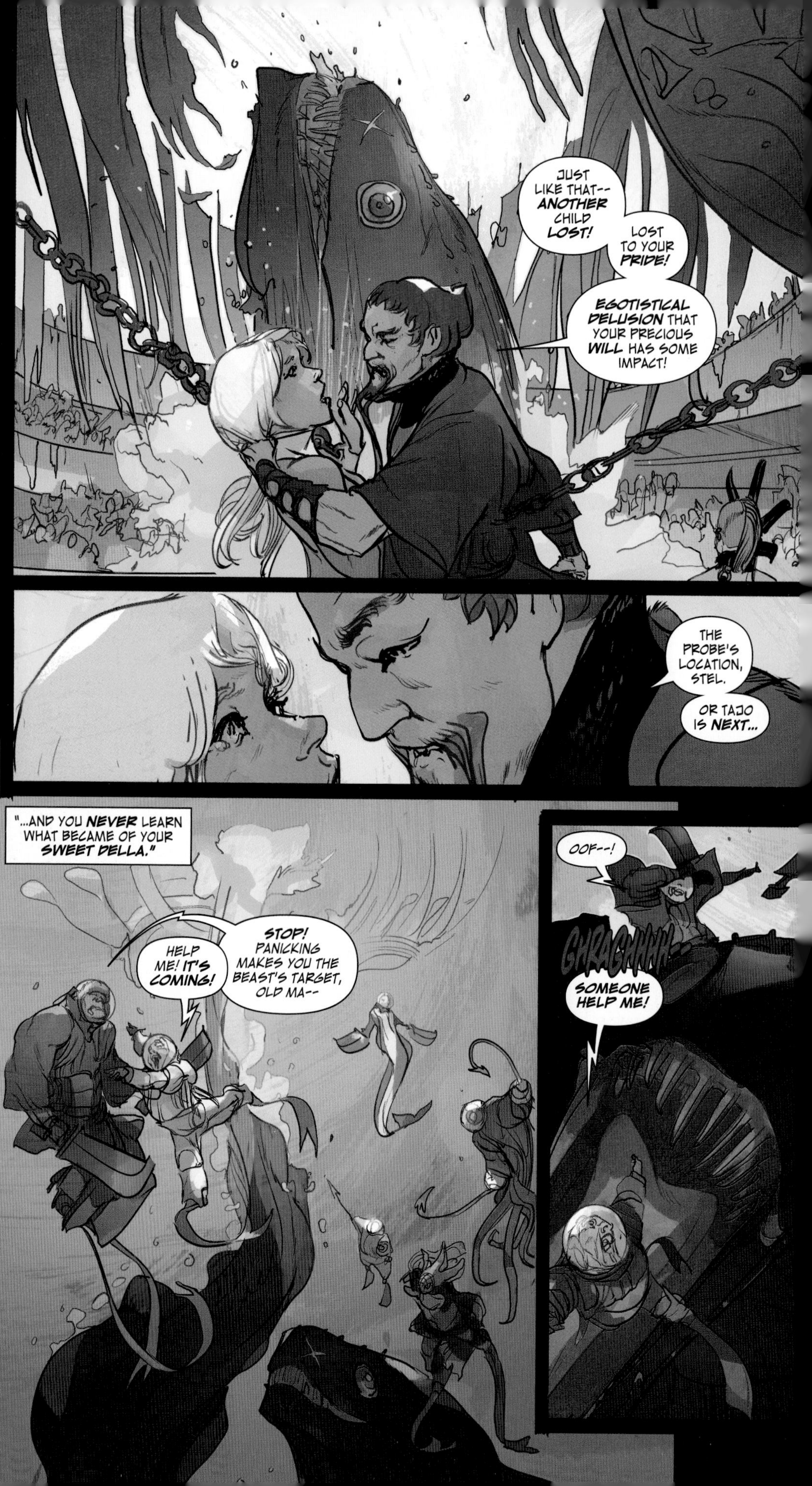
JUST LIKE THAT-- ANOTHER CHILD LOST!
LOST TO YOUR PRIDE!
EGOTISTICAL DELUSION THAT YOUR PRECIOUS WILL HAS SOME IMPACT!
THE PROBE'S LOCATION, STEL.
OR TAJO IS NEXT...
"...AND YOU NEVER LEARN WHAT BECAME OF YOUR SWEET DELLA."
HELP ME! IT'S COMING!
STOP! PANICKING MAKES YOU THE BEAST'S TARGET, OLD MA--
OOF--!
GHRAGHHHH--
SOMEONE HELP ME!

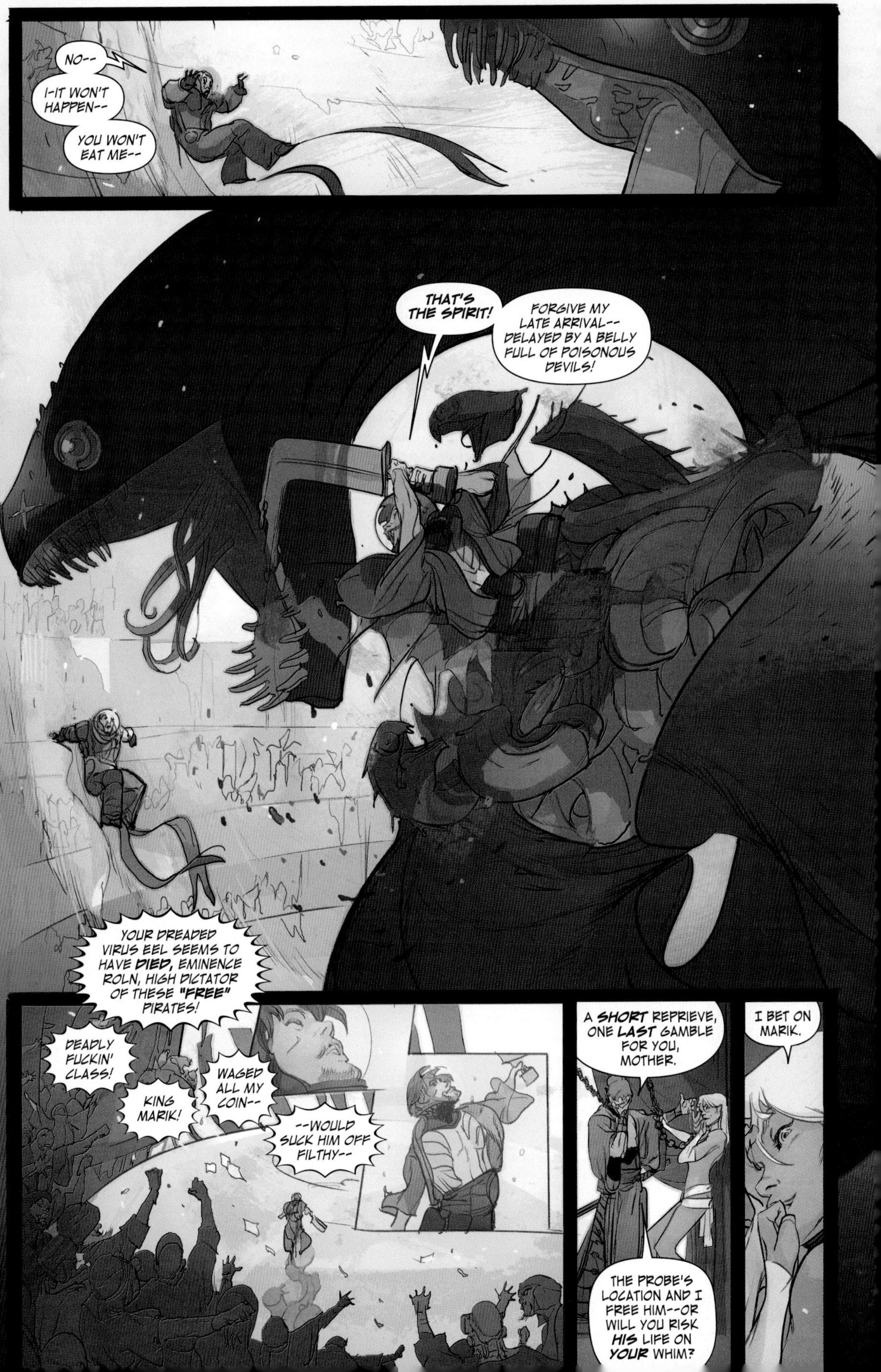
NO--
I-IT WON'T HAPPEN--
YOU WON'T EAT ME--
THAT'S THE SPIRIT!
FORGIVE MY LATE ARRIVAL--DELAYED BY A BELLY FULL OF POISONOUS DEVILS!
YOUR DREADED VIRUS EEL SEEMS TO HAVE DIED, EMINENCE ROLN, HIGH DICTATOR OF THESE "FREE" PIRATES!
DEADLY FUCKIN' CLASS!
KING MARIK!
WAGED ALL MY COIN--
--WOULD SUCK HIM OFF FILTHY--
A SHORT REPRIEVE, ONE LAST GAMBLE FOR YOU, MOTHER.
THE PROBE'S LOCATION AND I FREE HIM--OR WILL YOU RISK HIS LIFE ON YOUR WHIM?
I BET ON MARIK.

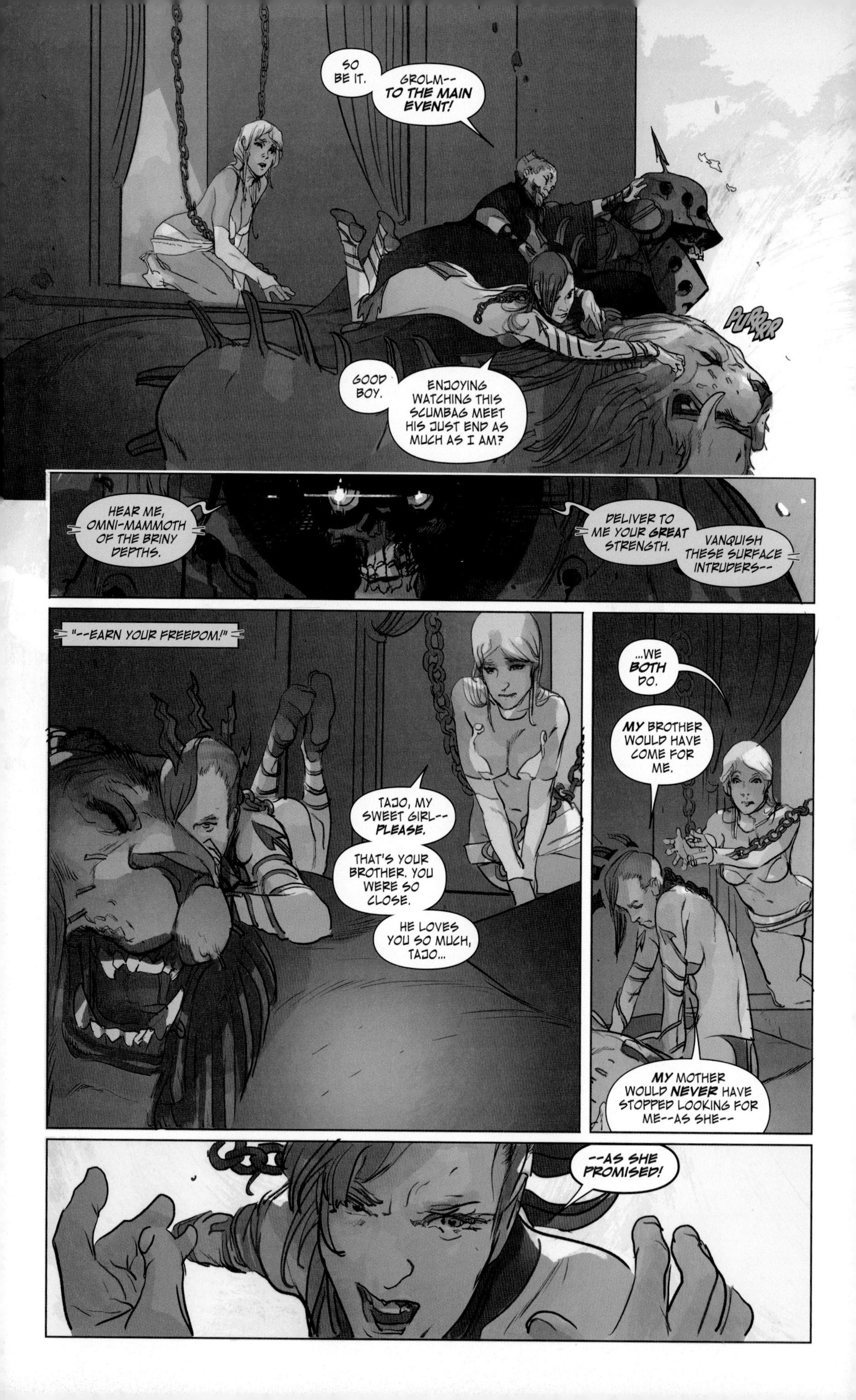
SO BE IT.
GROLM-- TO THE MAIN EVENT!
PURRR
GOOD BOY.
ENJOYING WATCHING THIS SCUMBAG MEET HIS JUST END AS MUCH AS I AM?
HEAR ME, OMNI-MAMMOTH OF THE BRINY DEPTHS.
DELIVER TO ME YOUR GREAT STRENGTH.
VANQUISH THESE SURFACE INTRUDERS--
"--EARN YOUR FREEDOM!"
TAJO, MY SWEET GIRL-- PLEASE.
THAT'S YOUR BROTHER. YOU WERE SO CLOSE.
HE LOVES YOU SO MUCH, TAJO...
...WE BOTH DO.
MY BROTHER WOULD HAVE COME FOR ME.
MY MOTHER WOULD NEVER HAVE STOPPED LOOKING FOR ME--AS SHE--
--AS SHE PROMISED!

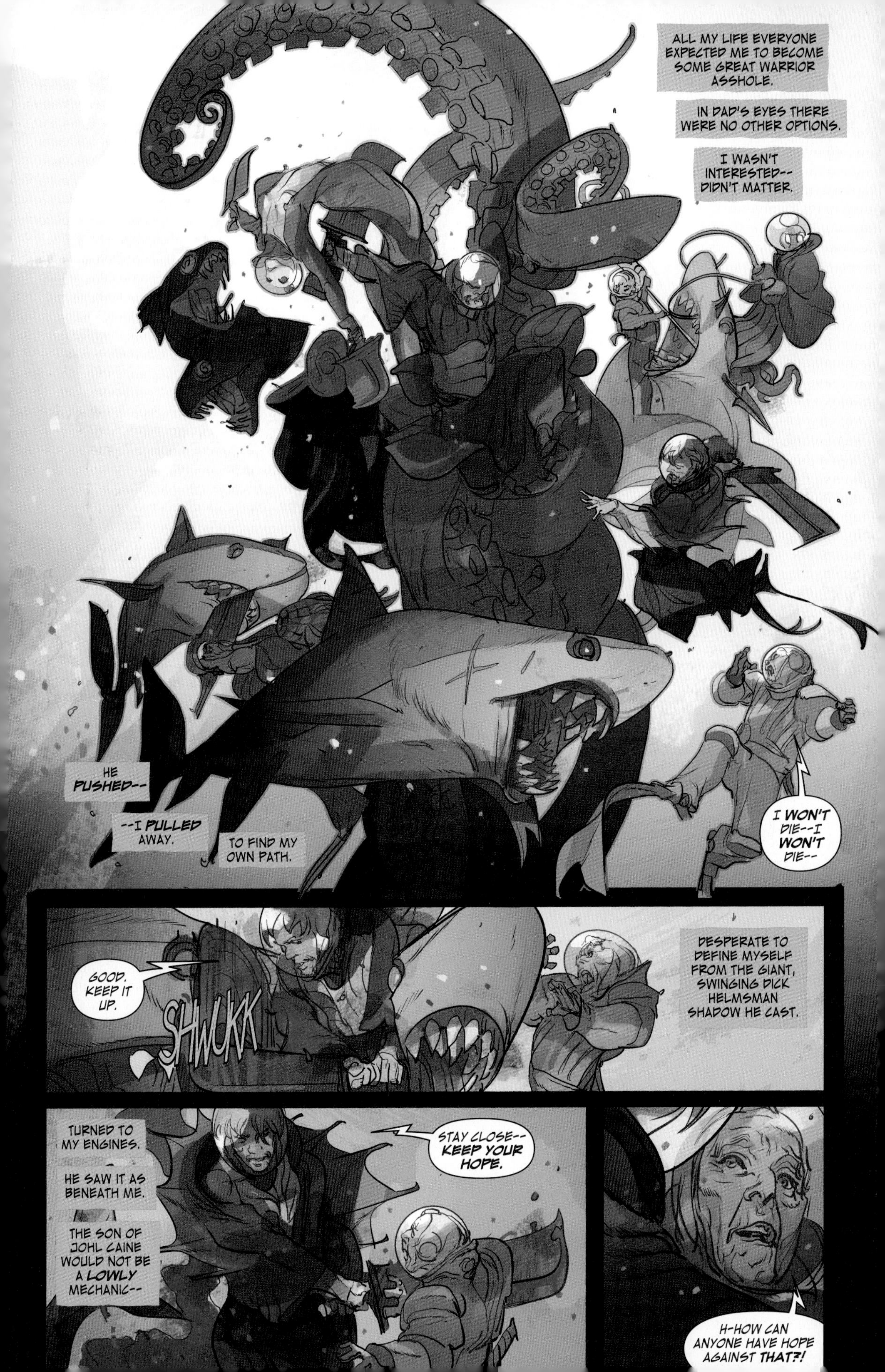
ALL MY LIFE EVERYONE EXPECTED ME TO BECOME SOME GREAT WARRIOR ASSHOLE.
IN DAD'S EYES THERE WERE NO OTHER OPTIONS.
I WASN'T INTERESTED--DIDN'T MATTER.
HE PUSHED--
--I PULLED AWAY.
TO FIND MY OWN PATH.
I WON'T DIE--I WON'T DIE--
GOOD. KEEP IT UP.
SHWUKK
DESPERATE TO DEFINE MYSELF FROM THE GIANT, SWINGING DICK HELMSMAN SHADOW HE CAST.
TURNED TO MY ENGINES.
HE SAW IT AS BENEATH ME.
THE SON OF JOHL CAINE WOULD NOT BE A LOWLY MECHANIC--
STAY CLOSE--KEEP YOUR HOPE.
H-HOW CAN ANYONE HAVE HOPE AGAINST THAT?!

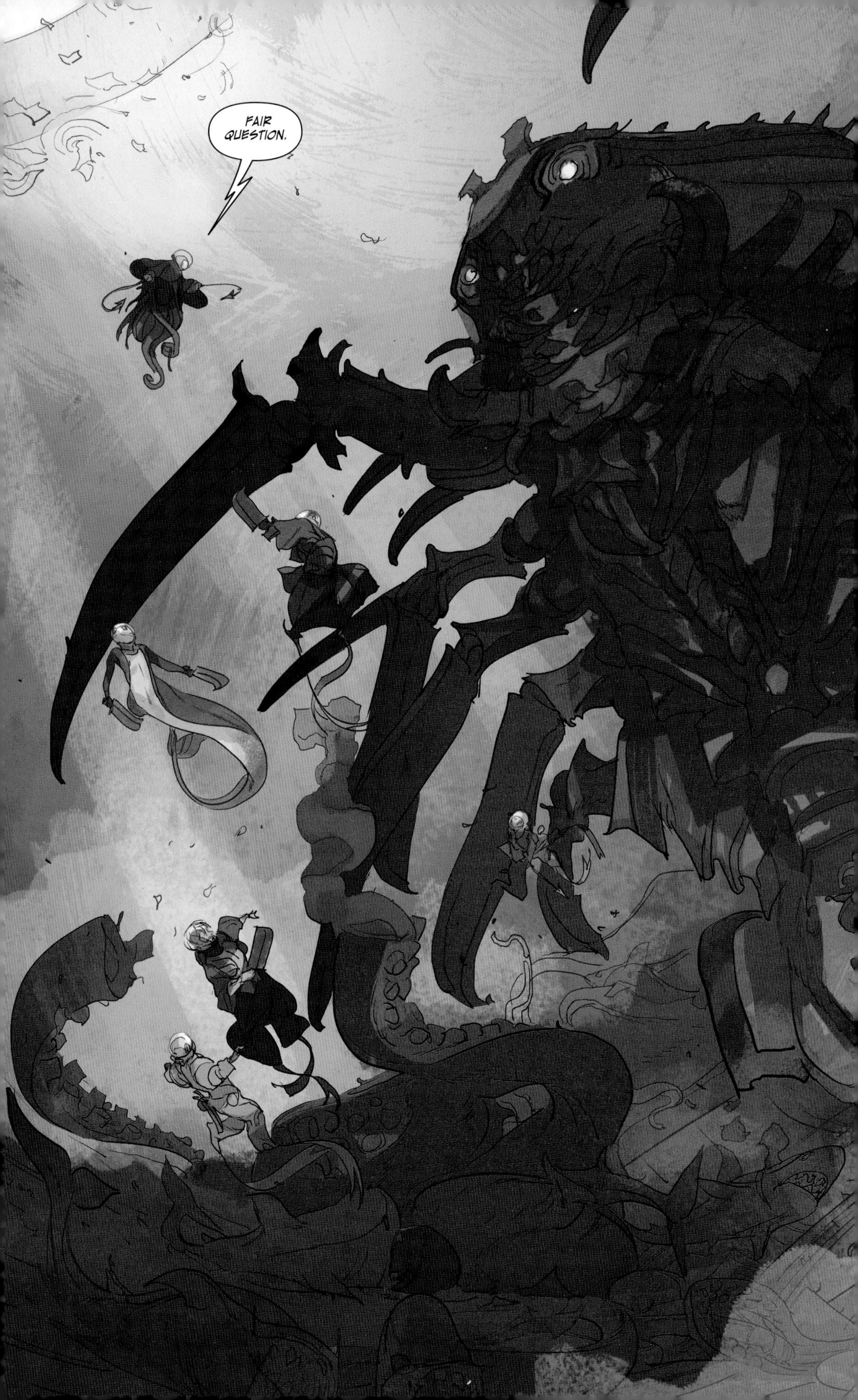
FAIR QUESTION.

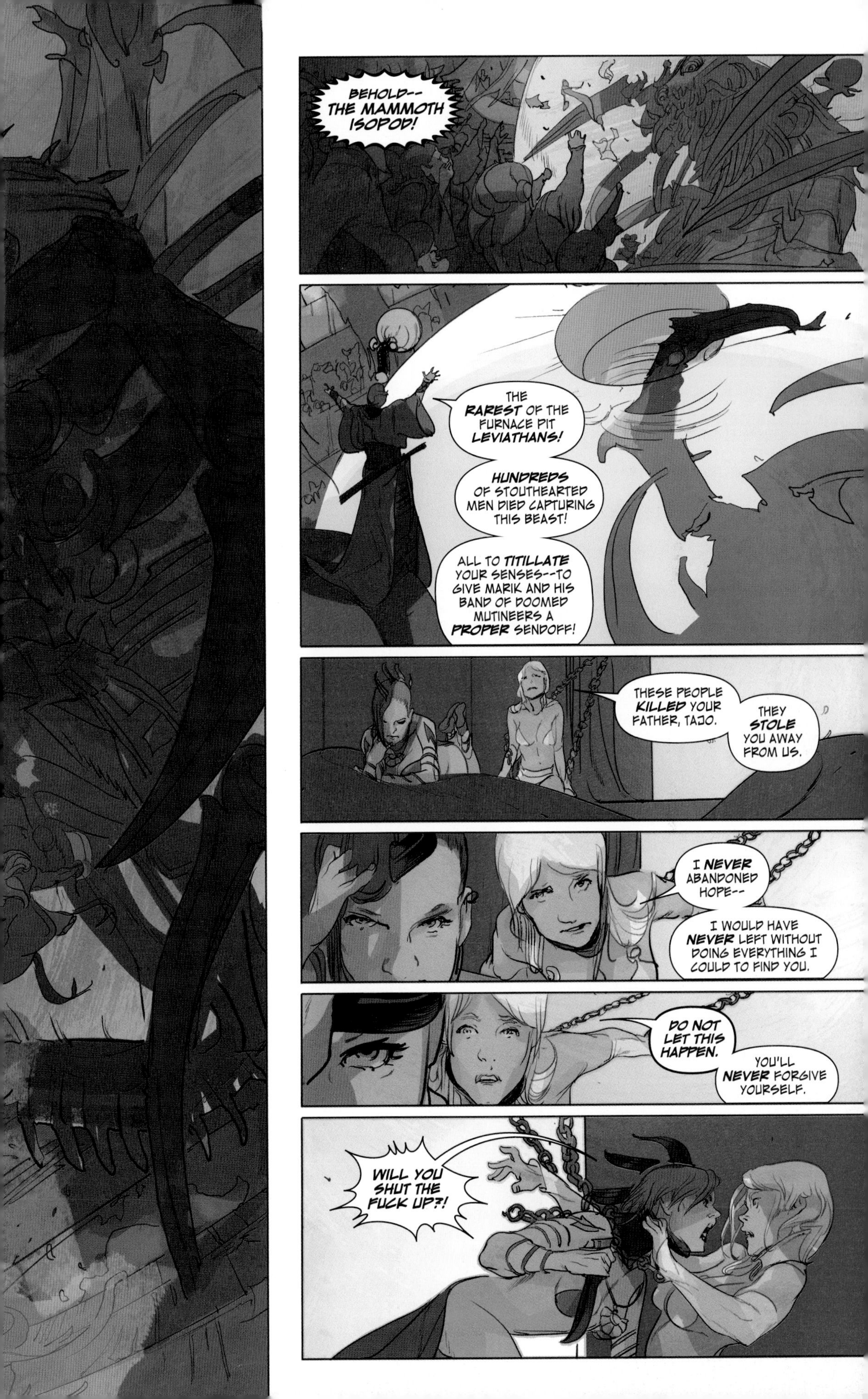
BEHOLD-- THE MAMMOTH ISOPOD!
THE RAREST OF THE FURNACE PIT LEVIATHANS!
HUNDREDS OF STOUTHEARTED MEN DIED CAPTURING THIS BEAST!
ALL TO TITILLATE YOUR SENSES--TO GIVE MARIK AND HIS BAND OF DOOMED MUTINEERS A PROPER SENDOFF!
THESE PEOPLE KILLED YOUR FATHER, TAJO.
THEY STOLE YOU AWAY FROM US.
I NEVER ABANDONED HOPE--
I WOULD HAVE NEVER LEFT WITHOUT DOING EVERYTHING I COULD TO FIND YOU.
DO NOT LET THIS HAPPEN.
YOU'LL NEVER FORGIVE YOURSELF.
WILL YOU SHUT THE FUCK UP?!

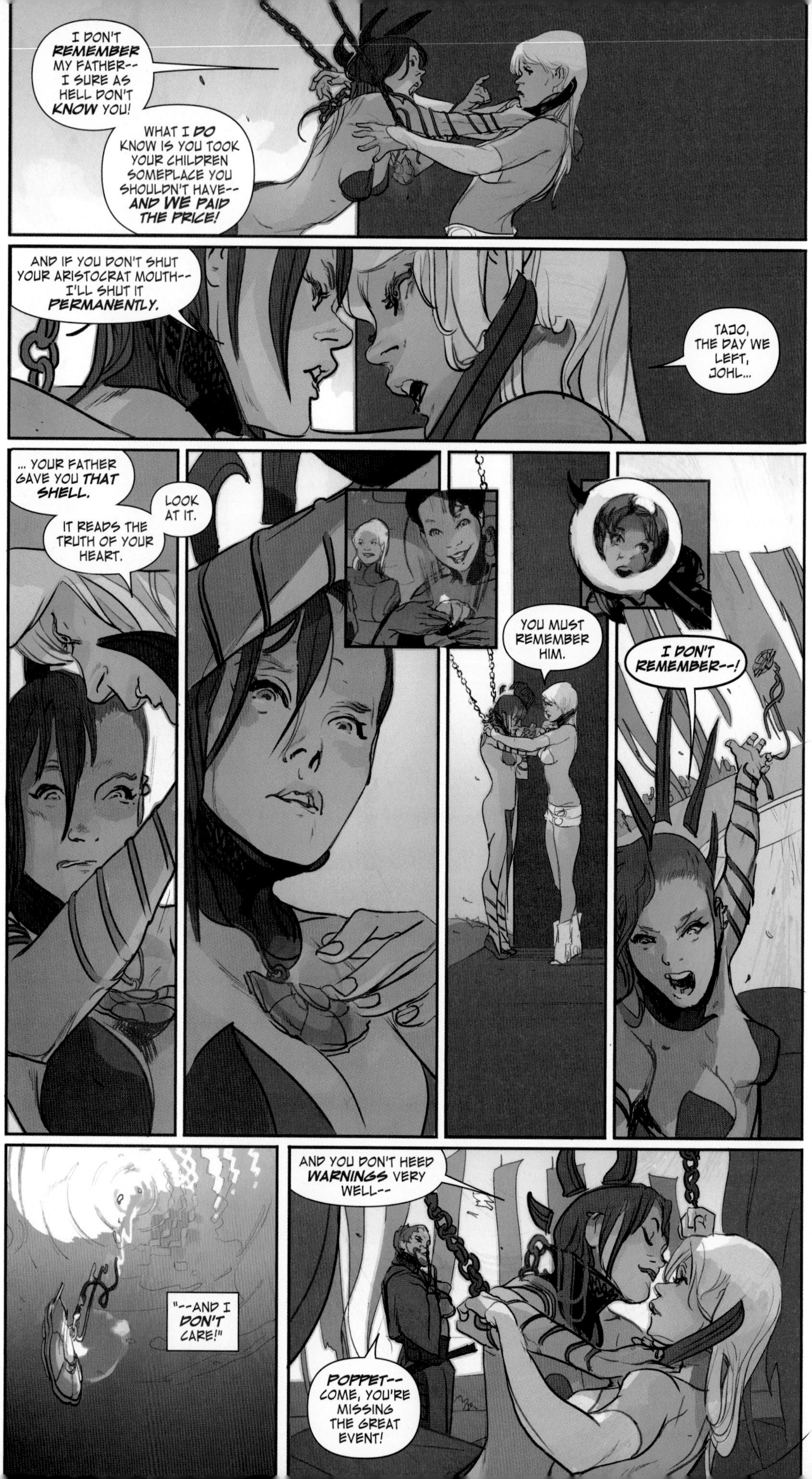
I DON'T REMEMBER MY FATHER-- I SURE AS HELL DON'T KNOW YOU!
WHAT I DO KNOW IS YOU TOOK YOUR CHILDREN SOMEPLACE YOU SHOULDN'T HAVE-- AND WE PAID THE PRICE!
AND IF YOU DON'T SHUT YOUR ARISTOCRAT MOUTH-- I'LL SHUT IT PERMANENTLY.
TAJO, THE DAY WE LEFT, JOHL...
... YOUR FATHER GAVE YOU THAT SHELL.
IT READS THE TRUTH OF YOUR HEART.
LOOK AT IT.
YOU MUST REMEMBER HIM.
I DON'T REMEMBER--!
"--AND I DON'T CARE!"
AND YOU DON'T HEED WARNINGS VERY WELL--
POPPET-- COME, YOU'RE MISSING THE GREAT EVENT!

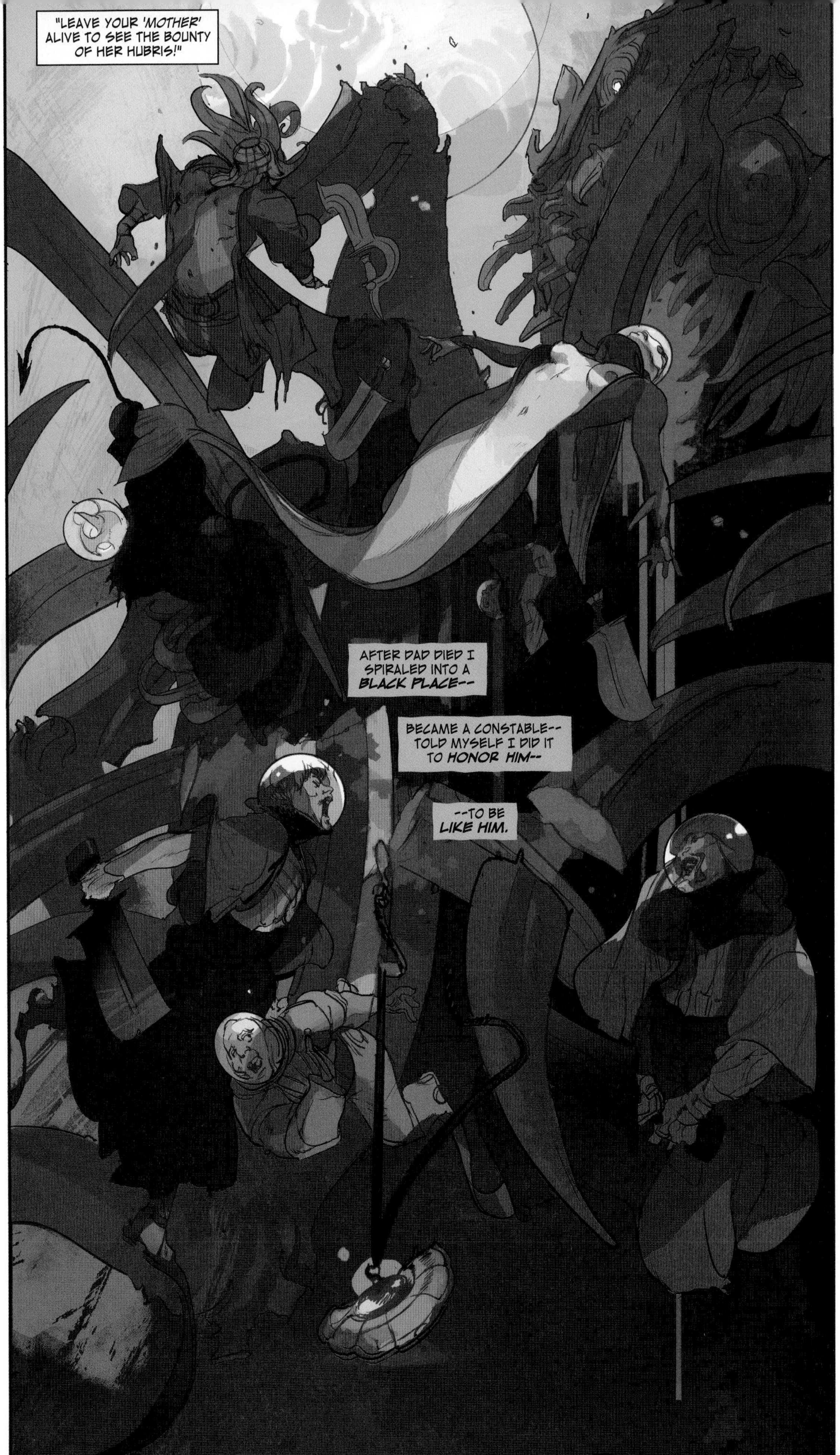
"LEAVE YOUR 'MOTHER' ALIVE TO SEE THE BOUNTY OF HER HUBRIS!"
AFTER DAD DIED I SPIRALED INTO A BLACK PLACE--
BECAME A CONSTABLE--TOLD MYSELF I DID IT TO HONOR HIM--
--TO BE LIKE HIM.

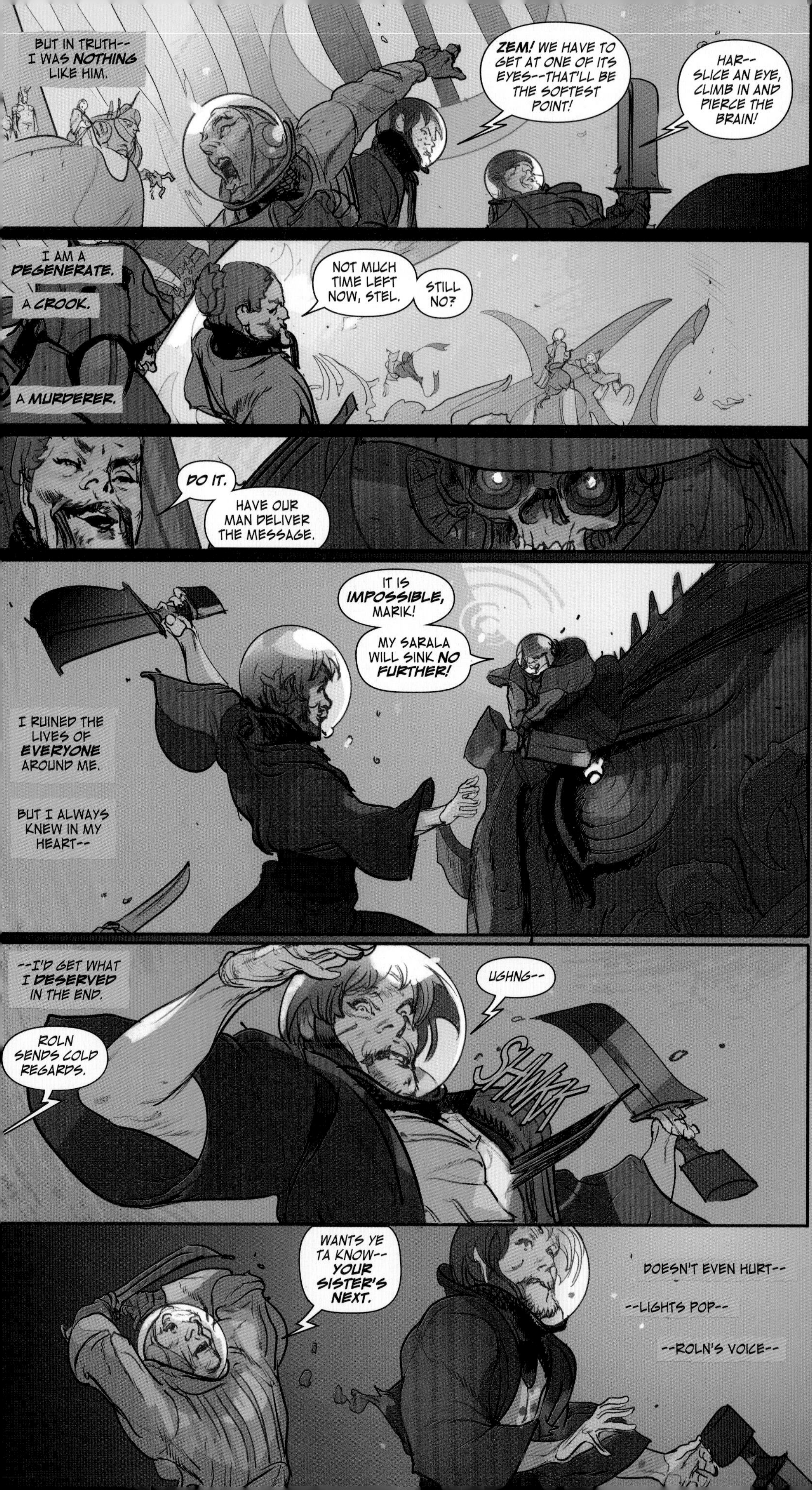
BUT IN TRUTH-- I WAS NOTHING LIKE HIM.
ZEM! WE HAVE TO GET AT ONE OF ITS EYES--THAT'LL BE THE SOFTEST POINT!
HAR-- SLICE AN EYE, CLIMB IN AND PIERCE THE BRAIN!
I AM A DEGENERATE.
A CROOK.
NOT MUCH TIME LEFT NOW, STEL.
STILL NO?
A MURDERER.
DO IT.
HAVE OUR MAN DELIVER THE MESSAGE.
IT IS IMPOSSIBLE, MARIK!
MY SARALA WILL SINK NO FURTHER!
I RUINED THE LIVES OF EVERYONE AROUND ME.
BUT I ALWAYS KNEW IN MY HEART--
--I'D GET WHAT I DESERVED IN THE END.
UGHNG--
ROLN SENDS COLD REGARDS.
SHNKK
WANTS YE TA KNOW-- YOUR SISTER'S NEXT.
DOESN'T EVEN HURT--
--LIGHTS POP--
--ROLN'S VOICE--

"WHAT DID YOU THINK I WAS GOING TO DO WITH YOU, BOY?"

RAHHGH--!

COWARD!

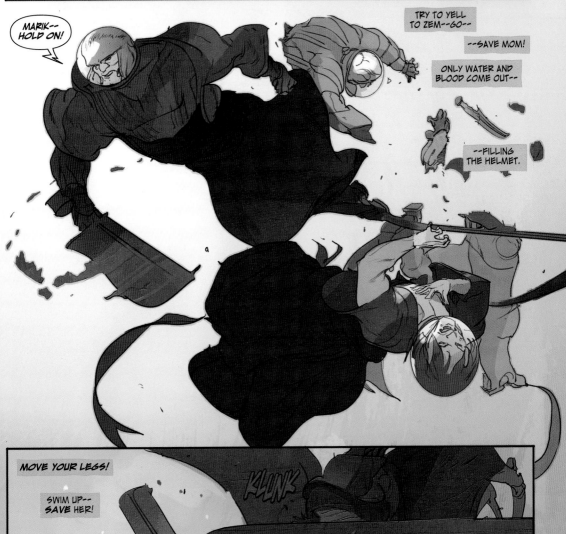

MARIK-- HOLD ON!

TRY TO YELL TO ZEM--GO--

--SAVE MOM!

ONLY WATER AND BLOOD COME OUT--

--FILLING THE HELMET.

MOVE YOUR LEGS!

SWIM UP-- SAVE HER!

KLUNK

OOF!

NO RESPONSE--

NO RETURNING FROM THIS--

AFTER A LIFE OF *FAILING* AT *EVERY* THING I EVER DID--

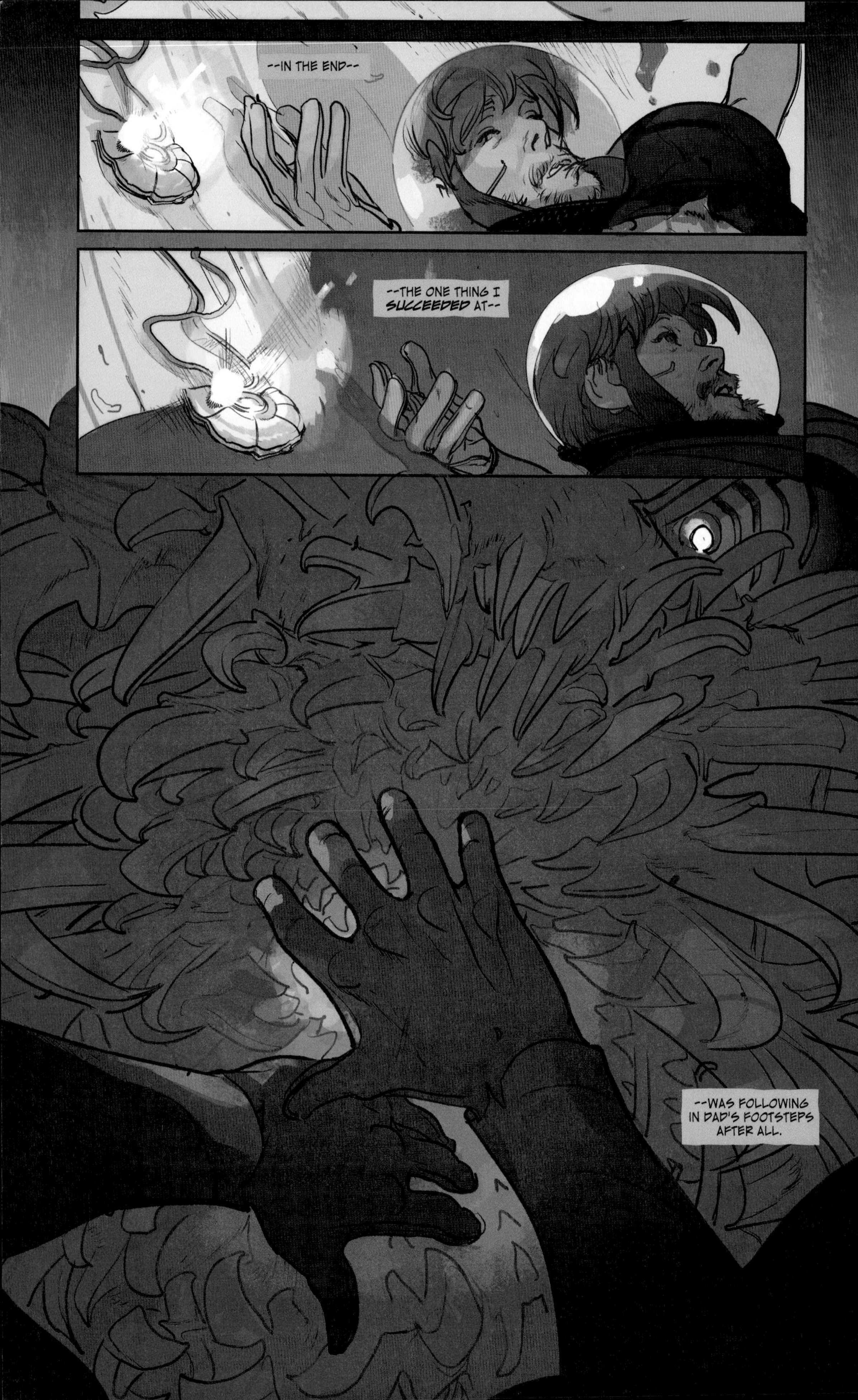
--IN THE END--
--THE ONE THING I SUCCEEDED AT--
--WAS FOLLOWING IN DAD'S FOOTSTEPS AFTER ALL.

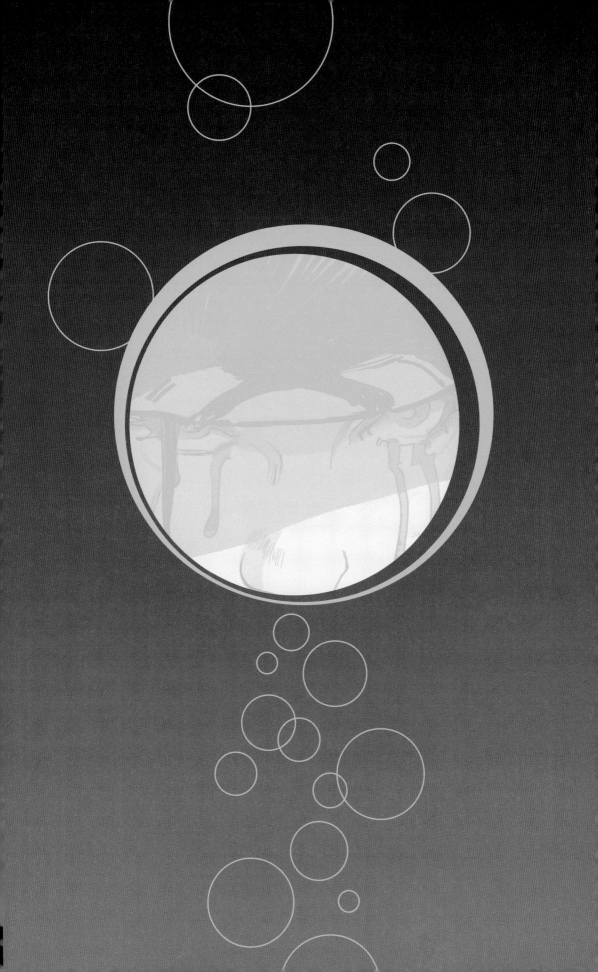

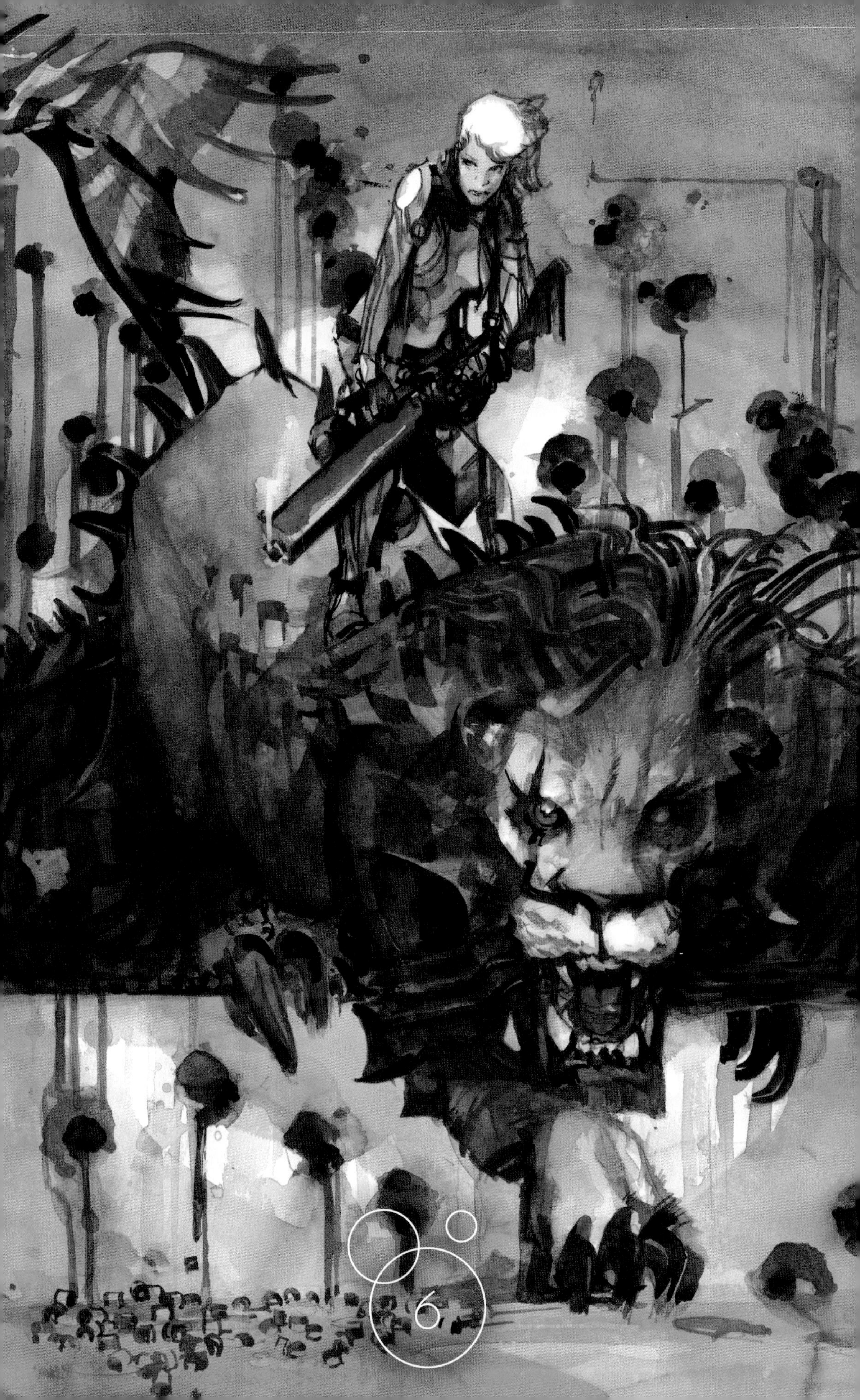
6

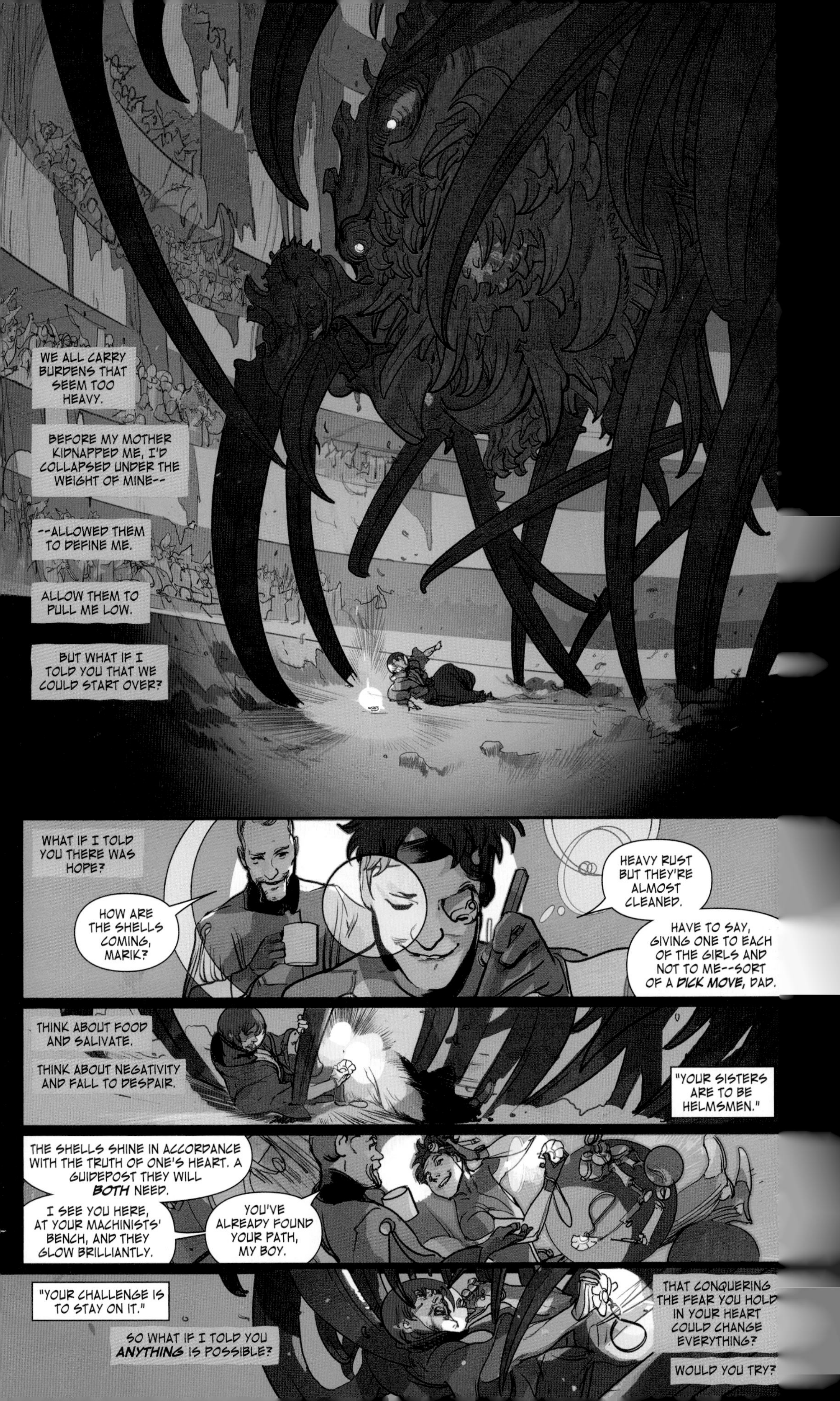

WE ALL CARRY BURDENS THAT SEEM TOO HEAVY.
BEFORE MY MOTHER KIDNAPPED ME, I'D COLLAPSED UNDER THE WEIGHT OF MINE--
--ALLOWED THEM TO DEFINE ME.
ALLOW THEM TO PULL ME LOW.
BUT WHAT IF I TOLD YOU THAT WE COULD START OVER?
WHAT IF I TOLD YOU THERE WAS HOPE?
HOW ARE THE SHELLS COMING, MARIK?
HEAVY RUST BUT THEY'RE ALMOST CLEANED.
HAVE TO SAY, GIVING ONE TO EACH OF THE GIRLS AND NOT TO ME--SORT OF A DICK MOVE, DAD.
THINK ABOUT FOOD AND SALIVATE.
THINK ABOUT NEGATIVITY AND FALL TO DESPAIR.
"YOUR SISTERS ARE TO BE HELMSMEN."
THE SHELLS SHINE IN ACCORDANCE WITH THE TRUTH OF ONE'S HEART. A GUIDEPOST THEY WILL BOTH NEED.
I SEE YOU HERE, AT YOUR MACHINISTS' BENCH, AND THEY GLOW BRILLIANTLY.
YOU'VE ALREADY FOUND YOUR PATH, MY BOY.
"YOUR CHALLENGE IS TO STAY ON IT."
SO WHAT IF I TOLD YOU ANYTHING IS POSSIBLE?
THAT CONQUERING THE FEAR YOU HOLD IN YOUR HEART COULD CHANGE EVERYTHING?
WOULD YOU TRY?

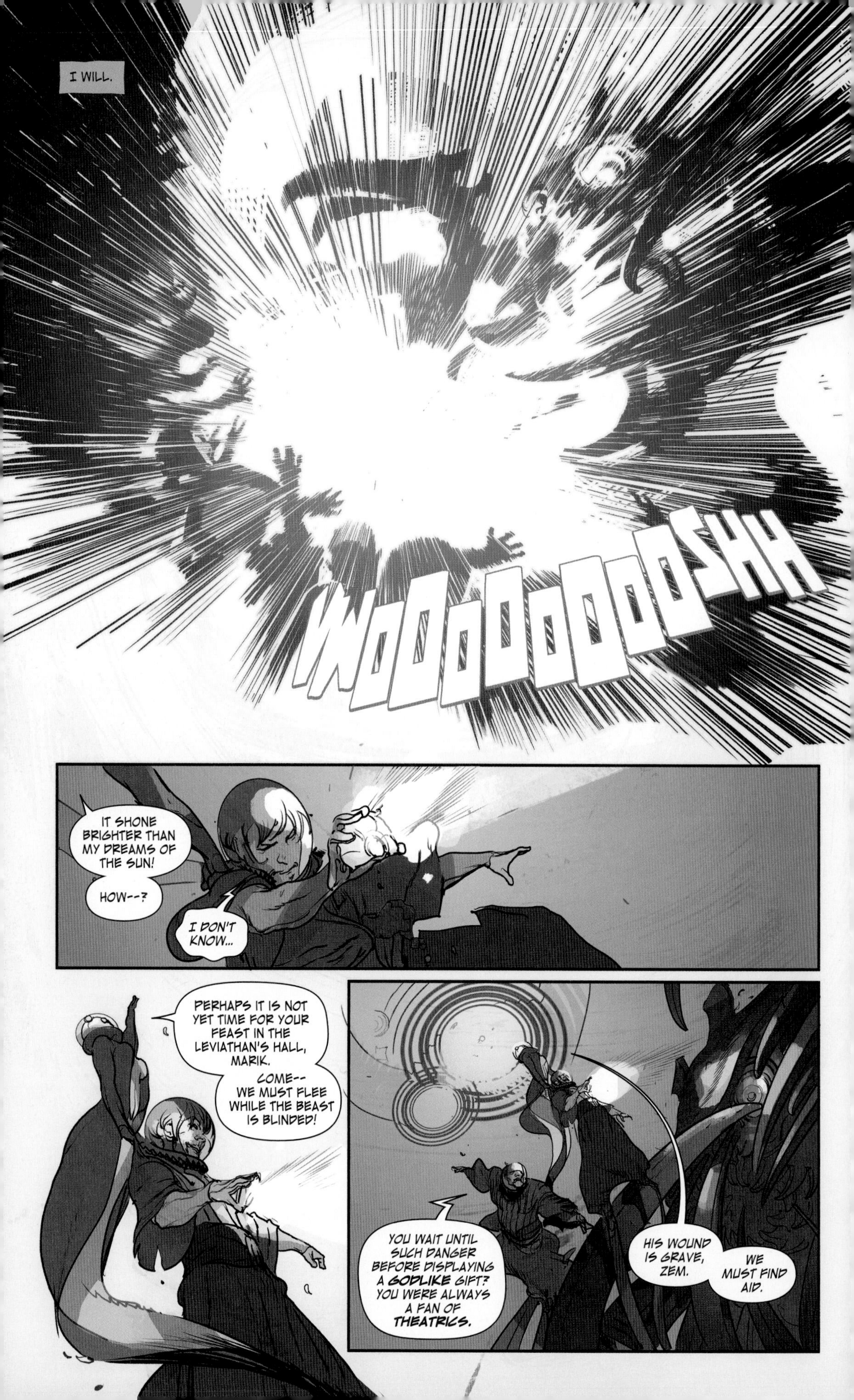
I WILL.
WOOOOOOOOOSHH
IT SHONE BRIGHTER THAN MY DREAMS OF THE SUN!
HOW--?
I DON'T KNOW...
PERHAPS IT IS NOT YET TIME FOR YOUR FEAST IN THE LEVIATHAN'S HALL, MARIK.
COME-- WE MUST FLEE WHILE THE BEAST IS BLINDED!
YOU WAIT UNTIL SUCH DANGER BEFORE DISPLAYING A GODLIKE GIFT? YOU WERE ALWAYS A FAN OF THEATRICS.
HIS WOUND IS GRAVE, ZEM.
WE MUST FIND AID.

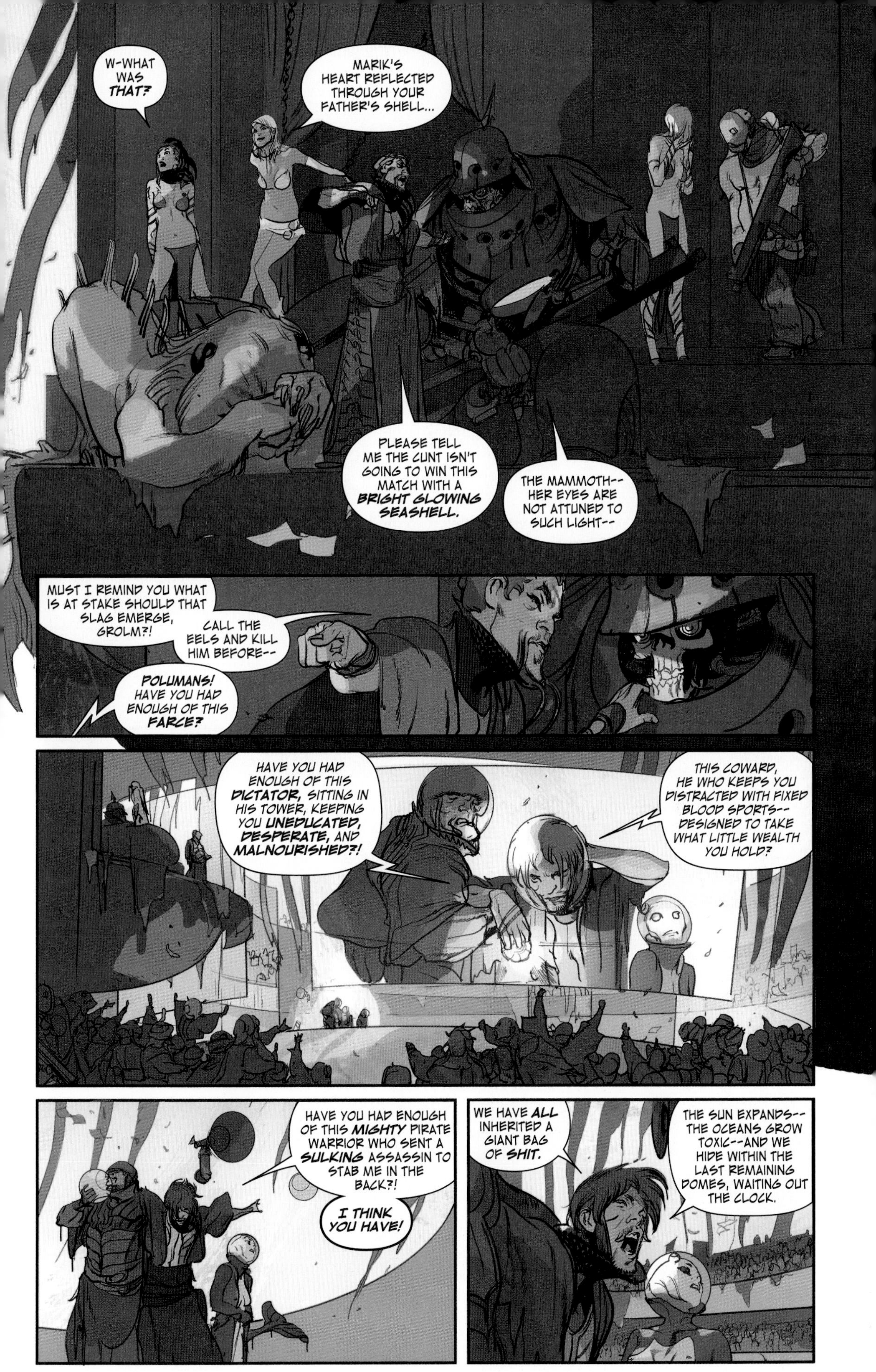
W-WHAT WAS THAT?
MARIK'S HEART REFLECTED THROUGH YOUR FATHER'S SHELL...
PLEASE TELL ME THE CUNT ISN'T GOING TO WIN THIS MATCH WITH A BRIGHT GLOWING SEASHELL.
THE MAMMOTH-- HER EYES ARE NOT ATTUNED TO SUCH LIGHT--
MUST I REMIND YOU WHAT IS AT STAKE SHOULD THAT SLAG EMERGE, GROLM?!
CALL THE EELS AND KILL HIM BEFORE--
POLUMANS! HAVE YOU HAD ENOUGH OF THIS FARCE?
HAVE YOU HAD ENOUGH OF THIS DICTATOR, SITTING IN HIS TOWER, KEEPING YOU UNEDUCATED, DESPERATE, AND MALNOURISHED?!
THIS COWARD, HE WHO KEEPS YOU DISTRACTED WITH FIXED BLOOD SPORTS-- DESIGNED TO TAKE WHAT LITTLE WEALTH YOU HOLD?
HAVE YOU HAD ENOUGH OF THIS MIGHTY PIRATE WARRIOR WHO SENT A SULKING ASSASSIN TO STAB ME IN THE BACK?!
I THINK YOU HAVE!
WE HAVE ALL INHERITED A GIANT BAG OF SHIT.
THE SUN EXPANDS-- THE OCEANS GROW TOXIC--AND WE HIDE WITHIN THE LAST REMAINING DOMES, WAITING OUT THE CLOCK.

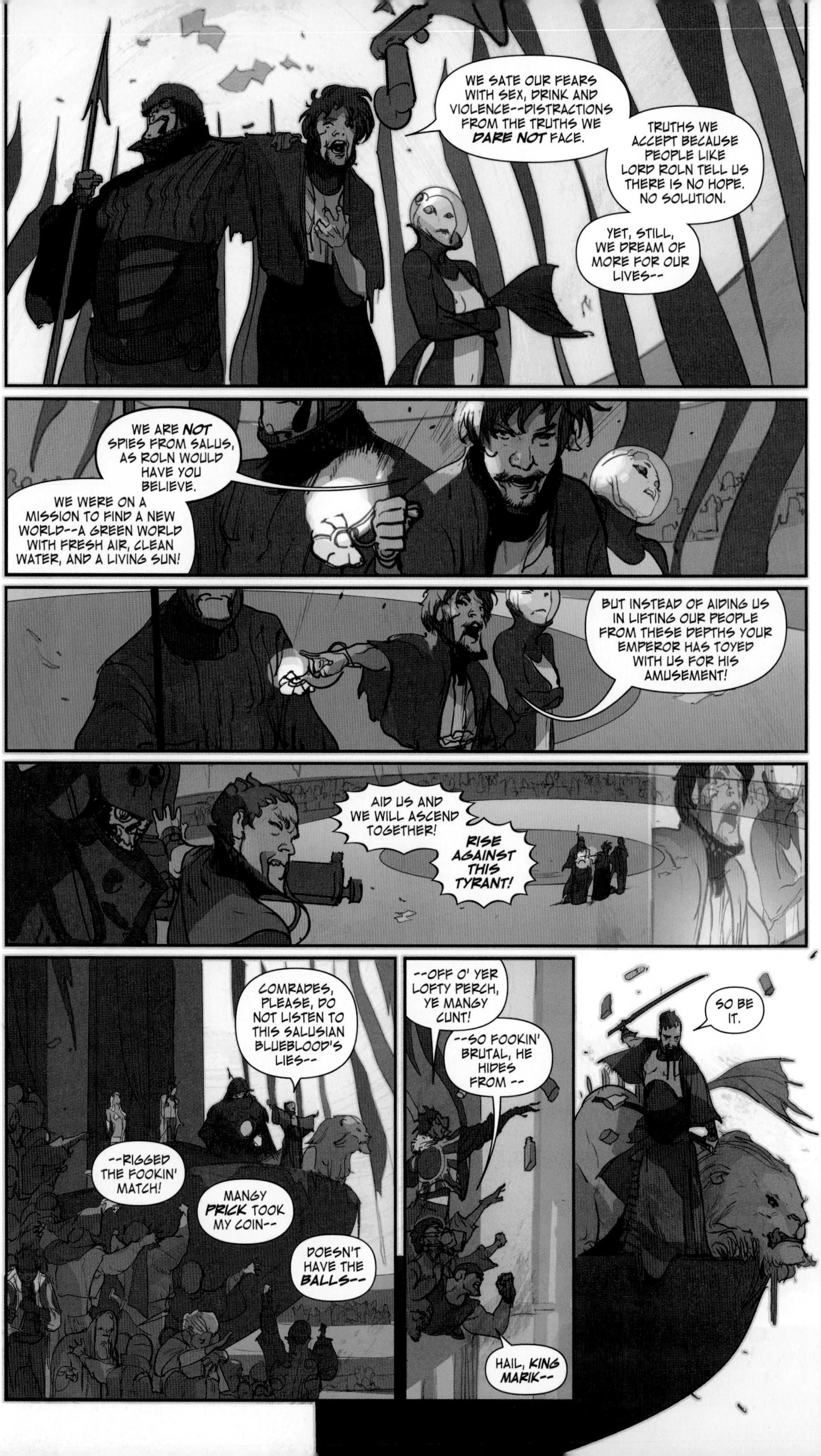
WE SATE OUR FEARS WITH SEX, DRINK AND VIOLENCE--DISTRACTIONS FROM THE TRUTHS WE **DARE NOT** FACE.
TRUTHS WE ACCEPT BECAUSE PEOPLE LIKE LORD ROLN TELL US THERE IS NO HOPE. NO SOLUTION.
YET, STILL, WE DREAM OF MORE FOR OUR LIVES--
WE ARE **NOT** SPIES FROM SALUS, AS ROLN WOULD HAVE YOU BELIEVE.
WE WERE ON A MISSION TO FIND A NEW WORLD--A GREEN WORLD WITH FRESH AIR, CLEAN WATER, AND A LIVING SUN!
BUT INSTEAD OF AIDING US IN LIFTING OUR PEOPLE FROM THESE DEPTHS YOUR EMPEROR HAS TOYED WITH US FOR HIS AMUSEMENT!
AID US AND WE WILL ASCEND TOGETHER!
**RISE AGAINST THIS TYRANT!**
COMRADES, PLEASE, DO NOT LISTEN TO THIS SALUSIAN BLUEBLOOD'S LIES--
--RIGGED THE FOOKIN' MATCH!
MANGY **PRICK** TOOK MY COIN--
DOESN'T HAVE THE **BALLS**--
--OFF O' YER LOFTY PERCH, YE MANGY CUNT!
--SO FOOKIN' BRUTAL, HE HIDES FROM --
HAIL, **KING MARIK**--
SO BE IT.

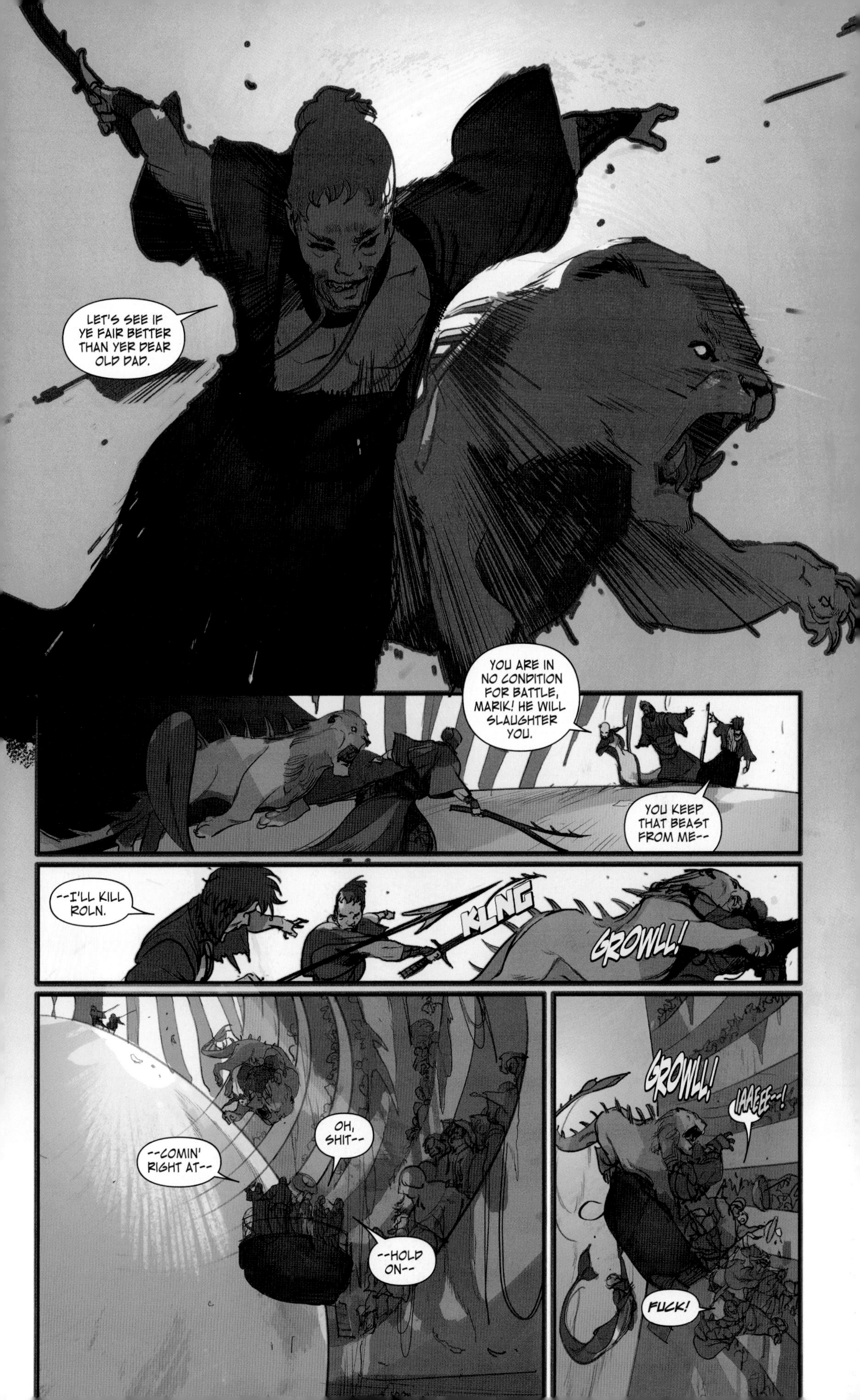
LET'S SEE IF YE FAIR BETTER THAN YER DEAR OLD DAD.
YOU ARE IN NO CONDITION FOR BATTLE, MARIK! HE WILL SLAUGHTER YOU.
YOU KEEP THAT BEAST FROM ME--
--I'LL KILL ROLN.
KLNG
GROWLL!
--COMIN' RIGHT AT--
OH, SHIT--
--HOLD ON--
GROWLL!
IAAEEE--!
FUCK!

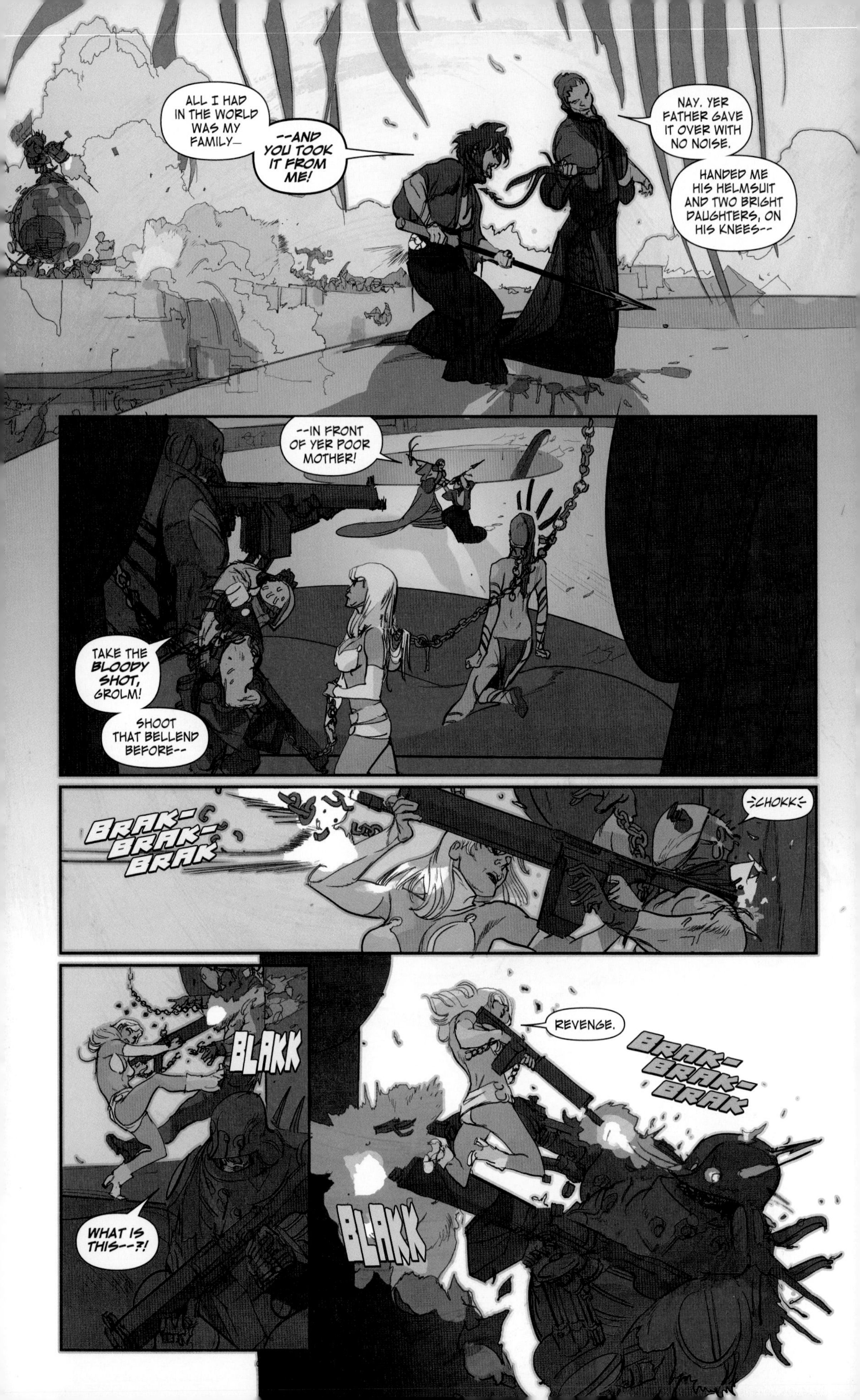
ALL I HAD IN THE WORLD WAS MY FAMILY—
--AND YOU TOOK IT FROM ME!
NAY. YER FATHER GAVE IT OVER WITH NO NOISE.
HANDED ME HIS HELMSUIT AND TWO BRIGHT DAUGHTERS, ON HIS KNEES--
--IN FRONT OF YER POOR MOTHER!
TAKE THE BLOODY SHOT, GROLM!
SHOOT THAT BELLEND BEFORE--
BRAK-BRAK-BRAK
CHOKK
BLAKK
WHAT IS THIS--?!
REVENGE.
BRAK-BRAK-BRAK
BLAKK

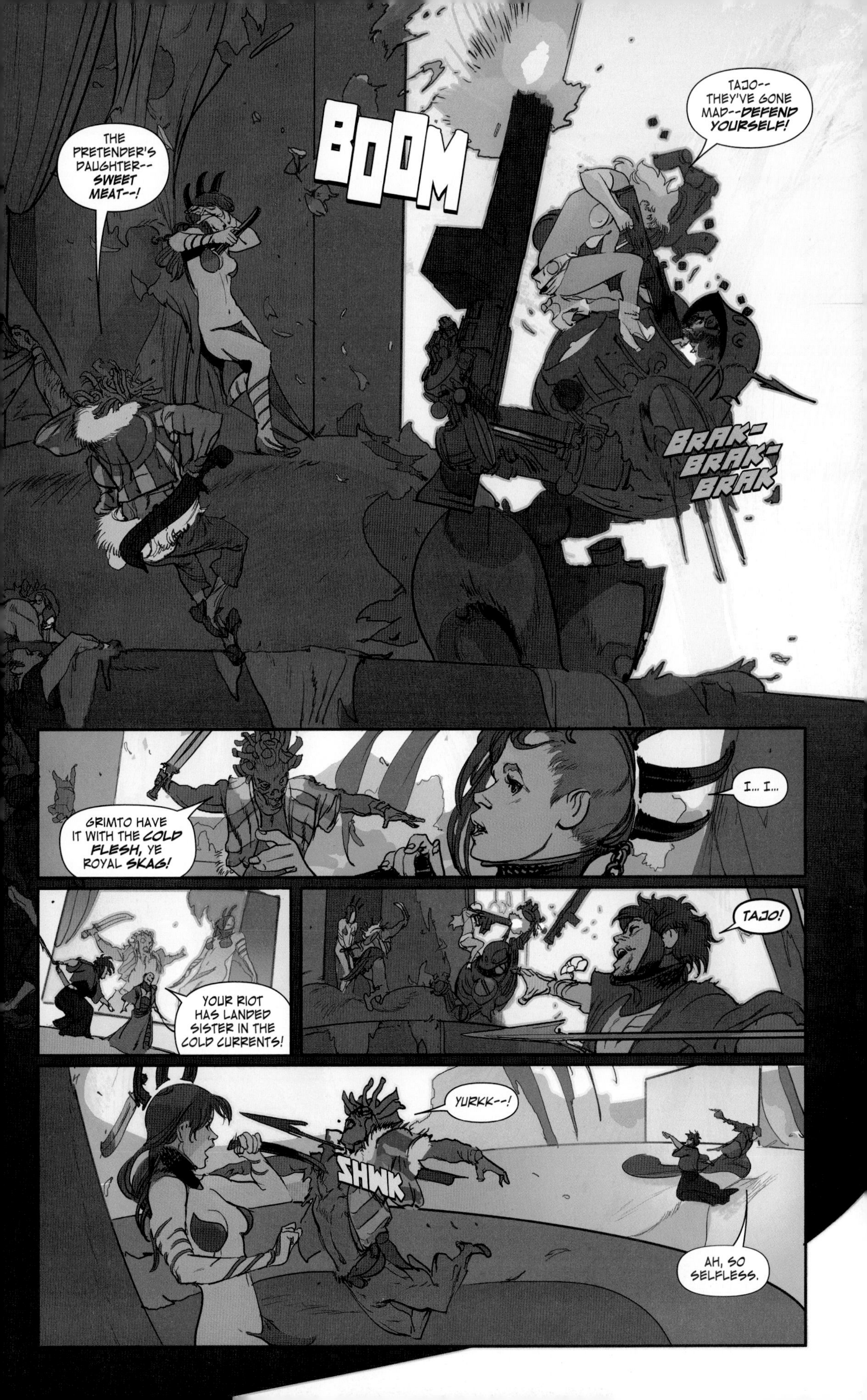
THE PRETENDER'S DAUGHTER-- SWEET MEAT--!
BOOM
TAJO-- THEY'VE GONE MAD--DEFEND YOURSELF!
BRAK-BRAK-BRAK
GRIMTO HAVE IT WITH THE COLD FLESH, YE ROYAL SKAG!
I... I...
YOUR RIOT HAS LANDED SISTER IN THE COLD CURRENTS!
TAJO!
YURKK--!
SHWK
AH, SO SELFLESS.

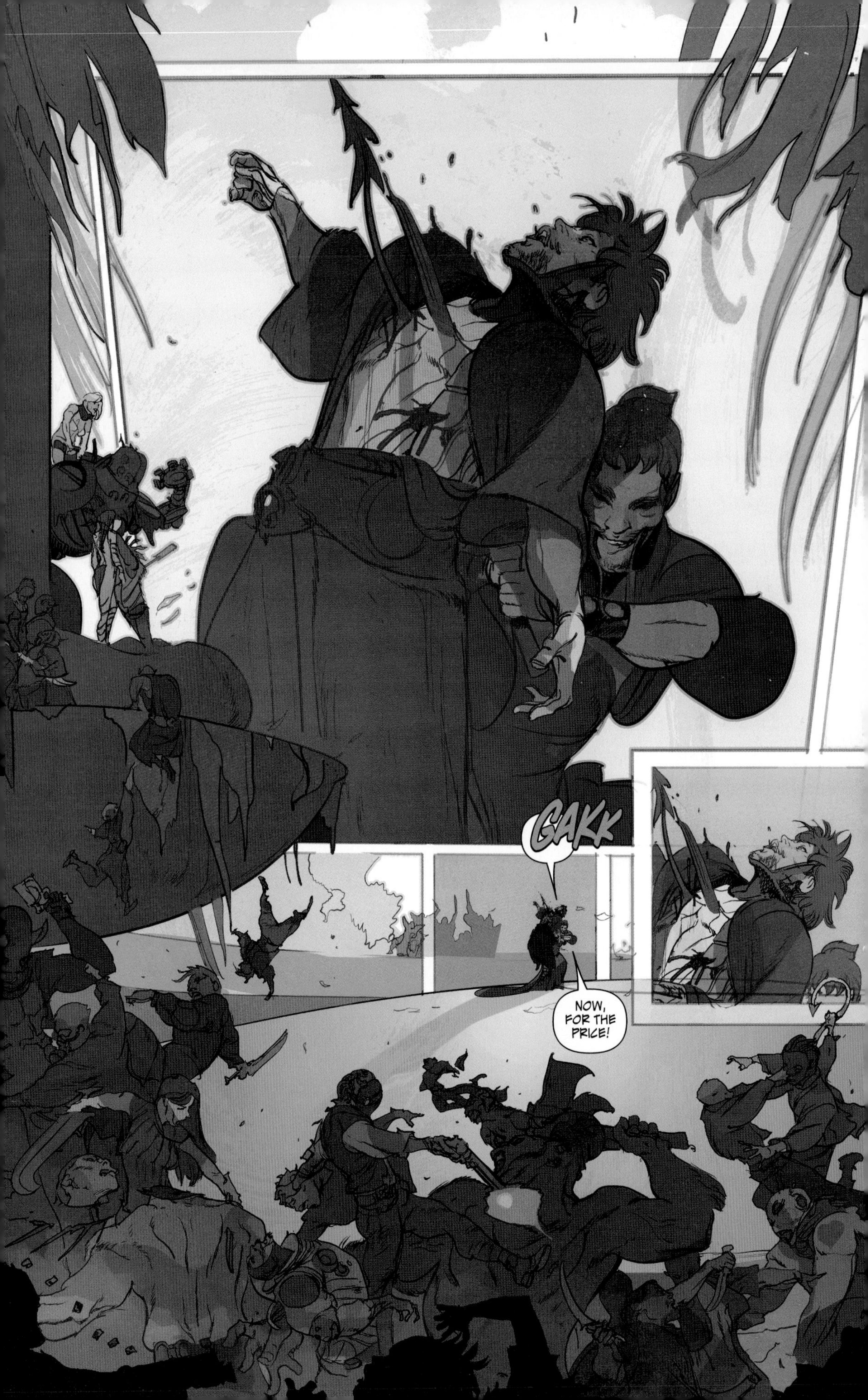
GAKK
NOW, FOR THE PRICE!

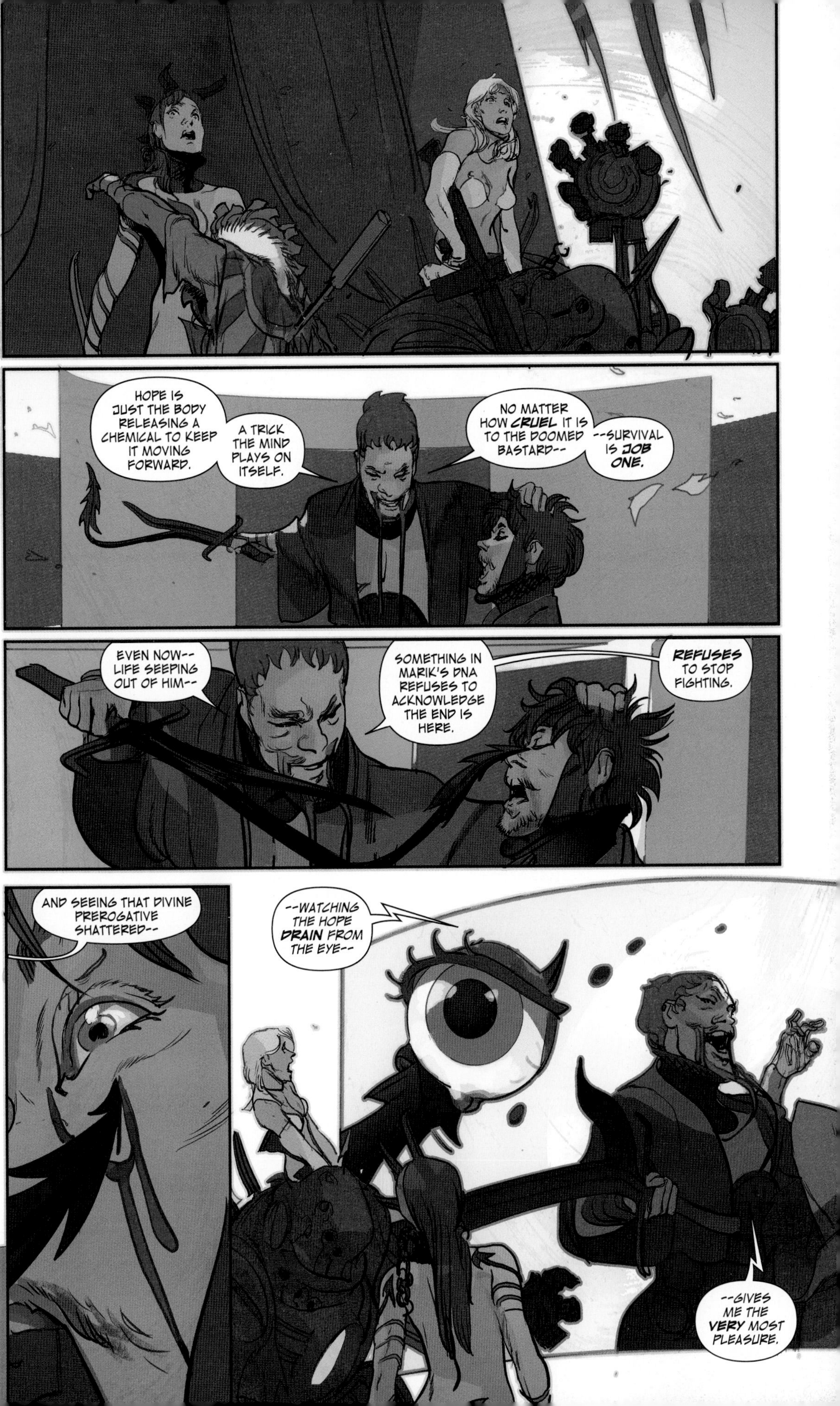
HOPE IS JUST THE BODY RELEASING A CHEMICAL TO KEEP IT MOVING FORWARD.
A TRICK THE MIND PLAYS ON ITSELF.
NO MATTER HOW CRUEL IT IS TO THE DOOMED BASTARD--
--SURVIVAL IS JOB ONE.
EVEN NOW--LIFE SEEPING OUT OF HIM--
SOMETHING IN MARIK'S DNA REFUSES TO ACKNOWLEDGE THE END IS HERE.
REFUSES TO STOP FIGHTING.
AND SEEING THAT DIVINE PREROGATIVE SHATTERED--
--WATCHING THE HOPE DRAIN FROM THE EYE--
--GIVES ME THE VERY MOST PLEASURE.

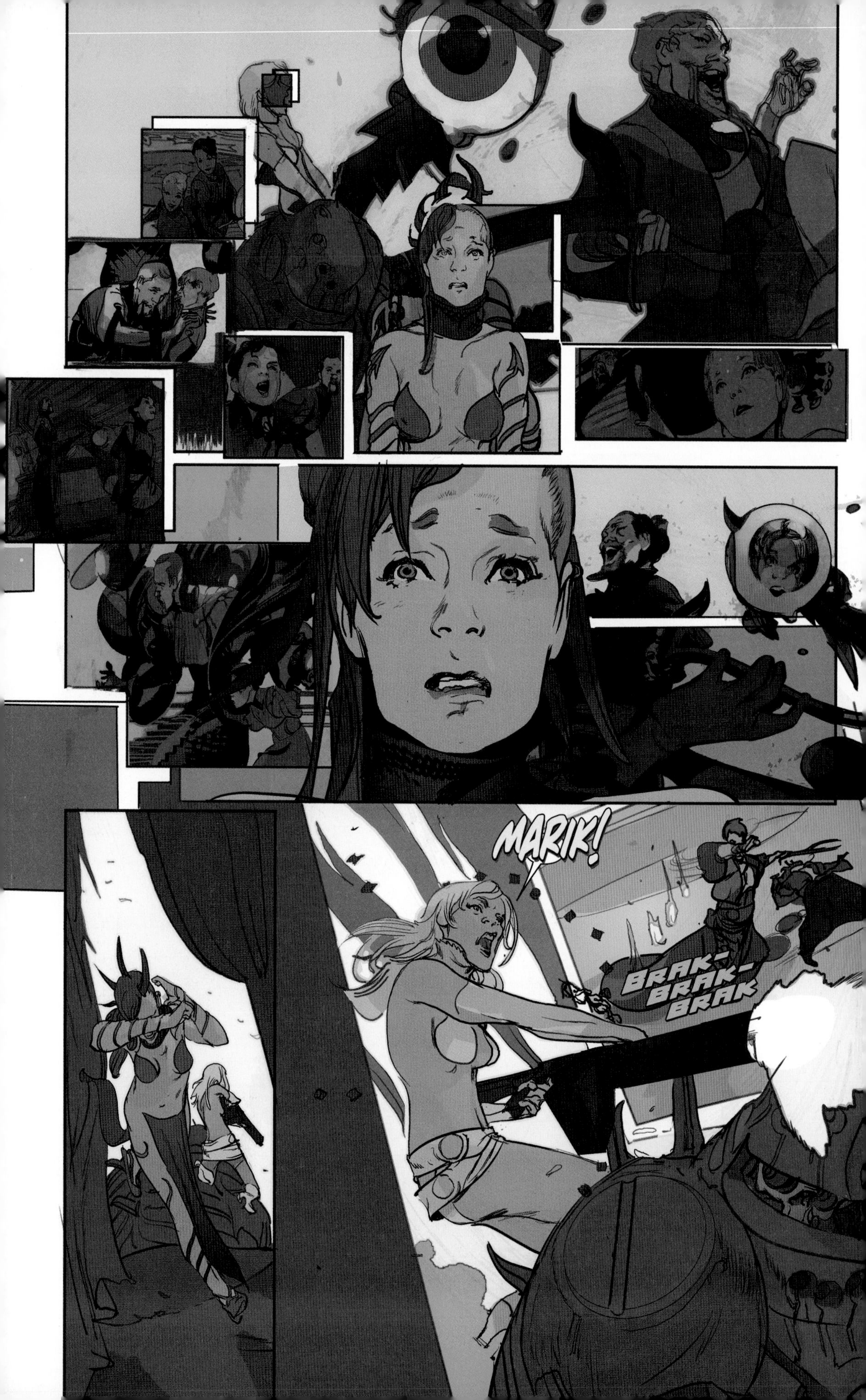
MARIK!
BRAK-BRAK-BRAK

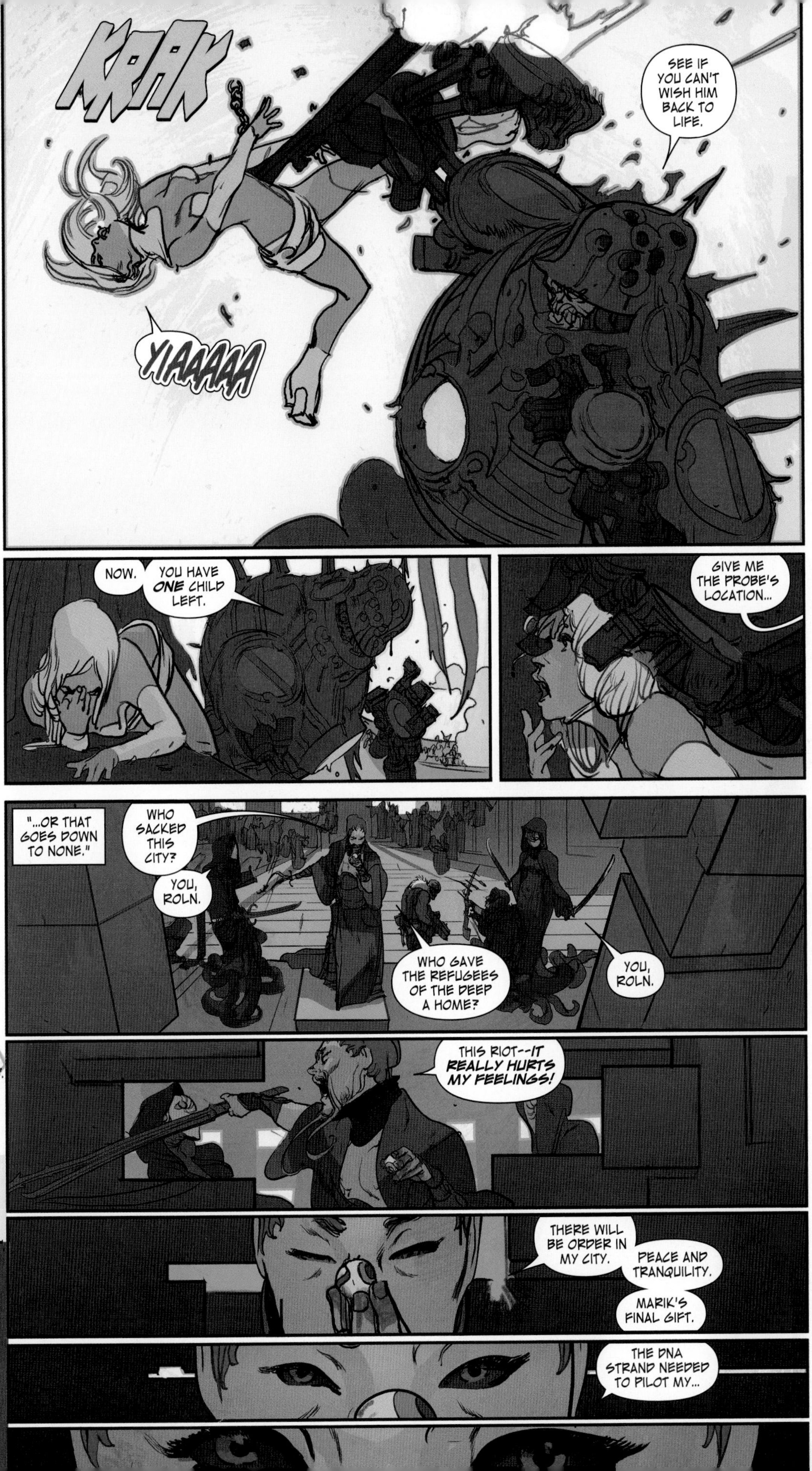
KRAK
SEE IF YOU CAN'T WISH HIM BACK TO LIFE.
YIAAAAA
NOW.
YOU HAVE ONE CHILD LEFT.
GIVE ME THE PROBE'S LOCATION...
"...OR THAT GOES DOWN TO NONE."
WHO SACKED THIS CITY?
YOU, ROLN.
WHO GAVE THE REFUGEES OF THE DEEP A HOME?
YOU, ROLN.
THIS RIOT--IT REALLY HURTS MY FEELINGS!
THERE WILL BE ORDER IN MY CITY.
PEACE AND TRANQUILITY.
MARIK'S FINAL GIFT.
THE DNA STRAND NEEDED TO PILOT MY...

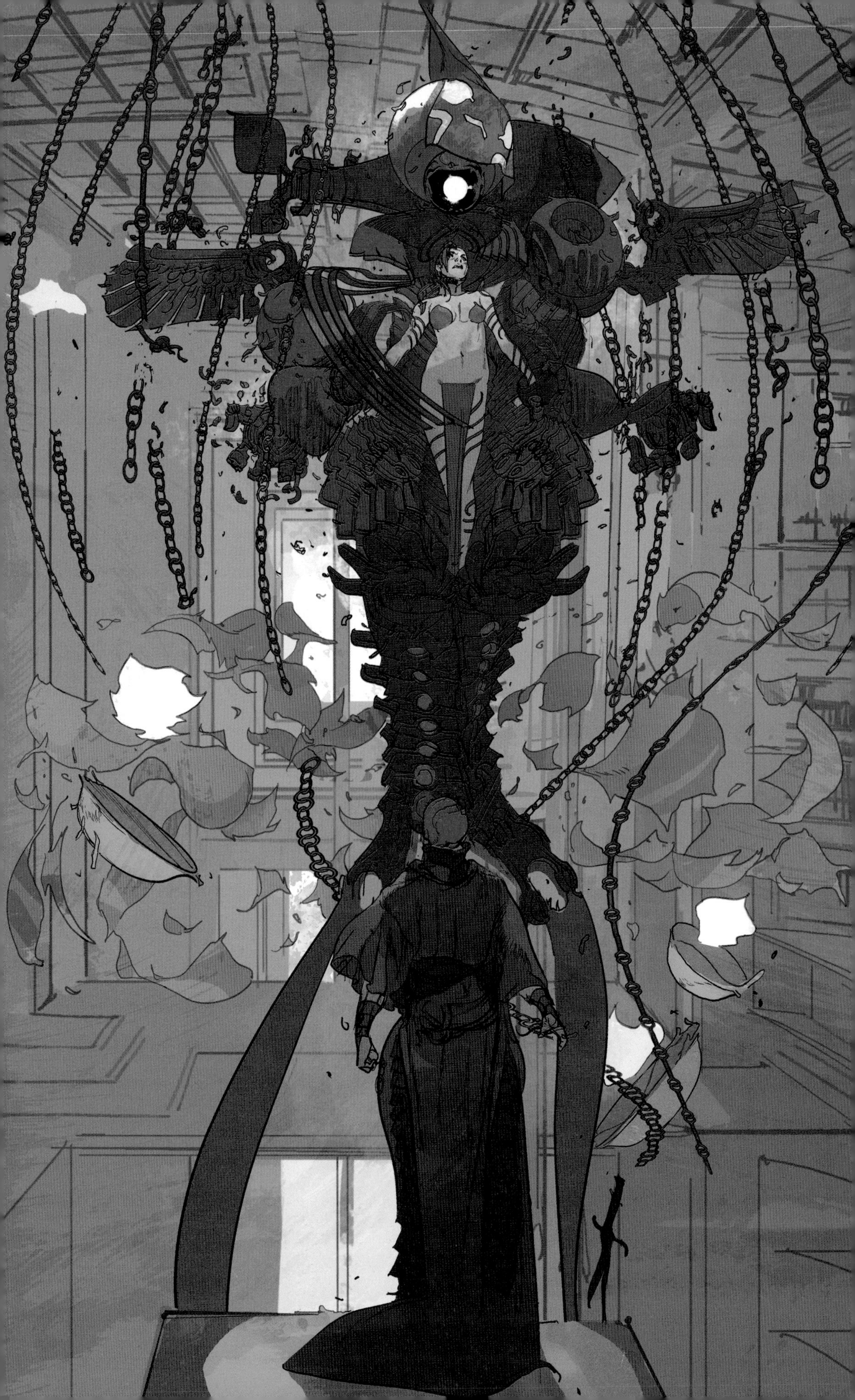

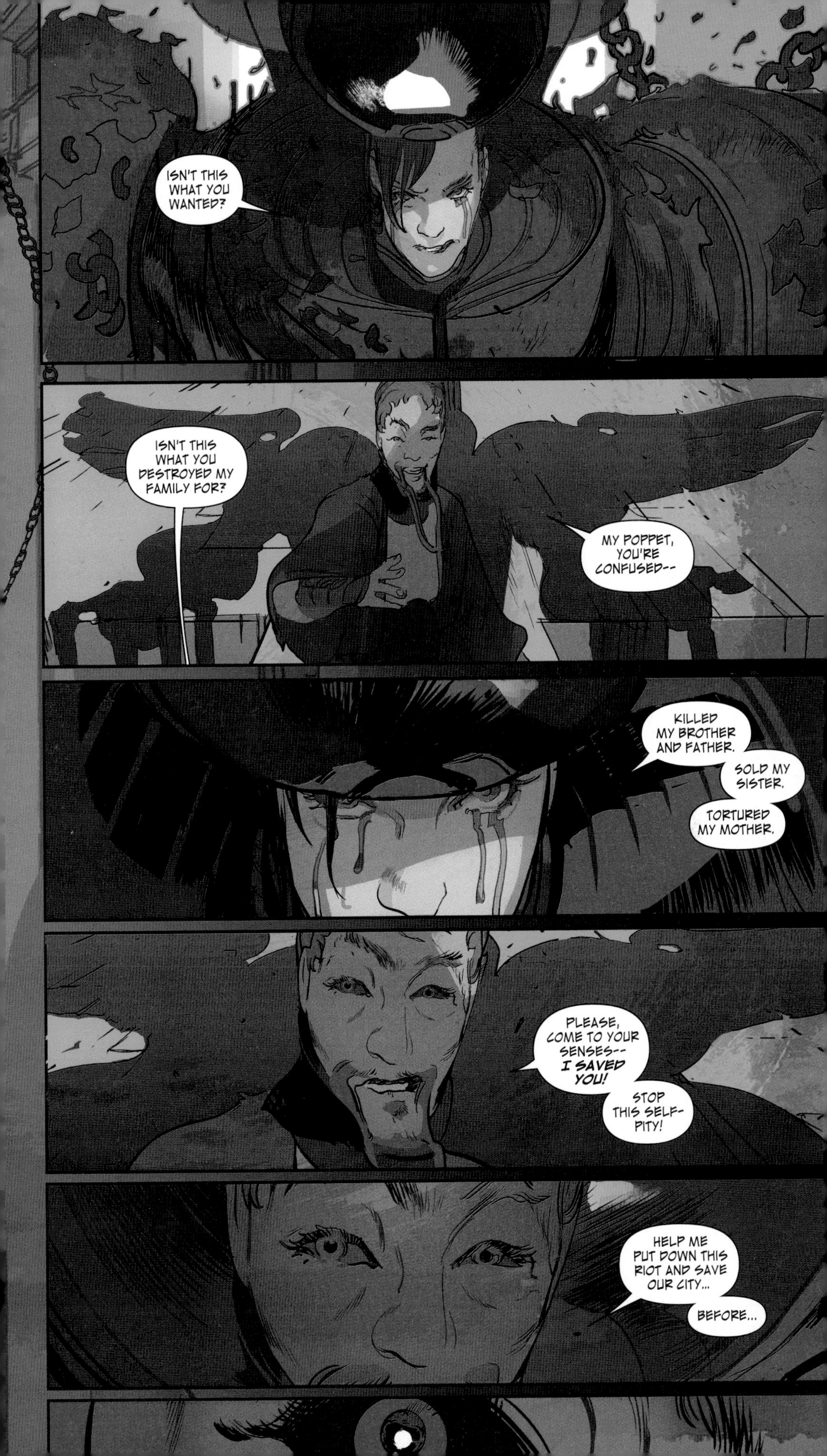

ISN'T THIS WHAT YOU WANTED?
ISN'T THIS WHAT YOU DESTROYED MY FAMILY FOR?
MY POPPET, YOU'RE CONFUSED--
KILLED MY BROTHER AND FATHER.
SOLD MY SISTER.
TORTURED MY MOTHER.
PLEASE, COME TO YOUR SENSES-- ***I SAVED YOU!***
STOP THIS SELF-PITY!
HELP ME PUT DOWN THIS RIOT AND SAVE OUR CITY...
BEFORE...

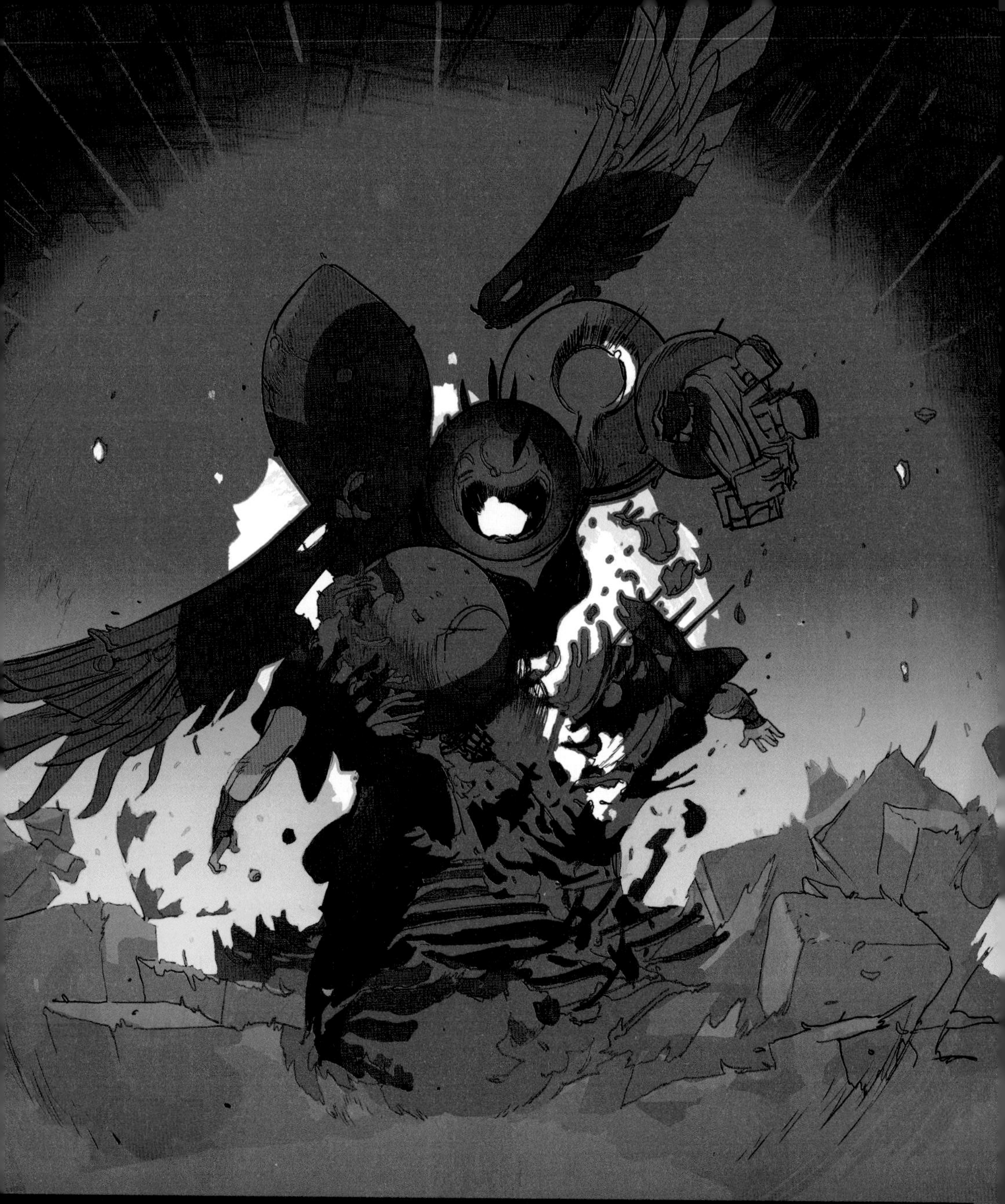
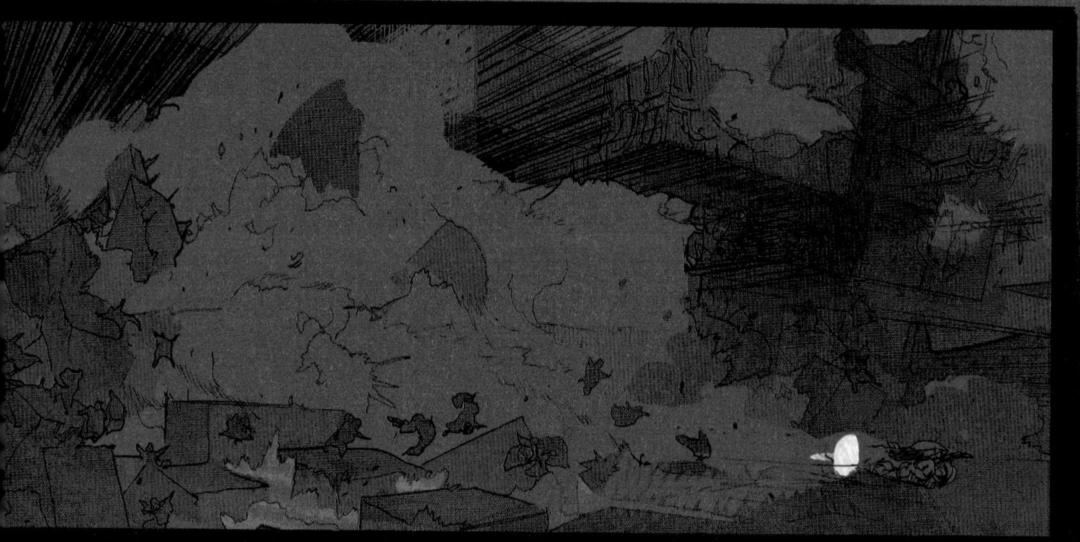

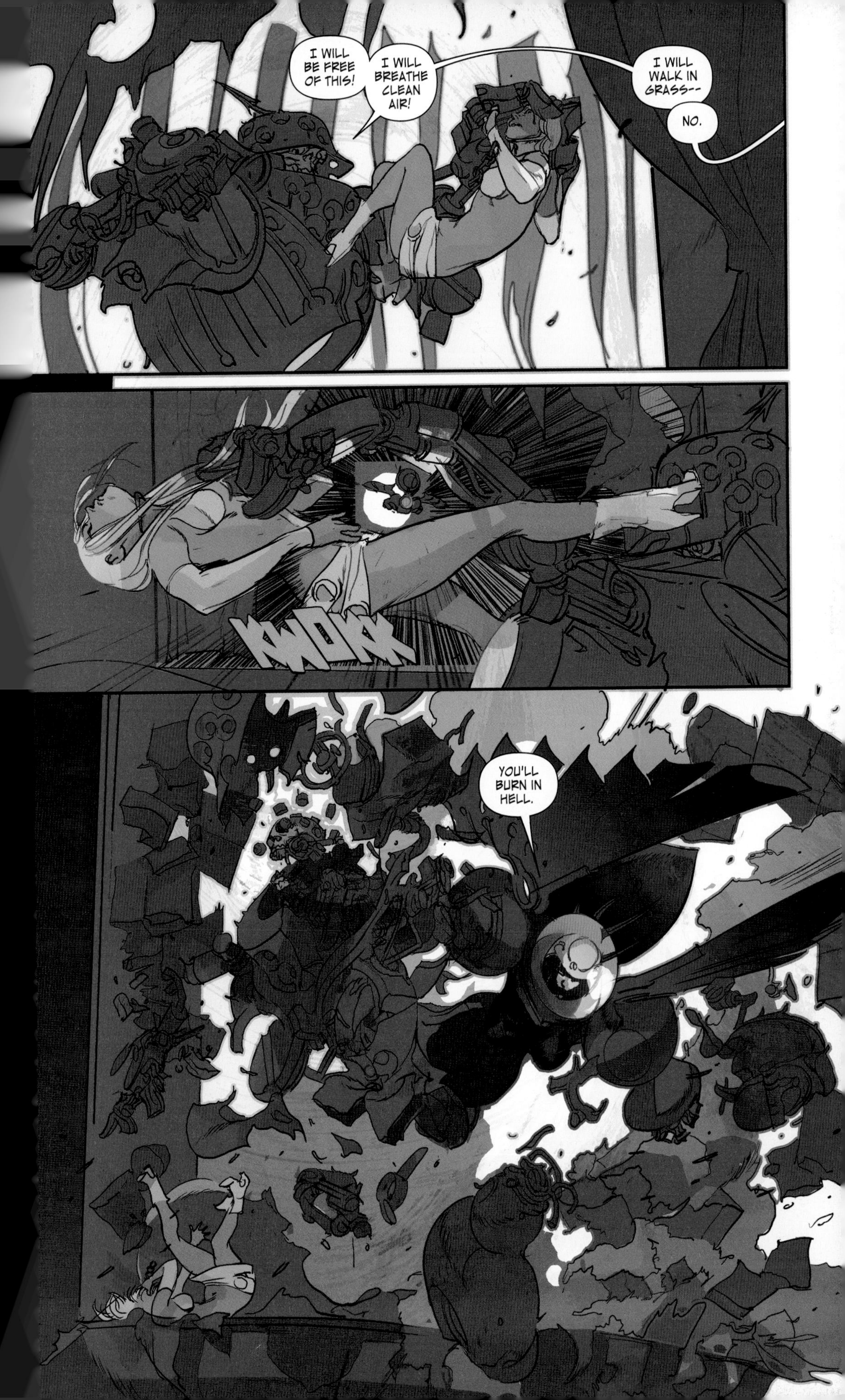
I WILL BE FREE OF THIS!
I WILL BREATHE CLEAN AIR!
I WILL WALK IN GRASS--
NO.
KWORK
YOU'LL BURN IN HELL.

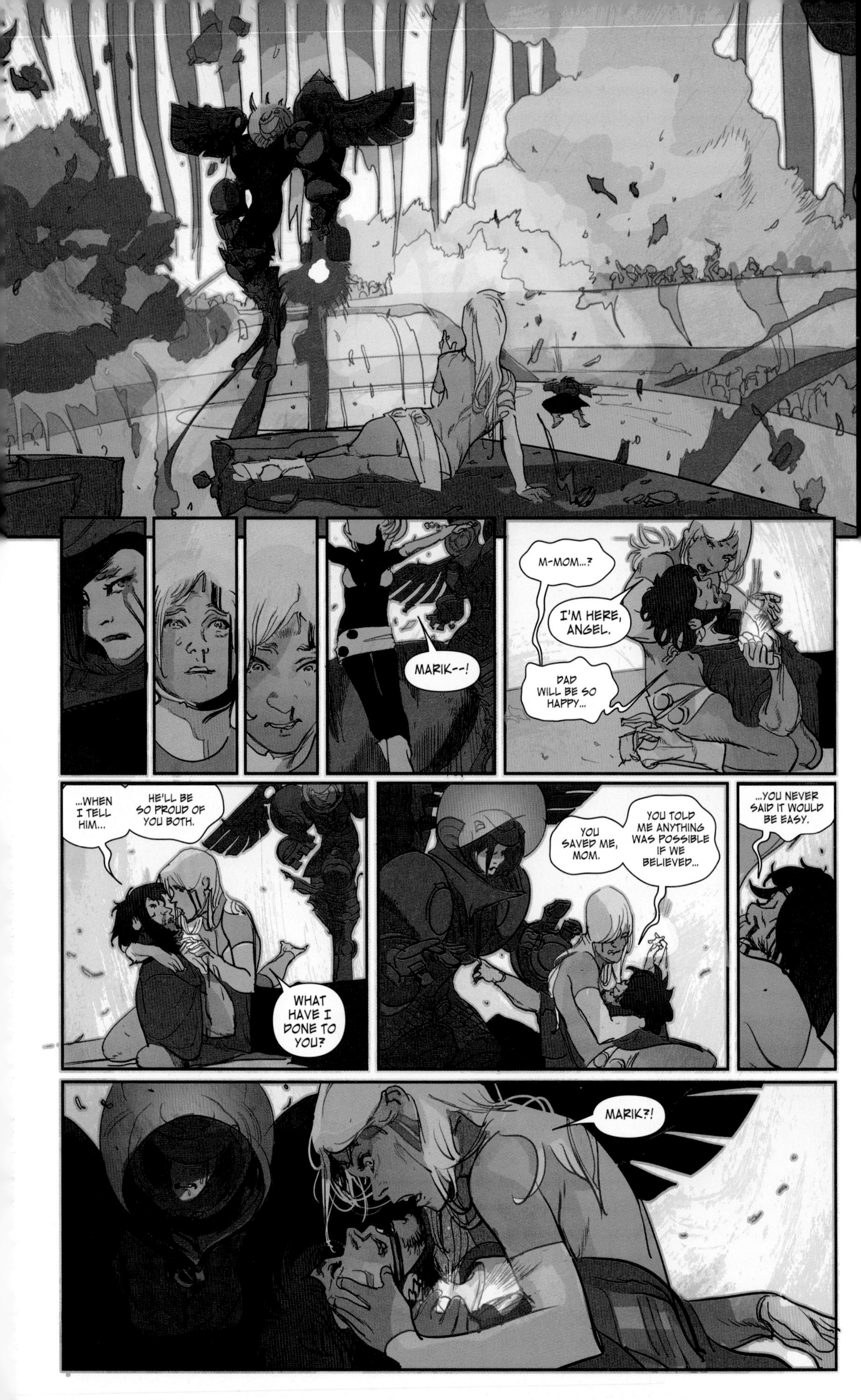
MARIK--!
M-MOM...?
I'M HERE, ANGEL.
DAD WILL BE SO HAPPY...
...WHEN I TELL HIM...
HE'LL BE SO PROUD OF YOU BOTH.
WHAT HAVE I DONE TO YOU?
YOU SAVED ME, MOM.
YOU TOLD ME ANYTHING WAS POSSIBLE IF WE BELIEVED...
...YOU NEVER SAID IT WOULD BE EASY.
MARIK?!

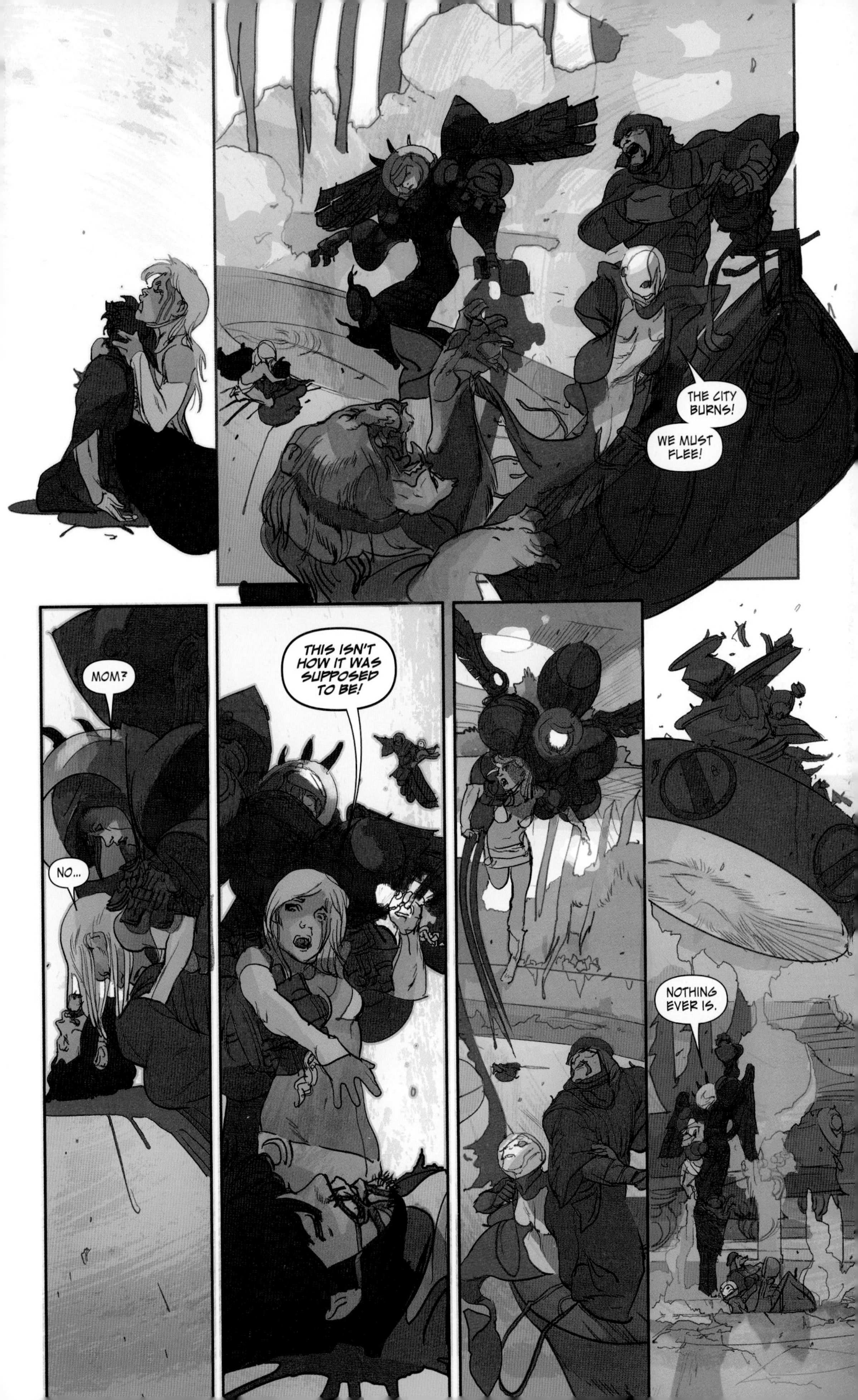
THE CITY BURNS!
WE MUST FLEE!
MOM?
NO...
THIS ISN'T HOW IT WAS SUPPOSED TO BE!
NOTHING EVER IS.

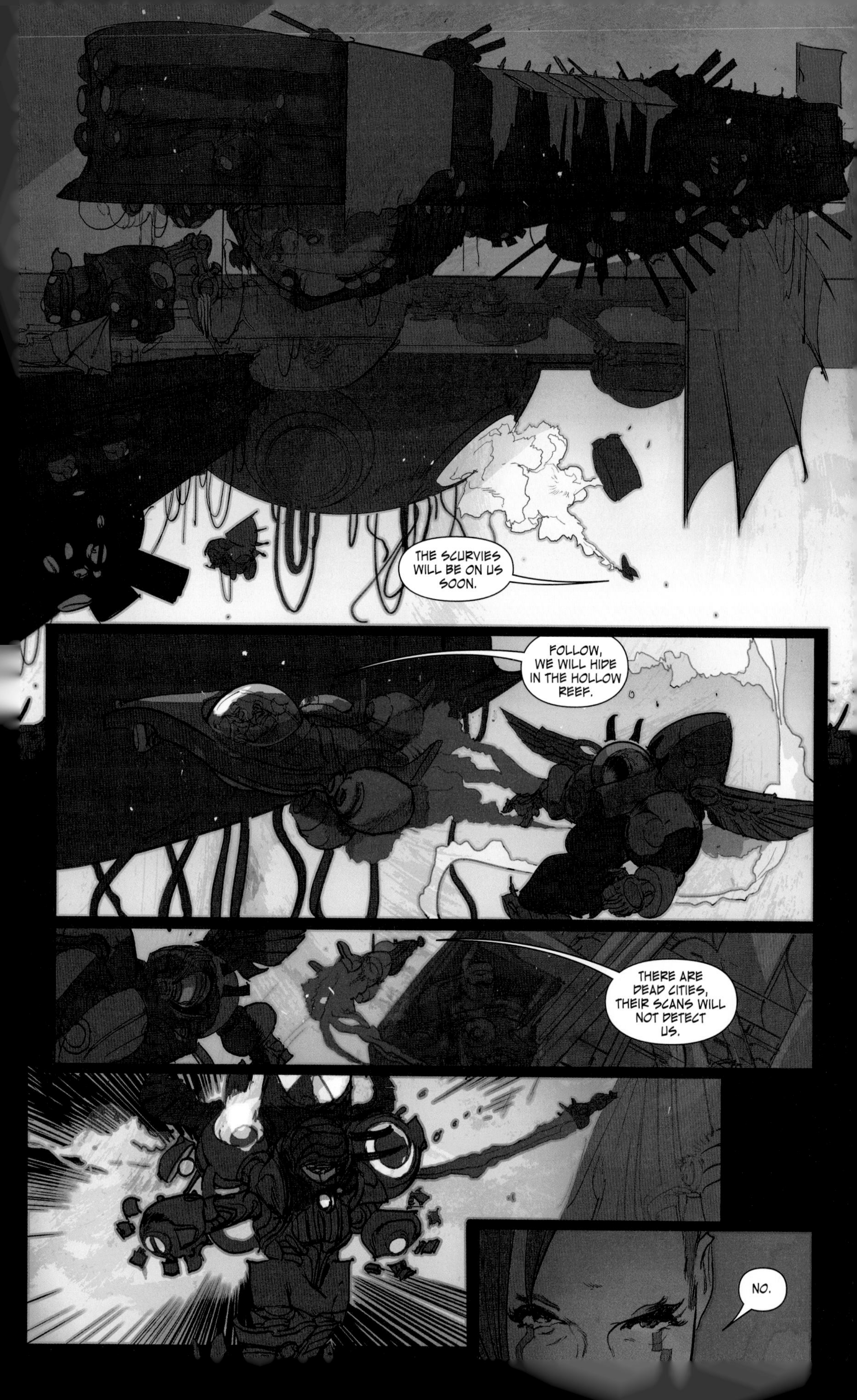
THE SCURVIES WILL BE ON US SOON.
FOLLOW, WE WILL HIDE IN THE HOLLOW REEF.
THERE ARE DEAD CITIES, THEIR SCANS WILL NOT DETECT US.
NO.

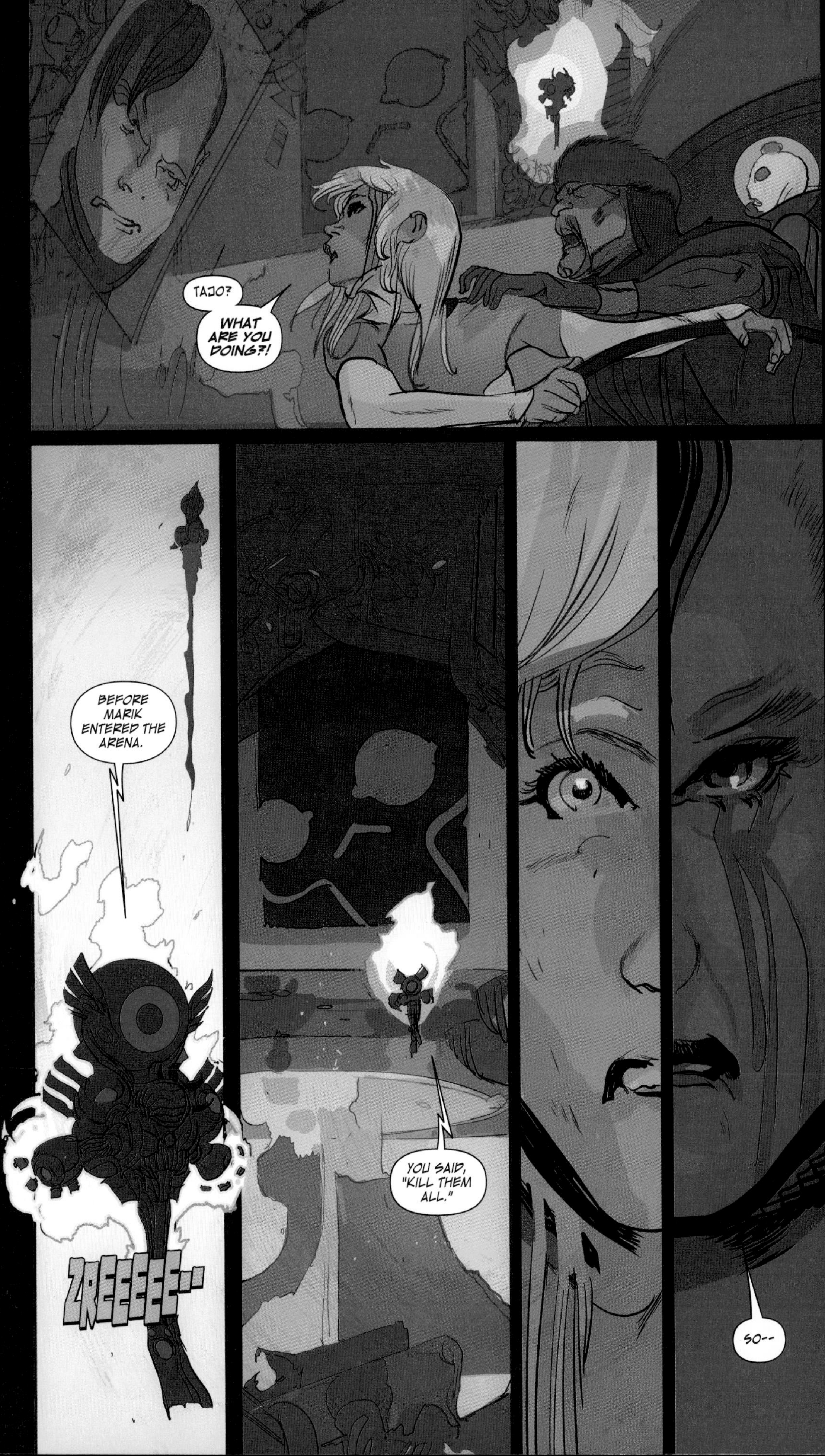
TAJO?
WHAT ARE YOU DOING?!
BEFORE MARIK ENTERED THE ARENA.
ZREEEEE--
YOU SAID, "KILL THEM ALL."
SO--

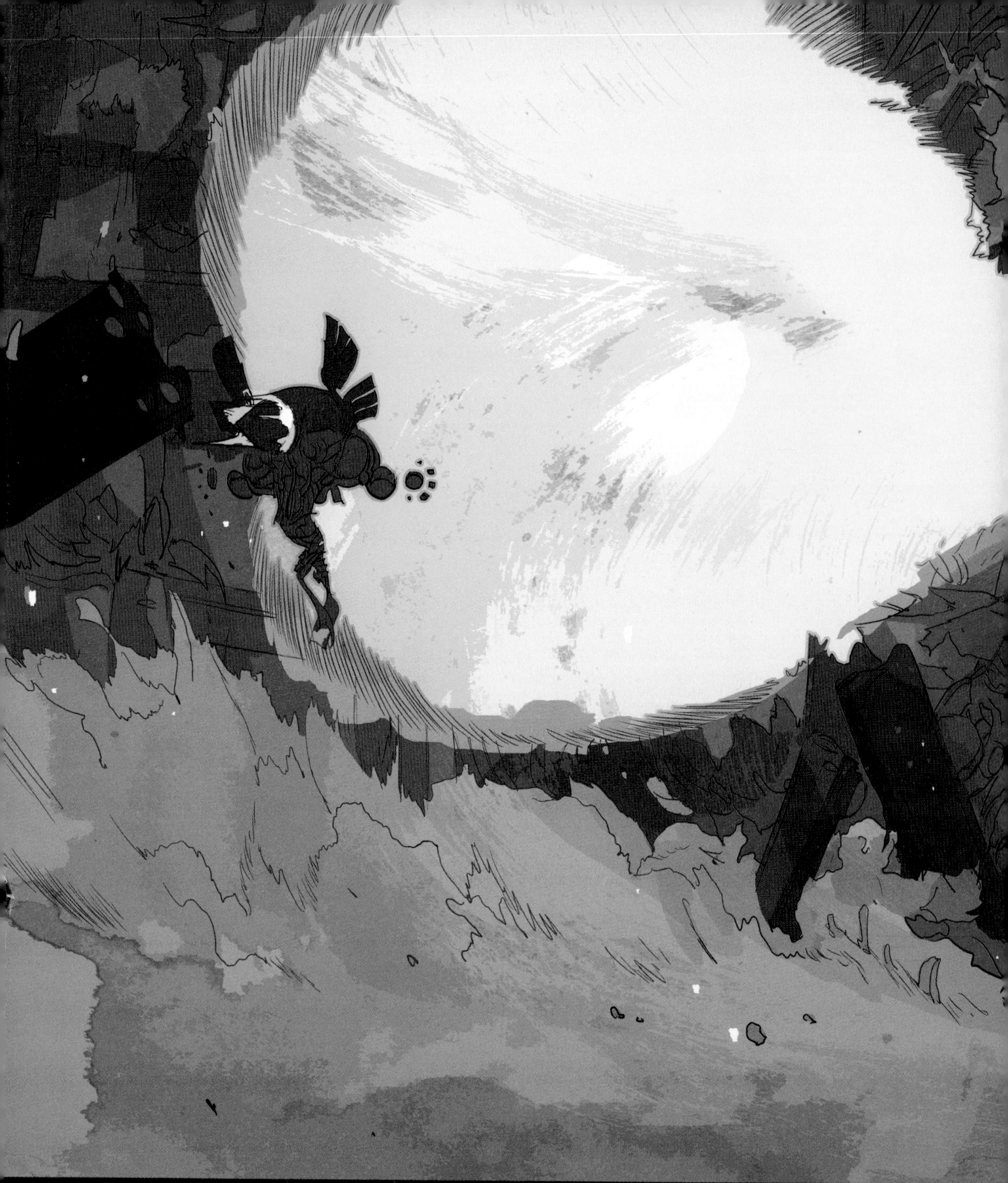
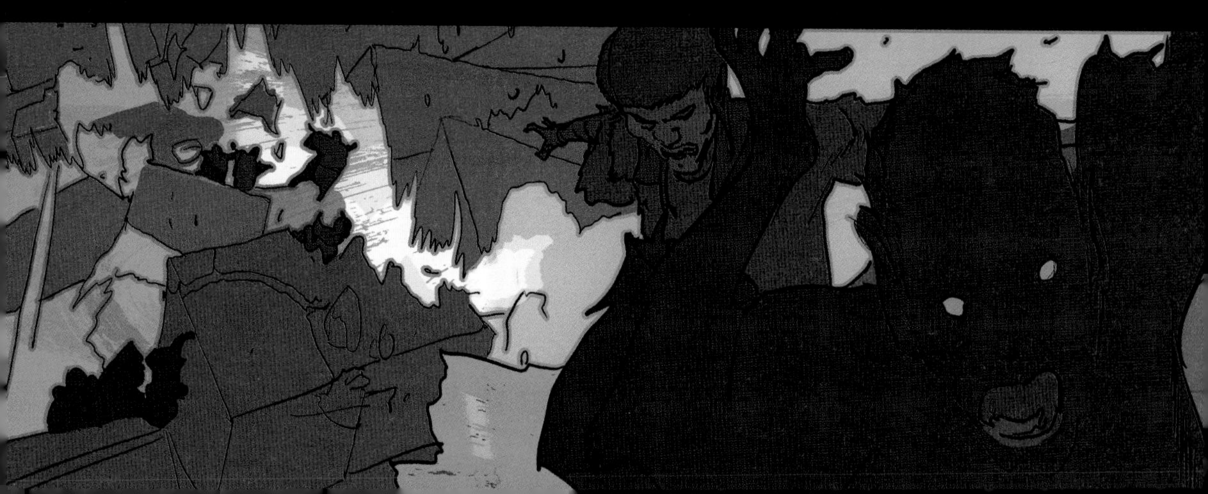

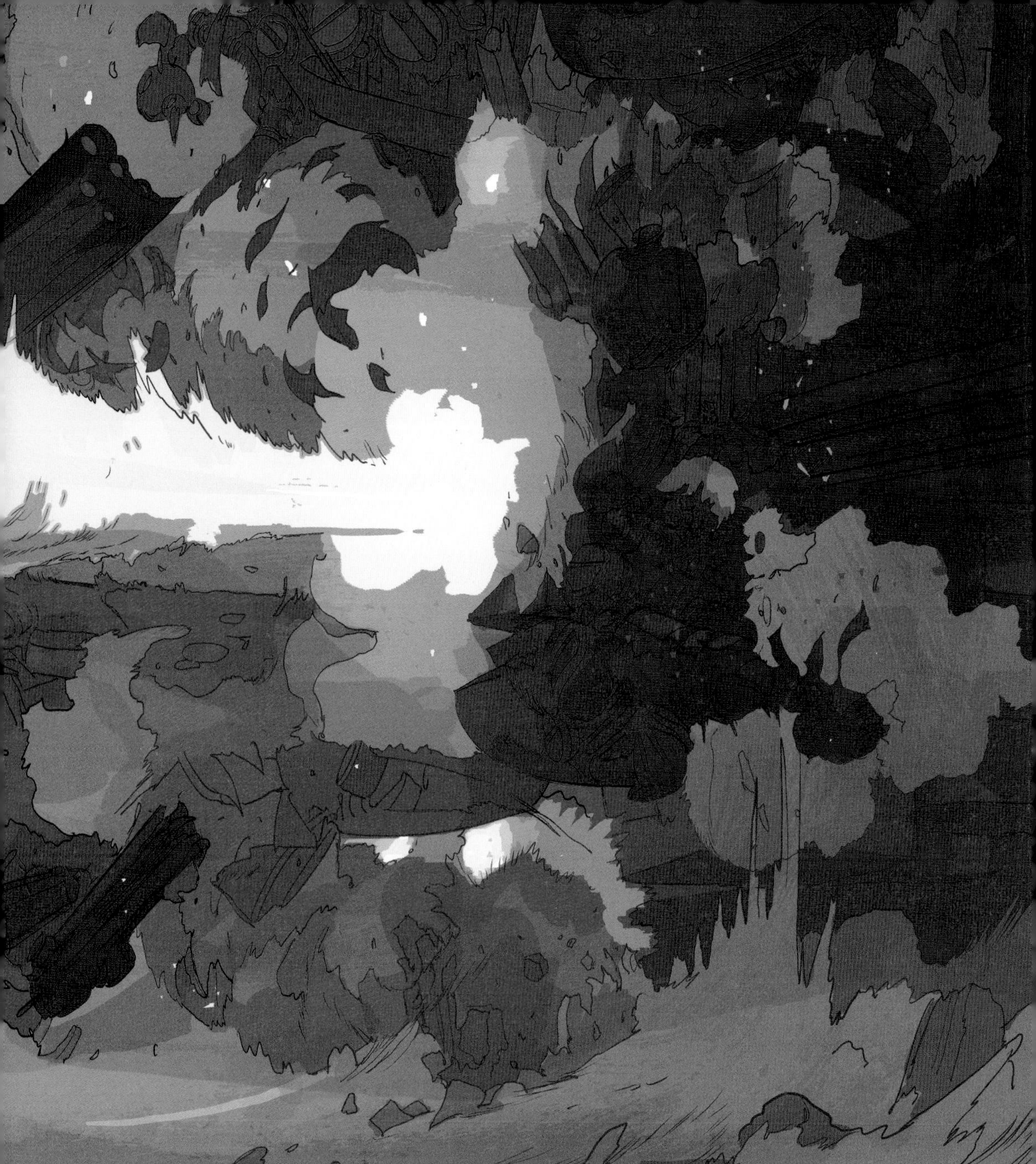

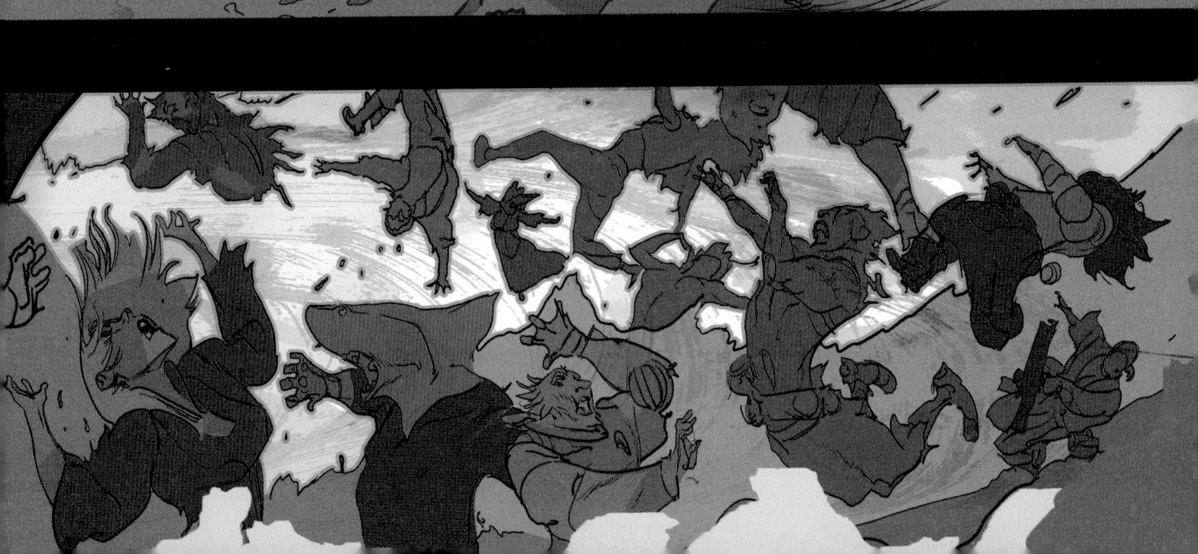

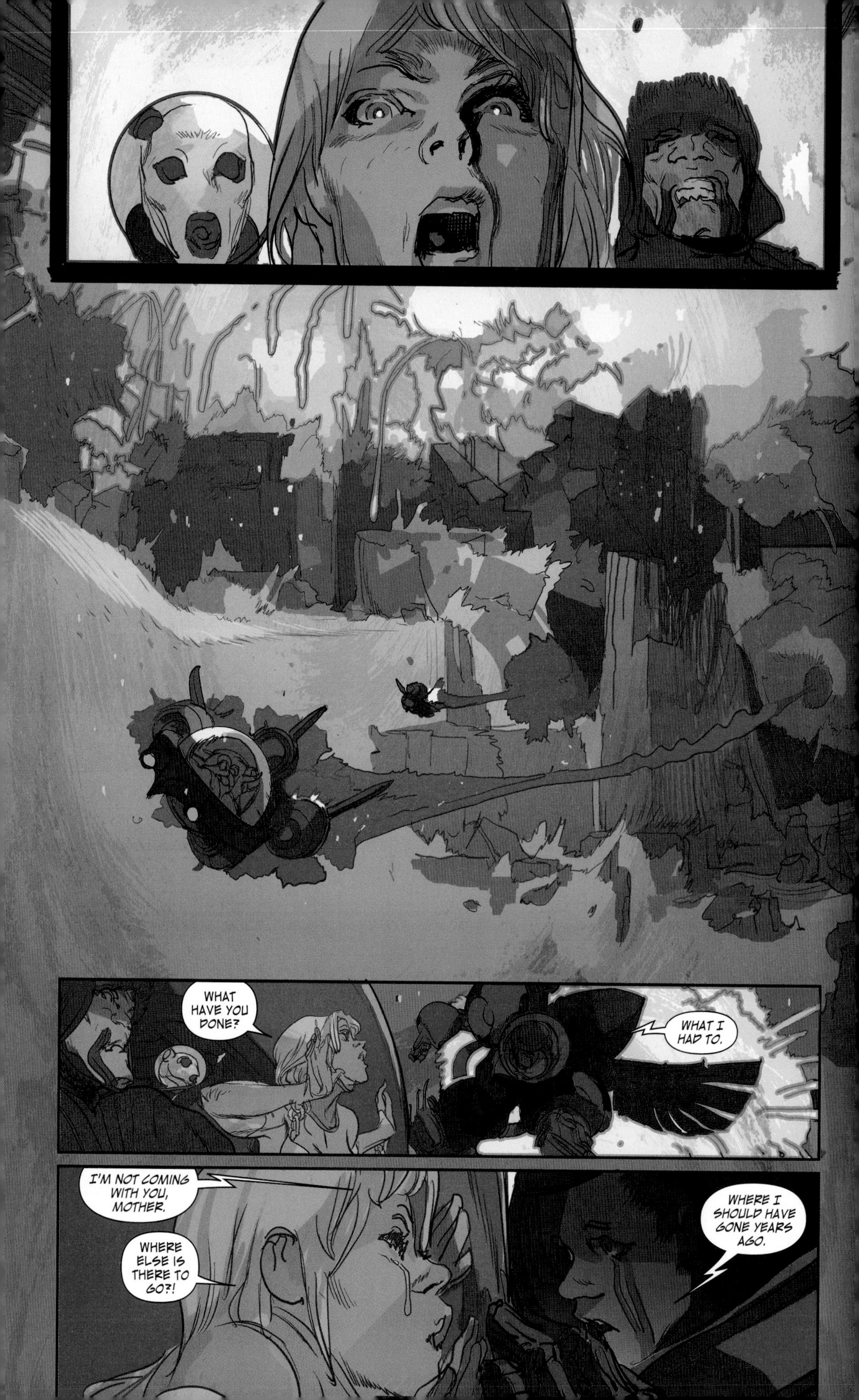
WHAT HAVE YOU DONE?
WHAT I HAD TO.
I'M NOT COMING WITH YOU, MOTHER.
WHERE ELSE IS THERE TO GO?!
WHERE I SHOULD HAVE GONE YEARS AGO.

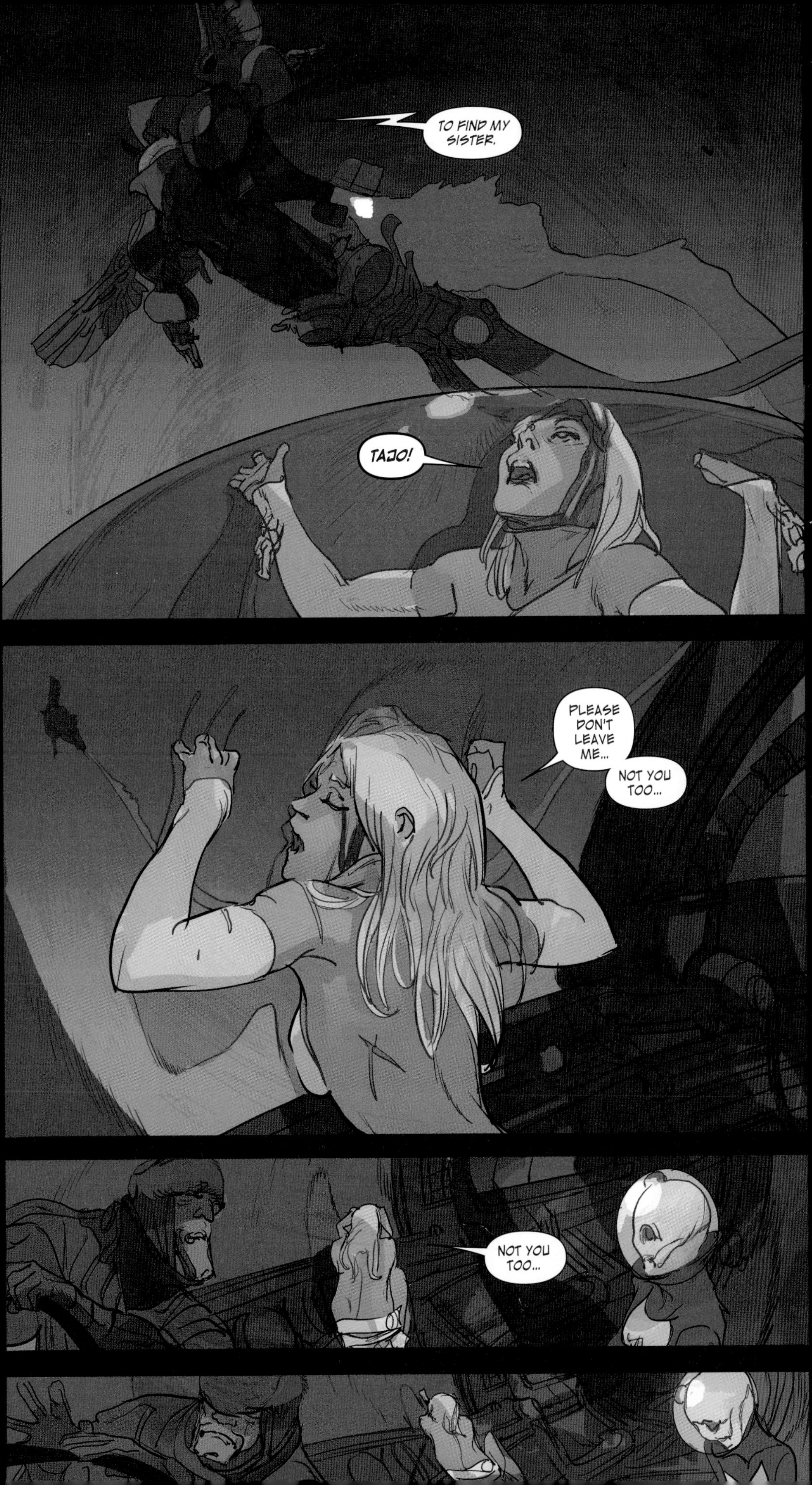
TO FIND MY SISTER.
TAJO!
PLEASE DON'T LEAVE ME...
NOT YOU TOO...
NOT YOU TOO...

"TO RESIST THE DEPTHS
OF THE WORLD'S SORROW,
THE TRUTH OF ONE'S HEART
MUST BE HONORED."

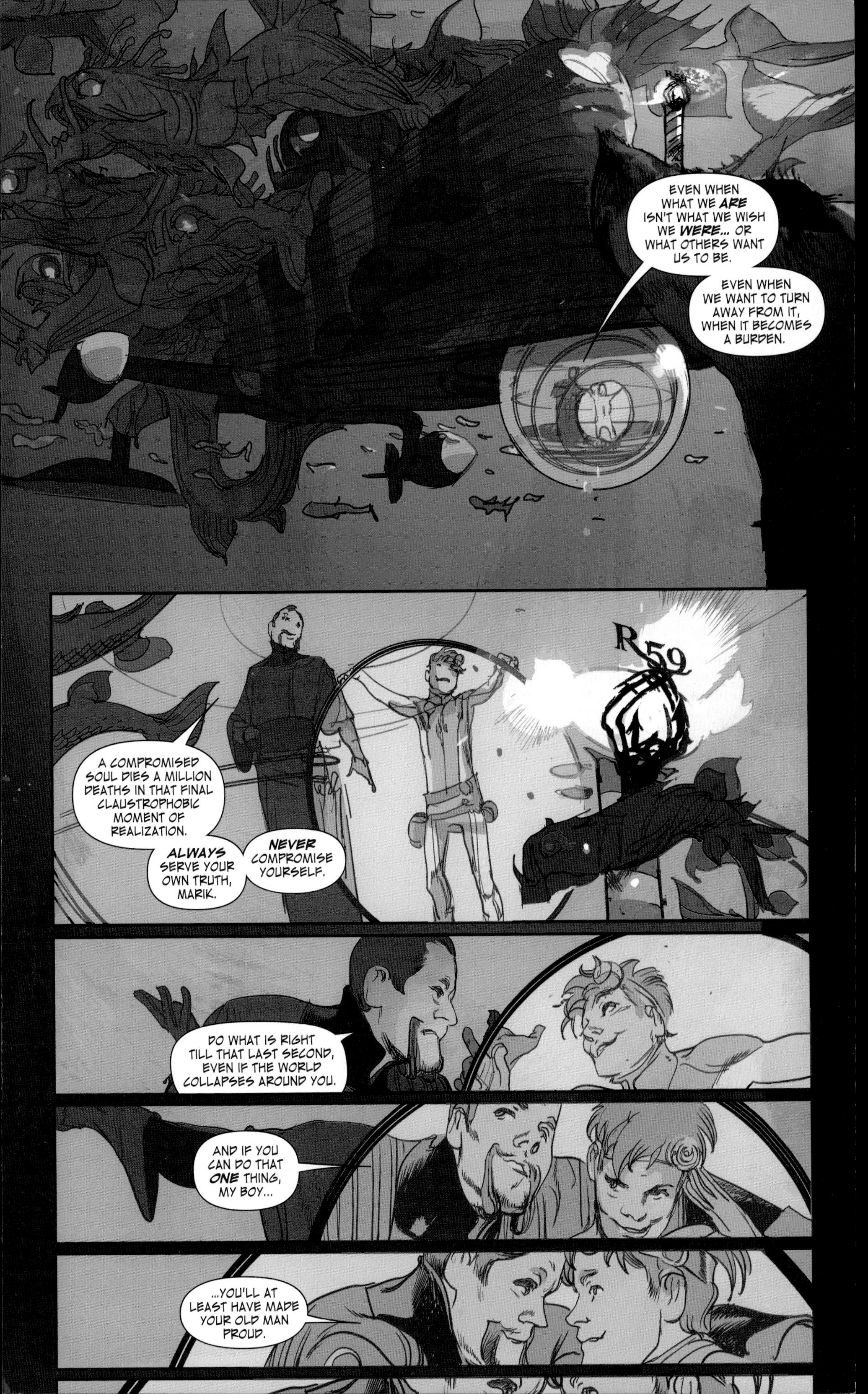
EVEN WHEN WHAT WE ARE ISN'T WHAT WE WISH WE WERE... OR WHAT OTHERS WANT US TO BE.
EVEN WHEN WE WANT TO TURN AWAY FROM IT, WHEN IT BECOMES A BURDEN.
R59
A COMPROMISED SOUL DIES A MILLION DEATHS IN THAT FINAL CLAUSTROPHOBIC MOMENT OF REALIZATION.
ALWAYS SERVE YOUR OWN TRUTH, MARIK.
NEVER COMPROMISE YOURSELF.
DO WHAT IS RIGHT TILL THAT LAST SECOND, EVEN IF THE WORLD COLLAPSES AROUND YOU.
AND IF YOU CAN DO THAT ONE THING, MY BOY...
...YOU'LL AT LEAST HAVE MADE YOUR OLD MAN PROUD.

#1 VARIANT BY GREG TOCCHINI

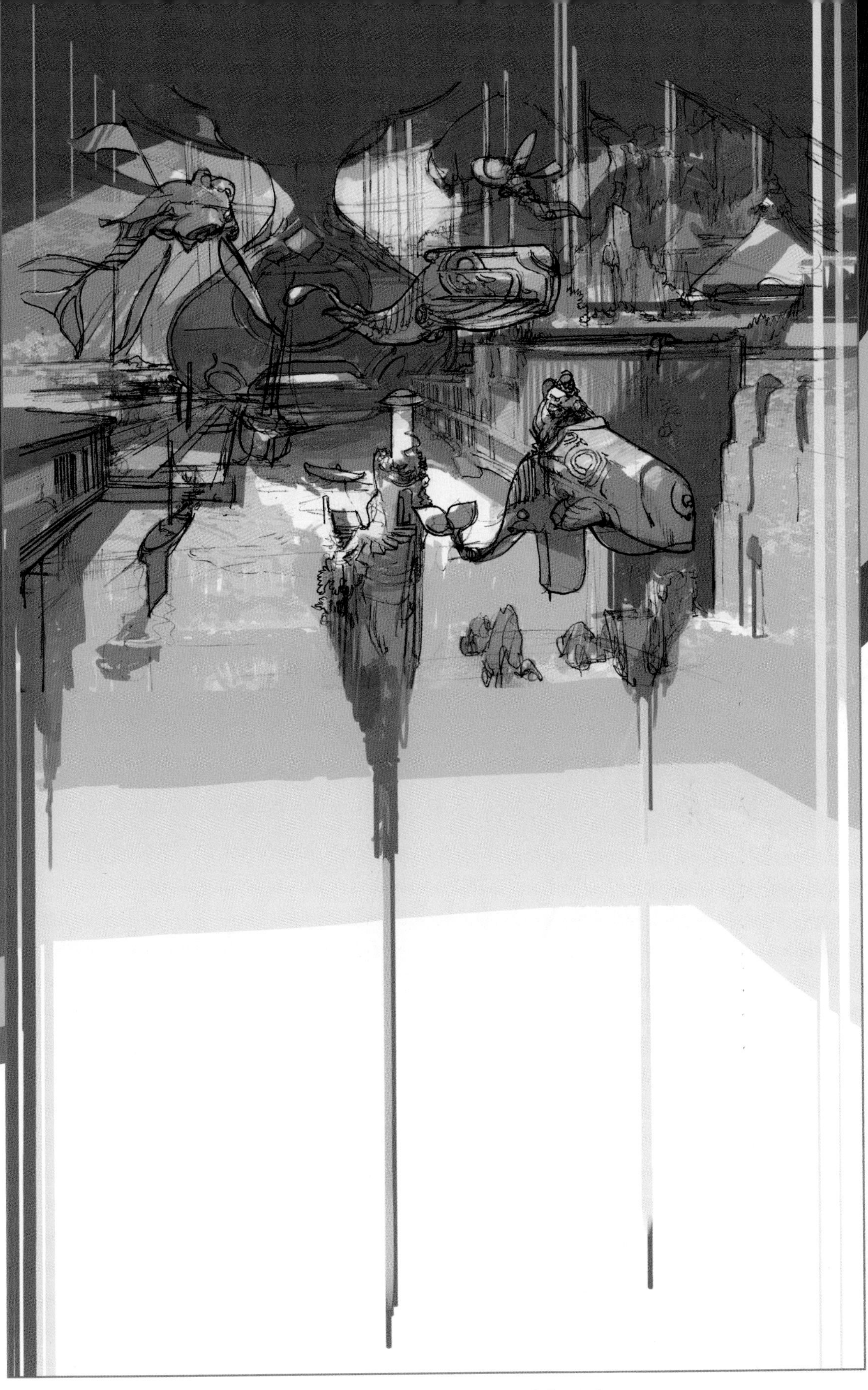

#1 VARIANT BY GREG TOCCHINI

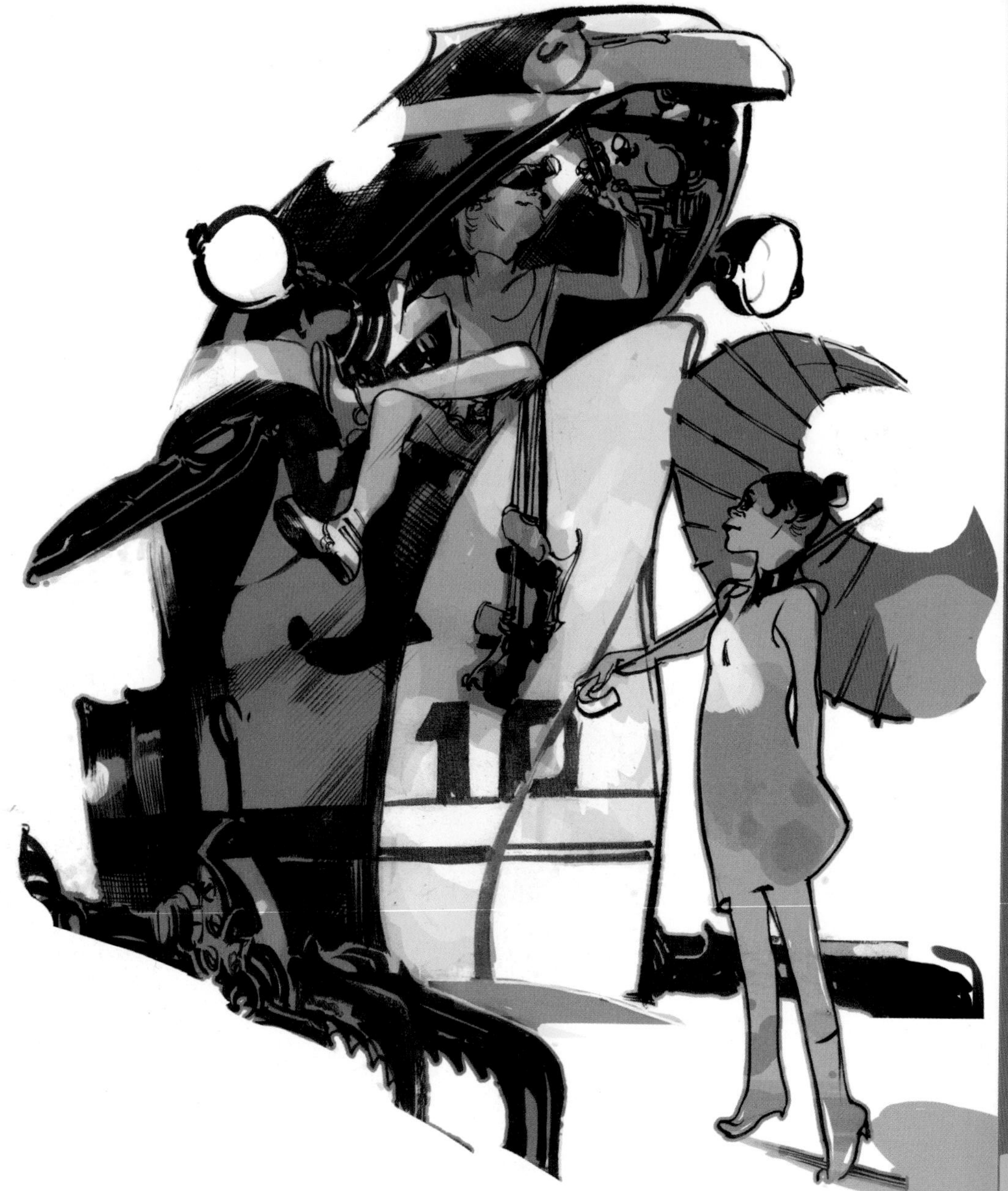

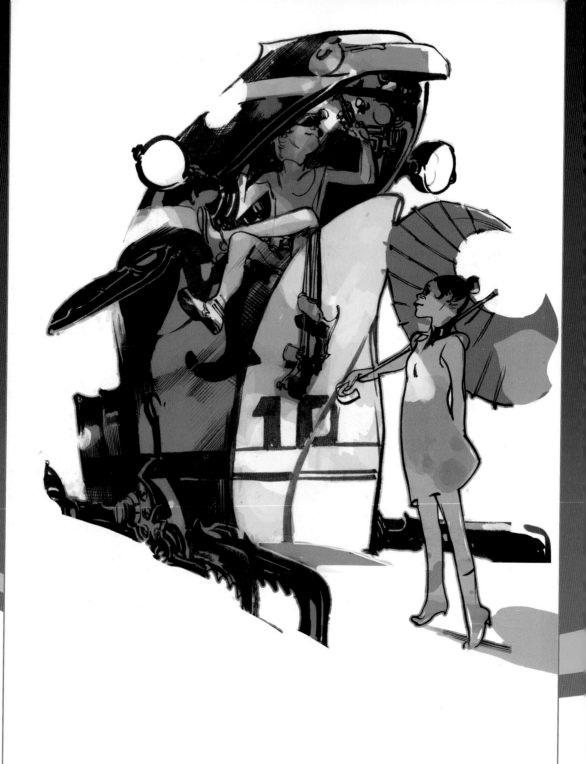

#1 VARIANT BY GREG TOCCHINI

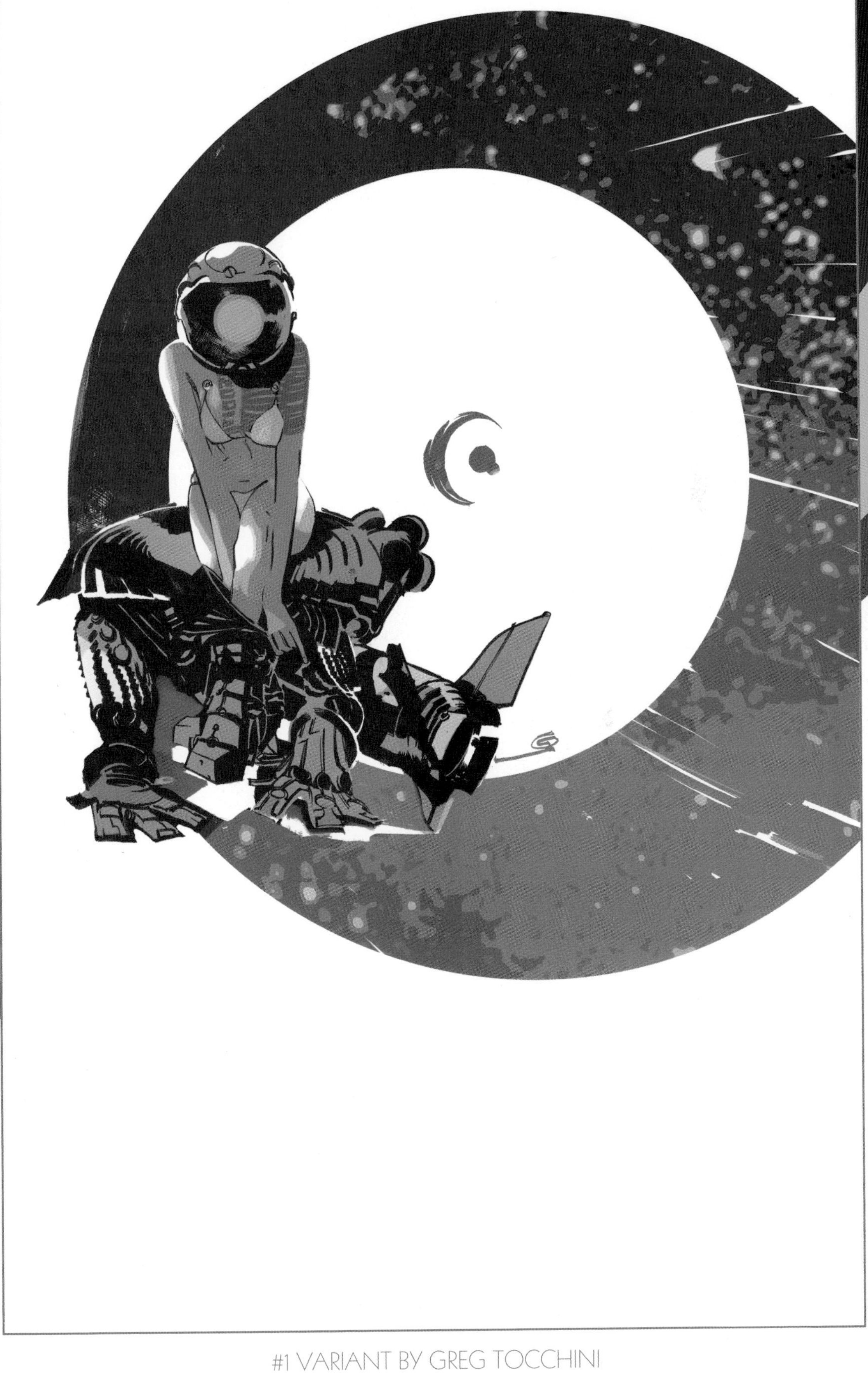

#1 VARIANT BY GREG TOCCHINI

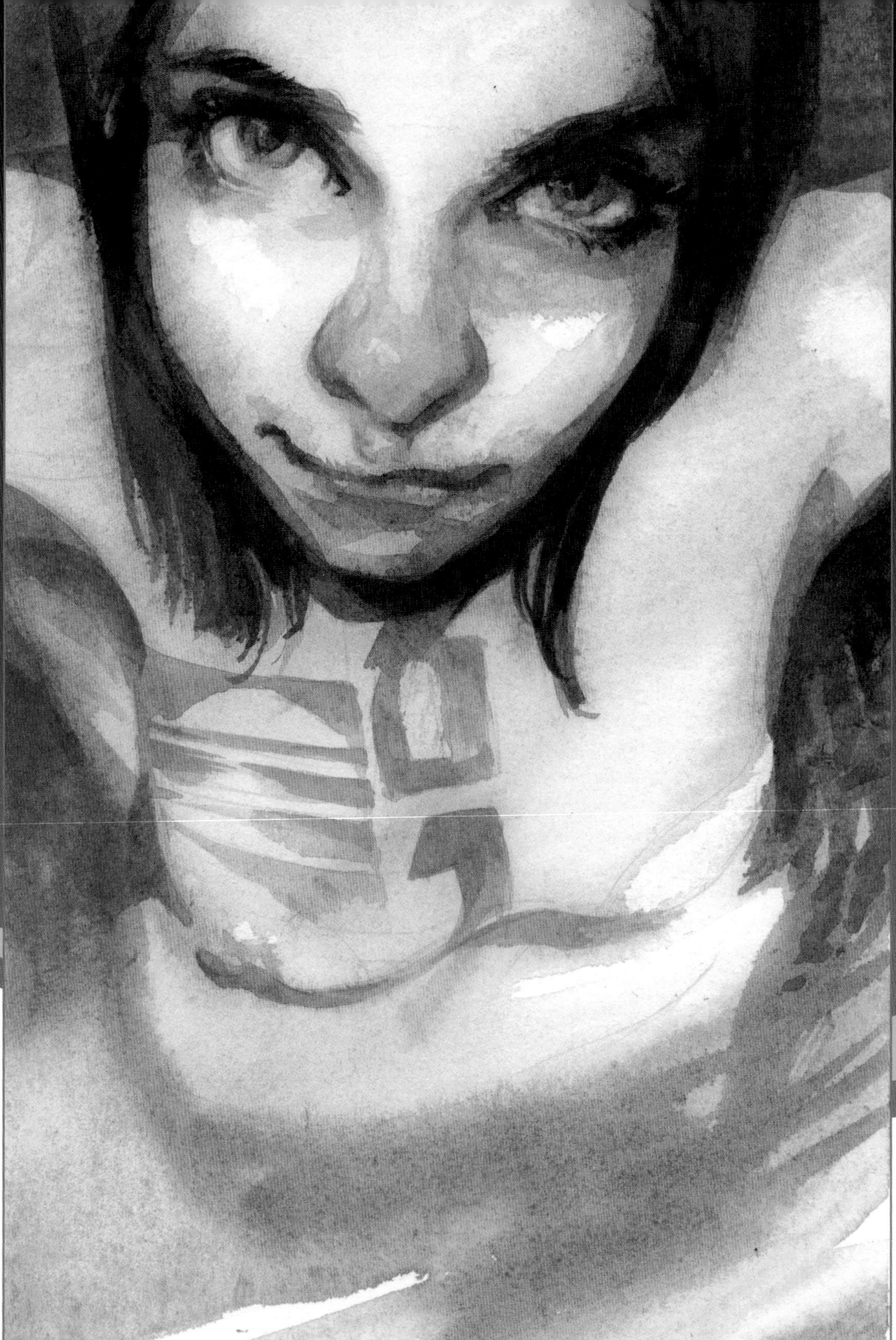

#1 VARIANT BY GREG TOCCHINI

LOW
SKETCHBOOK

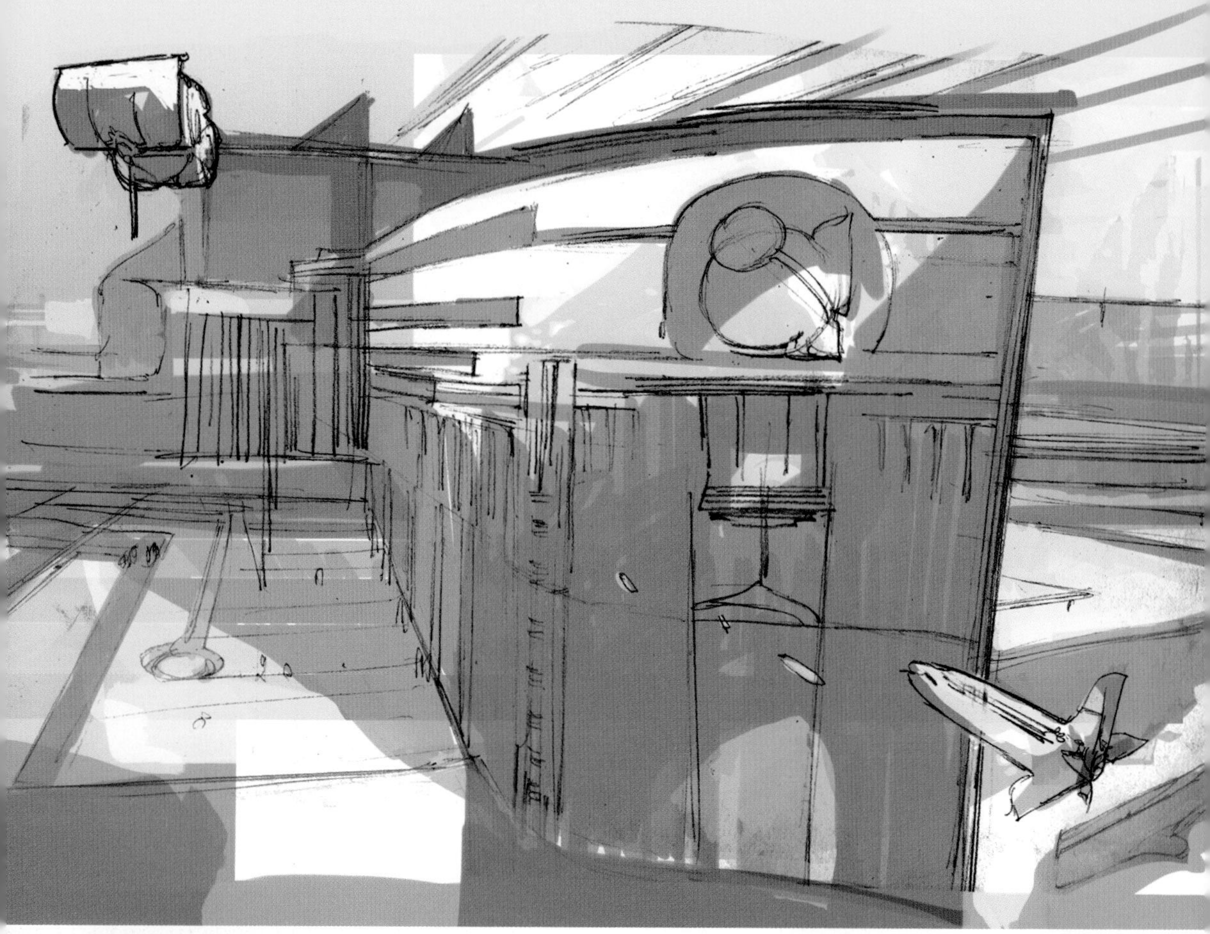

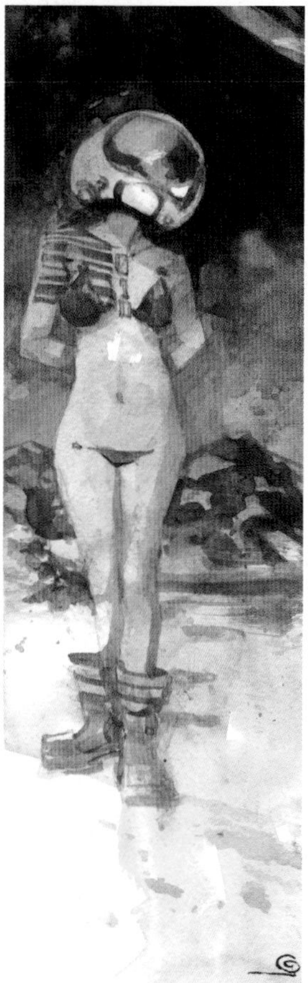

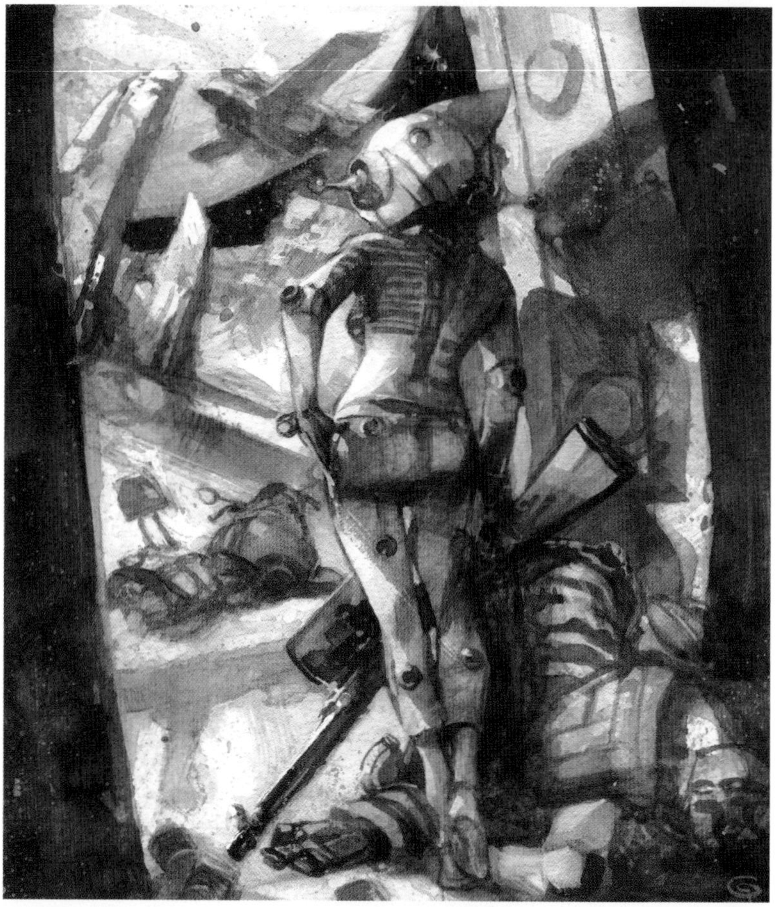

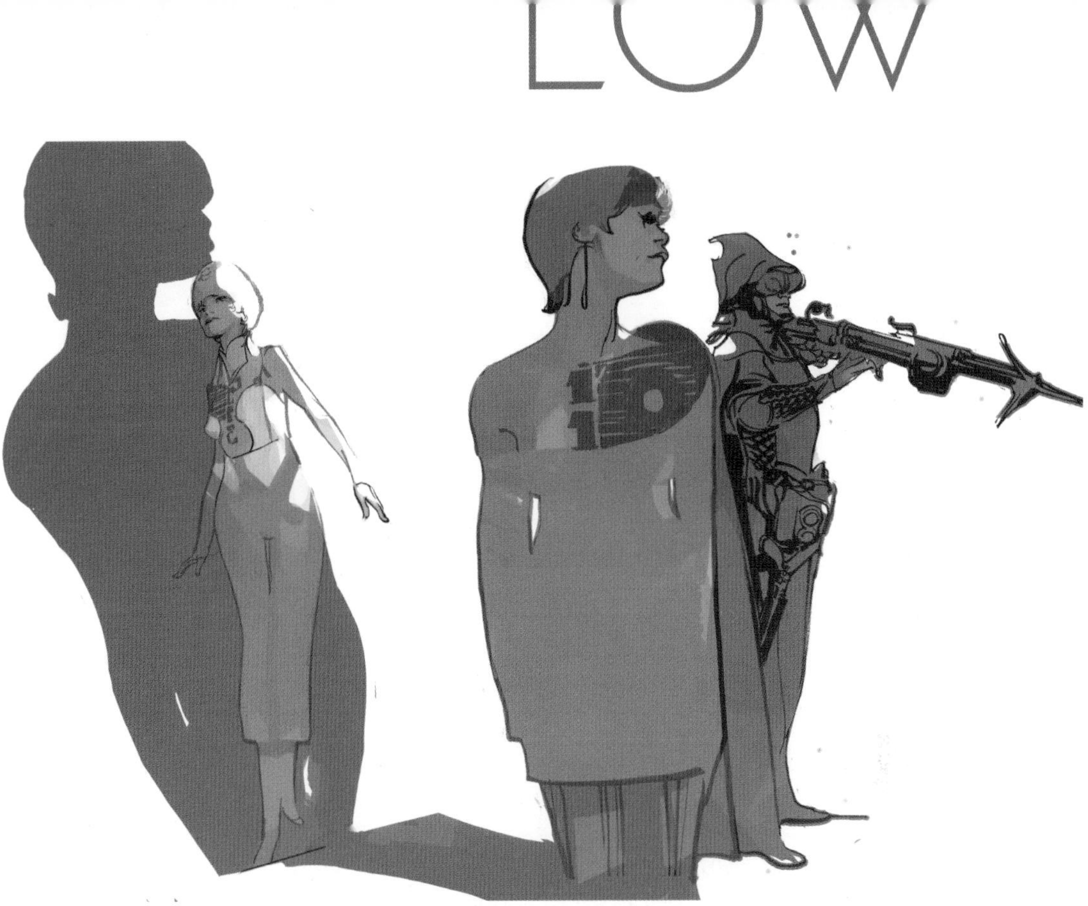
LOW

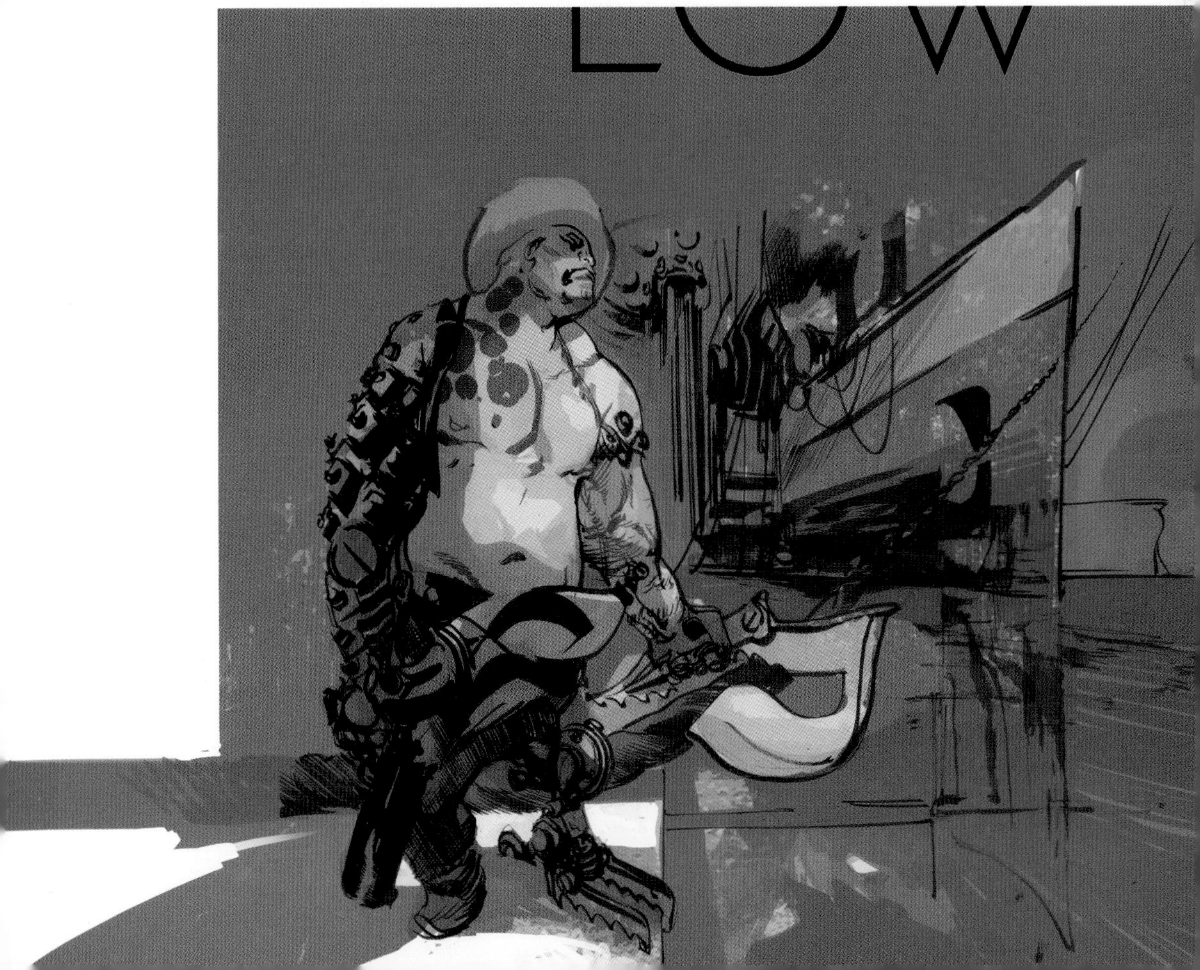
LOW

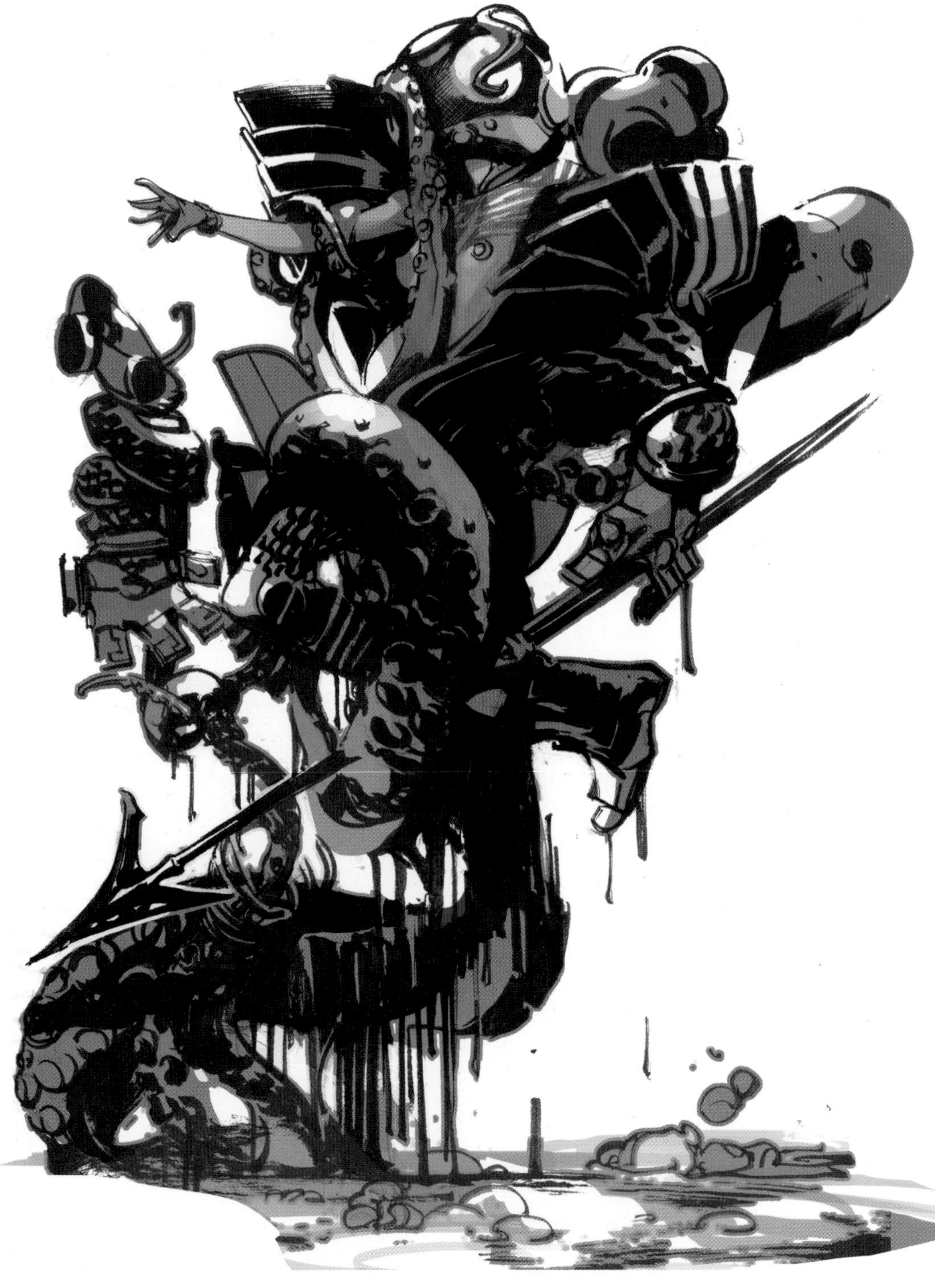

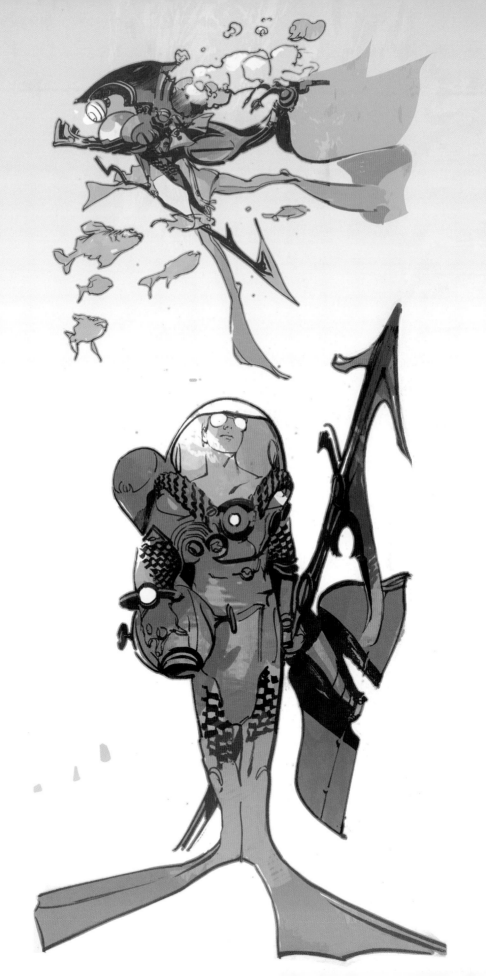

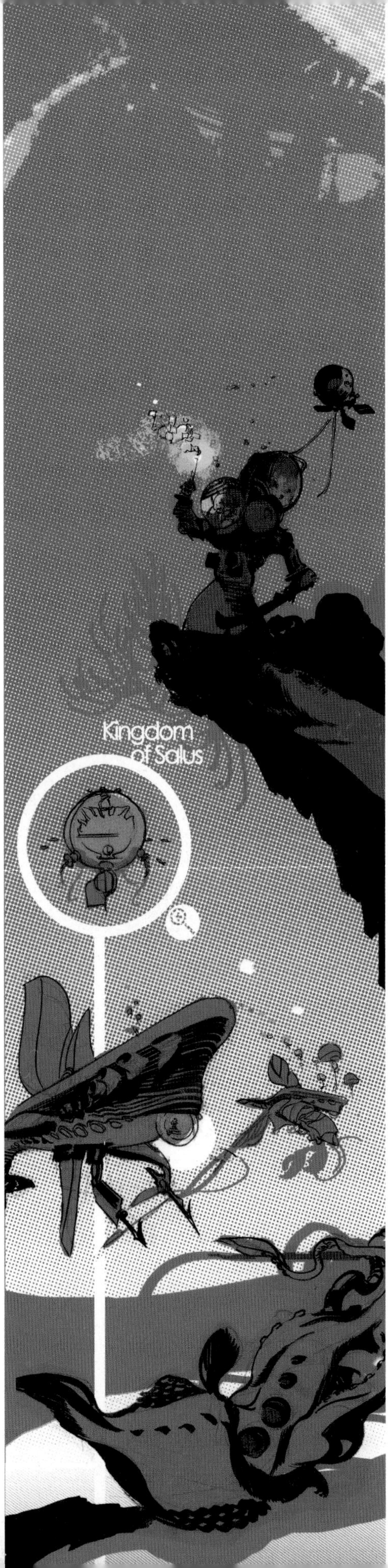
Kingdom of Salus

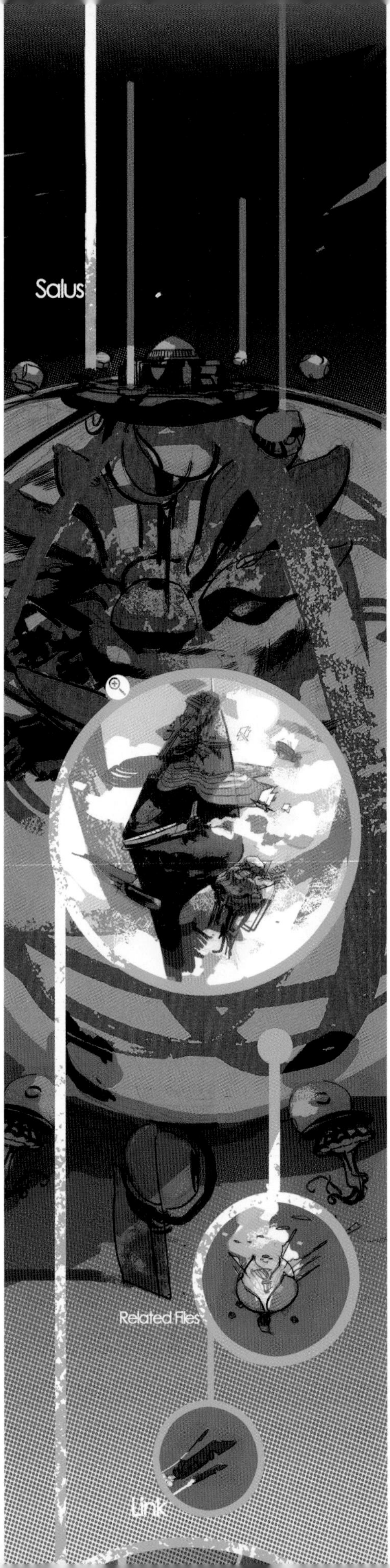
Salus
Related Files
Link

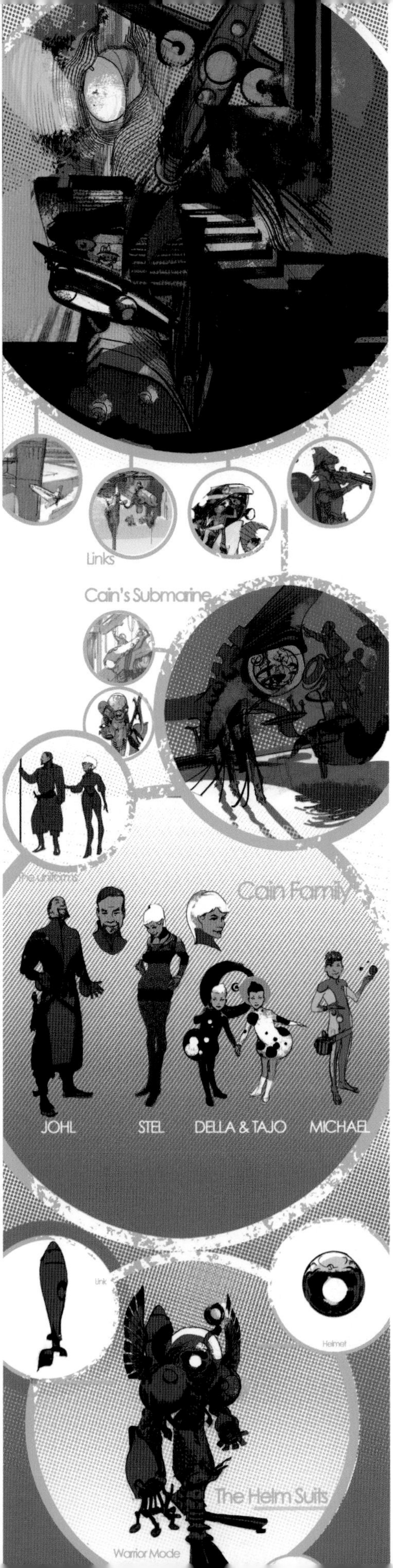
Links
Cain's Submarine
The Uniforms
Cain Family
JOHL
STEL
DELLA & TAJO
MICHAEL
Link
Helmet
The Helm Suits
Warrior Mode

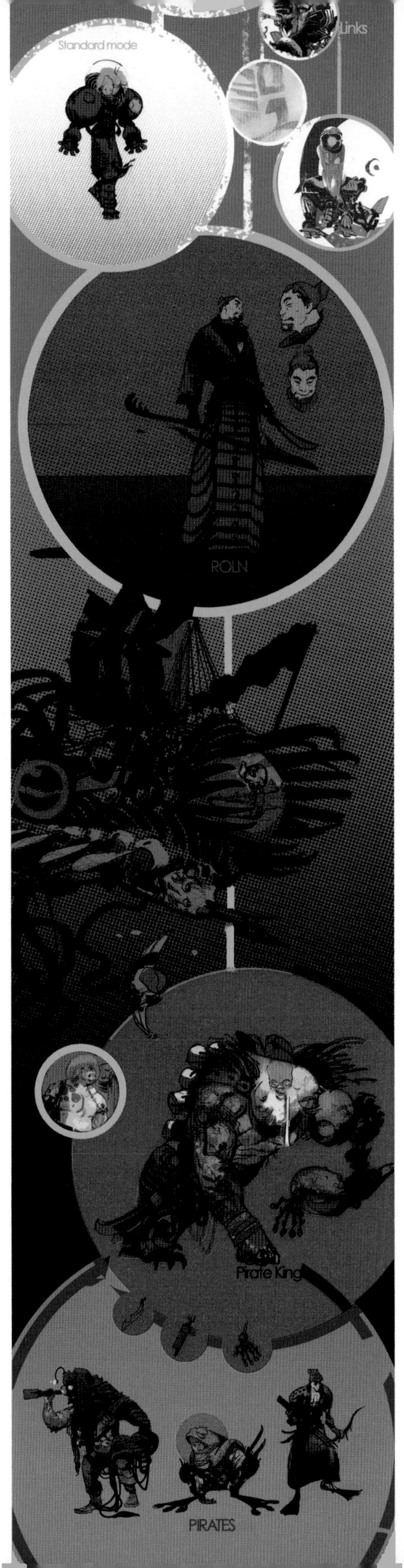
Standard mode
Links
ROLN
Pirate King
PIRATES

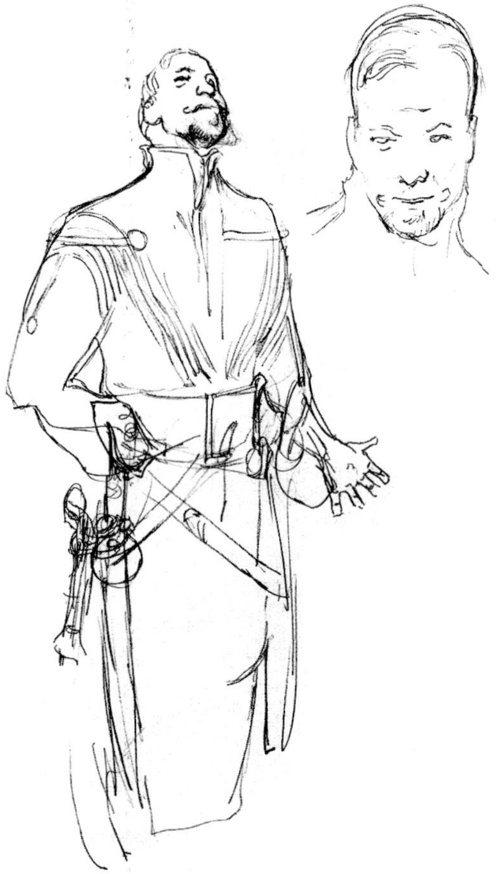

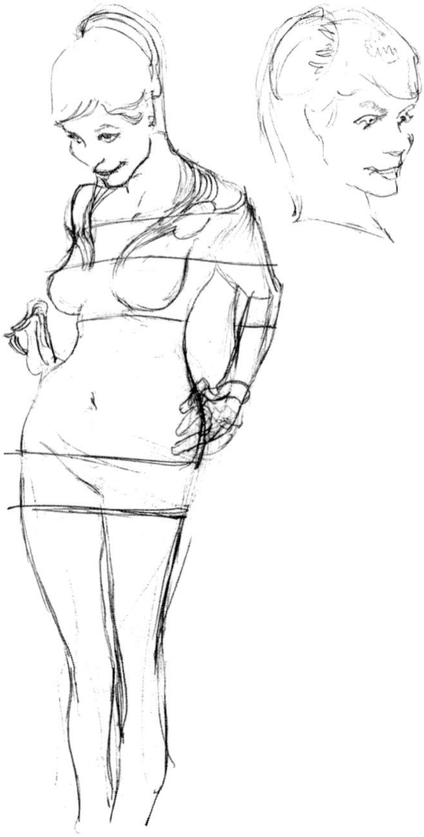

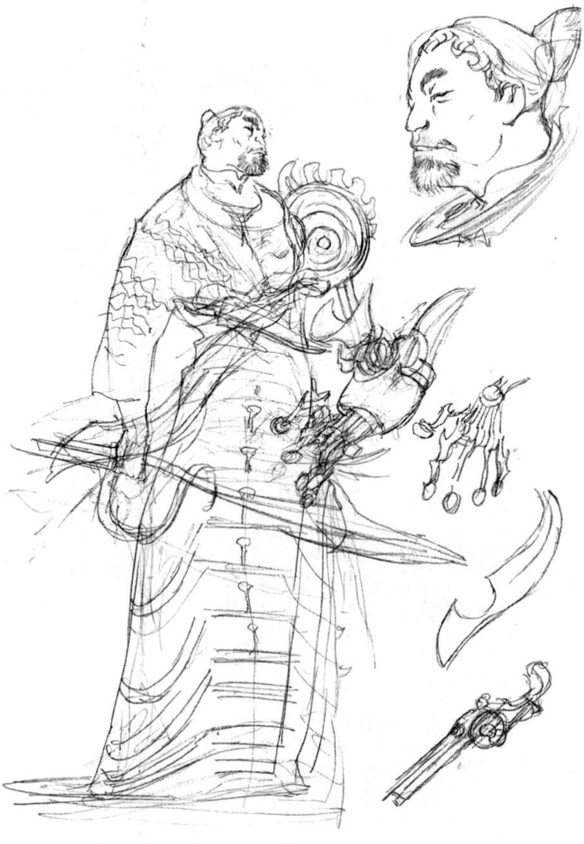

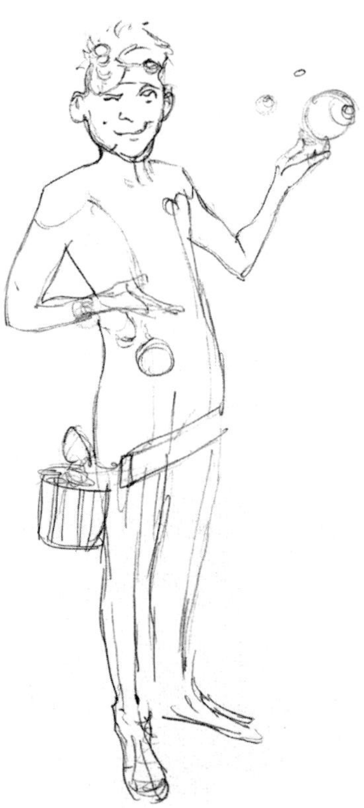

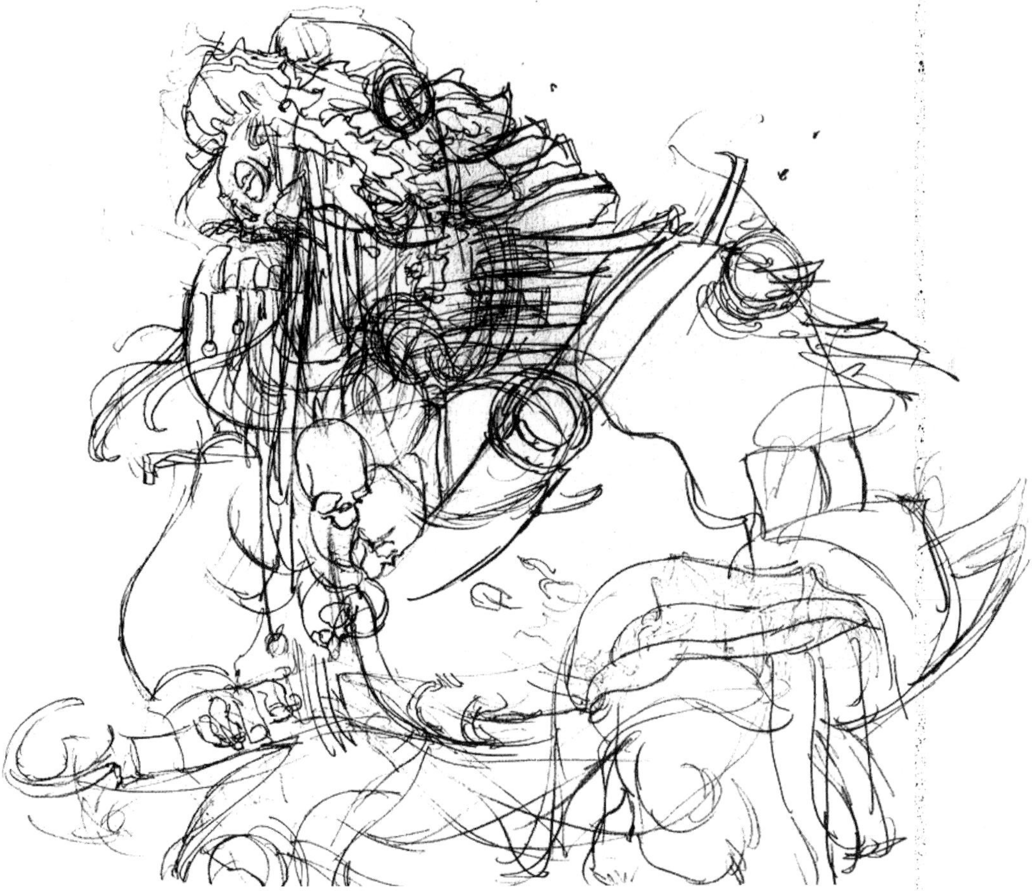

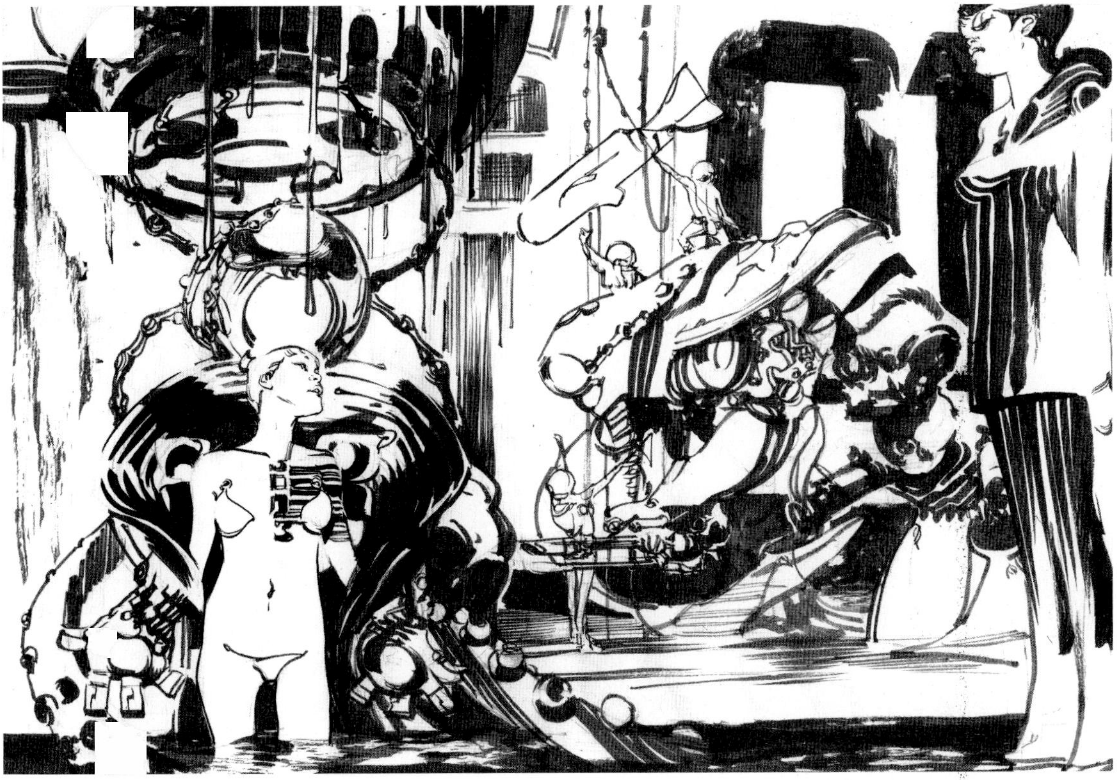

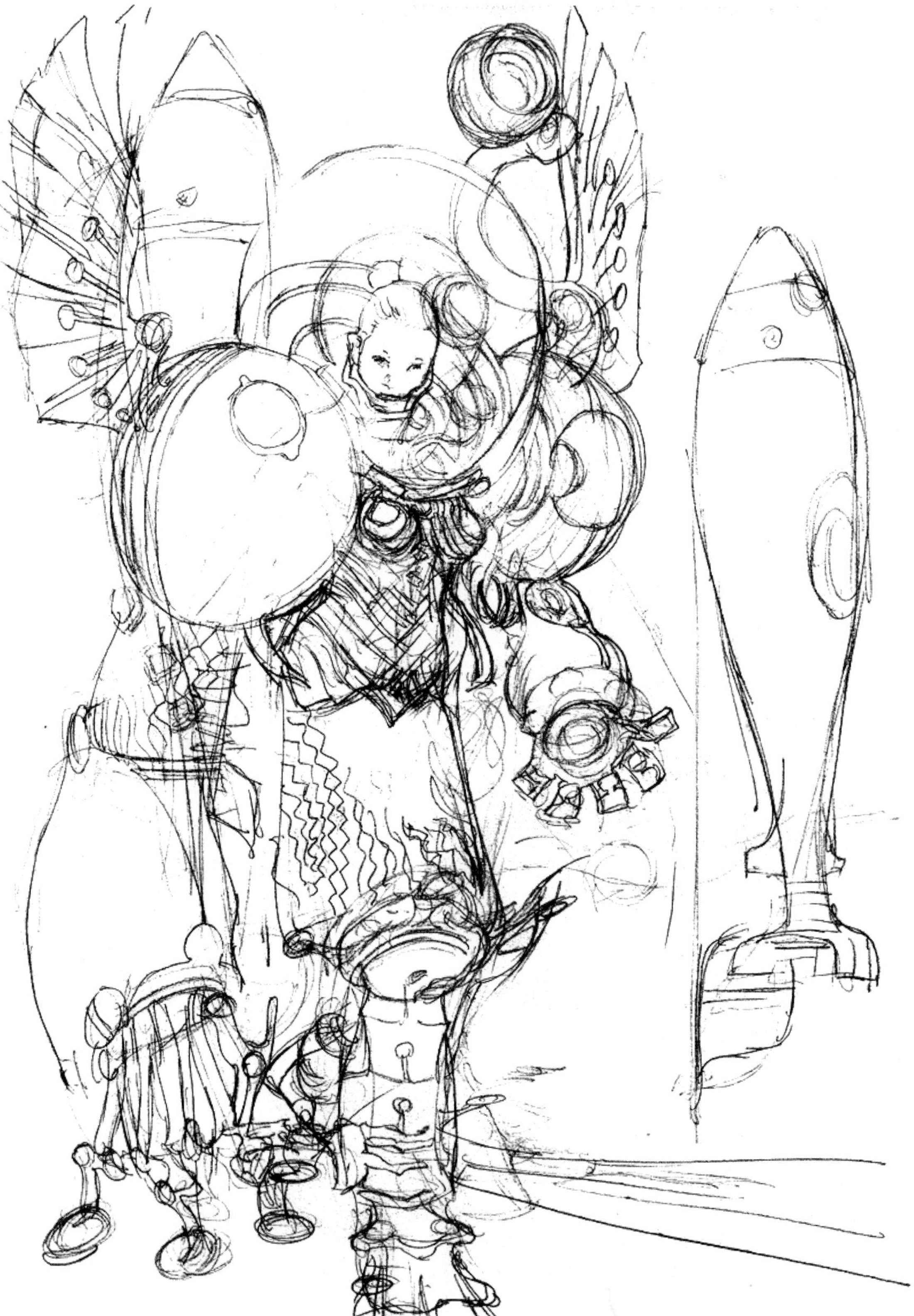